THE QUMRAN PARADIGM

SBL

Society of Biblical Literature

Early Judaism and Its Literature

Rodney A. Werline, Editor

Editorial Board:
Mark J. Boda
George J. Brooke
Esther Glickler Chazon
Steven D. Fraade
James S. McLaren

Number 43

THE QUMRAN PARADIGM

A CRITICAL EVALUATION OF SOME FOUNDATIONAL HYPOTHESES IN THE CONSTRUCTION OF THE QUMRAN SECT

Gwynned de Looijer

SBL Press
Atlanta

Copyright © 2015 by SBL Press

All rights reserved. No part of this work may be reproduced or transmitted in any form or by any means, electronic or mechanical, including photocopying and recording, or by means of any information storage or retrieval system, except as may be expressly permitted by the 1976 Copyright Act or in writing from the publisher. Requests for permission should be addressed in writing to the Rights and Permissions Office, SBL Press, 825 Houston Mill Road, Atlanta, GA 30329 USA.

Library of Congress Cataloging-in-Publication Data

Looijer, Gwynned de., author.
  The Qumran paradigm : a critical evaluation of some foundational hypotheses in the construction of the Qumran sect / by Gwynned de Looijer.
    p. cm. — (Early Judaism and its literature ; number 43)
  Includes bibliographical references and index.
  Summary: "Gwynned de Looijer reexamines the key hypotheses that have driven scholars' understandings of the Dead Sea Scrolls, the archaeological site of Khirbet Qumran, and the textual descriptions of the Essenes. She demonstrates that foundational hypotheses regarding a sect at Qumran have heavily influenced the way the texts found in the surrounding caves are interpreted. De Looijer's approach abandons those assumptions to illustrate that the Dead Sea Scrolls reflect a wider range of backgrounds reflecting the many diverse forms of Judaism that existed in the Second Temple period"— Provided by publisher.
  ISBN 978-0-88414-071-9 (pbk. : alk. paper) — ISBN 978-0-88414-072-6 (ebook) — ISBN 978-0-88414-073-3 (hardcover :
  alk. paper)
  1. Qumran community. 2. Dead Sea scrolls. 3. Judaism—History—Post-exilic period, 586 B.C.–210 A.D. I. Title.
  BM487.L66 2015
  296.8'15—dc23   2015025096

Printed on acid-free paper.

For my father, Bert de Looijer

Contents

Acknowledgments xi
Abbreviations xiii
Figures and Tables xvii

1. Introduction 1
   1.1. A Qumran Community? 4
   1.2. A Sectarian Library? 15
   1.3. Moving the Foundation Stone: Sectarianism as a
        Second Temple Phenomenon? 20
   1.4. Judea and Judaism in Second Temple Times:
        Power, Privilege, and Fragmentation 24
   1.5. The Qumran Paradigm: A Persistent Phenomenon? 30

2. Textual Classification of Presectarianism: On In-Between
   Texts and Formative Periods 37
   2.1. Dimant, A Sectarian Library and In-Between
        Sectarian Texts 39
   2.2. Evaluating Dimant's Qumran Library and Its
        Textual Classifications 48
   2.3. García Martínez's Groningen Hypothesis and a
        Formative Period of the Sect 62
   2.4. Evaluating García Martínez's Formative Period
        and Model of Chronological Development 76
   2.5. Conclusions: Classification Systems and Their
        Function in the Paradigm 85

3. The Provenance Of 4QMMT: A Case Of Qumran
   (Pre-)Sectarianism? 89
   3.1. The Task of This Chapter 90
   3.2. A History of Controversies 91

3.3. The Texts	92
3.4. Genre	107
3.5. Date	108
3.6. Historical Setting	111
3.7. From 4QMMT as (Pre-)Sectarian Tool to 4QMMT in Its Own Right	113
3.8. The Parameters of 4QMMT's Status as Foundational Document	115
3.9. Conclusions	138

4. Ideology as a Cohesive Strategy: The Development of Qumran Dualism..139

4.1. Dualism as a Qumran Characteristic	140
4.2. Dualism as an Aspect of Larger Socioreligious Phenomena	154
4.3. Dualism as a Concept in Religious Systems	167
4.4. Revisiting Types of Dualism at Qumran	172
4.5. Revisiting Frey's Patterns of Dualistic Thought and Their Developments	182
4.6. Revisiting Dualism in Its Socioreligious Milieu: Aspect or Core?	185
4.7. The Cohesive Ideology of Dualism: Building Block of the Qumran Paradigm?	187

5. The Zenith of Qumran Thought: The Case of Dualism and 1QS III, 13–IV, 26..189

5.1. The Text: The Treatise of the Two Spirits	190
5.2. Dating the Treatise	201
5.3. Textual Correspondences and Sociohistorical Setting	204
5.4. Dualism in the Treatise	209
5.5. The Treatise and Its Position in the Sapiential Pattern of Qumran Dualism	231
5.6. Two Ways: A Case Study	248
5.7. The Cohesive Function of Dualism at Qumran	251

6. The Qumran Paradigm: Toward a Revisionist Approach......................253

6.1. The Pyramid Structure of the Qumran Paradigm	255
6.2. The Proposed Alternatives: Protest Reinforces the Paradigm	257

6.3. What Can We Learn from 4QMMT and the Treatise?	260
6.4. Proposals for Future Research	261
6.5. Conclusion	268

Bibliography 271

Index of Primary Texts 287
Index of Modern Authors 295

Acknowledgments

One of the main arguments of this book is that texts do not emerge as the result of solitary contemplation, but rather as the reflection of a process in which the active engagement with others is of vital importance. Accordingly, this work is a reflection not only of my own thoughts and ideas, but it also was shaped by the many conversations and discussions, both academic and leisurely, that I have had with colleagues and friends.

This book is a reworking of my PhD dissertation, and I am grateful to the people who then helped me structure and shape my work: First and foremost, I thank my supervisors, John Barclay, Lutz Doering, and Loren Stuckenbruck. I especially thank John Barclay, whose clear mindedness and professionalism I greatly admire and to whom I am very grateful for taking on a project outside of his subject area. Also, I have learned much from Lutz Doering, whose fundamentally different views of Qumran kept me on my toes and whose near-photographic knowledge of relevant literature has profoundly humbled me. A very special thanks to Loren Stuckenbruck, whose relentless interest, enthusiasm, support, and friendship have made the gravel road of dissertation writing worth traveling.

During this project, many people challenged, helped, and supported me in many ways and I would like to thank them for that: Kate Hampshire and Johannes Haubold for seeing what was right in front of me; Jürgen Zangenberg for his keen interest in the topic; my examiners Stuart Weeks and Philip Davies for their candid comments and creative suggestions for further research; Mary Ledger and Ed Kaneen, for believing in me and providing practical support; Eibert Tigchelaar, for always being scarily critical and cheerfully helpful at the same time (a true gift); Brian Black for our shared joy in talking "text" and "history" anthropologically; Tobias Nicklas, for his kind advice and positive attitude throughout the years; Douglas Davies for his brilliant ideas and for being Douglas Davies; Frans Louwers for his steady friendship and true southern hospitality at the Dutch side of the North Sea (NU EVEN NIET!); Helen Ball and Jamie

Tehrani at the Anthropology Department for giving me the opportunity to teach; Ellen Middleton and Susan Tait, without whom the Theology and Religion Department simply would not have been the same; and finally, Robert Hayward for his generosity and kindness and for being an extraordinary language teacher! Of course, my gratitude extends to the British Arts and Humanities Research Council for granting me a scholarship, which has helped me tremendously throughout the years. Finally, I am very honored that Rod Werline has kindly accepted my manuscript to be published in the Early Judaism and Its Literature series, and I am grateful for all the help from the people at SBL Press, particularly Nicole Tilford.

In Durham, I have been part of a truly international academic community, thus enjoying the company of friends and colleagues from all over the globe, especially: Christian Schneider, Simon Walsh (my Teacher of Righteousness!), Eduardo Díaz-Amado, Nidhani de-Andrado, Karin Neutel, Yulia Egorova, Susana Carro-Ripalda, Jan de Ruiter, Justin Mihoc, and Claudia Merli. A special thank you to Dorothe Bertschmann, for her warm friendship, her willingness to have poignant and challenging theological conversations, and her encouragement regarding my work.

Finally, I am deeply indebted to Iain Edgar, who over time became a most loyal supporter, cooking meals at the end of long days of revising and finally reading through the final versions of my chapters on the search for typos and "Dutchisms." Any mistakes that might occur in this final version are, of course, my own!

Abbreviations

1QpHab	Pesher Habakkuk
1QS	Rule of the Community
AB	Anchor Bible
AGJU	Arbeiten zur Geschichte des antiken Judentums und des Urchristentums
A.J.	Josephus, *Antiquitates judaicae*
ANYAS	Annals of the New York Academy of Sciences
BAAS	*Bulletin of the Anglo-American Archaeological Society*
BARIS	British Archaeological Reports International Series
BASOR	*Bulletin of the American Schools of Oriental Research*
BDB	Brown, Francis, S. R. Driver, and Charles A. Briggs. *A Hebrew and English Lexicon of the Old Testament*.
BETL	Bibliotheca Ephemeridum Theologicarum Lovaniensium
BH	Biblical Hebrew
BibInt	Biblical Interpretation Series
BibSem	The Biblical Seminar
B.J.	Josephus, *Bellum judaicum*
BJSUCSD	Biblical and Judaic Studies from the University of California, San Diego
BRLJ	Brill Reference Library of Judaism
ca.	circa (approximately)
CBC	Cambridge Bible Commentary
CBQ	*Catholic Biblical Quarterly*
CD	Cairo Genizah copy of the Damascus Document
CEJL	Commentaries on Early Jewish Literature
CJA	Christianity and Judaism in Antiquity
CQS	Companion to the Qumran Scrolls
CRINT	Compendia Rerum Iudaicarum ad Novum Testamentum
CurBR	*Currents in Biblical Research*
DD	Damascus Document

DJD	Discoveries in the Judaean Desert
DSD	*Dead Sea Discoveries*
DSS	Dead Sea Scrolls
DSSSE	García Martínez, Florentino, and Eibert J. C. Tigchelaar. *The Dead Sea Scrolls Study Edition*. 2 vols. Leiden: Brill; Grand Rapids: Eerdmans, 1997.
HCS	Hellenistic Culture and Society
FO	*Folia Orientalia*
frag(s).	fragment(s)
HSS	Harvard Semitic Studies
JAJSup	Supplements to the Journal of Ancient Judaism
JBL	*Journal of Biblical Literature*
JJS	*Journal of Jewish Studies*
JRA	*Journal of Roman Archaeology*
JQR	*Jewish Quarterly Review*
JSJ	*Journal for the Study of Judaism in the Persian, Hellenistic, and Roman Periods*
JSJSup	Supplements to the Journal for the Study of Judaism
JSPSup	Journal for the Study of the Pseudepigrapha Supplement Series
LSTS	Library of Second Temple Studies
MH	Mishnaic Hebrew
MS(S)	manuscript(s)
Nat.	Pliny the Elder, *Naturalis historia*
NEA	*Near Eastern Archaeology*
Prob.	Philo, *Quod omnis probus liber sit*
QH	Qumran(ic) Hebrew
RB	*Revue Biblique*
RelSoc	Religion and Society
RevQ	*Revue de Qumran*
RHR	*Revue de l'histoire de religions*
SBLDS	Society of Biblical Literature Dissertation Series
SBT	Studies in Biblical Theology
ScrHier	Scripta Hierosolymitana
SemeiaSt	Semeia Studies
SHR	Studies in the Histories of Religion
SJLA	Studies in Judaism in Late Antiquity
STDJ	Studies of the Texts of the Desert of Judah
SUNT	Studien zur Umwelt des Neuen Testaments

SymS	Symposium Series
TSAJ	Texts and Studies in Ancient Judaism
VTSup	Supplement to Vetus Testamentum
WUNT	Wissenschaftliche Untersuchungen zum Neuen Testament

Figures and Tables

Figures

1. Schematic Overview of Dimant's Theory of a Sectarian Library — 44
2. Schematic Table of García Martínez's Groningen Hypothesis 1 — 64
3. Schematic Table of García Martínez's Groningen Hypothesis 2 — 66
4. García Martínez's Assessment of the Development of Eschatology at Qumran — 68
5. García Martínez's Groningen Hypothesis with Its Inconsistencies — 83
6. Overview of Meyers's Assessment of Influences on Jewish Dualism — 156
7. The Pyramid Structure — 256
8. The Antipyramid Structure — 259

Tables

1. Summary of García Martínez's Formative Period — 70
2. 4QMMT, according to DJD X — 93
3. 4QMMT, according to Von Weissenberg (43) and Ben-Dov in DJD XXI — 94
4. Overview of Collins's Assessment of Influences on the Development of Apocalypticism — 158
5. Frey's versus Bianchi's Definition of Dualism(s) — 181
6. Frey's Two Patterns of Dualism Schematically Described — 183
7. Overview of S Documents and Their Dates (according to DJD XXVI) — 203
8. Frey's Three Levels of Dualism in the Treatise — 210

9. Schematic Overview of the List of Virtues and Vices in the
   Treatise IV, 2–14   223
10. Overview of Frey's Pattern of Sapiential Dualism   232
11. Possible Dualistic Elements in CD (following Frey)   245

an Essene identification of the scrolls. Furthermore, the presuppositions regarding the content of the scrolls and their resemblance to the Essenes as described in the classical sources led to a specific interpretation of the site of Khirbet Qumran, which at the time was mainly thought to be unique as a result of the absence of any comparable geographical and Hellenistic/Herodian contemporary archaeological sites in the Judean desert.[9] In this light, scholars interpreted the perceived archaeological uniqueness of the site as reflecting Essene peculiarities. These three elements together—content of the scrolls, information from the classical sources, and peculiarities at the site—thus created the paradigm mentioned above.[10]

A second and subsequent important influence on the establishment of the Qumran paradigm was the proposition that the textual finds were representative of and coherently meaningful to the inhabitants of the archaeological site.[11] Moreover, the Qumran scrolls were not only presupposed to represent accurately the socioreligious reality of a community residing at Khirbet Qumran, but they were also perceived as an accurate and meaningful representation of a once existent and deliberately chosen sectarian library.

Finally, the underlying and less openly acknowledged building block from which much of the paradigm was constructed is the presumed social reality of sect and sectarianism, as put forward by many scholars on the basis of Josephus's account of the four "philosophies."[12] To take the notion of sectarianism as the cornerstone of Second Temple society is not without

---

Phillip Callaway, *The History of the Qumran Community: An Investigation*, JSPSup 3 (Sheffield: JSOT Press, 1988).

9. See de Vaux, *Archaeology and the Dead Sea Scrolls*, 112.

10. I hereby thank Prof. Jürgen Zangenberg for his comments and willingness to meet and reflect with me. His reference to the Qumran triangle stems from our first talk on March 20, 2012.

11. This proposition is clearly witnessed in the two citations at the beginning of this chapter.

12. In *Bellum judaicum* (2.119, 122, 124, 137, 141–142) Josephus refers to "parties" (*haireseis*), which is often translated as the less neutral "sects." The translation of *haireseis* as "sects" brings up, sociologically, Christian connotations of sectarianism and provokes a tendency to interpret events in textual worlds in terms of dualistic categories. In Josephus's *Antiquitates judaicae* (and in *B.J.* 2.119), the term "philosophies" is used, which in the ancient world is used for groups that try to convert others to their point of view. Therefore, there is an inherent tension between the two terms that Josephus uses not only with regard to the Essenes, but with regard to all mentioned Jewish groups.

problems and creates certain presuppositions about the origin, nature, and function of the scrolls, as well as, above all, the quality and character of groups and group formation.

The first tenet of the Qumran paradigm basically has laid the foundation for various hypotheses with regard to the identification and history of a perceived radical socioreligious organization (or sect),[13] while the second tenet has persisted in maintaining the idea of a characteristic collection or library, partly to categorize texts by separating the sectarian from the nonsectarian ones and partly to demonstrate the uniqueness of the Qumran community within Second Temple Judaism.[14] The third tenet, the presumed connection between ideology and social reality, which shall be the main focus of the present work, is more essential and fundamental for the way scholars have approached the peculiarities of the Qumran situation itself.[15] The following sections will discuss each of these tenets in more detail.

1.1. A Qumran Community?

In the history of Qumran studies, a development has taken place from the presumption that the manuscripts found in the Qumran caves reflected a single community, residing at Khirbet Qumran and authoring all hidden manuscripts, to the notion that the manuscripts reflect more than one community and were not all written at or in the immediate environs of Khirbet Qumran. Over the last six decades, scholars have developed several models to explain "Qumran," of which three hypotheses about the

---

13. See above, nn. 1, 2, and 4; e.g., Florentino García Martínez, "Qumran Origins and Early History: A Groningen Hypothesis," *FO* 25 (1988): 113–36.

14. See Devorah Dimant, "The Qumran Manuscripts: Contents and Significance," in *Time to Prepare the Way in the Wilderness: Papers on the Qumran Scrolls by Fellows of the Institute for Advanced Studies of the Hebrew University, Jerusalem, 1989–1990*, ed. Devorah Dimant and Lawrence H. Schiffman, STDJ 16 (Leiden: Brill, 1995), 23–58.

15. The first to use the term "sect" was Louis Ginzberg in 1922 while describing the community behind the CD fragments of the Cairo Genizah (*An Unknown Jewish Sect* [New York: Jewish Theological Seminary of America, 1970]). Critical of this indiscriminate usage of "sect" is, for instance, Jutta Jokiranta, "'Sectarianism' of the Qumran 'Sect': Sociological Notes," *RevQ* 20 (2001): 223–39. See also Schofield, *From Qumran to the Yaḥad*, 21–33. However, less specifically, scholars have addressed the inherent effect of the (historical) usage and connotations of sectarianism over a number of decades.

1. INTRODUCTION

origins of the scrolls and their preservers seem to be considered most viable within the field. A fourth hypothesis, which argues for Saducean origins is discussed here as a persistent dissonant proposal that has been thought by some to hold merit.[16] The four hypotheses to be described and evaluated may thus be listed as follows: (1) the Essene hypothesis; (2) the Groningen hypothesis; (3) the multicommunity (Essene) hypothesis; and (4) a dissonant opinion: the Saducean hypothesis.

1.1.1. The Essene Hypothesis

Since the discovery of the Dead Sea Scrolls, the so-called "Essene hypothesis" has had a strong influence on Qumran scholarship and basically provided the parameters for the still prevalent Qumran paradigm. This hypothesis was first proposed by Eleazar Sukenik and André Dupont-Sommer.[17] Based on the idea that the Rule of the Community was "a kind of book of regulations for the conduct of members of a brotherhood or sect,"[18] Sukenik made the connection between the community behind the rule and what was written in the classical sources about the Essenes. As such, he concluded that the entirety of manuscripts that formed the Dead Sea Scrolls were the main library of an Essene community, a sectarian group which resided "on the western side of the Dead Sea, in the vicinity of En-Gedi."[19] After publication of the first books and articles proposing this Essene identification, Roland de Vaux's excavations of Khirbet Qumran led him to conclude that the site was an Essene settlement from the middle of the second century BCE.[20] As is well known, the identification of the Qumran community with the Essenes primarily rests on what Josephus, Pliny the Elder, and Philo reported about them.[21]

---

16. Schiffman himself never really argues for the Qumranites to be Sadducean but rather follows Ginzberg's model of "an unknown Jewish Sect." Nevertheless, he argues that Qumran halakah has many similarities with Sadducean halakah; see Lawrence Schiffman, *The Halakhah at Qumran*, SJLA 16 (Leiden: Brill, 1975); also, *Qumran and Jerusalem: Studies in the Dead Sea Scrolls and the History of Judaism* (Grand Rapids: Eerdmans, 2010).
17. Sukenik, *Megillot Genuzot*; André Dupont-Sommer, *The Dead Sea Scrolls: A Preliminary Survey*, trans. M. Rowley (Oxford: Blackwell, 1952).
18. Sukenik, *Megillot Genuzot*, 16.
19. Ibid.; see also n. 1.
20. De Vaux, *Archaeology and the Dead Sea Scrolls*, 134–37.
21. Ibid., 137; cf. n. 2.

Various scholars have raised critical questions regarding such straightforward identification of Qumran as Essene. For instance, Steve Mason noted that classical sources need to be approached with scrutiny, since they might reflect the classical author's own agenda.[22] In particular, according to Mason, Josephus's account of the Essenes is "thoroughly Josephan, part of the historian's rhetorical and apologetic presentation of Judaism."[23] In a comparison of the historical sources, Philip Callaway also demonstrated that, in addition to similarities, these ancient reports are not entirely congruous with the Qumran texts. On this basis, he contested a straightforward identification of the Qumran community with the Essene movement.[24] In his article "Who Cares and Why Does It Matter? Qumran and the Essenes, Once Again!" Albert Baumgarten systematically addressed the question of Essene identification.[25] He compared the descriptions of the Essenes in the aforementioned classical sources to both textual and archaeological evidence (i.e., women buried in the cemetery; the presence of a latrine inside the Qumran walls) from Khirbet Qumran. In his conclusion, he pleaded that so many discrepancies beg for the Qumran-Essene identification "to be jettisoned as an unnecessary burden" to Second Temple scholarship.[26] Finally, Carol Newsom rightly added that the word "Essene" does not occur in the Scrolls. She concluded: "Even though there is good warrant for describing the community at least as 'Essene-like,' it is probably better scholarly practice not to use the terms Qumran and Essene as though they were interchangeable."[27] Currently, many scholars are convinced that the original Essene hypothesis can—in

---

22. Steve Mason, "What Josephus Says about the Essenes in His *Judean War*," http://orion.mscc.huji.ac.il/symposiums/programs/Mason00-1.shtml; http://orion.mscc.huji.ac.il/symposiums/programs/Mason00-2.shtml.

23. See the discussion of Mason's argument in John. J. Collins, *Beyond the Qumran Community: The Sectarian Movement of the Dead Sea Scrolls* (Grand Rapids: Eerdmans, 2010), 122–24.

24. See Callaway, *History of the Qumran Community*, 63–87 for the main discussion between Dupont-Sommer and Driver.

25. Albert I. Baumgarten, "Who Cares and What Does It Matter? Qumran and the Essenes, Once Again!" *DSD* 11 (2004): 174–90.

26. Ibid., 190.

27. Carol Newsom, "'Sectually Explicit' Literature from Qumran," in *The Hebrew Bible and Its Interpreters*, ed. William H. C. Propp, Baruch Halpern, and David N. Freedman, BJSUCSD 1 (Winona Lake, IN: Eisenbrauns, 1990), 168.

its strict sense—no longer be maintained.²⁸ These arguments give sufficient reason not to take the Essene hypothesis as a point of departure.

1.1.2. THE GRONINGEN HYPOTHESIS

Due to unease with the univocal identification of the Qumranites as Essene as advanced by the Essene hypothesis, some scholars developed modified or new views of the Qumran community in its pluralistic environment. For instance, Philip Davies argued that the Essene movement is the parent movement to the Qumran sect, while others have argued that the Qumran sect gradually parted from the Essene movement and developed its own ideology.²⁹ Along similar lines, in 1988, Florentino García Martínez published his influential Groningen hypothesis. His hypothesis marked a coherent attempt "to relate to each other the apparently contradictory data furnished by the Dead Sea manuscripts as to the primitive history of the Qumran Community."³⁰ Five basic propositions characterize this approach:³¹

(1) A clear distinction must be made between the origins of the Essene movement and the origins of the Qumran community.

---

28. See John J. Collins, "Forms of Community in the Dead Sea Scrolls," in *Emanuel: Studies in Hebrew Bible, Septuagint and Dead Sea Scrolls in Honor of Emanuel Tov*, ed. Shalom M. Paul et al. (Leiden: Brill, 2003), 97–112; and "The Yaḥad and the 'Qumran Community,'" in *Biblical Traditions in Transmission: Essays in Honour of Michael A. Knibb*, ed. Charlotte Hempel and Judith Lieu, JSJSup 111 (Leiden: Brill, 2006), 81–96. However, quite recently, the late Edna Ullman-Margalit has reconstructed the "Qumran triangle" on rational grounds and concludes that the Essene hypothesis is still the best model for explaining the Qumran situation; see Edna Ullman-Margalit, "Interpretative Circles: The Case of the Dead Sea Scrolls," in *The Dead Sea Scrolls and Contemporary Culture: Proceedings Held at the Israel Museum, Jerusalem (July 6–8, 2008)*, ed. Adolfo Roitman, Lawrence Schiffman, and Shani Tzoref, STDJ 93 (Leiden: Brill, 2011), 649–66.

29. Philip Davies, *Sects and Scrolls: Essays on Qumran and Related Topics* (Atlanta: Scholars Press, 1996), 69–82. Another version of such an offshoot theory is advanced by Gabriele Boccaccini, who roots the Essene movement in "Enochic Judaism" and sees the Qumran community as a radical split-off group from that movement; see *Beyond the Essene Hypothesis: The Parting of the Ways between Qumran and Enochic Judaism* (Grand Rapids: Eerdmans, 1998).

30. García Martínez, "Qumran Origins," 113.

31. Ibid.

(2) The origins of the Essene movement lay within the Palestinian apocalyptic tradition (late third to early second century BCE).
(3) The Qumran movement originates as a split-off from the larger Essene movement over the teachings of the Teacher of Righteousness. Those who were loyal to the Teacher eventually established themselves at Qumran.
(4) The "Wicked Priest" is a collective term and points to the sequence of Hasmonean high priests in a chronological order.
(5) The formative period of the community is placed within a larger perspective, which takes "ideological development, halakhic elements and political conflicts" into account to reconstruct the community's split and subsequent settlement at Qumran.

Thus, the Groningen hypothesis aimed to provide a historical framework in which the Qumran sectarian texts and the *yahad* community can be positioned. Furthermore, it also attempted to explain the dissimilarities between certain core manuscripts, for example, the Damascus Document (CD/DD) and the Community Rule (1QS). Moreover, it sketched possible reasons behind the *yahad*'s retreat into the wilderness and provides a model of identity.

For our purposes, it is important to address the core element that moved García Martínez's proposal away from the Essene hypothesis, that is, the discordant split-off that made the Qumran community distinct from its Essene parent movement. The basis of a split-off theory lies in the presupposition that in 1QS and CD/DD different sectarian groups are addressed. According to García Martínez, the main reasons for the alleged split-off (other than the Teacher's emphasis on eschatology, unknown to the Essenes[32]) are the cultic calendar, norms of purity in the temple and Jerusalem, and halakot concerning tithes, impurity, and marriage.[33] However, the problem in his analysis lies in the way he explained

---

32. This might also be evidence against a connection between Essenism and the apocalyptic tradition.

33. Note that much of García Martínez's argument is based upon two documents, 11QT[a] (11Q19) and 4QMMT[a] (4Q394), both of which he closely links to the Qumran community. The Temple Scroll (11QT[a]) is placed in the sect's formative period, while 4QMMT[a] is seen as a document authored after the sect's split-off. However, both documents do not contain any of the typical sectarian terminology that would identify them as *yahadic* texts.

and interpreted the occurrence of differences in and between texts. Some of the arguments in these disputes are important to our evaluation.

First, according to Josephus, two different orders of Essenes—celibate and marrying—"were in agreement with one another on the way of life, usages and customs" (*B.J.* 2.160).[34] Accordingly, and despite Callaway's emphasis on inconsistencies, Todd Beall has shown that the classical accounts often agree with the Rule of the Community.[35] If García Martínez is correct in his Essene identification, these two observations speak against a discordant split-off. Second, the idea of a calendrical dispute as a major split-off factor needs to be approached with care. The argumentation depends heavily on the chronological placement of CD/DD, a point that is not always clear in García Martínez's reasoning. Moreover, the classical sources do not report any calendrical disputes and hence do not give us any additional arguments on which García Martínez can base his "Essene parent and Qumran split-off" theory. A third split-off factor, namely, García Martínez's assessment that the Teacher of Righteousness introduced eschatology to Qumran, which "is precisely one of the elements not brought out in the classical description of Essenism," also needs to be evaluated cautiously. This argument seems somewhat in tension with one of the pillars of the Groningen hypothesis, namely, the notion that both the Essenes and the Qumran sect are thought to stem from the Palestinian apocalyptic tradition.[36]

In conclusion, these uncertainties and contradictions call into question García Martínez's identification of the *yahad* as a split-off group from a larger Essene movement and thus weaken the Groningen hypothesis's basic framework of a parent and break away-movement. Moreover, if the idea of a discordant break between the Essene parent movement and the Qumran sect can indeed be called into question, we also need to critically reassess García Martínez's presupposition of a formative period in the establishment of the community that highlights the differences and developments between the parent and daughter's ideology. García Martínez found the textual basis for a split-off in the ideological development from parent to daughter in two documents, namely, 4QMMT[a] (4Q394) and

---

34. See Collins, "Yaḥad and the 'Qumran Community,'" 92.
35. See Todd Beall, *Josephus' Description of the Essenes Illustrated by the Dead Sea Scrolls* (Cambridge: Cambridge University Press, 1988).
36. Florentino García Martínez, *Qumranica Minora I: Qumran Origins and Apocalypticism*, ed. Eibert J. C. Tigchelaar, STDJ 63 (Leiden: Brill, 2007), 12–14.

11QT^a (Temple Scroll/11Q19). However, the reconstruction of 4QMMT^a depends heavily on 11QT^a, and both documents have their own problems regarding date, genre, and social location.[37] More generally, the criteria by which García Martínez distinguished between formative writings and *yahadic* writings are not always clear, especially in light of the fact that many texts demonstrate redaction and diachronic development and/or are present in various copies, often with textual variants.[38]

It is therefore not surprising that recent scholarship has moved towards more complex theories of assembly. Even though the Groningen hypothesis has long been helpful as a theoretical framework to further investigate key issues in Qumran studies, with the steady publication of the Scrolls, the basic presuppositions of this hypothesis can no longer be maintained.

1.1.3. The Multicommunity (Essene) Hypothesis

Due to the extensive publication of the Scrolls since 1991, scholars have developed new theories regarding the identity of the group(s) reflected in the Qumran texts. Recently, Eyal Regev proposed the notion of a larger, more complex movement behind the S (Rule of the Community) and D (Damascus Document) traditions. Regev suggests an organizational structure in which small local groups together form a larger organization.[39] He distinguished between the communities of the *yahad* as they occur in the S tradition, which he considered to be "an organisation of autonomous, democratic communities with no definite leader" and the D communities, who lived in camps and were ruled by authoritative leaders.[40] In his analysis, he considered D to be more hierarchical and complex, which leads him to conclude that D has a later origin than S. His conclusion reflected a more radical stance: "D was not a direct continuation or adaptation of S, but an entirely different movement, which adopted certain precepts

---

37. I will elaborate on this topic in chapters 2 and 3.

38. Similar methodological remarks are made by Charlotte Hempel, "The Groningen Hypothesis: Strengths and Weaknesses," in *Enoch and Qumran Origins: New Light on a Forgotten Connection*, ed. Gabriele Boccaccini (Grand Rapids: Eerdmans, 2005), 249–55; also, Schofield, *From Qumran to the Yaḥad*, 38–40.

39. Eyal Regev, "The Yahad and the Damascus Covenant: Structure, Organization, and Relationship," *RevQ* 21 (2003): 233–62; also *Sectarianism in Qumran: A Cross-Cultural Perspective*, RelSoc 45 (Berlin: de Gruyter, 2007).

40. See Schofield, *From Qumran to the Yaḥad*, 43.

and concepts from S and revised them extensively."[41] Hence, according to Regev, the *yahad* was a collective of small, local communities, loosely organized by one central governing power, the "Many."

John J. Collins has also argued that the Qumran texts give evidence for "multiple small assemblies within a larger umbrella organization."[42] In his understanding of the Damascus Document (D), the Community Rule (1QS, 4Q256/4Q258), and the Rule of the Congregation (1Q28a), he reached the following conclusions:

> The Damascus Document provides for "camps" whose members marry and have children, but also for "men of perfect holiness," with whom these are in contrast. The Community Rule describes a yahad, which is not a single settlement but an "umbrella union."... But the Community Rule also describes an elite group, set apart within the yahad, which goes into the wilderness to prepare the way of the Lord.... Finally, the Rule of the Congregation looks to a time in which "all Israel" will follow the regulations of the sect, but still assigns special authority and status to the "council of the community" in the future age."[43]

Hence, Collins, based on his understanding of the relationship between CD/DD and 1QS (plus 1Q28b), argued against the split-off theory held by the Groningen hypothesis. Instead, he provided a framework of diversification that attempts to address the issue of textual diversities. His notion of the existence of "two orders of Essenes who represented different options within the sect, not dissenting factions" as reflected in the S and D traditions has been met with skepticism.[44] One of the most ardent opponents of Collins's proposal is Sarianna Metso. Even though Metso agreed with Collins that the S and D traditions are harmonized through redaction and bear witness both to a large complex and a small, more primitive organization, she firmly stood against Collins's use of 1QS VI, 1–8 as a decisive heuristic tool to build his case. Metso argued that this passage, which envisions small, geographically dispersed communities (cf. 1QS VI, 2 "all their residences" and 1QS VI, 3 "every place where there are ten men [of/from] the community council"), is

---

41. Regev, "Yahad and the Damascus Covenant," 262.
42. Collins, "Forms of Community," 97–112.
43. Ibid., 112.
44. Ibid., 110.

in fact an interpolation to guide traveling members of the community.⁴⁵ Alison Schofield agreed with Metso that Collins "glosses over some of the complexities in the relationship between D and S" by stating that these documents merely represent different forms of community, that is, two different Essene orders. However, she did not concur with Metso's objections with regard to 1QS VI, 1–8, as she held that even if these lines were an interpolation, it must be an early one as the lines occur in every manuscript. She therefore thought that these lines might represent the redactor's meaningful and deliberate strategy to make the text reflect the contemporary *yahad* community structure.⁴⁶

Schofield's own textual research on S led her to argue that the S tradition reflects a radial-dialogic model of semi-independent development. According to this anthropological model of the development of traditions, the various S documents reflect sociologically a multitude of decentralized communities, whose rules and regulations rippled out from their ideological center. Subsequently, the S documents developed in dialogue with or over against the ideology of the central body of the Jewish Other (i.e., the Jerusalem temple), yet semi-independently from their own ideological center in order to meet local circumstances. In her proposal for a radial-dialogic model, Schofield attempted to move away sociologically and historically from the previous models of chronological development, such as the Groningen hypothesis, without neglecting diachronic developments within the S and D traditions, which she interprets sociogeographically.

In contradistinction to the satellite proposals of Regev, Collins, Metso, and Schofield, Charlotte Hempel has argued that "some of the primitive and small-scale communal scenarios ... reflect the life of the forebears of the *yahad*."⁴⁷ Hempel argued against an umbrella framework or a central

---

45. Sarianna Metso, "Whom Does the Term Yahad Identify?" in Hempel and Lieu, *Biblical Traditions in Transmission*, 213–35.

46. Schofield, *From Qumran to the Yaḥad*, 45.

47. Charlotte Hempel, "Emerging Communal Life in the S Tradition," in *Defining Identities: We, You and the Other in the Dead Sea Scrolls; Proceedings of the Fifth Meeting of the IOQS in Groningen*, ed. Florentino García Martínez and Mladen Popović, STDJ 70 (Leiden: Brill, 2008), 43–61. More recently, Hempel repeated her position as she acknowledges a closeness in interpretation to Metso, as she calls her diachronic approach "temporal" or "fossil," while calling Collins's and Schofield's approaches as "spatially spread-out;" see Hempel, "1QS 6:2c–4a: Satellites or Precursors of the Yahad?" in Roitman, Schiffman, and Tzoref, *Dead Sea Scrolls and Contemporary Culture*, 31–40.

organization. Rather, she reconstructed the D and S traditions chronologically, identifying these texts' multilayeredness and diachronic development. Instead of the existence of a framework or central organization to all small-scale "communal scenarios," Hempel proposed to investigate these forms of community in their own right as the forebears of the later *yahad*, who do not (yet) seem to have separated themselves from others. In what Hempel considered later textual material, she identified an emerging community that is more focused on cultic and priestly ideology, but which nonetheless only holds a moderate dissident perspective.

A common denominator for all these theories is their rejection of previous scholarship's idea of the *yahad*'s singular separation, which is equally challenged by recent archaeological evidence. Recent archaeological studies that focus on the Qumran site have discovered same-type pottery between Qumran and the Hasmonean and Herodian palaces in Jericho.[48] Other archaeological studies have suggested an agricultural, secular function of Qumran.[49] For instance, Yizhar Hirschfeld has argued that Qumran, after being abandoned as a Hasmonean fortress, functioned as a regional agricultural trading estate.[50] Also Yitzhak Magen and Yuval Peleg have recently suggested that Qumran firstly functioned as a Hasmonean military outpost, after which it was thought to function as a pottery-producing site.[51] These archaeological studies provide evidence that Qumran was "an integral part of the regional economy."[52] With emerging evidence demanding the need to reexamine hypotheses

---

48. Katherina Galor, Jean Baptiste Humbert, and Jürgen Zangenberg, eds., *Qumran, The Site of the Dead Sea Scrolls: Archaeological Interpretations and Debates; Proceedings of a Conference Held at Brown University, November 17–19, 2002*, STDJ 57 (Leiden: Brill, 2006); especially the essay by Rachel Bar-Nathan, "Qumran and the Hasmonean and Herodian Winter Palaces of Jericho: The Implication of the Pottery Finds on the Interpretation of the Settlement at Qumran," 263–77.

49. Pauline Donceel-Voûte, "'Coenaculum': La salle a l'étage du locus 30 a Khirbet Qumrân sur la mer morte," in *Banquets d'orient*, ed. Rika Gyselen, ResOr 4 (Leuven: Peeters, 1992), 61–84.

50. Yizhar Hirschfeld, *Qumran in Context: Reassessing the Archaeological Evidence* (Peabody, MA: Hendrickson, 2004).

51. Yitzhak Magen and Yuval Peleg, *The Qumran Excavations, 1993–2004: Preliminary Report* (Jerusalem: Israeli Antiquities Authority, 2007).

52. Jean-Baptiste Humbert, "Interpreting the Qumran Site," *NEA* 63 (2000): 140–43; see also "Some Remarks on the Archaeology of Qumran," in Galor, Humbert, and Zangenberg, *Qumran, The Site of the Dead Sea Scrolls*, 19–39.

and assumptions, Jürgen Zangenberg's statement is no doubt true, that "the more archaeological material becomes available, the less unique and isolated Qumran becomes."[53]

1.1.4. A Dissonant Opinion: The Sadducee Hypothesis

From the beginning, one scholar has rejected the straightforward identification of the sectarian Qumran community with the Essenes—Lawrence Schiffman. Schiffman correctly noted a tendency of "reverse methodology"; that is, Qumran scholars searched for halakic evidence to make the Josephan Essene identification already with "preconceived views on the nature of the sect" in mind.[54] Over the last decades, Schiffman has consistently proposed that the *yahad* was closely related to the Sadducees. On the basis of 4QMMT, which he held to be a final attempt to convince a "false Jerusalemite high priesthood," Schiffman argued that these (successors of a group of) Sadducees were unable to accept the replacement of the Zadokite priesthood with the Hasmonean dynasty; hence the self-identification "Sons of Zadok" (in D and S).[55] Schiffman drew his conclusion more specifically from the occurrence of certain halakot in the sectarian documents, which demonstrate great resemblance to Sadducean halakot known from the later rabbinic literature. He primarily used the Temple Scroll (11QT^a) and the Halakic Letter (4QMMT) to build evidence for his case. He explained the dissimilarities by postulating that the Qumran *yahad* diverged from a broader Sadducean group at a later stage in time. Schiffman also thought that the D tradition "deals with satellite communities, while the *Rule* [of the Community] deals with the main center."[56]

---

53. Galor, Humbert, and Zangenberg, *Qumran, The Site of the Dead Sea Scrolls*, 9.
54. Schiffman, *Halakhah at Qumran*, 2.
55. See Philip Davies, who argues against this self-identification, in "Sects from Texts: On the Problems of Doing Sociology of the Qumran Literature," in *New Directions in Qumran Studies: Proceedings of the Bristol Colloquium on the Dead Sea Scrolls, 8–10 September 2003*, ed. Jonathan Campbell, William J. Lyons, and Lloyd Pietersen, LSTS 52 (London: T&T Clark, 2005), 79.
56. Lawrence Schiffman, *Reclaiming the Dead Sea Scrolls: Their True Meaning for Judaism and Christianity* (Philadelphia: Jewish Publication Society, 1994; repr., New York: Doubleday, 1995), 274.

Schiffman's theory has found limited support among Qumran scholars.[57] Many have brought forward the argument that discussions and disputes about the interpretation of Jewish law were at the core of Second Temple Judaism.[58] Also, the "Sadducean positions" in the highly reconstructed legal section B of 4QMMT are few and according to some not nearly enough to sustain a straightforward Sadducean identification. Moreover, like García Martínez's Groningen hypothesis, Schiffman's case leans heavily on 11QT[a] and 4QMMT, both of which are unclear in relation to a possible *yahadic* or even a pre-*yahadic* origin.

These four hypotheses were attempts to explain the social world behind the Qumran documents. Sociohistorical reconstructions commenced with the Essene hypothesis, and many other theories have sprung from its basic foundations. Textually, scholars have tried to theorize about the provenance of these manuscripts found in the caves. In the following section, the idea of a sectarian library is discussed.

1.2. A Sectarian Library?

In studying the *yahad*, we mostly rely on information we derive from the nine hundred manuscripts found in the Qumran caves. The Qumran paradigm especially rests upon the way scholars have assessed the function, meaning, and coherence of these manuscripts. To arrive at a comprehensive picture of a community on the basis of texts is not only a tricky business laden with a degree of arbitrary decisions but also demands some sort of categorization of texts. The notion of a coherent, meaningful, and representative collection, which is often referred to as the Qumran library, is a cornerstone in the theories of the existence of a Qumran community.

---

57. Some scholars have argued for a comparable halakic approach between Qumran texts (predominantly 4QMMT[a] [4Q394]) and Sadducean legal positions; see Jacob Sussman, "The History of *Halakhah* and the Dead Sea Scrolls—Preliminary Observation on *Miqsat Maʾase Ha-Torah* (4QMMT)," *Tarbiz* 59 (1990): 11–76; Aharon Shemesh, *Halakhah in the Making: The Development of Jewish Law from Qumran to the Rabbis*, Taubman Lectures in Jewish Studies (Berkeley: University of California Press, 2009), 17–18; Aharon Shemesh and Cana Werman, "Halakhah at Qumran: Genre and Authority," *DSD* 10 (2003): 104–29.

58. E.g., James VanderKam, *The Dead Sea Scrolls Today* (Grand Rapids: Eerdmans, 1994), 93–95.

The first to speak of a "Qumran library" were two influential scholars of the first hour: Józef T. Milik and Frank Moore Cross.[59] Hence, from the beginning of Qumran scholarship, the notion of a library has brought about connotations of a meaningful interrelatedness of the texts found in the caves, which subsequently allow for a sectarian community as their writers, owners, preservers, and redactors. Accordingly, in a series of articles, Devorah Dimant has advocated for the coherence of the "Qumran collection," which, according to her, reflects uniqueness "in its size and literary character."[60] Dimant concluded that the Qumran manuscripts form a representative and meaningful collection. Moreover, she seemed convinced that the manuscripts known today represent the whole of the manuscripts that once were hidden in the caves, and she considered the collection an intentional, well-chosen, and uniform sectarian library.[61]

With the connection to the site and the notion of a meaningful coherent library of a particular community presupposed, the Qumran collection needed an inventory with regard to contents. Until recently, the commonplace categorization of the manuscripts and fragments from the caves took place according to neat oppositional categories: "biblical" and "nonbiblical," "sectarian" and "nonsectarian." The exact criteria on the basis of which texts were categorized have been the object of many debates, the most influential of which will be discussed here.

---

59. See Milik, *Ten Years of Discovery*; and Cross, *Ancient Library of Qumran*.

60. Dimant, "Qumran Manuscripts: Contents and Significance," 23–57; see also Dimant, "Between Sectarian and Non-sectarian: The Case of the *Apocryphon of Joshua*," in *Reworking the Bible: Apocryphal Texts at Qumran; Proceedings of a Joint Symposium by the Orion Center for the Study of the Dead Sea Scrolls and Associated Literature and the Hebrew University Institute for Advanced Studies Research Group on Qumran, 15–17 January, 2002*, ed. Esther G. Chazon, Devorah Dimant, and Ruth A. Clements, STDJ 58 (Leiden: Brill, 2005), 105–34; Dimant, "Sectarian and Non-sectarian Texts from Qumran: The Pertinence and Usage of a Taxonomy," *RevQ* 24 (2009): 7–18; Dimant, "The Qumran Aramaic Texts and the Qumran Community," in *Flores Florentino: Dead Sea Scrolls and Other Early Jewish Studies in Honour of Florentino García Martínez*, ed. Anton Hilhorst, Émile Puech, and Eibert J. C. Tigchelaar, JSJSup 122 (Leiden: Brill, 2007), 197–207; also, Dimant, "Between Sectarian and Non-sectarian Texts: The Case of Belial and Mastema," in Roitman, Schiffman, and Tzoref, *Dead Sea Scrolls and Contemporary Culture*, 235–56.

61. Dimant does not seem to give any weight to the fact that over two millennia, texts and other archaeological evidence must have got lost forever, and hence it is difficult to prove that the current assembly of texts is representative of what once was there.

The first to label certain texts sectarian were Dupont-Sommer[62] and Géza Vermes.[63] Their early categorization was uncomplicated: all nonbiblical documents found in the Qumran caves were considered to be sectarian. In 1983, Hartmut Stegemann first outlined criteria to evaluate specific Qumran texts as sectarian. He only considered a small number of texts to be sectarian, namely, those texts that reflected the recognizable authoritativeness of the Teacher of Righteousness, which elaborated upon the rules of the Qumran community, or which used distinct terminology tying them to such texts.[64]

In 1995, Dimant proposed to establish a systematic classification of all Qumran scrolls according to their sectarian or nonsectarian character as well as their content.[65] She first proposed three main categories: (1) biblical works, (2) works containing community terminology (CT), and (3) works not containing community terminology (NCT).[66] Such a classification naturally requires determining criteria for "community terminology." Dimant recognized four main criteria to signify the CT texts: "(1) The practices and organization of a particular community, (2) the history of this community and its contemporary circumstances, (3) the theological and metaphysical outlook of that community, and (4) the peculiar biblical exegesis espoused by that community."[67]

The distinction between sectarian and nonsectarian texts has driven scholars to identify sectarian features. Like Dimant, Armin Lange focused on sectarian terminology to evaluate a text as sectarian. Following the example of Stegemann, he set criteria based on certain features in the text:[68]

---

62. Dupont-Sommer, *The Essene Writings from Qumran*.

63. Géza Vermes, *The Dead Sea Scrolls: Qumran in Perspective* (Cleveland: Collins World, 1977).

64. Hartmut Stegemann, "Die Bedeutung der Qumranfünde für die Erforschung der Apokalyptik," in *Apocalypticism in the Mediterranean World and the Near East: Proceedings of the International Colloquium on Apocalypticism, Uppsala, August 12–17, 1979*, ed. D. Hellholm (Tübingen: Mohr Siebeck, 1983), 495–530.

65. Dimant, "Qumran Manuscripts," 23–58.

66. Ibid., 26–30.

67. Ibid., 27–28.

68. Armin Lange, "Kriterien essenischer Texte," in *Qumran Kontrovers: Beiträge zu den Textfunden vom Toten Meer*, ed. Jörg Frey and Hartmut Stegemann, Einblicke 6 (Paderborn: Bonifatius, 2003), 59–69. Under the influence of the discovery of a large number of so-called parabiblical or rewritten Bible texts, Lange advances a categorization tool for this body of texts, still on the basis of the foundational distinction

the absence of the Tetragrammaton (except for quotations from scripture), a specific ideology, a 364-day calendar, strict halakah and torah observance, cosmic-ethic dualism and eschatology, a critical attitude towards the priestly order in Jerusalem, specificity of genre (i.e., pesharim), and finally distinct terminology. However, Hempel has argued that only two of these criteria unambiguously distinguish a text as sectarian:[69] specific terminology (Teacher of Righteousness, Wicked Priest, Man of Lies) and literary genres unique to Qumran and therefore presumably of Qumranic authorship (pesharim).

Under the influence of the steady publication of the Scrolls and heavily informed by the desire to explain the origins of a Qumran community, several additional propositions to further differentiate between the different nonbiblical manuscripts of the Qumran library were made.

García Martínez proposed a fourfold classification of nonbiblical texts in accordance with his Groningen hypothesis: (1) sectarian works, (2) works of the formative period, (3) works reflecting Essene thought, and (4) works belonging to the apocalyptic tradition, which gave rise to Essenism.[70] Moreover, García Martínez already problematized his own proposition, as he recognized different layers within certain texts. He therefore argued for the occurrence of a certain sectarian development; that is, he raises the possibility that the Qumran community elaborated upon, adapted, and modernized texts so as to fit their specific ideology. Another proposal was suggested by Torleif Elgvin, who attempted to honor Emanuel Tov's argument for the existence of a specific Qumran scribal school,[71] and has the following classification: (1) works copied according to the Qumran scribal system, (2) works copied for the *yahad*, (3) works composed by

---

between sectarian and nonsectarian texts: see Lange, "From Paratext to Commentary," in Roitman, Schiffman, and Tzoref, *Dead Sea Scrolls and Contemporary Culture*, 195–216.

69. Charlotte Hempel, "Kriterien zur Bestimmung 'essenischer Verfasserschaft' von Qumrantexten," in Frey and Stegemann, *Qumran Kontrovers*, 71–85.

70. García Martínez, *Qumranica Minora I*, 3–29.

71. Emanuel Tov, *Scribal Practices and Approaches Reflected in the Texts Found in the Judean Desert*, STDJ 54 (Leiden: Brill, 2004). Tov's proposal that the Qumran manuscripts reflect a specific scribal culture, which ties the Qumran caves together, has influenced the theories of various scholars that claim the "representativeness of the Qumran collection" as a library. However, Tov's proposal seems to ignore some considerations in the material culture evidence from Qumran that call into question straightforward links between the caves.

the "parents" of the *yaḥad*, that is, "Essenes," "presectarians," "Enochians," or "apocalyptics," and (4) works of a wider Jewish setting (non-Essene).[72] Gabriele Boccaccini identified an emerging taxonomic consensus on the classification of three distinct groups of texts: (1) texts distinct by ideology and style produced by a single community (sectarian); (2) texts with only some sectarian features, belonging to either a parent movement or brother/sister movement; and (3) texts where sectarian elements are marginal or completely absent, including biblical texts.[73]

Finally, Dimant called for a further refinement of her earlier classification once it became clear that some Qumran texts lack "sectarian characteristic nomenclature and style but embrace notions shared with the sectarian ideology."[74] Realizing that those texts that lack specific sectarian terminology or style cannot be simply classified as sectarian or nonsectarian, Dimant proposed to assign such writings to an intermediate "in-between" category. This new category is to be placed in between what Dimant considers to be sectarian literature proper and "writings devoid of any connection to the community."[75] According to Dimant, candidates for such an in-between sectarian and nonsectarian category are texts like the Temple Scroll and the book of Jubilees. Generally speaking, Dimant recognized Qumranic works that "rework the Bible"[76] as belonging to this in-between category.

Scholars such as García Martínez and Eibert Tigchelaar have lately challenged the categorization into sectarian and nonsectarian (and also Dimant's in-between) texts.[77] After his initial Groningen hypothesis clas-

---

72. Torleif Elgvin, "The *Yaḥad* Is More Than Qumran," in Boccaccini, *Enoch and Qumran Origins*, 273–79.
73. Boccaccini, *Beyond the Essene Hypothesis*, 57–58.
74. Dimant, "*Apocryphon of Joshua*," 106.
75. Ibid.
76. Naturally, the term is problematic since in Qumran times there was no canonized Bible.
77. Eibert J. C. Tigchelaar, "The Dead Sea Scrolls," in *Eerdmans Dictionary of Early Judaism*, ed. John J. Collins and Daniel Harlow (Grand Rapids: Eerdmans, 2010), 163–80; see also Tigchelaar, "Classifications of the Collection of the Dead Sea Scrolls and the Case of *Apocryphon of Jeremiah C*," *JSJ* 43 (2012): 519–50; Florentino García Martínez, "Sectario, No-Sectario, O Qué? Problemas de una taxonomía correcta de los textos qumránicos," *RevQ* 23 (2008): 383–94.

sification, in which he proposed a fourfold distinction among the Qumran literature,[78] García Martínez proposed

> de abandoner los esfuerzos de clasificación anacrónicos de los manuscritos de la colección qumránica como textos 'bíblicos o no bíblicos' y 'sectarios o no sectarios', y ... de considerar el conjunto de la colección como un conglomerado de textos religiosos más o menos autoritativos para el grupo que los recogió, los conservó y, en determinados casos, los compuso.[79]

In his proposal to abandon the sectarian/nonsectarian dichotomy, García Martínez critically evaluated all earlier attempts to classify the Qumran literature. He convincingly demonstrates that Dimant's classifications are too simplified to do justice to the complexity of Qumran.[80] According to García Martínez, the abandonment of classifications in terms of sectarian or nonsectarian would help us to appreciate how a specific group within its original historical setting in the Second Temple period handled religious texts and managed their own unique collection of manuscripts. However, in this new proposal the idea of a Qumranic sectarian library, a meaningful collection that can be tied to one community or group, is maintained.

1.3. Moving the Foundation Stone: Sectarianism as a Second Temple Phenomenon?

The concept of sectarianism is commonly used to describe the fragmentation within Jewish society in the Second Temple period. The use of the term "sect," which originated in (Christian) Western sociology, was enhanced by translations of Josephus's description of group divisions, which he labeled "philosophies" or *haereseis*. Consequently, various groups with diverse legalistic and socioreligious ideas were scaled on the basis of their perceived tension with a common Judaism and—to a lesser or larger extent— classified as sects. Also within the field of Qumran studies, the terms sect and sectarianism are frequently employed. The existence of sociological

---

78. García Martínez, *Qumranica Minora I*, 9.
79. García Martínez, "Sectario, No-Sectario," 393.
80. For instance, in the case of the Aramaic Levi Document, the Qumran text demonstrates differences from the documents found in the Cairo Genizah. Hence, classification of such a document as sectarian/nonsectarian would be difficult.

sects within the Second Temple period and, more specifically, the sectarian character of the Qumran community are more or less presupposed. However, in the employment of these terms, their actual meaning is by no means clear. For instance, Schiffman defines a sect as "a religious ideology that may develop the characteristics of a political party in order to defend its way of life."[81] Baumgarten, however, defines sect as "a voluntary association of protest, which utilizes boundary making mechanisms—the social means of differentiating between insiders and outsiders—to distinguish between its own members and those otherwise normally regarded as belonging to the same national or religious entity."[82] Schofield, who clearly acknowledges the complexity of Second Temple society, holds that a characteristic tenet of sects is that they are simultaneously part of and antagonistic to a larger religious community. She reaches the following definition: "A sect is a group which identifies with and simultaneously sets up ideological boundary markers against a larger religious body."[83] Joseph Blenkinsopp attempts to assign certain characteristics to the notion of sect: "the well-known sects … including the Qumran *yaḥad* … deviated from generally accepted social norms, some of them shared common space, and all of them obeyed a charismatic leader." However, on the basis of sociological notions of sectarianism, he argues that "being set apart"-ness is the most decisive aspect in identifying a sect.[84] Davies defines a sect as "a social group of like-minded persons that lies within a larger social entity but which, as opposed to a party, does not understand itself as belonging within that larger group, but outside it. Its boundaries exclude members of the larger group and there is no overlap."[85] The commonality in all these definitions is their sensitivity to the sect's tension with the outside world. However, the various definitions differ rather extensively with regard to the degree of tension, separation, and isolation.

---

81. Schiffman, *Reclaiming the Dead Sea Scrolls*, 72–73.

82. Albert I. Baumgarten, *The Flourishing of Jewish Sects in the Maccabean Era: An Interpretation*, JSJSup 55 (Leiden: Brill, 1997), 7.

83. Schofield, *From Qumran to the Yaḥad*, 28.

84. Joseph Blenkinsopp, "The Qumran Sect in the Context of Second Temple Sectarianism," in Campbell, Lyons, and Pietersen, *New Directions in Qumran Studies*, 11.

85. Davies, "Sects from Texts," 70. Davies's definition is heavily influenced by Bryan Wilson's work on sects, e.g., Bryan Wilson, *Religious Sects: A Sociological Study*, World University Library (London: Weidenfeld & Nicholson, 1970).

Jutta Jokiranta has recognized the variety of terminology and criticized the indiscriminate use of the terms *sect* and *sectarianism* for different designations in different contexts.[86] Hence, while some scholars consciously choose elaborate definitions, containing all sorts of inherent problems, others have used the term sect casually, presupposing that any reader will implicitly understand what is meant by the employment of the term.[87] Broadening definitions, in which the term sect can easily equal the terms "group," "movement," or "faction," run the risk of losing their explanatory power altogether, as they complicate the identification and quality of a specific group phenomenon, such as a Qumran community. Stricter definitions, which contain the sense of "being set apart"-ness from wider society are equally problematic: first, because of their often pejorative connotations (stemming from the term's Christian roots), and, second, because they implicitly presuppose a unified socio-religious outside world, that is, a "church."[88] Hence, by ascribing terms like sect and sectarianism to the social phenomenon of group formation or societal fragmentation, one also opens the door to all sorts of confusion with regard to the diverse semantic fields of these terms.

Partly this confusion is fueled by the development of the sociological field of the study of sectarianism itself. Within the sociological field, critique has been uttered about various aspects of the usage of models of sect and sectarianism: models are supposed to be anachronistic and

---

86. "Thus, for the same groups, one may call them 'parties' or 'factions,' the other separates between 'reform movements' and 'sects,' and a third may speak of 'reformist sects' and 'introversionist sects' ... and we can only guess how readers of Qumran Studies in different countries and cultures understand the term" (Jokiranta, "Sociological Notes," 224).

87. This tendency started even before the discovery of the Dead Sea Scrolls, when the Damascus Document was discovered in the Cairo Genizah; see Solomon Schechter, *Fragments of a Zadokite Work*, Documents of Jewish Sectaries 1 (Cambridge: University Press, 1910); see also Ginzberg, *Unknown Jewish Sect*.

88. The first notion of the term sect can be found in the work of sociologist Max Weber. Weber's thoughts on sects can be found throughout his work, but he is nowhere specific. His most important contribution might be *Wirtschaft und Gesellschaft* (Tübingen: Mohr Siebeck, 1925). Weber's student, Ernst Troeltsch, the German sociologist and theologian, placed the terms church and sect in a dichotomous relationship and created an ideal-type of church and an ideal-type of sect, identifiable through oppositional characteristics; see Ernst Troeltsch, *The Social Teaching of the Christian Churches*, trans. Olive Myon (New York: Macmillan, 1931).

ethnocentric; that is, they were designed with specific cultural, socioeconomic, and historical settings in mind. Also, models reflect a specific philosophical history, which limits their compatibility and commensurability in cross-cultural analyses. Furthermore, it is often stated that models are oversimplifications that tend to block out dissonant data.[89] Pieter Craffert argues that "once within the framework of a particular model, it is difficult, if not impossible, to consider viewpoints which do not belong to that framework."[90] Therefore, what he calls a model's "goodness of fit" is difficult to establish. Even though there might be a fit between the model and the empirical data, in itself this "is not necessarily a confirmation that it is either a good model or an appropriate model for that set [of data]."[91]

Moreover, typologies and models of sect and sectarianism depend heavily upon antagonistic dependencies and as such on the oppositional concept of the outside world—a sect's social environment. In describing the Qumran texts as a coherent sectarian library and the Qumranites as sectarians, the notion of sectarianism not only drives the perception, classification, and interpretation of its contents, but it also presupposes a social context that reflects a diversified or contrasting common Judaism. Even if one wants to cling to the idea of a sectarian Qumran community and its library, research on group formation has shown that although socioreligious groups in tension tend to perceive the outside world ideologically as a monolithic stronghold of evil, the sociohistorical reality is that these groups develop "as intensified versions of a shared mainstream culture and not as alien movements imported into it."[92] Moreover, in environments where sects are dominant, a binary typological structure seems to lose

---

89. See Pieter Craffert, "An Exercise in the Critical Use of Models: The 'Goodness of Fit' of Wilson's Sect Model," in *Social Scientific Models for Interpreting the Bible: Essays by the Context Group in Honor of Bruce J. Malina*, ed. John J. Pilch, BibInt 53 (Leiden: Brill, 2001), 23. See further Stephen Barton, "Early Christianity and the Sociology of the Sect," in *The Open Text: New Directions for Biblical Studies?* ed. Francis Watson (London: SCM, 1993), 144.

90. Craffert, "Exercise in the Critical Use of Models," 23.

91. Ibid.

92. Maxine Grossman, "Cultivating Identity: Textual Virtuosity and 'Insider' Status," in García Martínez and Popović, *Defining Identities*, 1–11; see also Frederik Barth, *Ethnic Groups and Boundaries: The Social Organization of Cultural Difference* (Propect Heights, IL: Waveland, 1998).

much of its analytical power and explanatory strength with regard to the cultural complexity of society as a whole.⁹³

Thus having evaluated the sociohistorical theories of the history of the Qumran community, the classification theories with regard to its library, and its underlying ideological framework of sectarianism, we now need to address what we know of the historical world within which Qumran functioned. This historical world, or at least what we can reconstruct of it, will be discussed in broad strokes in the next section.

1.4. Judea and Judaism in Second Temple Times: Power, Privilege, and Fragmentation

In order to understand the Qumran situation and its place within the larger contemporary society, we need to obtain information about its larger socioreligious and political context. As we now know, with the help of advanced techniques of carbon-14 testing, AMS testing, paleography, archaeology, and the historical allusions in the Scrolls,⁹⁴ all Qumran documents, with the exception of the Copper Scroll (3Q15) from Cave 3, can be dated between the late-third/early-second century BCE and the destruction of the Second Temple in 70 CE. Hence, if we can take these dates as a point of departure, we would have to focus on Judaism in the Hellenistic, Maccabean, and Roman periods. However, we might also want to consider the historical background against which Jewish groups came into existence. Davies, who considers Judaism multiform in nature, has argued that Jewish group formation has its roots in exilic times and became manifest in the early Persian period.⁹⁵ Similarly, Lester Grabbe holds that "sects and movements have a long history in Judaic religion, perhaps going back to preexilic times but most likely being present already in the Persian period."⁹⁶ Even though Grabbe admits that such a preexilic origin of

---

93. See Jokiranta, "Sociological Notes," 31; Barton, "Early Christianity and the Sociology of the Sect," 158; Craffert, "Exercise in the Critical Use of Models," 24.

94. For a general overview of these methods, see, e.g., James VanderKam and Peter Flint, *The Meaning of the Dead Sea Scrolls: Their Significance for Understanding the Bible, Judaism, Jesus, and Christianity* (London: T&T Clark, 2002), 3–55.

95. Philip Davies, "Sect Formation in Early Judaism," in *Sectarianism in Early Judaism: Sociological Advances*, ed. David Chalcraft (London: Equinox, 2007), 143–44.

96. Lester Grabbe, *Judaic Religion in the Second Temple Period: Belief and Practice from the Exile to Yavneh* (London: Routledge, 2000), 207.

1. INTRODUCTION 25

sectarianism is hard to prove, Blenkinsopp argues that biblical records of the time of the kingdoms contain evidence for group formation within ancient Israel.[97] Here, he finds evidence for the "existence of distinctive subgroups" in the models of charismatic leadership as provided in the description of Elijah and Elisha.[98] With respect to a Persian origin, Blenkinsopp, like Davies, provides more certainty, by pointing to the insider/outsider terminology in Ezra-Nehemiah. Hence, a brief overview of Qumran's socioreligious and political context needs to reckon with preexisting influences from at least the Persian period (538–332 BCE).

Richard Horsley has researched the origins of the Judean temple-state under Persian rule.[99] He finds that the Persian imperial politics of the rebuilding of the temple and reinstating the high priesthood was decisive in the foundations of the political-religious struggles that eventually led to the coming into being of multiple Jewish sects. He names basically four conflicts that contributed to the rise of Jewish sectarianism:

(1) The division between those who remained in the land after the Babylonian conquest and those who returned from exile, encouraged and reinstated by the Persian ruler;
(2) The division between the peasantry and the Jerusalemite aristocracy, who were centered around the high priesthood;
(3) Conflicts between various priestly fractions; and
(4) Power struggles between local magnates and between local magnates and the Persian ruler.[100]

Horsley concludes that, even though the high priesthood might have perceived itself as the functional ruler of the Judean temple state, in effect they represented a "political-economic as well as a religious institution that served as the instrument of imperial rule in Judea."[101]

---

97. Blenkinsopp, "Qumran Sect in the Context of Second Temple Sectarianism," 10–25.
98. Ibid., 10–11.
99. Richard Horsley, *Scribes, Visionaries and the Politics of Second Temple Judea* (Louisville: Westminster John Knox, 2007).
100. Ibid., 22–31. Horsley clearly follows Lenski's theory of agrarian society; see Gerhard Lenski, *Power and Privilege: A Theory of Social Stratification*, McGraw-Hill Series in Sociology (New York: McGraw-Hill, 1966), 190–296.
101. Horsley, *Scribes, Visionaries, and the Politics*, 32.

Grabbe is very critical of historical reconstructions concerning the Persian era, simply because the sources are not always reliable, sometimes skimpy and problematic, and, during certain centuries, almost nonexistent (especially 465–404 BCE).[102] He does, however, acknowledge that the Persian era has sown the seeds of a decisive religious outlook (including angelology, demonology, and eschatology) and has brought about an early formation of what later would become a Jewish canon of scripture.

The Hellenistic period (332–63 BCE) provides much more information and a much clearer view of the rise of Jewish factions. After Alexander the Great's death in 323 BCE, rivalries between the Seleucid and Ptolemaic empires left Judea in a constant state of war and chaos. Judea was mainly exploited for taxes and Hellenistic influences were considerable. Greek language was widespread and some of the Jerusalemite aristocracy seemed to have evaluated this hellenization of Jewish culture favorably.[103] However, the reign of the Seleucid ruler Antiochus IV Epiphanes (175–164 BCE) and his hellenizing program initially split the nation into two opposing parties: (1) the Hellenists among whom were many from the educated and aristocratic classes, and (2) the Devout/Hasidim, who were considered to represent the traditional views of the scribes. It was only Antiochus's attempt to abolish Jewish religion altogether that turned not only the small group of the Hasidim but also the majority of the people against hellenization and ultimately resulted in the Maccabean revolt.

In his study of Jewish society in the Second Temple period, Baumgarten positions the emergence of Jewish sectarianism in these Maccabean times, and he basically identifies five "decisive factors" responsible for the flourishing of sects: (1) the encounter with Hellenism; (2) the rising literacy levels; (3) urbanization and the loss of "reference"; (4) the inherent eschatological tension within Judaism and its search for redemption; and (5) priestly reform resulting in a renewed emphasis on the correct observance of the law.[104] Baumgarten evaluates sectarianism as a relatively

---

102. Lester Grabbe, *Yehud: A History of the Persian Province of Judah*, vol. 1 of *A History of the Jews and Judaism in the Second Temple Period*, LSTS 47 (London: T&T Clark, 2004).

103. See Emil Schürer, *History of the Jewish People in the Age of Jesus Christ (175 B.C–A.D. 135)*, ed. Géza Vermes, Fergus Millar, and Martin Black, rev. and enl. ed. (Edinburgh: T&T Clark, 2004).

104. Baumgarten, *Flourishing of Jewish Sects*, 7. Grabbe considers Baumgarten's "decisive factors" for the rise of sectarianism merely hypothetical.

minor phenomenon (sects supposedly made up 6 percent of the total population). Accordingly, he claims that society's low literacy levels demonstrate that sects were elitist.[105] Moreover, he does not associate these sects with high boundaries, as he asserts a certain openness: people were able to check out several sectarian groups before making a choice for one of them.[106] Finally, Baumgarten postulates that sects were not very different but artificially "blew up" their legalistic differences in order to attract potential members.[107] In a recent article, Davies—somewhat in line with Baumgarten—has argued that the reasons for sectarianism lay in politics, disguised and legitimized by (religious) ideology.[108] This is certainly true for the Maccabean position. While Mattathias and Judas Maccabeus initially fought for the preservation of Jewish religion against the hellenizing program of Antiochus IV, Judas's quest changed after Antiochus V Eupator had guaranteed the rights of the Jews in 162 BCE.[109] Now, politics and internal struggles for power between the high priesthood and the political leader(s) became more pronounced, as did the wish to expand the land. Rulers and high priests sought for alliances with foreign powers to secure their positions over against one another.[110] In 143/142 BCE, Simon managed to achieve Jewish freedom in return for his loyalty to the Syrian king

---

105. Baumgarten's estimates depend heavily on Josephus and Philo and are to be addressed with caution. Moreover, there seems to be some tension within Baumgarten's reasoning, as he, on the one hand, presumes the rise of literacy levels to cause sectarianism, while, on the other hand, he presumes that low literacy levels cause sectarian groups to be relatively small and elitist.

106. This observation is based on Josephus, who, according to Baumgartner, "learned all there was to learn from all schools and sources" (Baumgarten, *Flourishing of Jewish Sects,* 52). Baumgarten emphasizes a sect's voluntary character and downplays one of the main characteristics of a sect, i.e., the existence of high social boundaries between insiders and outsiders. However, an example of the existence of such social boundaries can be found in the Rule of the Community's entrance requirements; see Matthias Klinghardt, "The Manual of Discipline in the Light of Statutes of Hellenistic Associations," in *Methods of Investigation of the Dead Sea Scrolls and the Khirbet Qumran Site: Present Realities and Future Prospects,* ed. Michael O. Wise et al., ANYAS 722 (New York: The New York Academy of Sciences, 1994), 251–70.

107. According to Baumgarten, legal authority and the explanation of the law were not decisive factors for sectarianism, neither were calendar and legal practice; Baumgarten, *Flourishing of Jewish Sects,* 79–80.

108. Davies, "Sect Formation in Early Judaism," 136.

109. See Schürer, *History of the Jewish People,* 125–242.

110. Ibid., 175–88.

Demetrius. At this time the Jews started their own chronology: "Documents and treatises were dated according to the years of Simon, High Priest and Prince of the Jews."[111] But, Simon wanted more, and on 18 Elul 140 BCE a popular decree was ordered: Simon should be high priest, military commander, and ethnarch of the Jews, and he should be "their leader and high priest forever until a trustworthy prophet should arise" (1 Macc 14:41).[112] Hence, the formerly hereditary post of high priest was transformed into "a high-priestly and princely dynasty, that of the Hasmoneans."[113]

Gerhard Lenski has researched agrarian societies and their way of dealing with power and privilege.[114] The reign of the Hasmoneans demonstrates an especially high degree of congruency with Lenski's findings. Not only do agrarian societies tend to be conquest states,[115] but they also tend to turn to internal struggles if struggles with foreign enemies—mainly over the possession of the land—are lacking. Internally, conflicts can persist between (1) the ruler and the governing classes, (2) governing classes among themselves, (3) the governing classes and the retainer class, and (4) the retainer class and the peasant class.[116] Horsley finds that imperial struggles between the Ptolemies and the Seleucids already gave rise to Judean power struggles between aristocratic groups. And after the foundation of the independent Hasmonean state, these internal tensions between social groups within Jewish society became even more evident. Now, an even closer link between religion and politics was established, since for a period, the high priest and the political leader were one and the same person. Accordingly, Lenski finds that in most agrarian societies religion is "a matter of concern to state authorities."[117] Like Baumgarten and Davies, he points out that power struggles were hardly ever over principles or religious matters, "rather they were struggles between opposing factions of the privileged classes, each seeking their own special advantage,

---

111. Ibid., 190; see 1 Macc 13:33-42, 14:27.
112. Ibid., 193.
113. Ibid., 194.
114. Lenski, *Power and Privilege*, 190-296.
115. "Social units formed through the forcible subjugation of one group by another" (ibid., 195).
116. Ibid., 190-296, with regard to this social stratification, especially fig. 1, 284. The retainer class is considered to be "a small army of officials, professional soldiers, household servants and personal retainers, all of whom served them [the ruler and the governing classes] in a variety of more or less specialized capacities," 243.
117. Ibid., 209.

or, occasionally, a small segment of the common people seeking political advantage and preferment for themselves."[118] Hence, the state in itself can be seen as the "supreme prize for struggle," since "gaining power and control over the state was to win control of the most powerful instrument of self-aggrandizement found in agrarian societies."[119] Also, Lenski finds a natural basis for symbiosis between political rulers and the priestly class: only the priestly blessing would secure and legitimize an abusive political system that took the greater part of the common people's revenues for the elite's enrichment. Since literacy levels were relatively low, the priestly class was often influential in matters of administration and education, in other words, in all matters that required scribal qualities. However, Horsley argues that "power struggle between factions of the Jerusalemite aristocracy [priestly and non-priestly] would have adversely affected the relative positions of Levites, ordinary priests, temple singers, 'scribes of the Temple' and others involved in and dependent on the operation of the temple-state."[120] Hence, political and economic objectives were often religiously legitimized, since identification with the right political and religious group became an individual's resource or obstacle to advancement in society.[121]

Thus, the Hasmoneans played an ambivalent role in these power struggles: They started out on the side of the most devout, but their later political aspirations made them close ranks with the influential nobility (mainly Sadducees), who had a more worldly focus. John Hyrcanus (135/134–104 BCE) even broke with the Pharisees, a break that became even more severe under Alexander Jannaeus (103–176 BCE), as he neglected his high-priestly duties in favor of his worldly rule. His political successor, his wife Alexandra (76–67 BCE), restored the bond with the Pharisees. After her predominantly peaceful reign, her sons Aristobulus II and Hyrcanus II fought one another for the rule of the Jewish state, which led to the Roman general Pompey's interference: the independent Jewish state came to an end (63 BCE) as Palestine was controlled by the Roman governor of Syria. Only the care of the temple was left to Jewish (Hasmonean) control. The time between Pompey's arrival in Jerusalem and the end of the Bar Kokhba revolt (63 BCE–135 CE) can mainly be

---

118. Ibid., 211.
119. Ibid., 210.
120. Horsley, *Scribes, Visionaries, and the Politics*, 51.
121. Lenski, *Power and Privilege*, 285.

characterized by struggle for influence, power, and privilege. In 57–55 BCE, Judea was divided into five Roman districts, each with its own Sanhedrin. Finally, it was Herod who seized power (37–4 BCE) by defeating and disposing of his enemies. Herod's allegiance to Rome and Hellenistic culture was strong. Even though he officially did not interfere with the powerful Pharisaic party and seemed to have respect for the temple cult, in reality he appointed and dismissed high priests to his liking, built a number of pagan temples throughout Palestine, took away most of the Sanhedrin's power and virtually murdered what was left of the Hasmonean family.

Undoubtedly the seeds for Jewish factionism/sectarianism were planted in exilic and Persian times, but its flourishing is closely connected to external imperial power struggles, to its economic consequences for Jewish society, and to internal struggles that were far more complex than initially thought. Next to the obvious disputes over legal matters, societal divisions, which eventually led to the formation of factions and groups, were also the result of social tensions between ethnic groups, between classes, between city-dwellers and peasants, and between aristocratic and priestly groups struggling for power. Hence, I would like to work from the idea that Judaic society in Second Temple times was a multifaceted and fragmented disunity in a complex cultural area, during a time and age which in modern terms we would call globalizing, a time, in which internally and externally based threats contributed to an already existing socioreligious identity crisis, which forced Judaism to renegotiate its boundaries of self-understanding. These negotiations were influenced by internal and external social, historical, political, and economic factors and ultimately led to an increasing power base for scriptural centrality over against the diminishing power of the temple cult.

It is in this complex and dynamic world that the documents of Qumran find their home. Theories about the meaning and function of Khirbet Qumran and the socioreligious world of the Qumran documents must reckon with this broader societal complexity.

1.5. The Qumran Paradigm: A Persistent Phenomenon?

The preceding sections have discussed the prevalent perceptions of the Qumran inside world and the sociohistorical situation of the outside world of Second Temple society. Within these settings, Qumran scholarship has found its theoretical niche in coming to terms with the textual and material evidence found at Khirbet Qumran. Over the last few decades, the Qumran paradigm, that is, the consensus view of a Qumran Essene-like sectarian community that set itself apart from others, has been called into question. Under the influence of the almost complete publication of the scrolls, interdisciplinary research, and our better understanding of the history of Judaism, the scholarly field of Qumran studies has questioned the early parameters of the Qumran paradigm in all sorts of ways and in all sorts of areas. The areas on which these questions are focused can be broadly divided into five recognizable clusters:

(1) Archaeological questions, such as: Is the original archaeology technically correct, and do its results allow for the conclusions drawn by de Vaux? Does the archaeological evidence reflect a segregated Qumran Essene-like sect? How do the texts and the archaeological evidence relate? Are the texts and the site connected? What is the significance of the cemetery?

(2) Ideological questions, such as: Are the Qumranites identical to Josephus's Essenes, and what is the evidence? Are there women in Qumran? Is there such a thing as Qumran theology? To what degree do the texts have a sectarian outlook? How to determine a sectarian text? Is sect useful as a sociological term? What are the specific characteristics of Qumran sectarianism? How does Qumran sectarianism build its identity and self-definition? Is the concept of dualism a core characteristic of Qumran theology? Does dualistic thinking occur in all sectarian texts, and if so, is the dualistic framework identical in all these texts?

(3) Literary questions, such as: How do CD and 1QS relate to one another? How do we assess the occurrence and relationship of the Hebrew and Aramaic Qumran corpus? Does the difference in language signify a different sociohistorical provenance? Can the Qumran texts be categorized? Do these categorizations aid or obstruct the analysis? Are there alternative ways to evaluate the texts? What is the relation between the various categories of texts within the Qumran library? Why does the library contain so many parabiblical works? Do they make a coherent and constructive unity? How do we deal with the oppositional views among the texts?

(4) Sociohistorical questions, such as: What is the meaning of the Qumran library? Are all the texts produced at Qumran? What

is the sociohistorical origin of the Qumran community? Can we read for history and social location in the sectarian texts? What do we know about the organizational structure of the Qumran situation on the basis of the texts we have? Do the texts give us a clear view of Qumran's social reality? Do the Qumranites reside in Qumran only, or is there a bigger movement?

(5) Methodological questions are all those questions that relate to how clusters 1–4 work together. But also: Can we use social scientific, particularly sociological models of sect, to open up the texts and broaden our knowledge of Qumran? If we use social scientific methods, which ones work and which ones do not? How do we read for history in the Qumran sectarian texts?

Many of these questions that critically reassess the first theories about Qumran have recently been asked, and I have listed them here in an attempt to implicitly gather together the problems that can be identified on the basis of the discussions on the previous pages of this introduction. These questions, which address the difficulties and discussions regarding various aspects of the parameters of the Qumran paradigm and its adjustments, have at least awakened us to the complexity of Qumran. However, these critical questions are often asked and answered from within the boundaries of the Qumran paradigm itself.[122]

The cause for the occurrence of this self-fulfilling prophecy of the Qumran paradigm and its adjustments might be found in the fact that many of the question marks that have surfaced in recent scholarship relate to theses that have been mirror-reading ideology onto sociologically definable groups. The foregoing discussion regarding the various approaches to Qumran has demonstrated enough problems to cast doubt on the assumption that ideas in texts have to be equated with sociological groups. In this book, I will attempt to question such mirror reading between ideology and social identity and to explore whether it would be possible to answer these

---

122. A good example of this is Edna Ullmann-Margalit's book *Out of the Cave: A Philosophical Enquiry into the Dead Sea Scrolls Research* (Cambridge: Harvard University Press, 2006), which attempts to evaluate Qumran scholarship's methods, attitudes, evaluations, and theorizations. Meant as a critical evaluation of DSS scholarship and posing numerous interesting methodological questions, the book functions within the paradigm and therefore leads to conclusions that do not fundamentally challenge the interpretative circle that upholds the paradigm in the first place.

questions (and other questions of this sort) from another vantage point and hence put Qumran in a different perspective.

The chapters that follow reckon with the possibility that too much weight might have been put on specific peculiarities within a number of Qumran texts in order to identify a group that mirrors these peculiarities sociologically. This study questions whether we have not all too easily retrieved from these texts distinguishing features in order to read into them a sociological reality of a radical minority group, a distinctive self-marginalized Qumran sect that (1) segregated itself from others and did not partake (any longer?) in the vigorous socioreligious negotiations of its time, (2) had significantly more extreme or more peculiar ideas than contemporary others, (3) was placed or placed itself at the margins of Judaism, and, therefore, (4) cannot be considered to be a representative of the ideological and sociological discourse that redefined the boundaries and parameters of Judaism in this period.

To put it differently: To what degree do the distinguishing features found among the Qumran texts necessitate the postulate of a sectarian community that segregated itself socioreligiously, ideologically, and maybe even geographically from others? The material that I will cover in the next chapters explores, in different ways, certain aspects of such a mirror reading connecting ideology and social reality, with this background question in mind.

Chapter 2 explores the way in which scholars have classified and categorized the collection of Qumran texts. It focuses on the most influential proposals for the literary and sociohistorical classifications of texts and questions whether and to what extent such classifications influence and determine the positioning of certain texts in light of a sectarian paradigm. A deeper look into these classification systems is warranted, because, for all the differences in their approaches, similar textual material emerges as critical to their frameworks. Moreover, one of the critical side effects of these classification systems is the notion that these texts—implicitly or explicitly—need to be placed within a framework of chronological development. Therefore, this chapter also explores the implications of this notion of chronology and its relation to the Qumran paradigm.

Chapter 3 is a test case with regard to our analysis of the classification systems and its concept of chronological development, as it reevaluates the text of 4QMMT and its prevalent provenance as a foundational document of the Qumran sect. As 4QMMT is an example of a text which has played a major, but difficult, role in both literary and sociohistorical classifications of Qumran, this document makes an excellent test case to identify possible problems with classification systems in general and mirror reading of ideology and sociology in particular. Moreover, this chapter identifies and reevaluates those peculiar and unique elements within 4QMMT on the basis of which scholars have argued for the text's important provenance. As such, it is interested in the question whether the peculiarities within the text point towards a sectarian or *yahadic* provenance or whether they also allow for a wider scale of possible interpretations.

Chapter 4 explores another aspect that has proven to be an important contributor to the sustainability of the Qumran paradigm, that is, the notion of a recognizable ideological coherence among certain Qumran texts. This chapter explores the ideological outlook from a theoretical perspective: it questions the definition, boundaries, and Qumran-specific evaluation of the concept of dualism. An analysis of the theoretical foundation for the identification of dualism is a first step in evaluating theories about Qumran dualism. Hence, this chapter provides the groundwork for questions about the relation between a Qumran-specific evaluation of ideological coherence and the prevalent Qumran paradigm, which will be discussed in chapter five.

In chapter 5, the Treatise of the Two Spirits (1QS III, 13–IV, 26) is explored as a test case for the ideological peculiarities of Qumran dualism. It asks whether and to what extent the Treatise and other dualistically evaluated sectarian texts might be interrelated on the basis of their dualistic outlook and what the function of such an ideological link might be. Even though the provenance of the Treatise as the zenith of Qumran theology has changed over time and some scholars no longer take the text to be the pivotal expression of the sect's dualistic outlook, the dualism in the Treatise is commonly taken as an important representative of one of the ideological boundary-markers of the Qumran community. As such, this text is worth evaluating in light of its dualistic features and its position and function within the Qumran paradigm.

Thus, the main thread of this study, namely, the questioning of the close alliance between ideology and sociology, is signified by the special focus on two test cases, 4QMMT and the Treatise, both of which scholars have regarded as foundational documents, one for the sociohistorical blueprint of the Qumran sect's theology and the other for the ideological basis of the Qumran sect's cosmology and anthropology. While these documents have been considered decisive in distinguishing specific characteristics of the Qumran community, neither of these texts mentions a connection to a *yahad* or uses *yahadic* terminology. Nevertheless, scholars have domesticated these texts within the realm of a sectarian paradigm.

This study is primarily focused on methodological questions on the metalevel of Qumran scholarship and explicitly does not want to be an exegetical study. The analyses of 4QMMT and the Treatise must be seen as illustrative to the main attempt of this monograph to investigate methodological issues and difficulties in mirror reading ideology and social identity, with special attention to the influence of the Qumran paradigm. This study explicitly wants to leave room for other and more fundamentally revisionist propositions with regard to the provenance of certain Qumran texts, while stabilizing the validity of certain aspects of the paradigm for other specific texts. Therefore, the final chapter will propose that we approach the prevalent Qumran paradigm with more revisionist scrutiny and content ourselves with the possibility that the Qumran manuscripts might not deal with an isolated community but with one that actively participated within the shaping of ideas and traditions of Judaism in this period. As such, we might reconsider these texts from a different vantage point, namely, from the perspective that they have something to contribute to our understanding of the shaping of Jewish traditions as a whole in the first centuries BCE and CE.

2

Textual Classifications of Presectarianism:
On In-Between Texts and Formative Periods

The structure of the Qumran paradigm, as described earlier, has for many functioned as especially determinative when investigating the Qumran community, its place of residence, and its library. As a result, the starting point for studying the Qumran manuscripts has often been their particular relationship with the Qumran sect and their perceived position within a sectarian library. Therefore, this study begins by exploring the way scholars have categorized the collection of Qumran texts and, more specifically, how they have attempted to read the social history and reality behind those texts. It focuses on two of the most influential proposals for the classification and categorization of the Qumran documents: a literary classification (Dimant) and a sociohistorical classification (García Martínez).[1]

In the introduction, we have already briefly encountered these two scholars' classification systems. The reason for addressing them more closely here lies in the fact that, despite the differences in their approaches, similar issues emerge as critical to the evaluation of their analyses. In what follows, I have chosen to reconstruct these two scholars' influential contributions in the area of Qumran classifications in order to bring out those specific elements within their theories that—it is my contention—tie textual information to a sociological model of chronological development that inherently sustains the Qumran paradigm.[2]

---

1. I thank Prof. Eibert Tigchelaar for our lively Skype discussion in March 2012. He has also dedicated an article to the subject of classification, with a different focus; see Tigchelaar, "Classifications of the Collection," 519–50.

2. It is important for me to state that I am not attempting to attack or diminish any of the eminent scholars whose theories I criticize in this study. Qumran scholar-

First, I will reconstruct and discuss the literary classifications of Dimant. In her classification system, Dimant introduces categories that distinguish sectarian texts from nonsectarian texts on the basis of the occurrence of recognizable "Community Terminology." Texts that are not biblical and not strictly *yahadic* are considered to be nonsectarian. This nonsectarian category hence contains a variety of texts that have as their common denominator that they are supposed to fall outside of the realm of the *yahad*. Since some of these texts demonstrate ideological affinity with the sectarian category of texts, Dimant later introduces a third "in-between" category for texts that convey *yahad*-like ideas but do not reflect specific sectarian terminology. In what follows, Dimant's literary classification will be studied in depth, not only with a special focus on the phenomenon of in-between texts, but also with regard to the presectarian connotation that seems to underlie this particular category.

Second, I will turn to the sociohistorical classifications advanced by García Martínez. In this classification scheme, better known as the Groningen hypothesis, García Martínez attempts to categorize the Qumran texts in terms of their relationship to the strict sectarian or *yahadic* texts. As such, he attempts to sketch the sect's ideological prehistory and its early and developed history by positioning the Qumran texts on a line of chronological development. This way, each text has its own place within the (pre)history of the Qumran group. In García Martínez's model, any text that is not considered to be strictly *yahadic* is perceived to be presectarian. This chapter is interested in this phenomenon and will thus discuss García Martínez's idea of a formative period of the Qumran sect as an important pillar of the Groningen hypothesis.

Dimant's and García Martínez's proposals can be counted among the most influential in Scrolls scholarship and as such have had and continue to have a profound impact on the way scholars have approached the scrolls and theorized about their provenance. This chapter attempts to identify how their classifications find their basis in and function by the parameters of the Qumran paradigm.

---

ship is deeply indebted to their insights and will continue to benefit from all their work on the scrolls. Rather, this study attempts to point out that certain elements in these theories reinforce rather than question, adjust rather than openly approach the Qumran paradigm, and that methodologically some aspects of these theories are inflexible, thereby possibly holding back new avenues of investigation in the fascinating world of Qumran.

2. TEXTUAL CLASSIFICATIONS OF PRESECTARIANISM   39

2.1. Dimant, a Sectarian Library and In-Between Sectarian Texts

Before addressing Dimant's literary classification system, we first need to assess its foundation with which her literary categories form an interpretative circle; namely, Dimant's notion that the Qumran texts form a coherent, deliberate, selective, and representative collection, much like an ancient library. Both aspects of Dimant's system, the notion of library and the categories of texts within this library, will be discussed below.

2.1.1. A Coherent and Representative Library

The first scholars who called the Qumran collection of texts a library were Milik and Cross.[3] Milik merely used the term *library* as shorthand for "the entirety of manuscripts from the Qumran caves" and thus gave no arguments or criteria for the usage of the term. Equally, Cross did not attach criteria to the term *library*, as he merely attempted to give an overview of the manuscripts and fragments found in the caves. Hence, Dimant is the first scholar who consciously argues for a deliberate and representative Qumran library.[4]

In defining the Qumran manuscripts as a library, Dimant takes the important step of attaching a set of critical presuppositions to this notion. In her influential 1995 article in which Dimant advocates a literary assessment of the Qumran collection, she establishes the notion of library by concluding that the collection comprises a unique "size and literary character."[5] Methodologically, she presents her reconstruction of

---

3. Milik, *Ten Years of Discovery*, esp. ch. 2, "The Qumran Library," 20–41; Cross, *Ancient Library of Qumran*.

4. Dimant argued that, since Milik and Cross had an overview of all Qumran writings, they thus had the authority to label them as forming a library; see Dimant, "Qumran Manuscripts," 23–58. It should be noted that she might also have been influenced by de Vaux, who, around the same time, assumed that the Cave 4 documents were the contents of "la bibliothèque commune qui était normalement dans les batîments centraux" (as an architectural feature) and were hidden in haste (Maurice Baillet, Józef T. Milik, and Roland de Vaux, *Les "Petites Grottes" de Qumrân: Explorations de la falaise, les grottes 2Q, 3Q, 5Q, 6Q, 7Q à 10Q, le rouleau de cuivre*, DJD III [Oxford: Clarendon, 1962], 34).

5. Dimant warns against "the constant confusion between literary considerations and historical evaluations" and hence demonstrates awareness of the methodological dangers of reading social reality from ancient texts; see "Qumran Manuscripts," 25.

the "library as consisting of units of complete manuscripts"[6] in which "individual small manuscripts are given numerical value equal to those of large scrolls" in order to give an idea of the "components which constituted the original collection."[7] Even though Dimant demonstrates awareness of the fact that many manuscripts must be lost forever over time, badly damaged, illegible, maybe even too small to be identified, or inconclusive as to their connectivity, she nevertheless aims for and is convinced that her method will reconstruct "the library as an intact collection," which is thought to be an accurate and representative reflection of the original Qumran library.[8] Thus, implicitly, Dimant takes the notion of the Qumran manuscript forming a library as a given, even though she is careful to use the more neutral term "collection" throughout the 1995 article.

2.1.2. A Literary Classification of Texts within the Qumran Library

Bearing in mind that Dimant works from the presupposition of a coherent and representative library, we turn to her literary classification system of all known manuscripts and fragments from Qumran. Her initial classification of manuscripts identifies three distinct groups:[9]

(1) Biblical manuscripts. This category is not to be understood as fixing a canon—one did not exist at the time—however, it takes the later Hebrew Bible as its point of reference; for this reason apocryphal or pseudepigraphal writings are excluded from this category.[10]

(2) Works containing terminology linked with the Qumran community (CT). While particular ideas and concepts, for instance, like eschatology or communion with the angelic world, are in themselves not enough to assign a text to this CT group, they will be if they are combined with specific *yahadic* terminology, such as

---

6. Ibid., 26.
7. Ibid., 27.
8. Ibid., 26, 36.
9. Ibid., 26.
10. This decision naturally has consequences for the overall categorization and begs the question of authoritativeness at Qumran.

2. TEXTUAL CLASSIFICATIONS OF PRESECTARIANISM 41

Teacher of Righteousness, Man of Lies, Seekers of Smooth Things, Men of the Community, and so on.[11]

(3) Works not containing such (clusters of ideas and) terminology (NCT). Any text that lacks the specific *yahadic* terminology is in principle assigned to the NCT group.

As Dimant does not seem to address the category of biblical works any further, her classification system focuses entirely on the distinction between CT and NCT texts. As such, the distinguishing factor between these two categories is the presence or absence of "community terminology," that is, terminology that is thought to determine the sectarian character of a text.[12] As a result, Dimant's NCT category—the category of nonbiblical but also nonsectarian texts—consists of all those documents that cannot be clearly identified as containing typical sectarian terminology and thus cannot be assigned to the CT category (or to the biblical category). However, Dimant finds that with regard to certain types of text, a clear distinction between CT and NCT remains difficult. In these cases of doubt, Dimant decides to assign these particular texts also to the NCT category:[13]

(1) Halakic texts: Some halakic texts contain clear CT terminology. However, other texts have halakic rules that are identical to *yahadic* halakic rulings, but do not employ CT terminology.
(2) Calendrical, chronological, and astrological texts: Some texts also do not contain CT, even though they seem to have the same ideology.

---

11. There has been ample dispute about the exact terminology that would indicate whether a document is *yahadic*; e.g., Dimant argues that "Returners from Transgression" is a CT term, while Hempel has argued that the term is derived from Isa 59:20 and as such cannot be seen as specifically sectarian; see Charlotte Hempel, "The Qumran Sapiential Texts and the Rule Books," in *The Wisdom Texts from Qumran and the Development of Sapiential Thought*, ed. Charlotte Hempel, Armin Lange, and Hermann Lichtenberger, BETL 159 (Leuven: Peeters, 2002), 280 n. 12.

12. For a full overview, see Dimant, "Qumran Manuscripts," 37–58; some of the texts Dimant mentions have since been reassigned; e.g., Sapiential Work A and B have later become 4QInstruction (4Q418).

13. This acknowledgement later in her work leads to the classification of an "in-between" category, which will be addressed later in this section.

(3) A special position assigned to the Aramaic corpus: The Aramaic corpus forms 13 percent of the collection, and Dimant assigns all Aramaic manuscripts to the NCT category.[14]

2.1.3. Library and Classification Reinforce Each Other

Dimant's literary classification system not only attempts to categorize the entire body of Qumran texts into three exhaustive categories; it also reifies the notion of them reflecting a meaningful and deliberate library. The latter is concluded on the basis of two observations that Dimant makes after categorizing all known Qumran documents, that is, "the interrelatedness of the caves" and "the fundamental homogeneity of content and configuration." These two observations lead Dimant to conclude that the Qumran collection is intentional.

Dimant's argument for the interrelatedness of the caves strongly depends on the central role she ascribes to the documents in Cave 4. Her argument, of which individual elements demonstrate interdependency, goes as follows:

(1) Copies of the same works were found in all caves; that is, most caves (1, 2, 3, 5, 6, and 11) contain at least one work of the CT and NCT writing(s) found in Cave 4.
(2) The other caves connect to Cave 4, since they not only reflect the same content but also the same configuration (see below).
(3) The fact that Cave 4 is situated at the outskirts of the site proves that the site and all the caves are connected.

According to Dimant, this cave interrelatedness demonstrates that all the caves housed segments of one and the same collection. This conclusion is subsequently reinforced by the perceived fundamental homogeneity in the various caves' manuscript collections, both in "content and configuration":[15]

---

14. For a fuller understanding of her choices, see Dimant, "Qumran Aramaic Texts," 197–207.

15. Dimant, "Qumran Manuscripts," 31–32.

2. TEXTUAL CLASSIFICATIONS OF PRESECTARIANISM 43

(1) The overall collection consists of three more or less equal proportions of biblical, NCT, and CT manuscripts; a division that is also broadly reflected in each individual cave.

(2) No CT works were transmitted through known channels. Of the 190 nonbiblical NCT and CT works, only nine writings were previously known. These nine manuscripts were all NCT works (Ben Sira, Tobit, Letter of Jeremiah, Apocryphal Psalms, 1 Enoch, Testament of Levi, Jubilees, Testament of Naphtali, the Book of Giants), which were—with the exception of the Book of Giants— handed down by Christians, not Jews.

(3) The CT and NCT works differ in their distinctive genres: CT works are rules and pesharim, which are concerned with the community. NCT texts are pseudepigrapha, Hebrew and Aramaic, not found among the CT texts.

(4) The NCT and CT Qumran manuscripts have a limited number of styles and genres: CT writings consist of rule texts, halakic rulings, liturgical and poetical compositions, and sapiential works, while the NCT works are characterized as narrative, poetic, prophetic, and wisdom texts; parabiblical texts; pseudepigrapha in Hebrew; and apocalyptic, haggadic, and testamentary Aramaic compositions.

(5) The Qumran library is remarkable in its exclusion: the library has no Jewish-Greek writings (e.g., Wisdom of Solomon), no remnants of the pro-Hasmonean 1 Maccabees or the book of Judith, and no precursors to the later Tannaitic literature.

In the figure on page 44 I offer a schematic drawing of Dimant's hypothesis. The circles represent the caves, with Cave 4 as the largest one. According to Dimant, this cave connects to most other caves (1, 2, 3, 5, 6, and 11), because they contain at least *one* CT or NCT text that is also found in Cave 4. The other caves do not necessarily connect directly to Cave 4 but by their similarity in percentages of their content (one-third of each category). Finally, the figure demonstrates that according to Dimant's theory a web is formed, as all caves are interconnected on the basis of both criteria; the caves are supposed to be connected in a literary sense and Cave 4 has a physical connection to the site; therefore, Dimant argues that all caves are thus archaeologically connected to the site.

In her initial 1995 classification of the Qumran texts, Dimant has two major goals: First, to provide evidence for the theory that these documents

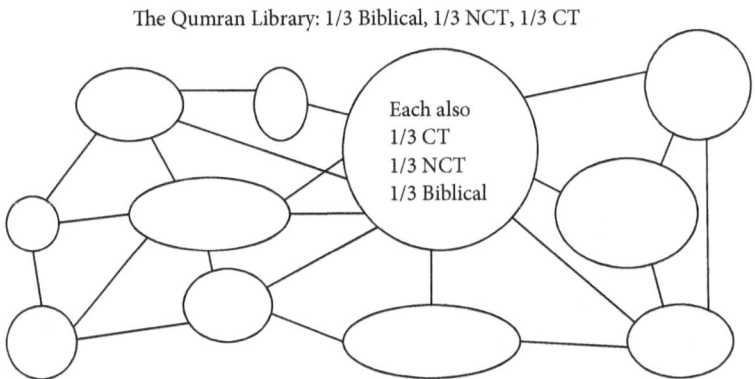

Figure 1. Schematic Overview of Dimant's Theory of a Sectarian Library.

represent a coherent library and, second, to classify these texts according to their presumed relationship to a sectarian group living at Khirbet Qumran. These two goals are best reflected in the conclusions of Dimant's influential article, which reports on the "uniform character of the entire collection."[16] Here, Dimant concludes: "The Qumran library is not just any library. Its homogeneous character and its selectiveness define it as a library of a specific circle or school, a school close to but not identical with the community."[17] Possible discrepancies are placed in a formative or parental sphere: "The Qumran Library would then be the specific literature produced by the community together with a body of literary works which they took over from their parent group."[18]

2.1.4. "In-Between" Sectarian Texts: Dimant's Adjusted Classification in 2005/2009

Under the influence of various criticisms[19] but mostly because the steady publication of texts provided scholars with more insight into the Qumran

---

16. Ibid., 35.
17. Ibid., 36.
18. Ibid.
19. E.g., Hempel ("Kriterien zur Bestimmung," 71–85, esp. 81) has argued that Dimant's initial criterion of a Qumran-specific ideology should be approached with caution. Hempel points out that similar ideology might prove no more than a simi-

2. TEXTUAL CLASSIFICATIONS OF PRESECTARIANISM 45

corpus, Dimant's initial classification system became in need of readjustment. In 2005, Dimant revisited her original classification system, now with a complete inventory of the Scrolls in hand. Dimant recognized that since the first wave of Qumran studies, several factors came to light that challenge the previous parameters of a sectarian library and reopen the question of sectarian and nonsectarian classifications:[20]

(1) a sizeable amount of Hebrew and Aramaic manuscripts lack sectarian or *yahadic* terminology;
(2) the collection consists of a large body of manuscripts that rework the Bible; and
(3) many of these parabiblical or reworked Bible manuscripts were not previously known but reflect connections to known Jewish literature of the Second Temple era.

Accordingly, and even though she remains steadfast in her assessment of a sectarian library on the basis of her cave-interrelatedness arguments, Dimant admits to the heterogeneous character of the collection, whose variety "raises questions about the nature and provenance of this library."[21]

As a result of these new findings, Dimant fine-tunes and updates her assessment of the different categories in her classification system.[22] First, and predominantly, Dimant's renewed classification aims for a clearer def-

---

lar socioreligious background, rather than a sectarian provenance. Furthermore, Hempel has methodological objections to the black and white classification of manuscripts in CT and NCT categories. Hempel argues that any classification system should take the complexity of tradition- and redaction-historical developments into account. Finally, Hempel criticizes Dimant for not providing criteria to distinguish between sectarian and presectarian texts, even though she clearly seems to acknowledge the existence of presectarian documents (or texts from a parent group) within the Qumran library.

20. Dimant, "Between Sectarian and Non-sectarian," 105–6.
21. Ibid., 105.
22. Dimant, "Sectarian and Non-sectarian Texts from Qumran," 7–18: An analysis of these particular indicators is undertaken, with the following methodological assumptions in mind: (1) the analysis limits itself to the sectarian (i.e., nonbiblical) literature; (2) the analysis is linguistic and literary; it does not take historical or sociological considerations into account; (3) since many writings are copies and (original) dating has proven difficult, the Qumran manuscripts are considered to form "a single contemporary entity"; and (4) the manuscripts and fragments are considered single units. Dimant recognizes that the layeredness of certain documents poses a difficulty

inition and identification of sectarian texts in order to be better equipped to categorize what is not sectarian proper. In this readjustment, Dimant's definition of CT texts is slightly broadened but remains the same in its focus: "works which display the terminology, style and ideas explicitly connected with the Qumran Community."[23] In other words, according to Dimant, CT works are "linked by particular *lexical locutions, phraseology* and *nomenclature.*"[24] These "lexical criteria from a representative group" (i.e., 1QS, CD, 1QSa [1Q28a], 1QSb [1Q28b], 1QM, 1QH[a], and the pesharim),[25] upon which the new classification system bases its CT assignments, fall into three main categories: (1) terms related to the organization of the community, such as *yahad*; (2) locutions alluding to the historical circumstances of the community, such as the sobriquets Man of Lies and Teacher of Righteousness; and (3) terms that denote religious ideas, such as dualistic terminology (Sons of Light/Sons of Darkness). Dimant argues that the first two categories are clear-cut, specific, and identifiable but that the third category of theological ideas causes problems, since they might resemble ideas in other nonsectarian documents, which may be adopted and developed by the Qumran community. Therefore, manuscripts can only be assigned to the CT category if they reflect all three criteria in an adequate frequency.[26]

Second, as Dimant clearly has diminished the number of writings in her CT category, she simultaneously recognizes that certain texts cannot simply be assigned as sectarian or nonsectarian on the basis of terminology and ideas.[27] That is, certain texts "lack sectarian characteristic nomenclature and style but embrace notions shared with the sectarian ideology."[28] Therefore, Dimant proposes to add a category to her original

---

but considers a disection of sectarian documents not desirable as long as there is no consensus about the basic taxonomy of sectarian works.

23. Dimant, "*Apocryphon of Joshua*," 106.

24. Dimant, "Sectarian and Non-sectarian Texts from Qumran," 8 (emphasis added).

25. Interestingly, while the definition has become more specific, the list of texts that Dimant assigns to the CT category seems to have become smaller: CD, 1QS, 1QM, 1QH[a], and the pesharim. Curiously, these works *themselves* provide Dimant's criteria "for establishing whether a text does or does not belong to the sectarian literature proper." See later in this chapter and Dimant, "*Apocryphon of Joshua*," 106.

26. Without quantification. Is frequency a fourth criterion?

27. Dimant notices that many of these texts are reworking the Bible.

28. Dimant, "*Apocryphon of Joshua*," 106.

three-tiered classification system (CT, NCT, biblical). This category, for which texts like Jubilees and the Temple Scroll (11QT^a) are thought to be good candidates, Dimant calls "in-between" texts as they are placed in-between the "sectarian literature proper" and "writings devoid of any connection to the community."[29]

2.1.4.1. The Apocryphon of Joshua: Dimant's Test Case

As a test case for her new category of in-between texts, Dimant analyzes the Apocryphon of Joshua (4Q378–379; 4Q522; perhaps 5Q9) and more specifically three passages in this text. The Joshua Apocryphon does not contain sectarian terminology, nor does it portray exclusive *yahadic* ideas. However, according to Dimant, the text conveys important analogies with the spheres of influence that eventually determined the Qumranites' ideology and styles: calendrical issues and Jubilee chronology as found in the book of Jubilees, priestly versus kingly leadership as reflected in the Temple Scroll, and the use of the pesher technique. Also, the text's closeness to Qumran sectarianism is presumed to be visible in the fact that the "clearly *yahadic*" 4QTestimonia (4Q175) quotes the Apocryphon.[30] Since the Apocryphon reflects its affiliation both with the *yahadic* works as well as a clearly observable wider frame of thought, Dimant assigns this text to the newly adopted in-between category.

2.1.5. Conclusion to This Section

As the preceding paragraphs demonstrate, Dimant's literary framework has consistently taken as a point of departure a sectarian Qumran library, authored, copied, studied, and preserved by the Qumran community. Even though Dimant has had to let go of the authorship and the homogeneity of the Qumran collection, the single most influential aspect of her classification theories lies in this very idea of a representative, coher-

---

29. Ibid.
30. Both texts, i.e., 4QTestimonia (4Q175) and the Apocryphon of Joshua (4Q378/4Q379), are disputed texts and considered *yahadic* by some scholars. Also scholars are far from in agreement on the nature and chronology of the interdependence between these texts. For instance, Eshel proposes that the Apocryphon cites 4Q175; see Hanan Eshel, "The Historical Background of the Pesher Interpreting Joshua's Curse on the Rebuilder of Jericho," *RevQ* 15 (1992): 409–20.

ent, and deliberate library from which categories are defined according to their relation and position to the focal point of the Qumran sect. The next section will systematically address the most important parameters of Dimant's theory and attempt to assess the influential implications of her notions of library and sect with regard to their function within the Qumran paradigm.

2.2. Evaluating Dimant's Qumran Library and Its Textual Classifications

As we have seen, Dimant's classification system is an attempt to categorize all the manuscripts found in the Qumran caves. In her theory and in the adjustments to it, certain elements can be identified that demonstrate inflexibility or that, literarily speaking, raise problems with regard to its classifying categories that can only be solved with the help of the Qumran paradigm. This section thus evaluates the interpretative circle that is formed by the two-tiered interdependent basis of Dimant's theories, namely, the deliberate collection (§2.2.1) and literary classification system (§2.2.2).

2.2.1. The Label "Library" Is Void of Criteria and Upholds a Specific Social Reality

As early theorists (Milik and Cross) labeled the collection of manuscripts a library, using the term loosely without criteria, they implicitly provoked the assumption that the 900 Qumran manuscript belonged together in a coherent collection, which hence logically led to the question: Whose library? In the early days of Qumran studies, Milik and Cross were working from a limited knowledge of the perceived peculiarities of both the site and the Cave 1 literature, and they theorized about the library belonging to a scribal "monastic group" living at Khirbet Qumran. As Scrolls scholarship advanced and more documents became available in the early 1990s, the need to readdress the question of these texts' nature and meaning became a central theme.

In her 1995 article, Dimant addresses this need by providing a preliminary literary classification, which builds upon the notion of a deliberate library. However, under the influence of Norman Golb's provocative theory that challenged the idea of cave/site-connectivity, textual coherence, and sectarianism in general, Dimant could no longer use the term *library* at

2. TEXTUAL CLASSIFICATIONS OF PRESECTARIANISM 49

face value.[31] The criteria on which Dimant builds her case for a deliberate library are often interlinked and arguments at times seem to circle back on themselves. These criteria are: (1) scholarly authority (§2.2.1.1); (2) connectivity and caves/site interconnectedness (§2.2.1.2); and (3) homogeneity in literary styles and genres, distinctions and exclusions (§2.2.1.3).

2.2.1.1. Using the Term *Library* Based on Scholarly Authority

Dimant ascribes the correctness of the term *library* partly to the authoritativeness of the first scholars who used the term, Milik and Cross, even though—as we saw above—these scholars never gave a clear definition or set of criteria for their usage of the term. Early on, Tov recognized the possible problems connected to the term *library* and proposed to use the term in a semantic sense, without drawing conclusions about the collection's contents or provenance.[32] Postponing the question of content, nature, and provenance, Tov argued that the term *library* ceases to be problematic if it is defined as "all the books, which the community owned and stored, without any implication that they used them or agreed with their contents" (contra García Martínez).[33] Tov's proposal is attractive, as it demonstrates awareness of the connotations attached to the term *library*. However, his proposal nevertheless sustains and enforces the presence of a sociological entity, a group of librarians, who actively assembled, maintained, and built this collection of books.[34]

The question that Tov deliberately postpones, namely, the question of the Qumran manuscripts' nature and provenance, is the prime question that Dimant's classification system wants to answer. In her stated intent of "reconstructing the library as an intact collection"[35] and thereby adopting the term *library* at face value, possibly on the basis of scholarly authority, the stage is set to find evidence to sustain the notion of a library and—

---

31. Norman Golb had advocated this view first in 1980 but defended his position more systematically in *Who Wrote the Dead Sea Scrolls? The Search for the Secret of Qumran* (London: O'Mara, 1995).

32. Emanuel Tov, "Hebrew Biblical Manuscripts from the Judaean Desert: Their Contribution to Textual Criticism," *JSS* 39 (1988): 5–37; see also Francesco Zanella, "Sectarian and Non-sectarian Texts: A Possible Semantic Approach," *RevQ* 24 (2009): 19–34.

33. Tov, "Hebrew Biblical Manuscripts," 10, emphasis added.

34. As Tov's later assertion of a Qumran scribal school clearly demonstrates.

35. Dimant, "Qumran Manuscripts," 26.

often unintentionally—block dissonant data. Also, in using specific terminology (CT and NCT) before analyzing the data, one runs the risk that the structure of the model (a library of a specific social group) becomes normative for the analysis.

2.2.1.2. A Library Based on Connectivity and Caves/Site-Interconnectedness

In Dimant's attempt to reconstruct the Qumran library, she naturally needs to prove that these manuscripts form a deliberate, meaningful, representative, and coherent collection. Therefore, Dimant argued for (1) an interrelatedness of the caves and (2) the homogeneity of the caves' contents. A third argument, which adds to the notion of a deliberate and meaningful library, springs from arguments (1) and (2) and builds the bridge of (3) caves/site-interconnectedness. However, these three arguments do not stand on their own, their validity is interlinked, and therefore, as arguments (1) and (2) might be proven inaccurate, this may also influence the evaluation of (3).

2.2.1.2.1. The Interrelatedness of the Caves. Dimant's observations regarding the interrelatedness of the caves is based on the caves' similarity in "content and configuration." Dimant argues that "the contents of the caves are essentially similar and interlinked," since "most of the caves ... contain at least one work ... represented by one or several copies in Cave 4."[36] However, this observation can only be made if one reasons from the centrality of Cave 4; that is, it describes the perceived relationship of the other caves to Cave 4, not to one another, and only based on CT and NCT works. In fact, from Dimant's work, the only conclusion that seems valid is the presence of all NCT and CT labeled manuscripts in Cave 4. Even more so, Dimant's table demonstrates that not a single manuscript of all the manuscripts she labels CT and NCT is present in all eleven caves.[37] And since Cave 4 contains 75 percent of all manuscripts, it is hardly a surprise that most manuscripts from the other caves are found in copy in the much larger Cave 4 collection.

---

36. Ibid., 30–33.
37. Ibid., 31.

2.2.1.2.2. The Fundamental Homogeneity. The argument of fundamental homogeneity is based upon several subarguments: (i) ratios, (ii) unknown NCT and CT works, (iii) limited styles and genres among the CT/NCT works, and (iv) (deliberate) exclusions of certain texts. The first subargument, ratios, is discussed in this section, since it is entangled with the argument of cave-interrelatedness. The other sub-arguments (ii, iii, and iv) are more literarily framed and are therefore discussed under §2.2.1.3 Homogeneity in Literary Styles and Genres, Distinctions, and Exclusions.

(i) Ratios. As Dimant's classification framework delivered a "more or less equal" one-third, one-third, one-third division of CT, NCT, and biblical texts, she argues that these ratios provide substantial grounds to assume these texts form a homogenous library. However, Dimant's own research demonstrates that only some caves align to these ratios for only *one* of the three textual categories. Moreover, the ratio argument is methodologically dependent on the criteria underlying the CT/NCT/biblical text division. Since these criteria determine the assignment of a text to a category, they also determine the ratios as these are based on "types of texts," CT/NCT/biblical, not on the actual presence of the same manuscripts. Furthermore, these ratios are based on the caves consisting of "units of complete manuscripts."[38] If we then consider the extreme fragmentariness of many of the Qumran Cave 4 writings and realize that Cave 4 makes up for 75 percent of the entire Qumran collection, we might realize the influence this cave exercises on the overall classification.

The fact that Dimant makes no distinction between whole manuscripts, partly preserved manuscripts, or fragments but assigns numerically equal value to all of them in order to construct an intact library demands the question whether such a decision is methodologically sound. Even if Dimant allows for a 10 percent fall-out, her division does not seem to reckon with or evaluate the consequences of unrecognizable fragments or heavily damaged manuscripts, nor does it take textual differences in various copies, diverse versions of one manuscript, incorporation of texts on one scroll, multilayeredness and redaction of texts, or the not unfamiliar scholarly debates over various fragments' assignment, connection, or/and manuscriptural home into account. Moreover, Dimant's argument also does not problematize the assignment of (parts of) documents to par-

---

38. Ibid., 26.

ticular caves. It is well known that the Bedouin who found many manuscripts and the first scholars after them have seriously obscured the original archaeological retrieval, which made the assignment of documents to caves difficult at times. Therefore, the interrelatedness of the caves, based upon similar ratios, and the original contents of the caves cannot be taken as a method of theorizing without extreme caution. Finally, and more generally, more insight into the entirety of the Qumran documents raises serious questions about these ratios, particularly as the importance of so-called rewritten Bible manuscripts has been demonstrated. In light of all these factors, the notion of cave homogeneity on the basis of ratios can no longer be maintained.

2.2.1.2.3. The Caves/Site-Interconnectedness. A fundamental second step in Dimant's theory of a "deliberate library" combines (1) and (2) to argue for (3) the cave/site connectedness or, in other words, the connectedness of the (homogenous and textually interconnected) caves and the Khirbet Qumran site. In Dimant's theory, the conclusion of interconnectedness between all the caves and the site can only be reached after the interconnectedness of the caves and the homogeneity of their contents are established, as it depends upon the centrality of Cave 4 as a linchpin. In light of the current archaeological insight that access to Cave 4 can only be obtained via the site, the inhabitants of the site are identified as the owners of the library. Dimant arrives at this conclusion, because her research has already established a fundamental connection between the caves based upon their textual "contents and configuration."[39]

However, if (1) and (2) are not proven, (3) cannot be maintained at face value. What is left is the access route from the site to Cave 4, whose proximity is likely to link this cave to the site. However, as we briefly discussed in chapter 1, the archaeological evidence as to whether the site and the caves (or some of the caves) can be connected is rather inconclusive. The proximity of some of the caves to the site is, of course, a case in point, but in light of the current lack of scholarly consensus, it might be better

---

39. Even though Dimant only stresses this point of access and proximity for Cave 4, Magness mentions Caves 7, 8, and 9 as otherwise inaccessible, while she only refers to Cave 4's proximity (500 meters) to the site; see Jodi Magness, *The Archaeology of Qumran and the Dead Sea Scrolls* (Grand Rapids: Eerdmans, 2002); also Kenneth Atkinson and Jodi Magness, "Josephus's Essenes and the Qumran Community," *JBL* 129 (2010): 317–42.

practice not to presume automatically a close relationship between caves and site.

2.2.1.3. Homogeneity in Literary Styles and Genres, Distinctions and Exclusions

At first sight, the subsequent arguments for the Qumran manuscripts forming a library seem more literary in nature and attempt to prove their homogeneity in character and deliberateness in text-choices: (ii) unknown NCT and CT works, (iii) limited styles and genres among the CT/NCT works, and (iv) (deliberate) exclusions of certain texts. However, these subarguments seem to be based upon a deeper level of presuppositions that sustain the Qumran paradigm:

(ii) Unknown NCT and CT works. A second subargument for the homogeneity of the library is the high amount of previously unknown CT and NCT works. To argue that "unfamiliarity by lack of outside sources" is evidence for the homogeneity of these texts seems rather odd ("we don't know them, so they must belong together"). However, if one assumes that Dimant theorizes from the preconception of an unfamiliar (sectarian) community's library, as might be derived from her CT/NCT division, the reasoning for making unfamiliarity an argument becomes clear. From this standpoint, it seems rather logical to give meaning to the fact that many Qumran texts were previously unknown, as the Qumranites were thought to have rather radical and extreme (i.e., at least not mainstream) Jewish ideas and ideologies. Hence, if one follows such reasoning, it would logically lead to the conclusion that their writings were unknown as they must have been unimportant and/or marginal to Second Temple Judaism as a whole. However, the argument that the Qumran manuscripts demonstrate homogeneity since (1) only 9 out of 190 NCT works were previously known and (2) "no CT works were transmitted through known channels" is not only an argument from silence; it also denies the general scarceness of textual sources from this period. Further, it neglects the Cairo Genizah manuscripts, which provided scholarship with the manuscripts of an "unknown Jewish sect,"[40] namely, the Damascus Document (CD), named by Dimant to be a CT work.

---

40. Schechter, *Fragments of a Zadokite Work*; see further Ginzberg, *Unknown Jewish Sect*.

(iii) Limited styles and genres among the CT/NCT works. This subargument of the supposed "limited styles and genres and clear-cut style/genre distinction in NCT and CT" has not convinced many scholars, since research has demonstrated that many Qumran texts exhibit composite structures and complex multilayeredness, as well as other textual shades of gray. Moreover, Dimant identifies a large variety of styles and genres among the CT and NCT manuscripts. Also, in leaving the category biblical manuscripts out of her analysis, while contemporarily the Hebrew Bible did not exist, Dimant limits the scope of the argument. As such, the above-mentioned shades of gray might be seen in another light if one takes the entirety of Qumran manuscripts into account. Most strikingly, what binds all these texts is their religious provenance, and since they use combinations of literary themes, strategies, and styles, a true literary classification would assign texts on the basis of literary criteria and themes, rather than in sociologically charged terms like CT/NCT works.

(iv) (Deliberate) exclusions of certain texts. Finally, the argument that the collection is deliberate on the basis of the absence of certain writings must be dismissed simply by the archaeological realization that many manuscripts have been lost over the course of two thousand years in the Judean desert, and thus one can never know whether the absence of a text is deliberate or simply a matter of worms eating texts. However, if we address the possibility that Dimant theorizes from a presumed framework of Qumran sectarianism and has a community with a specific outlook in mind, we might understand her argumentation better. Even though Dimant's argument of deliberate exclusion is seemingly based upon language (Wisdom of Solomon), genre (book of Judith), and style (1 Maccabees), the ideological or rather sociohistorical assumptions are hardly hidden under this thin layer of literary qualifications. A first hint to a possible deeper interpretative layer to this argument of exclusion, which in its nature might be more sociological, can be found in the statement that "no precursor to the later Tannaitic literature … nor to the New Testament" were found at Qumran.[41] As the fact that Qumran is never mentioned in the New Testament is never used as an argument for the homogeneity of the New Testament, one does not expect the absence of (precursors to the) New Testament material to be used as an argument for a Qumran

---

41. Dimant, "Qumran Manuscripts," 33.

2. TEXTUAL CLASSIFICATIONS OF PRESECTARIANISM 55

library. Hence, one suspects this exclusion category is not based upon literary criteria but is the result of reasoning backwards, starting from a presumed sectarian Qumran community with a particular socioreligious worldview and matching perception of opponents. In such a sociological framework, the absence of certain texts might be explained as deliberate exclusions of oppositional views. Hence, the absence of Wisdom of Solomon, which in its complex nature might be not the best candidate for a literary argument of exclusion on the basis of language; but sociologically one might presume a sectarian Jewish priestly community would want to exclude a non-Palestinian, possibly hellenized diaspora text. An even clearer case in point is Dimant's suggestion of deliberateness in the absence of the Psalms of Solomon, since this argument surely cannot be made on purely literary grounds: the extant Greek text clearly is translated from a Hebrew original; the literary genre is well-attested at Qumran; and the themes and styles are also most familiar among the Qumran literature.[42] Moreover, the already more sociohistorical aspects of the text—its Palestinian origin and its estimated 70–40 BCE original Hebrew date—also do not clarify why Dimant finds the text's absence significant for the fundamental homogeneity of the library. Therefore, one suspects that underneath the literary argument lies a more sociological reason to suggest deliberate exclusion, in this case an ideological one, as the text contains Sadducean/Pharisean themes of dispute and its author takes the position of the Pharisees. Most definitely, Dimant's underlying argument is overtly socioreligious and/or political in the case of 1 Maccabees, which most likely is not believed to be absent because of its literary genre (historiographical narrative), but rather because the text is overtly pro-Hasmonean.[43] In short, the presumption of deliberate exclusion is colored by sociological presuppositions of the particular religious outlook of a sectarian group in charge of the Qumran library and feeds the idea that our contemporary collection of manuscripts is representative

---

42. Themes such as suffering inflicted by foreign invasion; desecration of Jerusalem and the temple; rebuke of men-pleasers; and recognition of God's justice in rewarding the pious and in punishing the wicked. The author is devoted to the law, has a bitter hatred of the wicked for their unethical lawlessness, and demonstrates great hostility towards the Hasmonean rulers.

43. Even though most scholars would agree that the Qumran community was anti-Hasmonean, a few Qumran texts seem to demonstrate another outlook, for instance, the Prayer to King Jonathan (4Q448).

of the original Qumran collection. As such, Dimant's theory leaves little room for natural causes, coincidence, or simply unknown reasons for the absence of texts.

2.2.1.4. Conclusion to This Section: A Library?

As we have established, the individual arguments on which Dimant bases her conclusion of a coherent, representative, and socioreligiously particular library leave room for doubt. The conclusion of a coherent library seems influenced by taking as a point of departure the presupposition that the Qumran manuscripts form the coherent collection of a specific religious group, as is demonstrated by the fact that—at the outset—the classification of texts as CT, NCT, and biblical is already based upon the presupposition of such a sectarian community. Hence, if one theorizes and classifies with a central category of sectarianism already in mind, the notion of a coherent sectarian library becomes a given framework in which data are classified to fit the framework. Hence, the classification of texts will be centrally focused on the detection of a sectarian identity, by means of ideology, and distinct terminology. From this central focal point, all texts are assigned their place in the Qumranites' library. Hence, it is the theory of a sociological entity, a sectarian community and its perceived socioreligious distinctiveness, that underlies not only the notion of a coherent library but also the categorization of texts and manuscripts. Therefore, the next section takes a closer look at the functioning of Dimant's classification of sectarian, nonsectarian, and in-between texts.

2.2.2. Sectarian, Nonsectarian, and In-Between: The Story of Escaping Texts

While the former section has looked at the notion of library, here I address the functioning of Dimant's literary classification of the Qumran texts. As we have seen, the fact that the Qumran manuscripts are taken as a sectarian library invokes a classification system in which every Qumran text is classified according to its perceived position in relation to the thoughts, ideas, and literary expressions of a sociological entity, the Qumran community. As the category of biblical texts, whose presence in any Jewish religious library need not be explained, is regarded as self-evident, Dimant's categorization system is entirely preoccupied with distinguishing between sectarian and nonsectarian texts. Such a distinction has led to challenges

2. TEXTUAL CLASSIFICATIONS OF PRESECTARIANISM

to the overall taxonomy and various difficulties, part of which will be discussed here.

2.2.2.1. A Nonhistorical Literary Classification System Based upon Sociological Phenomena

As we have seen earlier, the hypothesis that the Qumran texts form a sectarian library was determined by the nature of Dimant's classification system. In turn, the presupposition of a sectarian library poses problems on Dimant's classification system, which over time has demonstrated several difficulties, which can be observed as follows:

(1) The sociological categorization of texts is problematic with regard to a literary analysis.
(2) The classification is based upon static criteria of terminology and ideology, and more and more texts do not fit in or escape these categories.
(3) The importance of the nonsectarian texts that escape all categories, predominantly the texts that rework the Bible, creates tension for the whole system of categorizations.
(4) Even after the introduction of an in-between category, several texts in question still manage to escape Dimant's classification.

Even though Dimant explicitly wants to stay away from historical reconstructions and all their difficulties, her classification system is heavily informed by specific geographical allocations and perceived socioreligious distinctiveness. In other words, the cave/site (or text/site) interrelatedness-argument provoked the adoption of a concept of a segregated, radical, sectarian, scribal entity. This view underlies the distinction between community terminology (CT) and no community terminology (NCT) that helped to provide evidence for the existence of a coherent library. Through this notion of a coherent sectarian library not only the terminology attached to the nonliterary sociological nature of this classification is adopted but inherently also all the sociological connotations and determinations attached to this terminology of sect.

Thus, Dimant needs to uphold a taxonomy in which the central sociological entity is clearly identifiable on the basis of its texts, which thus are to be recognizably sectarian or nonsectarian. As we have seen earlier, the sectarian category (CT), which thus is central to the entire taxonomy, is based on circular reasoning: the sectarian texts themselves determine what the criteria for assigning the CT label are. Hence, this CT category never really needs to address the problem of nonfitting or escaping texts, for it simply can—and does!—adjust its own criteria.[44] However, no such flexibility can be ascribed to the NCT (nonsectarian) texts as they form a broad category on the basis of no specific criteria other than that they do not fit either the sectarian or biblical profile.

Indeed, with the steady publication of the Dead Sea Scrolls, Dimant observed that her initial classification system posed problems and that more and more CT and NCT texts seemed to escape their categories for all sorts of reasons.[45] Having recognized a more complex reality and the texts' tendency for escaping categories, Dimant subsequently proposed to add a category "in-between" the sectarian and nonsectarian texts. This proposal seems not to take into account the fact that most of the in-between texts are parabiblical works, which thus cannot be easily categorized without also taking the category biblical texts into account. But more importantly, the texts that receive the in-between label inherently seem to attach themselves to an underlying sociohistorical connotation. This needs some explanation. Since the center from which the entire taxonomy is built, the notion of a Qumran sectarian community, determines what is sectarian from "the sectarian texts proper," it can also redefine the relationship with the outside world, in other words, with the other textual categories (nonsectarian and in-between texts). Hence, the nonsectarian texts are positioned further away from the sectarian center as they are defined to be "writings devoid of any connection to the community," while the in-between texts sociologically seem to move closer to the role of sectarian precursors, as they are defined to "lack sectarian characteristic nomenclature and style but embrace notions shared with the sectarian ideology."[46] As Dimant defines the Qumran library as "the specific literature produced by the community together with a body of literary works which they took over from their parent group,"[47] Dimant thus arrives at an implicit chronological framework, which is developmental and places these in-between texts in a particular presectarian relationship to the sectarian texts proper.

---

44. We have seen this phenomenon over time, as Dimant adjusted her list of sectarian texts.

45. See §§2.1.2 and 2.1.4 of this chapter.

46. Dimant, "*Apocryphon of Joshua*," 106.

47. Dimant, "Qumran Manuscripts," 36.

In other words, a possibly unwanted consequence of the adjustments to Dimant's classification system creates a framework that retraces the Qumranites' steps and implicitly holds that the NCT texts were earlier and possibly collected by the community's precursors; This begs the question of whether the subsequent in-between texts are to be seen as presectarian for they already narrow the scope by their shared sectarian ideology, which eventually can be observed in full force in the Qumran sectarian literature proper. Such an inherent notion of an underlying chronology, based upon the centrality of a sociological phenomenon, thus tends to seriously obstruct and obscure a true literary classification.

2.2.2.2. The Convenient Osmosis of the CT Category's Boundaries

Under the influence of García Martínez's criticism that Dimant does not set distinguishable criteria for the in-between category, Dimant needed to redefine her three categories (sectarian, nonsectarian, and in-between) more stringently.[48] Since the in-between and nonsectarian categories are derivatives from the sectarian category, the only possible way for Dimant to reach such a stricter definition is to redefine the boundaries of her central—and as we have seen most flexible—category of sectarian texts. Interestingly, however, the introduction of clearer CT criteria (particular lexical locutions, phraseology, and nomenclature) cannot prevent the recurrent phenomenon of escaping texts from resurfacing. As a result, in order to safeguard the provenance of certain key texts, additional—and often text-specific—criteria are used to make a case for the assignment to the desired category. That is, in the case of certain texts, the application of the three above-mentioned criteria turned out to be unsuccessful, and additional reasoning is used to close the escape gap retrospectively. For instance, Dimant assigns disputed documents like 4QInstruction and Songs of the Sabbath Sacrifice (4Q400–407; 11Q17) to the CT category solely on the basis of terminology and ideas parallel to the sectarian texts.[49]

---

48. Florentino García Martínez ("Sectario, No-Sectario, O Qué," 383–94) heavily criticized the somewhat tentative invention of this in-between category. He argued that this (third) category tries to establish the impossible: it wants to maintain a fundamental dichotomy between sectarian and nonsectarian texts while creating a third category, for which it is difficult to set stringently defined criteria.

49. See Dimant, "Sectarian and Non-sectarian Texts from Qumran," nn. 12 and 13. Note that terminology in 4Q415–418 is compared with 1QS III, 19; IV, 23–24,

Also, in the case of the Commentary on Genesis (4Q252; 4Q254), the text's employment of the term "Men of the Yahad" (4Q252 V, 5; 4Q254 4, 4) might be considered a clear indication of Dimant's sectarian provenance. However, since this term occurs only once, Dimant assigns the text to the NCT category, as she argued that a single occurrence "should not outweigh the bulk of the commentary."[50] Thus, the unquantified criterion of adequate frequency in the occurrence of certain terminology is introduced to assign certain texts to those categories that support the underlying theory of the paradigm.

This tendency can be best observed in regard to the—for the paradigm—important text of 4QMMT. Notwithstanding her criteria, Dimant assigns this text to her sectarian category, even though the text contains no CT terminology nor is it written in "the peculiar style of the sectarian scrolls."[51] Here, so it seems, the text's CT classification is entirely based upon 4QMMT's perceived subject matter or rather of the general Qumran scholars' interpretation thereof.[52]

2.2.3. Conclusions to the Analysis of Dimant's Classification System

In the preceding pages, I have tried to analyze Dimant's classification system and her notion of a deliberate, representative, and sectarian library. As one of the most influential taxonomies, Dimant's classification system has had a strong influence on the way scholars have approached the Qumran corpus. However, my analysis demonstrates that the taxonomy has inherent limitations, which need to be taken into account in future approaches to Qumran:

---

while parts of Songs of the Sabbath Sacrifice (4Q400–407) are compared with CD. Hence, one may question the "sectarian provenance" Dimant claims, as 1QS III, 13–IV, 26 is mostly accepted as an incorporation of a formerly independent text and CD as so multilayered that it remains difficult to assign which parts to consider *yahadic*.

50. Ibid., 12.

51. Ibid.

52. Dimant legitimates her decision by stating that, since the polemical 4QMMT was clearly addressed to outsiders, naturally, the Qumran sectarians would not have written in their sectarian style but in a rather contemporary literary style. Such argumentation seems rather contrived.

2. TEXTUAL CLASSIFICATIONS OF PRESECTARIANISM   61

(1) A classification system that takes the sociological term sectarian as its point of departure can never really be truly literary but instead has assumptions of a certain type of community in its background.
(2) The notion of a sectarian library and a categorization that inherently depends on the centrality of a sect together form an interpretative circle in which one becomes the logical consequence of the other. One of the key points of circular reasoning is the fact that certain chosen sectarian texts are assigned to set the criteria for the definition of what is a sectarian text, thus creating flexibility in allowing texts to be allocated according to theories that fit the paradigm.
(3) Moreover, the perception of a sectarian community aids an underlying pattern of retrospective theorizing in which a collection of texts becomes a meaningful and coherent library, which in turn positions individual texts according to their relationship to that perceived sectarian community. Methodologically, one runs the risk of blocking dissonant data and theorizing only from within the given paradigm.
(4) Such a categorization system may help to provide evidence for the deliberateness and coherence of the sectarian library, but within this framework, which is based upon the above mentioned interpretative circle, certain key texts seem to keep on escaping their assigned categories. Hence, the idea of a sectarian library seems to limit the assessment of the nature and provenance of the individual Qumran texts, for they can only be assessed and classified as part of a coherent library and in relation to the library's assumed sectarian views.

Moreover, the notion of a library as well as the categorizations force texts into a diachronic (or chronological) framework, in which sociohistorical qualifications rather than literary qualifications are leading.[53] This not

---

53. This phenomenon of diachrony can also be observed in Dimant's notion of "textual reworking of terms"; i.e., Dimant recognizes in some texts a typical and unique sectarian provenance in the way they rework their biblical foreground into a new combined meaning. She argues that a characteristic development in the use of terminology can be observed, in which lexical terms, (1) having rather broad semantic fields and (2) being applied with knowledge of surrounding textual witnesses, are restrictively used in the "undisputed sectarian texts." That is, Dimant hypothesizes that

only prevents the possibility of assessing them in their own right but also enforces the tendency to evaluate each text that is not sectarian proper as a more or less influential precursor to later sectarian thought and hence predating the Qumran community. As such Dimant's in-between category is, with respect to its functioning within the larger framework, the equivalent to García Martínez's formative period, which will be the focus of the next section.

2.3. García Martínez's Groningen Hypothesis and a Formative Period of the Sect

In the divide between a literary and a history-of-the-sect approach, the most influential protagonist of the latter has been García Martínez, who, together with his Groningen colleague Adam van der Woude, has launched the so-called "Groningen hypothesis" of early Qumran history.[54] García Martínez argues that the Groningen hypothesis, which partly builds on and partly supersedes the Qumran-Essene hypothesis, aims to provide a historical framework in which the Qumran sectarian texts and the *yahad* community can be positioned. Furthermore, it also attempts to explain the dissimilarities between certain core manuscripts by providing a chronological framework of historical development of the sect and its assumed precursors. Thus, the Groningen hypothesis assigns texts to historical categories of (group) identity. In the original 1988 article, as well as in a recent article that revisits the original hypothesis, García Martínez identifies five essential pillars of his Groningen hypothesis, which we have already mentioned briefly in our introductory chapter. This chapter will focus on the fifth pillar of the Groningen hypothesis: the notion of the "Qumran Sect's formative period," defined by García Martínez as a period "before its [the sect's] retreat to the desert" in which "the ideological development, the halakhic elements, and the political conflicts" can be identified that resulted in "the break which led to the community's establishing itself in Qumran."[55]

---

in these *yahadic* texts the same terms are semantically narrowed "to serve the Qumranites pre-occupation with themselves, their self-understanding and self-definition."

54. García Martínez, "Qumran Origins and Early History," 113–36; Florentino García Martínez and Adam van der Woude, "A 'Groningen' Hypothesis of Qumran Origins and Early History," *RevQ* 14 (1990): 521–42.

55. García Martínez, "Qumran Origins and Early History," 113–34; reprinted in

2. TEXTUAL CLASSIFICATIONS OF PRESECTARIANISM

The fact that the formative period is a significant building block in García Martínez's theory is demonstrated by its centrality among the major assumptions that form the foundations of the hypothesis:

(1) A theory that works from texts must be limited by paleography and archaeology. Hence, historical reconstructions ought to be limited by material evidence.
(2) A period of time (long or short) preceded the break between the Qumran group and the Essene movement in which ideological differentiation took place. Hence, García Martínez assumes a "pre-Qumranic phase or formative period, an extraordinarily fruitful period from which were to proceed writings which establish the ideological bases of the break with the Essene movement and during which there develop the conflicts which are to issue in the sectarian group's trek to the desert."[56]
(3) The nonbiblical Qumran literature is related either to the Qumran sect or to its predecessors. Thus, the writings form a coherent and representative reflection of a sectarian collection and therefore can be assessed as "compatible with its own ideology (and even more important with its halakhah), that is, as coming from the Essene movement or from the apocalyptic tradition which inspired it."[57] Hence, the Qumran nonbiblical writings can be classified as follows: (3.1) sectarian works; (3.2) works of the formative period; (3.3) works that reflect Essene thought (i.e., in accordance with the classical sources); and (3.4) works belonging to the apocalyptic tradition that gave rise to Essenism.
(4) The composite character of the basic works, the presence of different versions of the same document, and the clear multilayeredness within the documents reflect a certain historical evolution. These phenomena reflect an origin in the formative period of the sect and the need for adaptation "to the successive historical, theological and organizational developments in the community."[58]

García Martínez, *Qumranica Minora I: Qumran Origins and Apocalypticism*, ed. E. J. C. Tigchelaar, STDJ 63 (Leiden: Brill, 2007), 3–29.
  56. García Martínez, *Qumranica Minora I*, 8–9.
  57. Ibid.
  58. Ibid.

Thus, the pivotal position of the concept of a formative period within the Groningen hypothesis can be observed from assumptions (2), (3), and (4) above. Therefore, the next section deals with García Martínez's theory with regard to this period.

2.3.1. A Formative Period

The Groningen hypothesis's formative period is of special significance as it is thought to encompass all those literary expressions of an upcoming ideological parting of the ways between Essenism and the Qumranites. In other words, during this time-wise unspecified period of sect formation, the precursory textual witnesses to the later Qumran community were supposedly still recognizably Essene but already contained elements of future developments, especially where the halakah was concerned. Also, this formative period supposedly not only explains ideological differences between pre-Qumranic documents; it also clarifies the differences in additions to, and later incorporations of, ideologically differentiated documents into Qumran sectarian works as developments over time. Hence, the concept of a formative period is of vital importance to the explicatory power of the Groningen hypothesis, which schematically might be sketched as follows:

Figure 2. Schematic Table of García Martínez's Groningen Hypothesis 1.

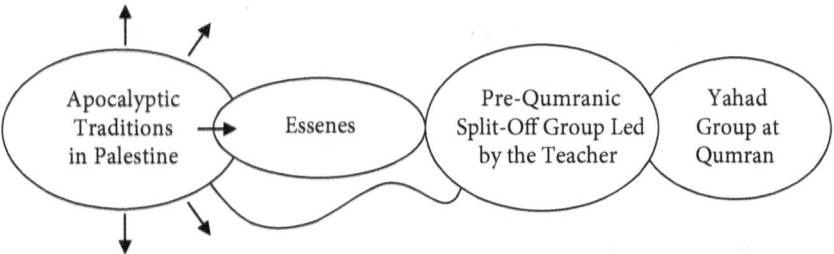

* The curved line represents García Martínez's notion that eschatology and calendrical problems, which according to him are not part of Essene ideology, were brought into the Qumran sect by the Teacher from apocalyptic traditions.

2.3.1.1. The Chronology of the Framework

In order to establish a framework of development, a chronological Qumranic timeline that runs from apocalyptic to Essene to formative disputa-

2. TEXTUAL CLASSIFICATIONS OF PRESECTARIANISM

tional to discordant split-off to Qumranic sectarian and that hence establishes a textual *terminus post quem* or foundation date for the Qumran community, García Martínez reconstructs an "early history of the community" on the basis of the rather sketchy and inconclusive historical allusions in the Scrolls, allusions which he predominantly finds in 1QpHab. His reconstruction consists of the following components:

(1) Archaeological periods of occupation (deVaux/Magness),[59] combined with
(2) The notion that the Wicked Priest is an umbrella term for a line of Hasmonean high priests, which can be historically identified with the help of 1QpHab.[60] In his reconstruction, García Martínez identifies merely Jonathan (161 BCE civil governor, but 152–143/142 BCE also high priest) and Simon (143/142–135/134 BCE) as the two high priests who provoked ideological and political conflict in the formative period of the Qumran sect.
(3) The proposed discordant split-off from the larger Essene movement, which, according to García Martínez, must have taken place under John Hyrcanus (134–104 BCE). This reconstruction is based upon John Hyrcanus's identification in 1QpHab XI, 2–8, in which the Wicked Priest "pursued the Teacher of Righteousness to his house of exile."[61]

---

59. Magness, *Archaeology of Qumran*, 68. De Vaux distinguishes Period Ia (ca. 130–100 BCE), Ib (ca. 100–31 BCE), II (4–1 BCE to 68 CE), and III (68 CE to 73–74 CE), while Magness argues for Ia (nonexistent), Ib (preearthquake 100–50 BCE to 31 BCE/postearthquake 31 BCE–9/8 BCE or maybe until 4 BCE), II (4–1 BCE to 68 CE), and III (same as de Vaux).

60. Adam van der Woude, "Wicked Priest or Wicked Priests? Reflections on the Identification of the Wicked Priest in the Habakkuk Commentary," *JJS* 33 (1982): 349–59; see also García Martínez, *Qumranica Minora I*, 24–29. The idea of a plurality of high priests was first put forward by William H. Brownlee, "The Historical Allusions of the Dead Sea Habakkuk Midrash," *BASOR* 126 (1952): 10–20 and later in "The Wicked Priest, the Man of Lies, and the Righteous Teacher: The Problem of Identity," *JQR* 73 (1982): 1–37.

61. It seems likely that, in his early hypothesis, García Martínez holds Qumran to be this "house of exile."

On the basis of this reconstruction, the Groningen hypothesis can now schematically be set in a rather "precise chronological framework for the development of the early history of the Community."[62]

According to García Martínez's hypothesis, this formative period ends at the moment of what he has called "the discordant split-off" of the Qumran group, which was initiated by the Teacher of Righteousness after his falling out with the Man of the Lie (1QpHab V, 9–12).[63] The schematic chronology of figure 3 demonstrates that the split-off is thought to have taken place in the early years of John Hyrcanus, while disputes and conflicts already were pregnant under Jonathan and Simon. Thus, even though García Martínez never discusses exact dates, his hypothesis implicitly confines the formative period of the Qumran sect broadly to about 161–125 BCE.

Figure 3. Schematic Table of García Martínez's Groningen Hypothesis 2.

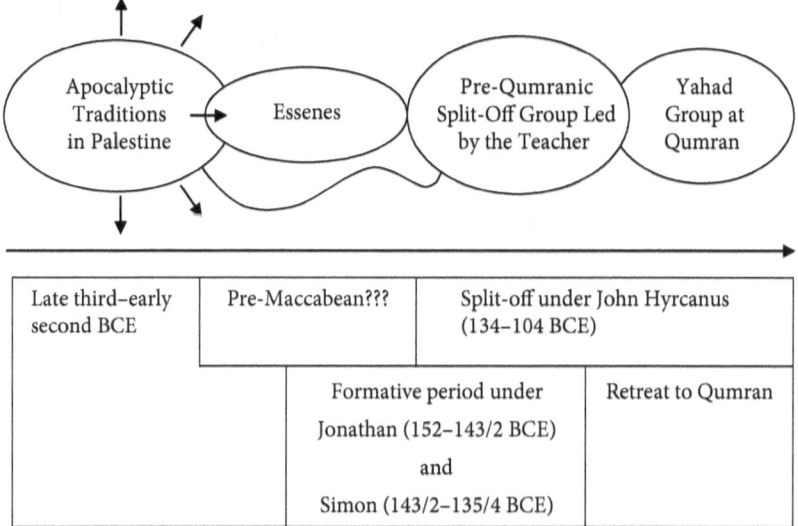

* For some reason García Martínez takes Jonathan's reign to run from 161 BCE, when he was not yet high priest but only governor of Israel.

* In the timeline I have prolonged the formative period beyond the split-off moment, to indicate that García Martínez holds 4QMMT to be a Qumranic post-split-off text but that he also believes the text still tries to influence the "leader of the Essenes" to admit he erred. Such an action would indicate that the split-off is not yet definite or beyond return. Moreover, CD is another document which García Martínez seems to assign to both the formative period and the time after the split-off (see below).

---

62. García Martínez, *Qumranica Minora I*, 26.

63. Interestingly, in this early phase of his hypothesis, García Martínez regards the Man of the Lie to be "the Head of the Essene Movement" (ibid., 25).

2. TEXTUAL CLASSIFICATIONS OF PRESECTARIANISM 67

2.3.1.2. The Reasons for the Split-Off

The cut off point from which the Qumran group became a separate entity must therefore be found in the perceived reasons for the split-off. García Martínez argues that the "discordant split-off" is the result of "the different interpretation of the Law laid down by the sectarian halakhot and ... the strong eschatological expectations of the Teacher of Righteousness."[64] Both of these reasons are argued for on the basis of perceived differences between the Qumran position and that of the parent movement, the Essenes.

2.2.1.2.1. Eschatology. According to García Martínez, the Teacher of Righteousness introduced a strong sense of eschatological hope in his message. These eschatological expectations are thought to have led to tensions in the broader Essene movement, since "eschatology is precisely one of the elements not brought out in the classical description of Essenism, but in the sectarian writings of Qumran it is prominent and shows a clear development."[65] García Martínez regards the Teacher's eschatological expectations to be reflected in various instances in 1QS, for example in 1QS VIII, 12b–16a:[66]

> And when these have become a community [ליחד] in Israel 13 according to these arrangements they are to be separated from the midst of the dwelling of the men of iniquity to walk into the wilderness to prepare there his [הואהא] path 14 as it is written [Isa 40:3]: In the wilderness prepare the way of the Lord [ייי ; cf. Isa 40:3 יהוה]; Make straight in the wilderness a highway for our Lord. 15 This (highway) is the study of the Torah/Law, which he has commanded through the hand of Moses in order to act according to all that has been revealed from age to age 16 and according to which the prophets have revealed in his holy spirit (*vacat*).

---

64. Ibid., 24.

65. Ibid., 17; contra Davies, who holds that the Qumran eschatology is a fulfillment of the Essene eschatology, which can be found in Jubilees, CD, and 4Q504; see Philip Davies, "Eschatology at Qumran," *JBL* 104 (1985): 39–55; see also Collins, "The Yaḥad and the 'Qumran Community,'" 81–96.

66. Even though the text does not mention the Teacher of Righteousness.

According to García Martínez, the eschatological expectations of the Teacher reflect the clear influence of the apocalyptic tradition, which similarly influenced Jubilees and the Animal Apocalypse (1 En. 85–90).[67] These two writings obviously are not Qumranic in origin but are influential in Qumran and therefore considered to be part of the community's formative period. García Martínez again places the developments of eschatology in a chronological order, attached to certain textual witnesses:

Figure 4. García Martínez's Assessment of the Development of Eschatology at Qumran.

Prophetic Eschatology	Apocalyptic Eschatology	Formative Teacher Eschatology
• Hebrew Bible	• Jubilees • Animal Apocalypse	• CD

2.2.1.2.2. Sectarian Halakah. García Martínez holds that the most significant reasons for the split-off, which he sees evidenced in CD I, 5b–12,[68] must be found in the "halakhah regulating practical life."[69] The two main documents García Martínez holds to indicate problems concerning legal or halakic matters are, chronologically, 11QT^a and 4QMMT. 11QT^a (11Q19 or Temple Scroll^a) is attributed to the formative period of the sect, that is, before the establishment of the community at Qumran, and is supposed to be authored by the Teacher himself. Therefore, 11QT^a is treated as a witness to the halakic disputes between the

---

67. Cf. John J. Collins, *Apocalypticism in the Dead Sea Scrolls* (London: Routledge, 1997), who argues that apocalyptic writings are not well attested at Qumran.

68. From this famous passage in CD, which narrates on the exile, the raising up of a "root," many scholars have tried to establish historical reconstructions about the foundation date of the Qumran community as well as the lifetime of the Teacher.

69. García Martínez, *Qumranica Minora I*, 17. See also Lawrence H. Schiffman, *Qumran and Jerusalem: Studies in the Dead Sea Scrolls and the History of Judaism* (Grand Rapids: Eerdmans, 2010), 5: "Jewish legal issues must stand at the center of all sectarianism in Second Temple Times." However, as we saw in chap. 1, Davies has argued that the obvious but often exaggerated disputes and differences regarding matters of halakah tend to disguise more profane, economical, political, or social points of contention; see Davies, "Sect Formation in Early Judaism," 136.

Teacher and "Greater Essenism" and his disputes "with other elements of the Judaism of the time."[70] García Martínez identifies the major elements of these disputes as: (1) prescriptions concerning feasts and sacrifices according to a sectarian calendar; (2) prescriptions concerning the temple, the city, and its related matters of purity; (3) the statute of the king; and (4) various halakot particularly relating to problems of purity, tithes, and marriage.[71]

The second witness concerning the development of sectarian halakah, 4QMMT, is especially thought to reflect the causes for the separation of the Qumran sect. Particularly one section of this highly fragmentary text, 4Q397 14–21, 7b–8c,[72] is considered to reflect a manifesto of separation. This passage has played a major role in the interpretation of the document's further contents and halakic statements.

García Martínez identifies in 4QMMT's supposed sectarian halakah four areas of dispute in which the Teacher's discordant interpretation of the law might have led to the alleged Qumranic split-off: (1) the cultic calendar; (2) prescriptions concerning the temple, the city, and its norms of purity; and (3) halakot relating to tithes, impurity, and marriage status.

Struck by the similarity of the halakic areas of conflict between 11QT^a and 4QMMT, García Martínez argues for—again, chronologically placed—a different provenance for both texts. Where 11QT^a is considered to be formative and preseparation, he places 4QMMT later and regards this text as an open letter written by the Teacher to the religious group from which the Qumranites separated.[73] Hence, he interprets 4QMMT as a polemical letter of an early Qumranic stage.[74] This early stage of separation is assumed since, apparently, the author of the letter still wants to negotiate and discuss matters of halakah in order to convince the Other to see the error of his/their ways.

---

70. García Martínez, *Qumranica Minora I*, 18.

71. Ibid.

72. *DSSSE* 2:801: "[And you know] we have segregated ourselves from the multitude of the peop[le] [and] from mingling in these affairs, and from associating wi[th them] in these things."

73. Interestingly, at a later stage, most scholars view 4QMMT as a letter addressed to the Jerusalemite high priestly establishment. García Martínez argues that it is precisely the lacking third component of 11QT^a, the statute of the king, which proves 4QMMT to be a later development with a more inner-sectarian programmatic character.

74. Qumranic is used to indicate post-split-off, not necessarily physically connected to Khirbet Qumran.

2.3.1.3. Summarizing the Theory of a Formative Period

Thus García Martínez concludes that the formative period contains the inceptions of visible differences between the Essene parent group and the Qumran group. First, in contradistinction to the Essenes, whose ideological and socioreligious outlook did not know eschatology, the Qumran group was characterized by the Teacher's apocalyptic influences that brought distinct eschatological expectations. Second, according to Josephus, the Essenes were admired by the Jerusalemite establishment and hence most likely accepted their calendar and subsequent festival cycle, while the Qumran group related to the Teacher's concepts of the periodization of history until the end time, which possibly inherently influenced their alternate position on calendrical and festival issues. Hence, under the influence of the Teacher of Righteousness, they supposedly changed their socioreligious Essene make-up and their halakic positions. García Martínez's hypothesis holds that the roots of these altering positions can be detected in the formative period of the Qumran sect, which thus consists of the following building blocks:

Table 1. Summary of García Martínez's Formative Period

Date:	ca. 161–125 BCE
Jerusalem Rule:	Jonathan (161/152–143/142 BCE)
	Simon (143/142–135/134 BCE)
	John Hyrcanus (134–104 B.E)
Qumran Rule:	Teacher of Righteousness (predesert)
Split-Off:	Early in John Hyrcanus's rule, ca. 134–125 BCE?
Issues:	Eschatology
	Apocalyptic influences
	Calendar and festivals
	Relation to the temple and temple cult
	Other halakic matters regarding purity, tithes, and matrimony
Texts:	11QT^a
	4QMMT
	CD
	Jubilees
	Book of Dreams (1 Enoch)

2.3.2. The Groningen Hypothesis in 2011, according to García Martínez Himself

In 2011, García Martínez readdressed his Groningen hypothesis with Baumgarten's question in mind as a central point of evaluation: "Has the Groningen Hypothesis reached the limits of its explanatory power, such that it is ripe for replacement ...?"[75] He recognizes that two fundamental contemporary insights, which were lacking at the first publication of the Groningen hypothesis, have become important for our understanding of Qumran: (1) After the full publication of the Scrolls, the formerly presupposed proportional division of the types of document (biblical, parabiblical, and sectarian) has changed, and the importance of parabiblical material has become clear. This so-called reworked Bible material accounts for the same number of texts as the biblical and sectarian texts taken together. (2) At the same time, it has become clear that these labels are anachronistic, far from neutral, and "inadequate to reflect historical reality."[76] Having observed this, García Martínez implicitly accepts the presence of multiple voices (representing multiple Jewish groups) within the Qumran texts, but he nevertheless—at the same time—holds on to the prime parameters of the Groningen hypothesis.

(1) The sectarian texts in the Qumran collection reflect a group or groups of Jews that were different from or opposed to the rest of the Jews of their time. These documents now form a minority of the total collection, but they do reflect the ideology and beliefs of the group that produced them.

(2) Even though the opposition (or Other) is differently defined in CD and 1QS, these two sectarian texts not only define themselves over against "all Israel" but also clearly give evidence to the existence of a parent and a split-off group. Hence, García Martínez holds on to a split-off group, the Qumran community that has brought together a library of manuscripts.

(3) This library is religious in nature and its outlook is sectarian: it reflects the sectarian group at Qumran. Moreover, García Martínez takes an even more radical stance than when he first formulated his hypoth-

---

75. Florentino García Martínez, "The Groningen Hypothesis Revisited," in *The Dead Sea Scrolls and Contemporary Culture: Proceedings of the International Conference Held at the Israel Museum, Jerusalem (July 6–8, 2008)*, ed. Adolfo D. Roitman, Lawrence H. Schiffman, and Shani Tzoref, STDJ 93 (Leiden: Brill, 2011), 17–30.

76. Ibid., 21.

esis in contextualizing the Qumran library as evidence of an authoritative canon-like collection, a Qumran Bible as it were:

> Now, we are much more aware that the only historical context we can apply with any certainty to the collection of compositions previously known (some as "biblical" and some as "non-biblical") as well as to the compositions previously unknown (some labeled "sectarian" and others "non-sectarian") is the Qumran context. For compositions previously unknown it is evident that the only context we can give them is the collection where they have been found, and while this context is independent of their origins it tells us at least that these previously unknown compositions were acceptable to and cherished by the group to a greater or lesser degree, in the same manner that the compositions which later will become "Bible" in Jewish, Christian or Ethiopic canons were acceptable to and cherished by the respective group to a greater or lesser degree.[77]

(4) In his understanding of the Qumran collection being a coherent library of authoritative manuscripts, specific for the Qumran sect, García Martínez moves towards the idea of a Qumran Bible and proposes to abandon the taxonomies of biblical and nonbiblical altogether. He proposes to approach all Qumran texts as authoritative for the Qumran sect: "The fact is that the whole collection of manuscripts found at Qumran ... is comprised of religious texts (in Hebrew or in Aramaic) whose formation has been influenced by other *preceding* religious texts that were considered as more or less authoritative. And the same authority conferring strategies are used in all of them."[78]

In a recent article that puts this earlier proposal in practice, García Martínez introduced a new method of analysis, which he calls "the authority-conferring strategy of the text."[79] Holding firm to the conviction of a representative Qumran library, he proposes to abandon the taxonomy of anachronistic labels and to replace them by an analysis of how the "core sectarian texts" (i.e., Damascus Document, Serekh, Hodayot, pesharim, War Scroll) reflect strategies "in order to invest their own compositions

---

77. Ibid., 26.
78. Ibid., 28, emphasis added.
79. Florentino García Martínez, "Beyond the Sectarian Divide: The 'Voice of the Teacher' as an Authority-Conferring Strategy in Some Qumran Texts," in *The Dead Sea Scrolls: Texts and Context*, ed. Charlotte Hempel, STDJ 90 (Leiden: Brill, 2010), 227–44.

with the same authoritative status of the other compositions their authors clearly recognized as authoritative ('Moses' and 'the Prophets,' but also compositions like Jubilees, Temple Scroll, Apocryphon of Joshua, Aramaic Levi)."[80] He demonstrates how these core sectarian texts attempt to claim authority by using strategies of divine inspiration and revelation (e.g., through the authoritative voice of the Teacher), strategies that were formerly used to demonstrate authority in biblical and other compositions. García Martínez's efforts to break open the anachronistic straightjacket of categorization and replace it with a more emic approach via a social group's understanding of authoritativeness and holy scripture is a commendable one and certainly demonstrates sensitivity to some obvious points, although they are often overlooked in Qumran studies:

(1) The writings from Qumran cannot be assumed to be exhaustive and must be treated as partial and coincidental for obvious reasons: (1.1) many of the Qumran finds are fragmentary scraps of scroll; (1.2) we do not know what the total contents of the caves around Qumran constituted at the moment the manuscripts were deposited in the caves.
(2) There was no such thing as a canon or a Bible, even though there seems to be an early notion of the authoritativeness in a division between the books of Moses and the books of the Prophets.
(3) Therefore, divisions in biblical and nonbiblical documents are anachronistic. Instead, the scholarly default setting should be authoritativeness for the community concerned.
(4) It recognizes the presence of more than one social group (and possibly more than a parent and a split-off group) in the core sectarian texts.
(5) It demonstrates that the strategies and techniques used in the Qumran sectarian writings are not unique but can be traced in formerly known compositions as well as in what later became the books of the Hebrew Bible.
(6) It demonstrates a certain awareness of continuity. Like Moses and the prophets before them, the contemporary generation of authority figures might also have been seen as being granted insights through divine revelation. This realization places the sec-

---

80. Ibid., 237.

tarian writings from Qumran, at least on a strategic and rhetorical level, in a long tradition and hence takes them—to a degree—out of their marginality.

However, underlying this newly proposed approach one can still observe the same parameters that uphold the old paradigm:

(1) There is a geographically definable Qumran sect with specific, rather radical ideas, which reflect the peculiar interpretations of an authority figure called the Teacher, who opposes mainstream Judaism.
(2) The writings are a representative collection of authoritative writings of this Qumran sect.
(3) As scholarship has clearly acknowledged the multitude of outlooks and voices in the various sectarian texts, García Martínez attempts to (partly) acknowledge these different groups, while holding on to the idea of a chronological development as the prime explanation for these differences in outlook.[81]

---

81. Ibid., 229–39. This new approach reflects the tension García Martínez is in, since he uses now one and then multiple, yet various, groups as being the owners of the Qumran collection. Here are just a few quotes from his article that illustrate how unclear and indecisive García Martínez is, how confused the reader might become when trying to figure out what exactly is still meant by the *yahad* or the Qumran community, or who are these other groups mentioned and how they relate to Qumran: "those core texts have revealed particular groups to us (the *yahad* group or the *mahanot* groups)" (229); "they show us a web of relationships among those groups, groups certainly interconnected, but in no way identical"(229); "groups that put together the collection" (230); "without elaborating here on the complicated matter of the relationship of the Damascus Document and the Serek, and consequently on the development and relationship of the communities for which these documents legislate" (231); "this figure of the past who was all-important for the different groups" (232); "the forming of the group of the Damascus Document" (233); "the activity of 'interpreting the law' is one of the basic characteristic of all the *yahad* groups" (234); "a constant function within the groups that gathered the manuscripts" (235); "divine revelation, produced by God's spirit, is now continuously accessible through exegesis which, within the group, reveals the true meaning of Torah for each age" (236); "the figure who has this function within the group, the 'Interpreter of the Torah'" (238); "what has been hidden from Israel is precisely those aspects of the Law of Moses that have been revealed to the members of the group" (238); "I think we can conclude that 'the voice of Teacher' is used within the collection of manuscripts as an authority-conferring

(4) The core sectarian writings reflect textual multilayeredness caused by the chronological development of the ideologies and beliefs that—from the precursors of the Qumran sect onwards—led to the unique positioning of the *yahad* in their age and time.

In abandoning the taxonomies, as well as letting go of his strictly historical reconstruction approach and replacing it by an approach of Qumran-centered contextualization, García Martínez seemingly obscures his Groningen hypothesis' idea of a formative period and subsequent textual chronology. However, he clearly retains the idea of a chronological development in which sectarian texts are influenced by preceding texts; since he also holds on to the main elements on which the concept of a formative period is based,[82] one may presume that even though the surface level of analysis has shifted—possibly under the influence of the realized importance of the so-called parabiblical texts—on a deeper level the parameters of the paradigm are still in place.[83]

Thus, this steady parameter of the original Groningen hypothesis—the notion of a formative period—is an important tool in tracing back historical origins and developments of a social entity called the Qumran community or *yahad*. Since the Qumran group is perceived to be a split-off group with a particular and distinctive sectarian outlook, the reverse trajectories to uncover the sect's origins and early history seek to identify presectarian sources and entities. Thus, in maintaining the notion of a formative period, two persistent main presuppositions can be detected: (1) the manuscripts found in the Qumran caves are the remains of a consistent, coherent, and meaningful sectarian library, assembled, owned, copied, written, and studied by the Qumran sect that lived at Khirbet Qumran; (2) "all the works found in Qumran that cannot be classified as strictly sectarian must have been composed before the split that gave rise of the Qumran group, because otherwise they would never have been

---

strategy for compositions that expand and adapt the Torah to the needs of the group, and that 'reveal' what in the Torah has remained 'hidden' from all Israel" (239).

82. I.e., a discordant split-off from a larger Essene body and a connection between the Qumran site and a Qumran sect with distinguishable sectarian ideas preserving a "deliberate collection of authoritative writings."

83. Therefore it is also safe to presume that the initial texts assigned to the formative period (11QT^a, 4QMMT, CD, Jubilees, 1 Enoch) are still considered to be formative.

accepted by the sect."[84] In the next section, I will critically reassess this notion of a formative period, especially in those elements that contribute to the theoretical framework of the Qumran paradigm and thus can make clear the function that formative texts play within García Martínez's theories.

2.4. Evaluating García Martínez's Formative Period and Model of Chronological Development

Over the years, scholars have grappled with the Groningen hypothesis and have also emphasized several theoretical weaknesses, which are connected to the idea of a formative period (and its underlying idea of a discordant split-off):[85] (1) the textual evidence for a discordant split-off is meager and not persuasive; (2) there are no clear criteria of how to distinguish between Essene and formative texts, nor between formative and Qumranic texts; (3) the paradoxes and contradictions within the various classical sources regarding the Essenes, as well as their authors' strategic objectives, obscure any sound Essene identification or distinction between Essene and Qumranic; (4) textual similarities do not necessarily reflect actual social reality;[86] (5) some documents might orthographically, ideologically, and rhetorically connect to a *yahad* but are far removed from its establishment in Qumran on the basis of dating and paleography;[87] and (6) Qumran might reflect a large collection of wider Jewish writings in which case *extra*sectarian would be better than *pre*sectarian. However, in most scholarly evaluations of García Martínez's theories, hardly any attempts are made to substantiate such fundamental criticisms by analyzing the hypothesis on a metalevel, in other words, on the basis of (the function of) its basic parameters and

---

84. García Martínez and van der Woude, "A 'Groningen' Hypothesis" in García Martínez, *Qumranica Minora I*, 31.

85. E.g., Gabriele Boccaccini, ed., *Enoch and Qumran Origins: New Light on a Forgotten Connection* (Grand Rapids: Eerdmans, 2005), esp. part 4: "The Groningen Hypothesis Revisited," 249–328.

86. See Albert Baumgarten, "Reflections on the Groningen Hypothesis," in Boccaccini, *Enoch and Qumran Origins*, 257. Baumgarten argues against simplified reconstructions of history on the basis of perceived similarities and differences. Hence, he warns against the methodological pitfall of researching "the idol of origins," which he considers often to be the researcher's wish to reconstruct an imagined and conceivable history instead of an accurately reconstructed past reality.

87. See Elgvin, "*Yahad* Is More Than Qumran," 273–79.

underlying assumptions. More often, scholars have either tried to replace (certain elements of) García Martínez's theory with their own alternative hypothetical elements, or they have commented on the content level of the theory.[88] More specifically, there are not many scholars who have systematically analyzed the *idea* of a formative period, which nevertheless is so essential to García Martínez's entire reconstruction of Qumran's early history. Hence, if one focuses and evaluates García Martínez's reconstruction of the early history of Qumran on its content level alone, one runs the risk of establishing variations within the prevailing paradigm, rather than systematically questioning the Qumran paradigm itself. This section takes another look at the formative period, especially questioning those elements that function to shape and sustain a social reality in which the notion of the Qumran sect takes center stage. In the pages to follow, the consequences of García Martínez's hypothesis will be discussed in order to identify where tension and problems occur and where precisely critical questions need to be asked.

2.4.1. Qumran Centrism Pushes All Dissonants into Presectarianism

As Dimant's categorizations seem to suffer from escaping texts, which seriously threaten to force her into recurrent reclassification in order to make them fit the paradigm, García Martínez's Groningen theory has proven to be much more flexible in its allocation of texts, since it is mostly interested in their historical positioning. Hence, because of its historical purpose, its prime interest is to establish a plausible lineage of diachronic devel-

---

88. E.g., Émile Puech, "The Essenes and Qumran, the Teacher and the Wicked Priest, the Origins," in Boccaccini, *Enoch and Qumran Origins*, 298–302. Puech reconstructs an alternative to García Martínez's early history of the sect and its formative period, while using mostly the same textual evidence. Yet, he changes one single parameter: He identifies the Wicked Priest, who pursues the Teacher of Righteousness to his place of exile in 1QpHab, as Jonathan. This replacement inherently places the birth of the Qumran group and its subsequent retreat to Qumran (and hence the whole historical framework including its parameters of persons, places, and events) some twenty years earlier and thus reverses the priority between 11QT^a and 4QMMT. Interestingly, if one compares Puech's and García Martínez's propositions and realizes that both theories are based on the same sources and read as similarly convincing, one can observe how appealing, but, at the same time, how contentious historical reconstructions on the basis of nonhistoriographical texts can be.

opments and perceived spheres of influence. Even though the Groningen hypothesis is as much tied to the problems of identifying the *yahadic* texts, the concepts of diachrony and chronology liberate the framework from the categorization problems that Dimant encounters for the simple reason that they implicitly arrange for all non-*yahadic* texts to be presectarian.

This presumed presectarianism of all non-*yahadic* texts is an implication of the sociological connotations attached to the underlying assumption that the Qumran manuscripts form the library of a sect. Sociologically, sects are perceived to be in tension with the outside world and as such are likely to self-identify by separation, segregation, and the ideological and social construction of (high) boundaries between insiders and outsiders.[89] Hence, the presumption of a sectarian library not only provides but also demands coherence. On the one hand, the notion of a sectarian library inherently provides coherence, since its users are thought to be members of a deviant organization, who are likely to be interested in preserving a library that accords with their ideology or at least whose contents can be meaningfully related to their worldviews. On the other hand, this very presumption demands the library's contents to be ideologically coherent. This double-edged sword of coherence thus leads to a Qumran sect centralism, which has far-reaching consequences as the perceived ideology of the sect becomes the main explanatory tool for the entire collection. Even if we set aside the proven difficulty of setting indisputable and sustainable criteria for the allocation of sectarian texts, the explanation for the presence of all nonsectarian texts will naturally be limited by the sociological notions of sectarianism. Hence, their presence can only be meaningfully explained in chronologically-based theories, which push dissonant and differing voices into the position of the sect's precursors. As a consequence, these theories are faced with the demand of sect centrism so as to construct a chronologically as well as ideologically meaningful lineage.

The weakness of such constructions lies not only in the tendency to downplay paradoxes and inconsistencies (see below), but also in the way it prevents us from studying individual texts in their own right. As Qumran sect centrism automatically relates texts to the Qumran sect, it limits interpretative horizons and possibilities to restricted semantic fields. More

---

89. In light of Judaism's multiformity, because we have seen that the usage of the term sect is often loosely defined (see chap. 1) and because these very connotations can influence or overly define the direction of research, it might be better to avoid or at least postpone the terminology and sociology of sect altogether.

importantly, Qumran centrism seriously tends to block conceptualizations that allow texts to reflect a different or wider social background. Hence, such a sect-centralizing concept never thinks of certain texts as contemporary to the *yahadic* texts or equally authoritative for other social groups, maybe even widely read and studied by various other contemporary Jewish groups. In short, Qumran centrism prevents theorizing more openly about the (possibly wider) provenance of inconclusive Qumran texts, which make up an important part of the collection. Specifically, these texts often lack explicit evidence of sectarian radicality and thus might allow for other possible interpretations than their assigned provenance in the early history of a small sect of two hundred people.

Thus, Qumran centrism also does not allow the Qumran community—if such an entity existed—to be considered as an active participant in a lively discussion on the parameters of Judaism (halakah, calendar, etc.) at the time and fixes it in its perceived socially, geographically, and ideologically segregated position. Moreover, it negates the possibility that the nonsectarian texts do not, or do not only, reflect Qumran sectarian ideas, ideologies, and practices in the making, but might provide evidence that these ideas were—in various versions and varieties—much more common and simultaneously developing in many more social settings than Qumran centrism would allow.

2.4.2. Formative Period: From Convenient Shelter to Invaluable Preservation Tool

The religious outlook of the Qumran community is perceived to have "a different theological outlook, a different calendar, a different *halakha*, etc., from the 'rest' of Judaism. Moreover, the texts also reveal that this group was a highly structured and tightly organized community whose members considered themselves to be an elect group, who have consciously *separated* from the rest of that Judaism."[90] In line with this perception, García Martínez argues that the sectarian library has an exclusivist character in

---

90. García Martínez, *Qumranica Minora I*, 34, emphasis original; this statement in itself raises a multitude of problems, such as "different," and (the assumption of) the existence of an identifiable "rest of Judaism," a notion that creates the imagery of a sectarian group over against an institutionalized, denominational, or church-like religion accepted by the majority of its contemporary society. Disputes regarding halakic matters and hence calendrical and festival issues lie at the heart of Judaism, especially

which "it does seem impossible that the community should have kept the religious literature of alien or clearly hostile groups."[91]

This assumption forces manuscripts with ostensibly different outlooks, ideologies, and halakic positions (and other minor and major differences) into a position in which they cannot threaten the concept of a homogenous sectarian library. As we have seen, one method of achieving this is to place all dissonant, or rather, all not 100 percent sectarian documents, *prior* to the formation of the sect.[92] However, the idea of presectarian categories only protects and preserves the uniqueness of the Qumran sect by referring the problems of diversity, difference, and (dis)similarity back in time; it cannot entirely explain these phenomena. While the presectarian pushback in time can identify and diachronically explain divergences from the perceived central sectarian position, it nevertheless needs to clarify the character of these divergences in relation to the later Qumran sectarianism, while at the same time preserve the unity of the entire library. In short, the presectarian categories have three vital functions in the overall framework of Qumran sectarianism: (1) they are recognizable identity markers, which can contain differences and similarities within their own unit; (2) they establish chronology and hence an explanatory frame of evolution; and (3) they keep Qumran sectarianism "clean" as they both deal diachronically with difference and provide an explanatory frame for inconveniences within Qumran sectarian texts. The most flexible asset within these presectarian categorizations has proven to be the extensible formative period, a convenient period of time in which the soon-to-be-formed Qumran sect experienced all sorts of influences upon its later ideological stance. The formative period is the linchpin that keeps the whole framework together: it functions not only as a bridge between all other categories; it also provides a shelter for all texts that—for various reasons—are difficult to position.

Hence, the formative period cleverly turns a weakness into a strength. While in Dimant's classification system texts like 4QMMT form a threat by

---

in the multigroup era of the Second Temple. Therefore, I consider the suggestion of Qumran versus "the rest of Judaism" unhelpful.

91. Ibid.

92. Ibid., 31: "All the works found in Qumran that cannot be classified as strictly sectarian must have been composed *before* the split that gave rise to the Qumran group, because otherwise they would never have been accepted by the sect" (emphasis original).

2. TEXTUAL CLASSIFICATIONS OF PRESECTARIANISM   81

their tendency to escape all categories, in García Martínez's proposal, such texts are placed in the formative period in which they form the chronological glue and primary building blocks of the development of Qumran sectarianism. In an overarching chronological framework of historical development that wishes to explain the presence of all Qumran manuscripts, the notion of a formative period functions as a preservation tool for the (re)construction of a unity in what otherwise may look as a rather varied, layered, and complexly related corpus of Jewish religious manuscripts.[93]

2.4.3. THE BUMPY ROAD TO SECTARIANISM: INCONSISTENCIES IN THE DEVELOPMENTAL FRAMEWORK

The functionalities of the formative period that I have discussed above—presectarization and the construction of unity—do have their own limitations and are bound to their own implicit criteria. One inherent limitation, which makes the formative period more than just a convenient rest-category for inconvenient texts, can be observed once one realizes that this category's documents are vitally important for the validity of the entire Groningen framework: Not only do these texts provide the evidence and the reasons for the *yahadic* split-off (4QMMT), they also preserve the sect's Essene identification (11QT^a). Moreover, the formative period aligns ideological, halakic, and organizational differences and idiosyncrasies in a variety of texts and molds them into the potentiality to be(come) *yahadic*. Finally, the formative period fixes the dating and provenance of various difficult-to-place documents by providing their date as being between approximately 166 BCE and 125 BCE[94] and their provenance by positioning them in a chronological order, inherently presuming developmental stages.

---

93. Moreover, García Martínez uses his historical reconstruction and, more specifically, his dating of the discordant split-off as a *terminus ante quem* and guiding tool to date (compositions of) difficult-to-date manuscripts as well as an explanation of why "only some of the so-called Old Testament Apocrypha or Pseudepigrapha—e.g., Ben Sira, Tobit and the *Epistle of Jeremiah* are represented in the caves and not other compositions of the same sort;" ibid., 36.

94. The formative period is fixed by its ending, i.e., the discordant split-off, which is dated early in John Hyrcanus's rule. Even though García Martínez connects Jonathan, Simon, and John Hyrcanus to the activities of the Teacher through 1QpHab, he specifically leaves open the possibility that the period commenced as early as the Maccabean uprising.

As such, the writings of the formative period together form a framework that is capable of diversity as they are thought to be witnesses of the sectarian development that eventually led to the discordant split-off of the Teacher's group from its Essene parent movement. This diversity is, however, not without focus: these writings are supposed to provide us with intimate insights into the areas of sectarian development. Logically, the formative period ought to consist of manuscripts that provide textual evidence of a growing sectarian discontent with and resistance to certain areas of Essene ideology and practice, while at the same time presenting new developments and ideas already in line with the later sectarian texts.

This understanding of the formative period might, however, be in tension with other assumptions of García Martínez's developmental model. For instance, if the Qumran community kept an ideologically homogenous library, and it was indeed "out of the question that it [the Qumran community] should have preserved and made use of works incompatible with its own ideology,"[95] why would they preserve the writings of their Essene parent movement, especially since their split-off is thought to be discordant? This is but one of the inconsistencies within García Martínez's reasoning; various aspects of the Groningen hypothesis are interconnected, partly overlapping and built upon one another. Moreover, they are mapped out on different levels: an overarching chronological framework, a periodization of time within this framework, an ideological unity in each period (except in the stormy formative period), a Darwinian notion of ideological evolution throughout the framework, and, finally, only a handful of documents to provide the literary evidence to either help construct the historical or the socioideological aspects of the framework. All these levels seem to hold inherent tensions and inconsistencies, which not only jeopardize the entire hypothesis, but also have implications for our analysis of the formative period.

In figure 5 (see page 84) I have tried to schematically expose some of the inconsistencies and inherent problems within the Groningen hypothesis.[96] These are a few examples of such inconsistencies that provoke the question of the validity and, hence, the underlying function of a formative period.

---

95. Ibid., 9.

96. Overall, there are too many inconsistencies to be exhaustive here. Moreover, the elaborate discussion of these issues falls outside the scope of this thesis.

2. TEXTUAL CLASSIFICATIONS OF PRESECTARIANISM 83

Figure 5. García Martínez's Groningen Hypothesis with Its Inconsistencies.

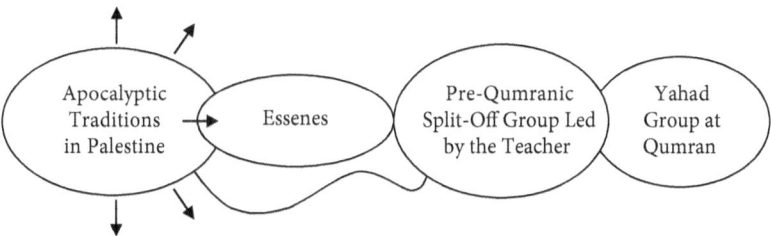

eschatology	no eschatology	eschatology	
idea of an eschatological temple	rejection of the temple and cult	idea of an eschatological temple	specific ideas about the temple
issues of calendar and festival cycle	no calendrical and festival cycle issues	issues of calendar and festival cycle	no polemics regarding calendar, harmonization of calendars
364-day calendar	calendar of the "rest of Judaism," unclear: 167 BCE Seleucid luni-solar calendar? Maccabees switched back? No sources!	the Teacher wants a "traditional calendar" (364-day calendar?) 4QMMT	calendrical texts show variety of calendars, from a solarized calendar like Jubilees to texts in which the 364-day calendar is synchronized with lunar phases
	admiration of the Jerusalem establishment		
		Sadducean halakot in 4QMMT	
		152 (161?)–34 BCE	John Hyrcanus pursues the Teacher to his place of exile (1QpHab XI, 2–8), i.e., ca. 134–104 BCE
			Qumran first occupation phases: de Vaux 130–100 BCE Magness 100/50–31BCE

(1) It is hard to imagine that such core apocalyptic issues as eschatology, its subsequent periodization of time, and the inherent calendrical problems and festival disputes were entirely dropped in their Essene predecessors' ideological make-up, only to be picked up by the Teacher to become the core issues of dispute and reason to split-off and retreat to Qumran.

(2) Even if we would accept this, the calendrical issues seem to be completely resolved in Qumran, but the calendrical texts the sect preserves

reflect a great variety (4QS^e [4Q259], 4QMMT^a [4Q394], 4Q320–330). Moreover, one can observe attempts to "synchronize the widely used lunar calendar with the solar calendar [i.e., 364-day calendar] which these texts consider the right one," to "synchronize the solar [364-day] calendar with a six-year cycle of the 24 priestly courses," or to "record which priestly course was in service."[97] García Martínez argues that the Qumranites apparently were aware of others "following a different calendar and accordingly they tried to synchronize both," and he finds that the way these various calendars are presented reflects "no hint of polemic."[98] I find it difficult to relate this obvious leniency and openness towards the views of others to the perceived segregation, radicality, and rigor of the Qumran sect.

(3) The same inconsistencies can be detected by García Martínez's perceived developmental theory regarding the attitudes towards the temple. The—for the formative period and split-off theory—vital conclusion, that calendrical issues and eschatology were not in the Essene ideology, is drawn on the basis of the classical sources that state that the Essenes were admired by the Jerusalemite establishment—the high-priestly and Hasmonean rulers. To sustain this argument alongside the developmental apocalyptic-Essene-Qumran argument of temple/cult issues and particularly the ideological Essene rejection of the temple seems rather hard to sustain.

In conclusion, the formative period has the function of presectarianization and unity-construction and resolves many of the tensions and problems within the sociohistorical framework of the Groningen hypothesis. The formative period functions as a two-way street: on the one hand, the formative period's presectarian character functions to preserve the *yahad*'s unique sectarian position and its library's ideological cleanliness by keeping potential discussion partners in their fixed posterior position (bottom up); but on the other hand, it functions as a vital funnel for the developmental theory of Qumran sectarianism (top down).

---

97. Ibid., 72. García Martínez's idea of a solar calendar is now considered to be incorrect. Therefore, I have put in between brackets the better term "364-day calendar"; see Jonathan Ben-Dov and Stéphane Saulnier, "Qumran Calendars: A Survey of Scholarship 1980–2007," *CurBR* 7 (2008): 131–79.

98. García Martínez, *Qumranica Minora I*, 76.

2.5. Conclusions: Classification Systems and Their Function in the Paradigm

In her 1995 literary classification, Dimant issues a fundamental critique of her colleague García Martínez's attempt to classify the nonbiblical texts from Qumran according to genres and contents.[99] Her main criticism asserts that García Martínez fails to make a "systematic distinction between community and non-community works" and that he includes the Aramaic texts "together with the Hebrew ones."[100] Paradoxically, Dimant's most important point of critique, not only of García Martínez, but of any scholar who has attempted to trace back the origins and history of the Qumran community on the basis of information in the Scrolls, is her conviction that texts can only be assessed on a literary, not on a sociological or historical level.[101] She argues that the original idea that these texts can be used to reach reliable historical reconstructions is profoundly flawed. Dimant particularly stresses that historical reconstructions based upon any combination of archaeological evidence regarding the habitation periods of Khirbet Qumran and textual evidence regarding the origins of the sect are still heavily debated. Therefore, Dimant concludes that no such reconstructed history can be suitable to establish either the dating (presectarian, sectarian) or the classification (sectarian, nonsectarian) of manuscripts.[102]

In this respect, Dimant's position is radically opposed to García Martínez's Groningen hypothesis, whose pivotal point is the establishment of an overall chronological framework to explain the history, development, and early origins of the Qumran community. As such, it is a historically focused classification system, which primarily attempts to date and allocate manuscripts diachronically in order to serve the sociohistorical purpose of positioning the perceived peculiarities of Qumran within Second Temple Judaism, while at the same time trying to find an overarching

---

99. See Florentino García Martínez, *Textos de Qumrán* (Madrid: Editorial Trotta, 1992).
100. Dimant, "Qumran Manuscripts," 24 n. 4.
101. Dimant, "Sectarian and Non-sectarian Texts from Qumran," 9; also n. 6. Of course, as we have seen, this criticism can also be applied to Dimant's own classification system.
102. Paradoxically, as we have seen, Dimant falls into her own pit, only via a different route.

explanation for the collection's textual and literary diversity. In turn, García Martínez has fundamental problems with Dimant's classification system, as his hypothesis is not served by a fundamental dichotomy between sectarian and nonsectarian, but rather he wants to understand the Qumran manuscripts as witnesses to a diachronic development of a particular Qumran-specific form of sectarianism. As such, García Martínez contests Dimant's assessment that the Aramaic manuscripts should be classified as nonsectarian solely on the basis of their language. More generally, he rejects Dimant's fundamental dichotomy of sectarian and nonsectarian texts, and he is critical of her subsequent in-between category: he argues that—in a fundamental dichotomy like Dimant's—texts cannot be "a little sectarian."[103] More specifically, he rightly observes that Dimant's in-between category consists mostly of reworked Bible texts and, hence, the recategorization cannot simply affect nonbiblical (sectarian/nonsectarian) texts but has to have an impact on all Qumran manuscripts, biblical and nonbiblical.[104]

Thus, García Martínez and Dimant take very different approaches, but they have the same goal: they wish to classify, categorize, and position the Qumran manuscripts in an overarching explanatory framework. This chapter has dealt with their two influential methods of classifying the Qumran documents and has attempted to lay bare those elements in their theories that seem to create tension and inflexibility by assessing their function within the Qumran paradigm. As we have seen, even though both scholars approach the Qumran texts very differently, the result of their theoretical frameworks asks questions of some of the same documents. Some texts seem to escape the boundaries of their literary and sociohistorical classification constructs, but at the same time they occupy a crucial position in these frameworks. This very phenomenon has caused Dimant and García Martínez to adjust their models of classification, but

---

103. García Martínez, "Sectario, No-Sectario, O Qué?" 383.

104. However, García Martínez's framework also builds upon Dimant's groundbreaking work, from which it takes its two primary contentions: The assumption of the existence of a Qumran community (1) that copied, wrote, read, studied, and owned a meaningful and deliberate collection of texts, which formed (2) its sectarian religious library. Thus, despite his rejection of Dimant's classification system and his counterproposition to abandon all taxonomies and textual classifications, García Martínez preserves the paradigm of a deliberate library of a sectarian group. These two paradigmatic pillars can be detected as the foundation stones of his recent analytical concept of authoritativeness.

at the same time has reinforced paradigmatic constructions of presectarianism and formative periods in both their theories. This convergence in Dimant and García Martínez's proposals calls for a more in-depth look into one of those texts that in each of their approaches turns out to be problematic. The most eye-catching example of such a problematic text that at the same time is highly important for the overall framework of both classification systems is 4QMMT. It is therefore this pivotal text that will be the focus of the next chapter.

3
THE PROVENANCE OF 4QMMT:
A CASE OF QUMRAN (PRE-)SECTARIANISM?

In the previous chapter, literary and sociohistorical classification systems were discussed, and we have seen that they have played an important role in the assessment of the provenance of certain key Qumran documents; 4QMMT or Miqṣat Ma'aśê ha-Torah ("Some Precepts of the Law") is one of those key texts from the Dead Sea. Scholars have throughout assessed this text to be the foundational document of the Qumran community, and as such, the text is thought to give a unique insight into the group's incipient theology. Since 4QMMT plays such a pivotal role in classification systems that implicitly or explicitly reconstruct the social reality behind the Qumran texts, this chapter seeks to reevaluate this text's position and function within the Qumran paradigm.

Scholarly consensus regarding 4QMMT's provenance as a foundational presectarian or very early *yahadic* text has proven to be vitally important to theories concerning the uniqueness of the Qumran sect, its split-off from a larger movement, its segregation from the Jerusalemite establishment and society as a whole, its position over against enemies and opponents, its stringent halakic system, and its sectarian calendar. 4QMMT is thought to provide the reasons for the Qumranites' very existence and to set the ground principles from which later *yahadic* rules and regulations of daily sectarian life spring. In this manner, 4QMMT is thought to be a uniquely and exclusively (pre-)Qumranic or (pre-)*yahadic* document, rather than a pseudepigraphal Second Temple text with a wider audience. 4QMMT thus holds a key position within the Qumran paradigm, while at the same time it tends to escape its confined categories within the classification systems we have discussed earlier. Therefore, this chapter takes another look at its provenance and its inherent function within the sociohistorical constructs that form the foundations of the Qumran paradigm.

3.1. The Task of this Chapter

As we have seen in the previous chapter, the identification of 4QMMT as foundational for the emerging sectarian identity of the Qumran community is far from straightforward and cannot easily be reconciled with the specific features of the text. For one, the text lacks sectarian terminology and literary style. Moreover, as we will see, the work is also notoriously difficult to date and its fragmentary state makes reliable reconstruction difficult. Moreover, the complexity of its structure raises questions about its genre and provenance.

Yet, the scholarly consensus that this text is to be evaluated as a foundational text for the Qumran community has remained more or less unchallenged. García Martínez strongly advocates that in the formative period of the Qumran community, 11QT^a (11Q19/Temple Scroll^a) represents the points of conflict between the Essene and the Teacher of Righteousness's halakic positions, while the chronologically later 4QMMT is a schismatic halakic letter, "which defines the reasons for the separation of the Qumran Sect."[1] Dimant shares this view: for her, 4QMMT is a polemical halakic letter, in which the Qumranites expressed their position to outsiders and as such defined their sectarian character.[2] In addition, Schiffman is convinced that this document is not only important for the understanding of the history of Jewish law, but in its Qumran context the letter aids in understanding more about the provenance of the Temple Scroll, while—at the same time—it purports to provide insight into the "early history of the community." Whereas García Martínez considers 4QMMT to be presectarian (i.e., part of the sect's formative period), and Dimant calls the text "undoubtedly *yahadic*,"[3] Schiffman seems more careful in positioning 4QMMT as he states: "It still remains to be determined if it [i.e., 4QMMT] is an actual letter, dating to the earliest days of the Qumran group, or if it is an 'apocryphal' text, written some years, or even decades, later to express the fundamental reasons for the break or schism with the Jerusalem establishment."[4] So, even though Schiffman contests the prov-

---

1. García Martínez, *Qumranica Minora I*, 17.
2. Devorah Dimant, "Israeli Scholarship on the Qumran Community," in *The Dead Sea Scrolls in Scholarly Perspective: A History of Research*, ed. Devorah Dimant, STDJ 99 (Leiden: Brill, 2012), 237–80.
3. Ibid., 162.
4. Schiffman, *Qumran and Jerusalem*, 113.

enance of the document as a contemporary foundational document that witnesses the break between the Essenes and the Qumranites and reckons with the possibility that this document merely narrates the reasons for the beginnings of the Qumranites' sectarian movement after the fact, he still reasons from within the prevalent Qumran paradigm as he subscribes to the consensus evaluation that 4QMMT reflects the reasons for a sectarian schism.

In this chapter, we reevaluate on what basis scholars have defined 4QMMT to be the prime witness of the Qumran sect's foundation and which elements are important in the evaluation of this position. How are the early evaluations of this text assessed, contested, challenged, critiqued, and reinforced by later scholarly research with regard to its peculiarities, sections, and themes?[5] This chapter's primary interest lies in the reasons why 4QMMT's position in the Qumran paradigm has remained so steadfast, especially in the face of scholarly arguments that, so it seems, directly affect the text's provenance and position. Therefore, this chapter seeks to answer the following three-tiered central question: (1) Does scholarly research satisfactorily confirm the provenance of this text as foundational to the Qumran community; (2) is there convincing evidence to establish and confirm the text's unique and exclusive relationship to the *yahad* as either "sectarian" (Dimant) or "presectarian" (García Martínez); and finally, (3) do our findings under (1) and (2) have consequences for the overall validity of the formative or presectarian pillar of the Qumran paradigm?

3.2. A History of Controversies

From the very beginning of its discovery, 4QMMT has been the center of conflict and controversy. Between 1953 and 1959, six manuscripts of the text (4Q394–399) were identified among the numerous Cave 4 fragments. From the very beginning, John Strugnell was assigned as the editor

---

5. DJD X and Strugnell's "Second Thoughts" will be taken as the primary commentaries, while the works of other scholars are considered here as later voices in the overall 4QMMT discussion: Elisha Qimron and John Strugnell, *Qumran Cave 4.V: Miqsat Ma'aseh Ha-Torah*, DJD X (Oxford: Clarendon, 1994); John Strugnell "MMT: Second Thoughts on a Forthcoming Edition," in *The Community of the Renewed Covenant: The Notre Dame Symposium on the Dead Sea Scrolls*, ed. Eugene Ulrich and James VanderKam, CJA 10 (Notre Dame: University of Notre Dame Press, 1994), 57–73.

of the text's DJD volume, but it was not until 1994 that he and his colleague Elisha Qimron were able to publish their composite text and full commentary on 4QMMT.[6] Throughout the project, much controversy and frustration crippled the investigation and publication of the composite text: Israel's contemporary political situation, problems with regard to funding, illegal publications by frustrated third parties, and various disagreements on the reconstruction and provenance of the text have been a constant and integral part of 4QMMT's history.[7] Moreover, the DJD X volume contains several paradoxes and opposing views, which reflect the disagreements between Strugnell and Qimron, who as a result dedicated separate appendixes to their respective views of the text. Their most eye-catching disagreement, on which Stegemann was asked to advise, concerned the fundamental aspect of the positioning of a paragraph (4Q398 11–13). Subsequently, Strugnell published an elaboration on his views in an article called "Second Thoughts."[8] The disagreements between Qimron and Strugnell not only concern such fundamental issues as the text's dating and genre but also affect the interpretation of 4QMMT's provenance as either a Qumranic or a pre-Qumranic (or rather *yahadic* or pre-*yahadic*) text.[9] These issues have remained topics of lively scholarly discussions. The most important scholarly disputes will, as far as they have consequences for our investigation, be discussed below.

3.3. The Texts

4QMMT comprises six manuscripts from Cave 4, all incomplete and fragmentary (4Q394–399). From these fragmentary manuscripts, the DJD X editors reconstructed a composite text, which consists of 130 lines. This composite text tries to follow the most complete manuscript at each occasion, but the fragmentariness and at times the lack of over-

---

6. Qimron and Strugnell, DJD X.

7. A full overview of these controversial proceedings can be found in Hanne von Weissenberg, *4QMMT: Reevaluating the Text, the Function and the Meaning of the Epilogue*, STDJ 82 (Leiden: Brill, 2009), 2–7.

8. Strugnell, "Second Thoughts," 57–73.

9. For an overview of the discussion, see Florentino García Martínez, "4QMMT in a Qumran Context," in *Reading 4QMMT: New Perspectives on Qumran Law and History*, ed. John Kampen and Moshe J. Bernstein, SymS 2 (Atlanta: Scholars Press, 1996), 15–27. Cf. Strugnell, "Second Thoughts" in which he expresses his doubt regarding the epistolary character of (part of) the text.

lap between the reconstructed manuscripts has forced the editors to use other texts and manuscripts in order to complete their reconstruction.[10] According to Qimron, "the reconstruction of approximately 130 extant lines of MMT probably constitutes 40% of the composite text."[11] He therefore warns against the usage of the composite text as a stand-alone manuscript and advises others to always consult the individual manuscripts behind the composite text. However, "in spite of this caveat, the composite text of *DJD X* has been regarded almost as the *textus receptus* of 4QMMT, and has remained virtually unchallenged in subsequent Qumran scholarship."[12]

Strugnell and Qimron divided the composite text into three major sections, which are often studied separately: section A, a 364-day calendar; section B, a series of halakic rulings, and section C, a hortatory epilogue. The six manuscripts of 4QMMT do not each contain material from all three sections. Quite strikingly, none of the manuscripts contains all three sections. Hanne Von Weissenberg has conveniently placed 4Q394–399 in two tables, so as to indicate which manuscript contains (parts of) which section.[13]

Table 2: 4QMMT, according to DJD X						
Calendar	4Q394 1–2, 3–4					
Halakot	4Q394	4Q395	4Q396	4Q397	4Q398 1–3	
Epilogue				4Q397	4Q398 11–17	4Q399

---

10. For instance, in his reconstruction of the text's halakic section B, but also in the interpretation thereof, Qimron relies heavily upon the halakah in 11QT^a (11Q19). For an overview of the (at points extremely thin) overlaps between the manuscripts and fragments, see von Weissenberg, *4QMMT*, 45–47.

11. Elisha Qimron, "The Nature of the Reconstructed Composite Text of 4QMMT," in Kampen and Bernstein, *Reading 4QMMT*, 9–13.

12. Von Weissenberg, *4QMMT*, 26.

13. Ibid., 41–43, tables 1 and 2; the issues of both tables will be discussed in the respective sections.

Table 3. 4QMMT, according to von Weissenberg (43) and Ben-Dov in DJD XXI						
Calendar	4Q394 3-4					
Halakot	4Q394	4Q395	4Q396	4Q397	4Q398 1-3, 5, 7	
Epilogue				4Q397	4Q398 11-17	4Q399

3.3.1. Section A: The Calendar

4QMMT's calendrical section A is preserved in only one manuscript, 4Q394. It consists of two very different types of fragments, 4Q394 1-2 (= 4QMMT A 1-18) and 4Q394 3-4 (= 4QMMT A 19-21).[14] As the differences between tables 2 and 3 demonstrate, scholars have questioned the structure of these section A fragments. DJD X holds that the fragments of an originally independently numbered document, 4Q327, belong to manuscript 4Q394 and renumber them 4Q394 1-2. In the course of Qumran scholarship, this provenance has been heavily debated: Nowadays, the former 4Q327 (representing lines 1-18 of section A) is commonly considered *not* to be part of 4Q394 but to represent another composition, 4QCalendrical Document D.[15] This leaves us with a calendrical section, consisting of three heavily reconstructed lines, section A 19-21 (i.e., 4Q394 3-4). These three lines contain the word Sabbath and the completion of the year in a reconstructed but, according to most scholars, likely number of 364 days.

The controversy about the calendar is not confined to the allocation of fragments 1-2, but rather comprises the question of whether a calendar can or cannot be considered a part of the original text of 4QMMT. Already in appendix 3 of DJD X Strugnell openly raises his doubts with regards to the originality of the calendrical section A. His doubts are rather funda-

---

14. The line numbers of the composite text are indicated in parentheses.
15. A reassessment of these fragments that has led to scholarly consensus regarding their exclusion is found in Shemaryahu Talmon, Jonathan Ben-Dov, and Uwe Glessmer, *Qumran Cave 4.XVI: Calendrical Texts*, DJD XXI (Oxford: Clarendon, 2001).

mental: Strugnell argued that "it is hard to relate the calendar to the rest of the work, whether form-critically or even in terms of subject-matter."[16] He considers the material evidence to link section A's calendar to sections B and C rather obscure, as its relation is only ascertained through one manuscript (4Q394).[17] Moreover, Strugnell finds especially section A's total absence of polemical language difficult to explain in light of what he considers to be the highly polemical sections B and C. Thus, based on material, form-critical, and content-level arguments, Strugnell argues that, for reasons unknown, only in 4Q394 the calendrical elements were placed before section B and that a calendar was not an original part of 4QMMT.[18]

Interestingly, unlike a majority of scholars, Strugnell never doubts that fragments 1–2 belonged to 4Q394. Unlike Strugnell, whose most important argument to exclude the entire calendrical section from the original 4QMMT is its absence of polemics,[19] most scholars have advocated on the basis of material, paleographical, and other technical arguments, to exclude the first eighteen lines of section A (4Q394 1–2).[20] Apart from these technical reasons for excluding fragments 1–2, only García Mar-

---

16. DJD X, appendix 3, 203–4.

17. The remaining three lines of section A preserve the beginning words of section B. On this basis, scholars disagree as to whether a calendar was an integral part of 4QMMT or must be considered to be a later sectarian addition, only occurring in 4Q394; see von Weissenberg, *4QMMT*, 36–38, 130–33.

18. In making this distinction between an individual manuscript, in this case 4Q394, and the original text of 4QMMT, Strugnell opens a rather peculiar door, through which later scholars may presume a pure and original 4QMMT which can be distinguished from its diversified Qumran manuscripts. Since 4QMMT only exists in a highly reconstructed form based on 4Q394–399, which came about only with the help of similar contents in texts like 11QT^a, it seems rather speculative to presume that we are able to distill a pure 4QMMT original or that certain inconvenient parts of individual manuscripts can be discarded on the basis of a presupposed Ur-text. Moreover, each manuscript ought to be assessed in its own right as to its structure, coherence, and order of fragments. If certain fragments are to be excluded from a manuscript, their exclusion should be based upon sound material, paleographical, and other methodologically verifiable evidence, not upon a presumed original that it is impossible to retrieve.

19. Strugnell includes section A 1–18, which represents merely lists of festivals and priestly rosters in a yearly scheme. This inclusion might have influenced his opinion regarding the nonpolemical nature of section A.

20. See von Weissenberg, *4QMMT*, 33–35; according to these arguments, frags. 3–4 remain part of 4QMMT.

tínez seems to advance an additional argument, based on the difference in calendrical content between 4Q394 1–2 and 3–4. According to García Martínez, the former would be merely a festival calendar listing, which enumerates the Sabbaths and festivals of the year without intercalation, while the latter contains a 364-day calendar that includes intercalation.[21] García Martínez's assessment of fragments 3–4 is especially problematic, since the fragmentariness of the material hardly allows us to draw any such conclusions, let alone to compare it with other calendrical material.[22] Therefore, García Martínez might have argued from a predisposition of a coherent sectarian document in which a known sectarian calendar would add to its perceived polemical stance. Indeed, perceiving 4QMMT as the schismatic foundational document of the sect, García Martínez advocates not "to exclude the calendar as an original part of the composition, as one of the key elements of the composition, and as one of the elements in which the 'we' group of the composition has separated itself from the others."[23] García Martínez's conclusions are sustained by Menahem Kister, who argued that the occurrence of a sectarian 364-day calendar in itself can be observed as a polemical statement. He holds polemics to be the main reason for adopting this sectarian calendar into 4QMMT at a later stage.[24]

Von Weissenberg agues that the calendar originally must have been a separate document and "not part of the earliest form of 4QMMT."[25] She thinks that the scribe of 4Q394 attached the calendar for reasons important to the community: calendrical matters and covenantal theology. The latter is suggested as von Weissenberg argues for the text to follow the

---

21. Florentino García Martínez, "Dos Notas Sobre 4QMMT," *RevQ* 16 (1993): 293–97.

22. 4Q394 3–4 (section A 19–21). The most important segments to support García Martínez's argument are reconstructed. The inference of intercalation is based upon the reconstruction of the word "added" [נוס]ף and what Qimron called "a tentative reconstruction" of line 19. The 364-day year ([שלוש מאת וש]שים וארבעה) is also reconstructed "according to the sectarian calendar" (DJD X, 44–45).

23. García Martínez, *Qumranica Minora 1*, 77–79; interestingly, García Martínez compares 4QMMT to a manuscript of 1QS and 4Q259, to which 4Q319 (4QOtot) is attached. However, there are many differences, not least since 4Q319 is attached to the end of 4Q259 and is primarily occupied with the priestly rosters.

24. Menahem Kister, "Studies in 4QMiqsat Ma'ase Ha-Torah and Related Texts: Law, Theology, Language and Calendar," *Tarbiz* 68 (1999): 317–71 (Hebrew).

25. Von Weissenberg, *4QMMT*, 133.

literary example of Deuteronomy, not so much on a structural, but on a conceptual level. Hence, just like Deuteronomy, it incorporates a festival calendar into its legal section.[26]

Overall, the scholarly consensus excludes fragments 1–2 from 4Q394, but opinions differ as to the originality of fragments 3–4 in the original version of 4QMMT. However, notwithstanding Strugnell's first doubts and the many debates that were to follow, the three-section structure of the DJD editors' composite text has survived to this day, and its calendar has played a major role in the Qumran sectarianism discussion.

3.3.2. Section B: The Halakah

As one can see in tables 2 and 3, the halakic section B is found in five of the six manuscripts of 4QMMT (4Q394–398). Document 4Q394 consists of section A and holds large parts of section B. Manuscripts 4Q395–396 contain only material from section B, and documents 4Q397 and 4Q398 contain material from both sections B and C. The physical nature of many of these manuscripts is very fragmentary. The beginning of section B, which is only preserved in 4Q394, is badly damaged. There is no material evidence for the transition between sections B and C. Only one manuscript, 4Q397, has material from both sections B and C. Overlaps between manuscripts are often very small and at times nonexistent, which immediately weakens the certainty of the reconstructions. Also the reconstruction of the composite text's halakah has been rather difficult, at times speculative, always as a compilation of the various 4QMMT manuscripts and often also informed by scripture or other relevant texts, such as the Temple Scroll.[27] As a result, the reconstructions that Qimron proposed for many of the halakot have often not convinced his coeditor Strugnell nor many others, like Moshe Bernstein and Ian Werrett, who seriously question many of his reconstructions.[28]

---

26. See §3.3.2 below. Interestingly, von Weissenberg agrees with the scholarly consensus that section A 1–18 does not belong to 4Q394. The remaining three calendrical lines (A 19–21) do not reflect a festival calendar.

27. Qimron, "Nature of the Reconstructed Composite Text of 4QMMT," 11–12.

28. For a critical assessment, specifically regarding section B, see Ian Werrett, *Ritual Purity and the Dead Sea Scrolls*, STDJ 72 (Leiden: Brill, 2007), 180–209. Also see Moshe Bernstein, "The Employment and Interpretation of Scripture in 4QMMT," in Kampen and Bernstein, *Reading 4QMMT*, 29–51.

Von Weissenberg has reassessed Strugnell and Qimron's evaluation and reconstruction of the text and has raised various questions on this subject, many of which address the rather speculative placement of certain fragments and the level of uncertainty raised by paleographical and material evidence regarding the origin and provenance of certain fragments.[29]

4QMMT's halakic section B is the most studied part of the document and—for several reasons—plays an important part in its assessment as a foundational document for the Qumran group. According to the DJD editors, section B, which starts with the words "these are some of our regulations," consists of a "long sequence of polemically formulated legal statements."[30] This consensus view holds that the section's legal statements are set in a particular form in which the legal position of the author's group ("we") is polemically set over against the halakic position of another group ("they"). In this supposedly polemical structure, the "we" group at times appeals, in direct address, to the legal knowledge of yet another group ("you" second-person plural), indicating that this "you" group knows that the legal position of the "we" group is right and that of the "they" group is wrong.

Understandably, the identification of these "we," "they," and "you" (plural) groups in section B is therefore quite important but certainly not unproblematic. First, none of the groups are named or historically referenced.[31] Also, the "they" group seems rather indefinable. Since the "they" reference only occurs in section B, scholars have attempted to identify them with the epilogue's רוב העם (partly reconstructed in C 7). However, such straightforward identification cannot be made, since the "they" references in section B seem to point to various different groups. According to von Weissenberg, the references to "they" occur in less than half of

---

29. Von Weissenberg, *4QMMT*, 38–63: von Weissenberg's study finds that the links between the three sections are established by only two manuscripts: only 4Q394 preserves a link between sections A and B, and only 4Q397 maintains a connection between 4QMMT's halakic and hortatory sections B and C. However, the latter connection is not demonstrated in a visible transition from section B to C, since the ending of section B and the beginning of section C are both lost in manuscript 4Q397. With regard to 4Q398, von Weissenberg's analysis seriously questions whether frags. 1–9 and 11–17 belong to the same manuscript. Rather, she suggests that frags. 1–9 might not belong to 4QMMT.

30. DJD X, 110.

31. For instance, Strugnell ("Second Thoughts," 70–71) already realized that none of the specific sobriquets of other Qumran texts could be identified in 4QMMT.

the halakot, and are not clearly related to one specific oppositional group. Moreover, she states that the only clear and certain "they" occurrence in B 35 "could refer to anybody."[32] The other occurrences of "they" point to specific groups, which interestingly also occur in Deuteronomy and Leviticus, like lepers and blind persons. The primary concern of the "we" groups with regards to these "they" groups seems to be how they should be dealt with in matters of ritual purity in the temple and the city.

The DJD X editors identify the halakic section's "they" group as the Pharisees with the help of section C. However, a straightforward identification of the "they" group(s) of section B with the Pharisees is problematic, since the presupposed oppositional legal positions can only be deduced from the inference that the "we" group's legal positions are Sadducean. These deductions of oppositional priestly and societal conduct may or may not reflect a social reality.

The second-person plural "you" occurs only twice unreconstructed, in both occasions asserting the addressees' awareness of a legal statement (B 68–70) and the current praxis of some priests (B 80–82). On this basis, no positive identification can be made, as one might even theorize that the "you" is used as a rhetorical device to focus the reader's attention.

Interestingly, even though the identification of the so-called dramatis personae has been a major topic in 4QMMT scholarship, no real attempts have been undertaken to question or challenge the identity of the "we" group. From the first evaluations of 4QMMT, the "we" group has been uncritically identified as the Qumran sect or its Essene predecessor(s). This straightforward identification of the "we" group with the Qumran sect has caused serious difficulties for the Qumran-Essene Hypothesis, as some of its halakic positions seemed to concur with the Tannaitic literature's recount of Sadducean halakic positions. The DJD editors therefore conclude that 4QMMT is "a document emanating from a priestly group related to the early Sadducees, and either identical with, or an ancestor of, the Qumran group."[33] As one of the first scholars who was given access to 4QMMT, Schiffman was so convinced that the "we" group's halakah reflected a Sadducean position, that he advocated for the Qumranites to be

---

32. Von Weissenberg, *4QMMT*, 136.
33. DJD X, 116–17. In their later work, Strugnell and Qimron take a different stand on this matter: Strugnell holds 4QMMT to be presectarian on the basis of its dissimilar theological outlook, and places the text in a developmental stage of the Qumran sect. However, Qimron remains convinced that the text is Qumranic.

Sadducees rather than Essenes.³⁴ Drawing less far-reaching conclusions, the recognition that some of the legal rulings expressed by the "we" group in 4QMMT demonstrate similarity to known Saducean legal interpretations has made scholars like García Martínez, Jacob Sussman, and Aharon Shemesh posit a Sadducean influence on the Qumran group.³⁵

The identification of the dramatis personae is closely related to the scholarly perception that 4QMMT ought to be understood as a polemical halakic text. The interconnectedness of the identity of the text's proponents and section B's halakah importantly influenced scholarly perceptions of the typical phrasing of the halakah, from which the uniqueness of Qumranic halakah was deduced. Again, as in the case of the dramatis personae, this uniqueness is established by considering section B in light of section C, as scholars find in the epilogue the underlying principles of 4QMMT's halakah. Moreover, in section C, the author of 4QMMT distinguishes between "clear" and "hidden" laws, on basis of which Schiffman arrives at a later sectarian halakah³⁶ containing the "two specific Qumranic characteristics" of *nigleh* and *nistar*.³⁷

The chosen halakic topics have puzzled scholars as at first glance they seem rather arbitrary and certainly not exhaustive. As purity issues, and more particularly the purity of the temple, city, and priesthood seem to stand at the heart of 4QMMT's "collection of laws," scholars have argued that section B reflects an interpriestly dispute. However, the fragmentary state

---

34. Schiffman, *Reclaiming the Dead Sea Scrolls*, 83–112; also, in moderate form, *Qumran and Jerusalem*, 15–43.

35. García Martínez, *Qumranica Minora I*, 67–103, esp. 81–82; Sussman, "History of *Halakhah*," 11–76; Shemesh, *Halakhah in the Making*. García Martínez criticizes Schiffman's Sadducean hypothesis as he finds only a small number of halakic positions concur with Sadducean halakah (e.g., the purity of the persons preparing the red heifer, and the purity issues surrounding liquid streams). More generally, García Martínez argues that it is not inconceivable for specific groups to agree with some groups on a number of halakic positions, while agreeing with other groups on different matters. Finally, and interestingly with regard to the overall positioning of 4QMMT, García Martínez points to section A's sectarian calendar to definitely discard the Sadducean hypothesis.

36. Schiffman, *Halakhah at Qumran*, 63–80, 112–42.

37. Schiffman identifies Qumran halakah by its categorization in *nigleh* (revealed law/torah/open and known to all) and *nistar* (hidden law/only the sect has the correct interpretation, through inspired biblical exegesis). Also, Schiffman argues that, next to the phenomena of *nigleh* and *nistar*, Qumran halakah is characterized by a unique combination of halakic views and particular sectarian regulations.

of the halakic section and hence its uncertain reconstructed composite text make it difficult to assess a clear understanding of its content and function. Recently scholars have challenged the polemical and sectarian nature of section B's halakah, as they argued that an independent reading of section B demonstrates no polemical stance. Rather than assuming a polemical argument against known opponents set out in twenty odd halakic statements, Shemesh and Cana Werman have proposed that these ostensibly particular halakic topics might together form the explication of exegetical difference, in which case the topics might correlate according to a "a is like b as c is like …"-formula instead of being individually significant.[38] However, Bernstein finds that, even though some of the language in 4QMMT is biblical, much of its content is too far removed from the biblical text to presume it to be biblical exegesis.[39] He also questions the "invariable position" of the DJD editors that "the impetus for restoration" that 4QMMT "must be polemicising on all points."[40] Indeed, Steven Fraade observed that the "opposing practice of the addressees" cannot be identified in any ruling in section B.[41] Moreover, Shemesh has argued that some halakic rulings in 4QMMT differ from the Qumran sectarian legal statements as they, contrary to Qumran halakah, explain how they reach their halakic or exegetical conclusions.[42] More generally, Hempel has recently observed section B's lack of sectarian outlook as she has argued that, "if we leave behind the comfortable theory of MMT's key role in Qumran origins and contemplate instead a broader halakic context, the text's significance may go far beyond the confines of a particular group."[43] Moreover, von Weissenberg, who has studied the fragments of the individual manuscripts of section B, finds hardly any meaningful variants or signs of redaction. On this basis, she concludes: "The lack of virtually all traces of redactional activity could reflect the nature of the

---

38. Shemesh and Werman, "Halakhah at Qumran," 104–29; Bernstein, "Employment and Interpretation of Scripture," 29–51.

39. Bernstein, "Employment and Interpretation of Scripture," 32, 46, 50–51.

40. Ibid., 43.

41. Steven Fraade, *Legal Fictions: Studies of Law and Narrative in the Discursive Worlds of Ancient Jewish Sectarians and Sages*, JSJSup 147 (Leiden: Brill, 2011), 73. Fraade states of the rules in section B "not one identifies an opposing practice of the opponent."

42. Aharon Shemesh, *Halakhah in the Making*, 35 n. 31.

43. Charlotte Hempel, "The Context of 4QMMT and Comfortable Theories," in *The Dead Sea Scrolls: Texts and Context*, ed. Charlotte Hempel, STDJ 90 (Leiden: Brill, 2010), 291.

halakhic section as non-communal Jewish legislation which is directed for all Israel in contrast to laws pertaining to community organization needing regular updating."[44] Indeed, section B is interested in the correct halakic observance for all Israel as it demonstrates concern for the people and the holiness of Israel. Here, von Weissenberg's conclusions implicitly point to another interesting feature, namely, that 4QMMT differs from commonly considered *yahadic* texts in the sense that these texts tend to have organizational rules and regulations, rather than halakic ones.[45]

Despite all these elements of uncertainty, in general, scholarly consensus tends to read 4QMMT's section B in conjunction with section C and holds the halakic section to reflect a polemical outlook, phrased in oppositional legal positions, from which insight can be obtained into (the development of) the Qumran sect's halakah. Moreover, the "they" opponents are commonly believed to be Pharisaic. The second-person plural "you" group (which needs to be distinguished from the second-person singular "you" in the epilogue) is hardly given attention but is commonly believed to be a group related to the Qumran sect.

Later in this chapter we shall return to these elements of section B and evaluate their role and function within the Qumran paradigm.

3.3.3. Section C: The Epilogue

4QMMT's epilogue, or section C, can be found in three manuscripts, namely 4Q397–399. The transition between section B and section C is lost. However, one manuscript, 4Q397, contains material from both sections B and C, on the basis of which the text's unity is decided.[46] Von Weissenberg has elaborately studied the overlaps and textual variants in 4Q397–399. She concludes that 4Q397 and 4Q398 have surprisingly little overlap, while even in the overlaps she records variant readings. She finds some textual variations and differences in wording and text-forms between the

---

44. Von Weissenberg, *4QMMT*, 79.

45. That is, with the exception of the complex and multilayered CD/DD.

46. According to Strugnell and Qimron, the resemblance between B 1 and C 26–30 establishes "a formal link" between the two. 4Q394 3–7, I, 4 and 4Q398 14–17, II, 6 both have מקצת דברינו (some of our words), while 4Q398 14–17, II, 3 has מקצת מעשי התורה (some works of the Torah). The question is whether these resemblances are enough to compensate for the missing junction between B and C, and 4Q394 is the only manuscript preserving B 1.

two manuscripts to the extent that these readings "cannot easily be combined into a single reliable composite text."[47] 4Q399 is the only manuscript that preserves text from the ending of the epilogue, even though it partly overlaps with 4Q398.[48] Von Weissenberg finds a considerable amount of difference between the two manuscripts and suggests that they contain important textual variants.[49]

Von Weissenbeg also addresses the long dispute between the editors of DJD X about the placement of 4Q398 11–13 in relation to 4Q397. The lack of agreement with regard to these fragments is well known. Since there is no parallel text or part overlap with these fragments in other manuscripts, the placement of 4Q398 11–13 is difficult.[50] Strugnell proposed to place the fragments at the beginning of the hortatory section, that is, before fragments 14–17. Qimron, rather, places them below the right parts of fragments 14–17. This position is reflected in the DJD composite text where fragments 14–17 correspond with C 9–16 and 25–32 while fragments 11–13 comprise C 18–24.[51] Von Weissenberg favors Strugnell's proposition for material reasons, but her extensive reexamination of the epilogue's textual material leads her to conclude that the entirety of the epilogue's composite text is problematic and at times materially impossible.[52]

The most notable example of the composite text's untrustworthiness is what von Weissenberg observed in lines C 10–12a: here, she finds that the composite text harmonizes the two textual witnesses from 4Q397 and 4Q398, while the extant fragments (in 4Q397 14–21, 10–12a and 4Q398 14–17, I, 2–4) demonstrate variant readings, which cannot be easily reconstructed, let alone harmonized.[53] Hence, von Weissenberg argues that

---

47. Von Weissenberg, *4QMMT*, 91.

48. The ending of the document is lost in 4Q398, even though a *vacat* after the last word preserved might indicate that the text ends.

49. Von Weissenberg, *4QMMT*, 85.

50. Qimron ("The Nature of the Reconstructed Composite Text," 12) even regards its placement as "physically unknown."

51. See DJD X, appendix 2; García Martínez, "4QMMT in a Qumran Context," in García Martínez, *Qumranica Minora I*, 91–103; von Weissenberg, *4QMMT*, 87–90; Qimron, "Nature of the Reconstructed Composite Text of 4QMMT," 12–13.

52. Von Weissenberg, *4QMMT*, 90–95.

53. Von Weissenberg's conclusion is disputed by Puech, who holds that her reading, based on DJD, for the section in which she claims there is no composite text (4Q397 14–21, 10–12a; 4Q398 14–17, I, 2–4), is untenable. Puech argues that the sections reflect mere variants within a generally common text; Émile Puech, "L'Épilogue

"the reconstructed composite text of the epilogue is relatively uncertain because of the variant readings and the rather small amounts of common material."[54] This conclusion is sustained by the editors of DJD X, who state: "Because of the fragmentary nature of the manuscripts and the uncertainty about the order of the text, the sequence of thought, the significance of the references to biblical historical figures and the linkage with section B are all far from clear."[55]

The subject matter of the epilogue is different in character from the halakic section. The latter seems to place great emphasis on priestly responsibilities (cf. B 12–13, 26–27), while section C does not reflect any of those central priestly concerns. Also, while the halakic section has many references to Leviticus and Numbers, the epilogue contains "language and terminology that is rich with allusions to Deuteronomy, a scriptural text which is significantly less interested in priestly matters and purity."[56] In contrast to the halakic concerns in section B, the epilogue exhorts its addressees to learn from Israel's past through its scripture in the realization that it is the end of days. Moreover, the author and his group seem to want to convince the addressee that "some of our words are true" (C 30) and to do right by both "you" and Israel (C 31–32). The references to scripture and Israel's past are eye-catching, as are the author's exhortation to his addressee(s) to learn from history. The language of (implied) curses and blessings points to a covenantal structure, which indicates the author's "concern for covenantal faithfulness."[57]

Also, with regard to the epilogue, a fair amount of scholarly attention has been given to the identification of the dramatis personae. As in section B, the "we" group is univocally regarded as the Qumran group or its predecessor. As the first-person plural "we" occurs in both sections B and C, it is evaluated by many scholars as a "unifying feature, … despite some differences in the applied verb forms resulting from the shift in topic and genre

---

de 4QMMT Revisité," in *A Teacher for All Generations: Essays in Honor of James C. VanderKam*, ed. E. F. Mason, JSJSup 153 (Leiden: Brill, 2012), 313ff., 322–25.

54. Von Weissenberg, *4QMMT*, 93.

55. DJD X, 111.

56. Von Weissenberg, *4QMMT* 117; cf. 121–22 where she nuances this distinction, as to the important reference to Deut 12:5 in the halakic section, thereby emphasizing the importance of Jerusalem and the temple for the author(s) of 4QMMT.

57. Ibid., 127–29; von Weissenberg thinks that 4QMMT in its entirety is modeled after the framework of biblical legal material in a covenantal pattern.

of the two sections."⁵⁸ Von Weissenberg finds two comparative models for 4QMMT's identification of the "we" group in the epilogue: Deut 1–3 and Neh 9–10, both of which stress the importance of a close connection between covenant and law. Moreover, in Deut 1–3, "we" includes the people of Israel, who are addressed in the second-person singular and plural ("you").⁵⁹

In the epilogue, the third-person plural "they" group does not occur. Qimron has initially tried to argue that "the majority of the people" in section C refers to the "they" group in section B, who in turn were, as we saw earlier, thought to be (connected to) the Pharisees. Also, Strugnell identified the "they" of the halakic section with this רוב העם in the epilogue.⁶⁰ Nowadays scholars have abandoned such a neat and simplistic solution.⁶¹ As we have seen, the "they" group identification is far from clear in section B. Moreover, the use of the third-person plural "they" in section B seems not to be oppositional but merely stating a general practice, the conduct of certain groups or the implied state of being of others.⁶² Also, the absence of the "they" group in general in section C warns us against the straightforward identification of section B's "they" with section C's only candidate for "they," the "multitude of the people."⁶³

Similarly, the identification of the "you" (second-person singular *and* plural) in the epilogue is far from straightforward. The plural "you" occurs twice in the halakic section, B 68 and B 70 (both in 4Q396), and once in the epilogue (C 8, 4Q397) where we merely find the independent pronoun אתם, while the verb is reconstructed. Instead, the epilogue introduces a second-person *singular* "you," which functions much more like a

---

58. Ibid., 134.
59. See below.
60. DJD X, 111.
61. See Hempel, "Comfortable Theories," 287–88.
62. For instance, von Weissenberg finds that the few straightforward "they" references (e.g., B 35) are only found in rulings about slaughter and sacrifice, and are clearly directed towards the proper execution of priestly duties.
63. Nevertheless the epilogue's "multitude of the people" plays another important role in the overall assessment of 4QMMT, namely, as an important argument for the presumption of polemics. In the sentence C 7–8 (4Q397 14–21) "[And you know that] we have segregated ourselves from the multitude [העם מרוב שפרשנו יודעים] of the pe[ople and] from mingling in these affairs, and from associating wi[th them] in these things." On the basis of this text, scholars have argued for the split-off of the Qumran sect on halakic grounds. This topic will be discussed later in this chapter.

direct address, that is, rather than being used in a general manner like the second-person *plural* in B 68, 70, and C 8. Strugnell suggests that this use of a second-person *singular* addressee is an indication of 4QMMT being a letter sent to a ruler of Israel.[64] This proposal rests upon the following three textual references: the author's exhortation in C 23 ("Think of the kings of Israel and contemplate their deeds") in combination with C 28 ("You have wisdom and knowledge of the Torah") and C 31–32 ("You will be doing what is righteous and good for you and for Israel"). Of course, such identification implicitly reads section C in light of the priestly overtones in section B and hence searches for a time in which both strands of power were united in one man's hand: the Hasmonean period.

Scholars have recently challenged this consensus. For instance, Fraade has pointed out that "it is commonplace in hortatory speech to switch between plural and singular forms of the second-person address" and "this can most clearly be seen in the very section of the book of Deuteronomy (30–31) upon which so much of section C is dependent for its scriptural language and allusions."[65] Fraade, who reads 4QMMT as an intramural educational tool, thus suggests that the singular and plural second-person usage in the epilogue might be a rhetorical device to maximize the effect of the exhortation as if it were addressed personally to every single member of the receiving audience.

Of course the text's last direct address, "for your good and that of Israel" (לטוב לך ולישראל), is considered decisive in those evaluations that take the addressee to be an influential spokesperson, possibly a ruler in Israel. Interestingly, von Weissenberg stresses that, if the above mentioned connection to Deuteronomy is correct, both 4QMMT's focus on priestly concerns and its address to "all Israel" need to be considered when evaluating the function, meaning, and positioning of this important text.

These subsections §§3.1–3 have demonstrated that the provenance of 4QMMT is difficult to establish with certainty for material as well as literary reasons. These difficulties are equally well attested to when it comes to establishing the text's genre, date, and social setting, three important issues that will be dealt with in §§3.4–6 below.

---

64. Also, the references to certain specific kings of Judah and to David have led scholars to believe that the second-person signular addressee of section C was a king or ruler of Israel.

65. Fraade, *Legal Fictions*, 76.

3.4. Genre

4QMMT is commonly referred to as a "polemical halakic letter." However, from its earliest publication onwards, the evaluation of the text's genre has proven difficult, due to the fragmentariness of the text, its lack of formal features, and the absence of comparable outside sources.[66] In the DJD X edition, Qimron argued that the presence of an explicit author and (an) addressee(s) strongly indicates that the genre of the text is that of a (personal or corporate/public) letter or a treatise.[67] Scholarly opinions with regard to the text's epistolary features are divided. Already in appendix 3 of the DJD volume, Strugnell points to the inconsistencies between 4QMMT's structure and character and the formal features of the genre of letter.[68] Scholars like Hempel and Joseph Baumgarten have pointed out that the perceived epistolary features in 4QMMT are much in line with later Tannaitic methods and formulae introducing legal statements.[69] In appendix 3 and later in "Second Thoughts," Strugnell suggests that 4QMMT might be a legal code: section B is a collection of laws and section C is its hortatory conclusion.[70] Bernstein and John Kampen contest Strugnell's view as it is thought to "disregard the combative aspect of section B." They argue that 4QMMT's halakic section is not simply "a

---

66. It remains difficult to tie the three rather different sections of the text together in an overarching framework, because its beginning is lost, its ending does not have any formal epistolary features, and the junctions between the sections are lost.

67. Qimron suggests 4QMMT might be a treatise, which is rejected by Strugnell; see DJD X, 113–14, 204.

68. DJD X, 204–5.

69. Charlotte Hempel, "The Laws of the Damascus Document and 4QMMT," 69–83 in *The Damascus Document: A Centennial of Discovery; Proceedings of the Third International Symposium of the Orion Center for the Study of the Dead Sea Scrolls and Associated Literature, 4–8 February 1998*, ed. Joseph M. Baumgarten, Esther G. Chazon, and Avital Pinnick, STDJ 34 (Leiden: Brill, 2000); Joseph M. Baumgarten, "The Laws of the Damascus Document—Between Bible and Mishnah," 17–26 in Baumgarten, Chazon, and Pinnick, *The Damascus Document*.

70. DJD X, appendix 3, 204: Strugnell's evaluation of a legal code is based upon his comparison with covenant formulae in Deuteronomy. In his final assessment in "Second Thoughts," Strugnell takes a "minimalist view," stating that 4QMMT is a legal document that was sent to someone, possibly an accepted ruler; "Second Thoughts," 57–73.

collection of laws but part of an argument."⁷¹ Hence, much of the debate regarding 4QMMT's genre revolves around the perception of the text's peculiarities. As we shall see, many of the issues regarding genre resurface once one starts to ask critical questions about the evaluation of 4QMMT as polemical.⁷² Currently, most scholars accept that 4QMMT is characterized by some epistolary features, among which rhetorical devices play a certain strategic literary part, but the idea that this text is a personal letter is largely abandoned.⁷³

3.5. Date

Strugnell and Qimron date the oldest manuscript of 4QMMT to 75 BCE and the latest to 50 CE.⁷⁴ The origin of the document is commonly thought to be older. In general, a date as early as 150 BCE is suggested. This early or presectarian dating is largely based upon a sociohistorical interpretation of information in the text, in other words, upon 4QMMT's perceived role and function within the early history and development of the Qumran sect. The presupposition of the Qumran paradigm ensures the highlighting and interpretation of some specific elements, which together form the basis for arguing such early dating. These elements are:

---

71. John Kampen and Moshe Bernstein, "Introduction," in *Reading MMT: New Perspectives on Qumran Law and History*, ed. John Kampen and Moshe Bernstein, SymS 2 (Atlanta: Scholars Press, 1996), 6.

72. See Fraade, *Legal Fictions*, 73: "Of the approximately twenty extant rules contained in section B of the composite text, *not one identifies an opposing practice of the addressees* (contrary to the impression gained from the characterizations of the text by scholars stressing its polemical nature)" (emphasis original). Other scholars who have questioned the text's polemical nature are Maxine Grossman, "Reading 4QMMT: Genre and History," *RevQ* 20 (2001): 3–22; Hempel, "Laws of the Damascus Document and 4QMMT," 70–71; and Hempel, "Comfortable Theories," 275–92.

73. Von Weissenberg remains rather inconclusive as she states that the text is a mixture of genres at best, and that it is easier to dismiss the personal letter-genre than to come up with a suitable alternative; *4QMMT*, 167. Also, see a recent reevaluation of 4QMMT's genre in Lutz Doering, *Ancient Jewish Letters and the Beginnings of Christian Epistolography*, WUNT 298 (Tübingen: Mohr Siebeck, 2012), 194–214.

74. They primarily base their evaluation on paleography: the manuscripts demonstrate late Hasmonean to early Herodian handwriting.

3. THE PROVENANCE OF 4QMMT   109

(1) The mild polemics of the text, specifically poignant in the respectful and friendly manner in which the second-person singular of the epilogue is addressed.[75]
(2) The "we" group is still in negotiation with its opponents.
(3) Polemical discussions with outsiders were thought to be allowed only during the Qumran sect's foundational years, that is, in the time of the Teacher of Righteousness. After the Qumran group's final segregation, polemics ceased to exist and were even forbidden (1QS IX, 16–17).[76]
(4) Inner-Qumranic evidence of 4QMMT in 4QpPs[a], which supposedly recalls that the Teacher of Righteousness had sent "precepts and laws" to the Wicked Priest.[77] Such evidence fixes 4QMMT in the perceived formative period of the sect, at the time the Teacher was in active leadership.
(5) 4QMMT's famous line "we have segregated ourselves from the majority of the people" (C 7) is thought to be evidence of Qumran sect's segregation.[78]
(6) The text is said to demonstrate a clear sectarian outlook that has similarities with the Qumranites' theology.[79] However, 4QMMT is thought to be "theologically less developed than the standard [sic] Qumran theology in its lack of dualistic language, typical community descriptions, apocalyptic ideas, and apocalyptic conscience."[80] Therefore, it is considered earlier.
(7) 4QMMT's choice of halakic topics contrasts with and is quite contrary to popular topics in the Qumran sectarian literature.[81]

---

75. Von Weissenberg, *4QMMT*, 15.
76. DJD X, 115.
77. 4QpPs[a] (4Q171) IV, 3, II, 8–9, which is a pesher on Ps 37:32–33, states, "Its interpretation concerns the Wicked [Pri]est, who sp[ie]s on the ju[st man and wants to] kill him ... and the law [התורה] which he sent him." The generic "law/torah" seems rather far off from 4QMMT's אלה מקצת דברינו.
78. This seems in tension with points (3) and (4).
79. At the same time, Strugnell and Qimron acknowledge that 4QMMT does not have any sectarian terminology or literary style, nor does it reflect any organizational rules and regulations that were found in sectarian texts like 1QS.
80. DJD X, 121.
81. The editors mention, for instance, 4QMMT's preoccupation with priestly matters of purity and its concern for the sanctity of the Jerusalem Temple; DJD X, 120–21.

On the basis of these factors, Strugnell and Qimron date 4QMMT "early in the history of the sect," at a time when the Qumranites formulated their theology. In line with the Qumran paradigm and sociohistorical reconstructions thereof, they date 4QMMT as originating between 159 and 152 BCE.[82]

Most scholars have more or less followed the editors in their assessment of this date. However, it is almost entirely based upon circumstantial evidence and the presupposition of certain sociohistorical circumstances. Fraade, who assigns a completely different provenance to the text, raised an important question with regard to the early dating of 4QMMT: If the relatively many copies of 4QMMT that were found at Qumran may be taken as an indication that the text was important to the Qumranites, how did it function within the community, if the text clearly "represents an early (pre-Qumranic) stage in the development of Qumran sectarian law and ideology"? Why, then, is 4QMMT still copied and studied more than a century after it originated, especially since the sect's theology and sociological outlook has further developed over time?[83] Were they not aware that the text was hopelessly outdated, or are our presuppositions and assumptions of the text in need of revision?

The problems with 4QMMT's dating and its subsequent historical setting are notorious, and the DJD X volume is full of circular reasoning to make the text fit its purpose of foundational document. This commonly accepted backtracing of evidence has many examples, such as the following: "If we assume that the work is to be explained as reflecting the history (or the prehistory) of the Qumran community, we must look for a time when the 'we' group, i.e., the writers, were in 'eirenic' discussion with the 'you' group—a group not so different from themselves as to be incapable of being won over to the writers' positions and practices."[84]

---

82. Their dating seems also based on the obscure break in the high priestly lineage over which Josephus and 1 Maccabees seem to disagree; see Josephus, *A.J.* 12.10, *B.J.* 5.408–412, and 1 Macc 10:18–20.

83. Fraade, *Legal Fictions*, 70–71. Fraade makes a case for 4QMMT's intramural use as a document of the sect's foundation and therefore an important text for its self-understanding and identification.

84. DJD X, 114.

3.6. Historical Setting

4QMMT offers little indication concerning its historical setting, and, hence, the presumed historical setting of the text is part of the presupposed character of the text as a foundational (pre-)Qumranic document. This assessment is predominantly carried by the conviction that the text witnesses the separation of the Qumran group from the wider society in section C: "We have segregated ourselves from the multitude of the peop[le] [and] from mingling in these affairs, and from associating wi[th them] in these things" (C 7–8; 4Q397 14–21, 7b–8). In this presumed setting, 4QMMT is often seen as a document that is addressed to outsiders, most possibly the Jerusalemite establishment. Based on C 32's "for your good and that of Israel," together with the references to various kings in Israel's history, the text is thought to be addressed to a Hasmonean ruler. According to such reasoning, the most likely candidates would be Simon and John Hyrcanus, as they held both the political and priestly powers. However, the Qumran paradigm, which takes the presupposed dates of the Qumranites' foundation and the Teacher of Righteousness's leadership into account, favors Jonathan as the most likely addressee.

The identification of the addressee as a Hasmonean ruler is thought to concur with textual references in 1QpHab, particularly its statement that the Wicked Priest was "loyal at the start of his office" (1QpHab VIII, 8b–11a). Both Kampen and George Brooke suggested that the addressee and the author of 4QMMT have a similar background, highlighted in the genuinely courteous tone of the letter with its emphasis on the addressee's wisdom and knowledge of the law (C 28).[85] From the presupposition that 4QMMT originates in the time of the Teacher's leadership and its second-person singular addressee is thought to be an Israelite ruler with both priestly and kingly powers (i.e., a Hasmonean), together with the idea of mild polemics and respectful addres, and in light of presumed comparable evidence about the Qumran sect in sectarian texts like 1QpPs^a, 1QpHab, and CD/DD, the date for the original manuscript of 4QMMT is fixed to a time of around 152 BCE, the year in which Jonathan seized the high priesthood alongside his already-established political powers.

---

85. John Kampen, "4QMMT and New Testament Studies," in Kampen and Bernstein, *Reading MMT*, 129–44.

As we have seen above, this early date does not however concur with the much later physical material of the extant manuscripts. The quantity of later copies (at least six, maybe seven) begs the question of why the Qumranites would preserve and copy an ancient, and in many respects archaic, halakic letter. Therefore, Fraade has suggested that 4QMMT might play an important role in the sect's self-understanding and hence might be used as an educational tool to remind the Qumranites of their beginnings. He hypothesizes that the extant manuscripts of 4QMMT might have been used as intramural pedagogical material with the aim of reinforcing the sect's choice of social separation.[86] Schiffman has argued that the Qumran manuscripts of 4QMMT might not be copies of an actual letter "dating to the earliest days of the Qumran group," but rather a much later apocryphal text, written to express and commemorate the reasons for the Qumranites' schism from the Jerusalemite establishment.[87] Schiffman thus seems to harmonize the two options of an older original and a later written commemorative document by focusing on the alleged sociohistorical reality that the text narrates. As such he defines the social world of 4QMMT as reflecting "the earliest, pre-Teacher stage in the offshoots of intra-priestly contention" in which Sadducean halakic views were held by those who later formed the Qumran sect.[88]

These proposals attempt to explain the presence of later manuscripts of 4QMMT, without losing the initially presupposed sociohistorical parameters along which the text is evaluated as a formative document. Maxine Grossman has demonstrated quite convincingly how shifting the presupposed parameters of the text with regard to genre changes our conceptions of 4QMMT's historical setting. Moreover, she demonstrates that proposed historical reconstructions on the basis of the text's perceived genre and function subsequently determine its date, authorship, addressees, and audience.[89]

Factually, without the help of sociohistorical presuppositions with regard to 4QMMT's setting, the content of the text itself gives us very little to go on. Several elements contribute to an understanding of the text's

---

86. Fraade, *Legal Fictions*, 69–91.
87. Schiffman, *Qumran and Jerusalem*, 112–13.
88. Ibid., 121–22; Possibly under the influence of García Martínez's Groningen hypothesis, Schiffman has recently placed 4QMMT's origin in the "sect's formative period" (138–39).
89. Grossman, "Reading *4QMMT*, Genre and History," 3–22.

social setting: its tripartite frame; its emphasis on Numbers, Leviticus, and Deuteronomy; its interest in halakic positions, which is thought to partly coincide with later Tannaitic sources' account of Sadducean halakah over against Pharisaic halakah; its exhortation to learn from Israel's history; and its clear conception to have reached the end of days. However, all this is certainly not enough for a solid identification of 4QMMT as a (pre-)Qumranic document.

3.7. From 4QMMT as (Pre-)Sectarian Tool to 4QMMT in Its Own Right

Investigations into 4QMMT have often chosen their point of departure from within the boundaries of the Qumran paradigm. Scholarly consensus holds 4QMMT to have played a distinct and crucial role in the foundation, theological formation, and subsequent social position of the Qumran community. Thus, most debates have focused on the question of whether this text belongs to either the early history of the Qumran community or to its formative period, in other words, whether the text is sectarian or presectarian.

The text of 4QMMT itself hardly gives any reason to closely link it to a sectarian community at Qumran at all: (1) 4QMMT differs in style, themes, outlook, and terminology from the undisputed *yahadic* texts. Moreover, the text does not refer to a *yahad*. (2) The text contains no data to establish a reasonably grounded sense of its date, historical setting, or the identity of its proponents. Moreover, the textual evidence of 4QMMT in general is difficult to assess because of the state and character of its manuscripts. (3) The lack of comparable sources, its fragmentary state, and complex structure have caused many technical, literary, and sociohistorical problems, which have proven to be a serious threat to the overall reliability and stability of the text's reconstruction. (4) Hence, this composite textual reconstruction depends upon innertextual interpretations and similarities to outside sources such as 11QT^a and CD/DD. These uncertain features and factors importantly diminish our capability to draw stable conclusions with regard to 4QMMT's provenance and hence should be a cause for caution. This caution is equally warranted as some of the features of 4QMMT demonstrate that the text might allow for a provenance that is broader and sometimes even independent from Qumran. Because of 4QMMT's peculiar tripartite structure (incomparable with any outside sources), questions can be asked as to the textual coherence of the three sections. Moreover, such questions implicitly touch upon evaluations regarding the originality of (each of the sections within) the structure as well as its specific function and meaning. Also, closely related to these issues of coherence are the observations of 4QMMT's literary style and language. Many scholars agree that in its style 4QMMT is unique and hence difficult to compare with other known texts. Bernstein argues that "in its style 4QMMT resembles neither 11QTemple ... nor other Qumran legal texts."[90] He observes that the differences predominantly lie in the formulation of 4QMMT's laws, its dealing with biblical texts, and its use of idiom.

However, the language of 4QMMT in itself does not provide a specific provenance for this text, since—as already stated—it lacks specific sectarian terminology and other *yahadic* features. Moreover, 4QMMT reflects a complex language structure, which combines a Biblical Hebrew (BH) style with grammatical features that resemble Mishnaic Hebrew (MH). This language structure obscures the allocation of the text. On the basis of his thorough investigation of the multiplex language features that occur in the 4QMMT manuscripts, Qimron concludes that the text predominantly "reflects the Hebrew spoken at Qumran" and that its dissimilarity with Qumranic Hebrew might be explained by the idea that 4QMMT is a very early (pre-)Qumranic document.[91] However, this assessment is rather misleading as the term *Qumranic Hebrew* (QH) does not implicitly connect a text to Qumran or the Qumran sect on a sociohistorical level.[92] On the contrary, the term *Qumranic Hebrew* is used for the entire period between late Biblical Hebrew and early Mishnaic Hebrew, and as such its usage only determines that a text written in Qumranic Hebrew dates between approximately 200 BCE and 70/100 CE.[93]

Interestingly, instead of causing caution, many of the text's features and peculiarities have been used to serve the overall purpose of molding 4QMMT into its important key position within scholarly theories about Qumran. Von Weissenberg has addressed this problem quite openly and concluded that the scholarly assessments and evaluations regarding 4QMMT's function and meaning suffer from "the uncertainty of the

---

90. Bernstein, "Employment and Interpretation of Scripture," 33.

91. DJD X, 108.

92. Qimron seems to hint at such a connection as he makes no distinction between the term QH and "the language spoken at Qumran."

93. I thank Prof. Eibert Tigchelaar for his kind help and patience in explaining Qimron's analysis of the language of 4QMMT.

assumption they are based on, namely, an understanding of 4QMMT as a letter sent to a high priest in Jerusalem, as well as of the development of the Qumran movement and its relation to other Jewish groups. If these assumptions are abandoned or revised, the arguments for the dating of the document need to be reconsidered." Moreover, she recognizes the scholarly tendency towards circular reasoning and concludes:

> The presumptions of both the genre and the historical setting of the document have an impact on our reading and interpretation of this text. Similarly, our reading and interpretation of the text influence our decision about its genre and historical setting.... The fact is that our reconstructions of the history of the Qumran community together with the assumptions we make concerning their theological and ideological development, affect the way we date, and how we understand the setting and function of the documents we read.[94]

The early assessment of 4QMMT has burdened the text with its (pre-)sectarian provenance and thereby shaped and influenced scholarly avenues of research. Without denying or forgetting the obvious fact that these manuscripts were found at Qumran (and, of course, this fact needs to count for something), one wonders how 4QMMT would have been assessed without its Qumranic burden. More interestingly, what information one might retrieve from this intriguing text with regard to its provenance within a wider Second Temple context if 4QMMT were evaluated in its own right, without presuming or presupposing its currently perceived function of polemical halakic foundational letter of the Qumran sect.

The former sections have dealt with the material and literary issues of the text, as well as its problems with regard to date, genre, and historical setting. The next section deals more specifically with those peculiarities in 4QMMT on which the scholarly evaluations of its provenance are predominantly based.

3.8. The Parameters of 4QMMT's Status as Foundational Document

The former sections have attempted to gather up the difficulties that surface when researching the provenance of 4QMMT. As we have seen, these

---

94. Von Weissenberg, *4QMMT*, 16–17, 24–25.

difficulties are numerous, and hence they provoke the question: How is it that, in the face of all this literary controversy and material instability, and with full recognition that only a few things are certain with regard to this text, scholarly views have remained steadfast in their evaluation of the authorship and provenance of 4QMMT as belonging to the realm of the Qumran sect? Throughout the years, scholars have acknowledged 4QMMT's lack of sectarian terminology, its lack of typically Qumranic style and ideology, and its discrepancies with perceived *yahadic* language, organizational, and theological outlook. Interestingly, these observations have not resulted in the abandonment of 4QMMT's overall assessment as a (pre-)Qumranic document, maybe even the Qumran sect's foundational document. Rather, surprisingly, these precise difficulties in 4QMMT seem to have become valuable assets with specifically allocated functions within the Qumran paradigm. These issues will be discussed in §§3.8.1–8.

3.8.1. The Identification of the Dramatis Personae

Much of the discussion regarding the provenance of 4QMMT has evolved around the identification of the so-called dramatis personae. As we have seen in §3.3.2 and §3.3.3, the inference of polemics and the identification of the "we," "they," and "you" groups and individuals are closely related. If, however, we consider the halakic section B in its own right, without a presupposition of polemics or in connection with section C, the text does not contain the clear polemical stance that the DJD editors (and later scholars) read into it. Moreover, in the actual text fragments (before reconstruction), the author(s) and/or "we" group in 4QMMT's halakic section merely express their own position forcefully, pointing out their convictions regarding the proper conduct and praxis of Jewish law.[95] Of course, the "we" group implicitly has a clear criticism of the contemporary legal practice and conduct. However, this criticism cannot simply be explained if merely the Jerusalemite priesthood is being addressed. Quite to the contrary, the "we" group seems more concerned with the moral decline (especially in matters of purity) of a larger range of society. Of course, the authors hold the priests partly responsible for the perceived societal decline, for the priests are seen as the guardians and overseers of Israel's relationship with God,

---

95. The "we" group is particularly concerned with matters of purity and impurity regarding sacrifice, the temple, its cult and the holiness of Jerusalem, matters of marriage, and how to deal with specific groups.

and hence responsible for the correct conduct of his people ("The priests ought to watch over all these things so they do not lead the people into sin"; B 12–13, 26–27).[96] In 4QMMT's halakic section, the conduct of the priesthood is certainly inherently criticized, but it is set within the bigger picture of purity concerns. These purity concerns seem most pressing where the temple and Jerusalem are concerned, but they ripple out from the sanctuary into the surrounding society.[97]

The descriptions of what the "we" group perceives as wrong conduct leading to impurity are described in a rather matter-of-fact manner as the stress lies on the group's own legal position. The second-person plural "you" addressee only occurs at the end of section B (B 68, 80), in both instances phrased nonpolemically. Qimron and Strugnell have heavily reconstructed line B 68 after the author's direct address to the "you" group to imply that the author and the "you" group share a common outlook. Others, however, have worked with the extant fragments and have refrained from inferring such a conclusion.[98] The second occurrence of the "you" group in B 80 merely attests that the addressees know of the things that occur in contemporary society, namely the practice of intermarriage. The author of 4QMMT is clear about his opinion regarding these matters, but we cannot infer from this section to have any knowledge about the "you" group's position. Hence, the clear-cut establishment of the text's polemical stance cannot be concluded on the basis of section B.[99]

Qimron and Strugnell's inference of polemics, then, is reached only by reading the halakic section with a presupposition of oppositional groups and interpreted in conjunction with section C: "this question [who are "we," "you," and "they"] is best postponed until we have looked at the evi-

---

96. Translation according to *DSSSE*. DJD X, 48, 86, comments on this as a biblical expression, e.g., Lev 22:16 "to make them bear guilt/punishment" (requiring a guilt offering). Either translation, however, places responsibility for the well-being of the people in the hands of the priests.

97. A good example of the fact that purity issues are thought to be a concern of others in society and not only of the priesthood, can, for instance, be found in the Tob 2:9, where a pious Jew is concerned with his ritual purity and observed *tebul yom* after touching a corpse.

98. E.g., *DSSSE*, 2:797; they chose not to reconstruct the passage after "you know" in 4Q397.

99. Hempel, "Laws of the Damascus Document and 4QMMT," 70–71, concludes that 4QMMT's halakic section B has a nonsectarian, rather general outlook.

dence of section C."[100] Moreover, Qimron and Strugnell use section C to identify the groups in section B, and—in accordance with the presupposed parameters of the Qumran paradigm—they subsequently determine the dating and historical setting of 4QMMT.[101] Hence, since this presupposition precludes any identification of the "we" group other than the Qumran sect, the other positions follow this prime identification. As an example, whereas in section A Strugnell expresses doubt about the calendar being part of 4QMMT at all, this same sectarian calendar now is regarded as an important piece of evidence in the identification of the "we" group as the Qumran sect.

Just as in the halakic section B, a fair amount of scholarly effort has been given to the possible identification of the dramatis personae in the epilogue. But equally uninvestigated as in section B, the "we" group is just presumed to be the Qumran sect or their predecessor(s) and is thus perceived as a unifying feature that ties sections B and C together. Von Weissenberg argues that the presence of the first-person plural in both the halakic section and the epilogue is rather unique, as she considers the use of a first person to be an indication of the author's consciously shaped group identity and specific set of rules. However, such group identity does not necessarily point to a sectarian provenance. Group differentiation often portrays images of self-understanding, which are built through defining oneself over against others, but in itself this does not imply sectarian exclusivism.[102]

As we have seen, the "they" group does not occur in section C, and earlier scholarly attempts to identify section B's "they" with "the multitude of the people" (C 7–8) are now largely abandoned (see §3.3.3).

In contradistinction to the plural "you" group in section B, the "you" addressee in section C occurs most often in the second-person singular.[103] Various questions can be asked with regard to this second-person singular direct address: (1) questions of identity in light of the positive and respectful terminology used; (2) the possibility of the "you" being included in

---

100. DJD X, 111.

101. See DJD X, 110–11.

102. For instance, Goodman has pointed out that matters of halakic dispute lie at the heart of Second Temple Judaism and do not necessarily need to be interpreted as causes for sectarianism; Martin Goodman, "Josephus and Variety in First-Century Judaism," in *Judaism in the Roman World: Collected Essays* (Leiden: Brill, 2007), 33–46.

103. The second-person plural "you" occurs only in the reconstructed text.

the "we";[104] (3) questions regarding the section's social location; and (4) the possible rhetorical function of using a direct address. The classic proposal holds that the second-person singular "you" can be identified as a Hasmonean ruler, based upon three textual references (C 23, C 28, and C 31–32). Of course, such an identification implicitly reads section C in light of the priestly overtones in section B and hence searches for a time in which both strands of power were united in one man's hand—the Hasmonean period. As we have seen, scholars have recently challenged this consensus. For instance, Fraade, who reads the text intramurally, believes the addressee to be an insider. However, Hempel has argued that, in order to establish ground for such a radically different reading, one also needs to provide evidence for the existence of walls between the inside and the outside. Indeed, in order to read 4QMMT intramurally and evaluate the addressee as an insider, one would have to prove sectarian features, which is precisely what is lacking if one reads 4QMMT without its background in the Qumran paradigm.

Specifically for section C, and closely related to the problem of identifying the proponents, is the rather unpolemical and respectful manner in which the "you" figure is addressed. This almost kind and inclusive way of speech seems not to fit with what scholars have identified as *yahadic* texts that demonstrate dualism and harsh polemical rebuking and cursing of opponents. The impression of mild persuasion on the part of the "we" group to convince the "you" group or individual to do the right thing might indeed point towards perceptions of inclusion rather than polemics.

The absence of harsh polemics and the politeness of address are supplemented by the notion that the epilogue has no clear sectarian features, ideas, or provenance. Moreover, the text seems directed to an established person of power and is obviously concerned with the fate of all Israel. Recently, scholars have challenged the consensus view that the important passage in C 7–8 points to a schism of the Qumran sect or any other sectarian schism (see §3.8.6). Scholars who hold on to the notion of a schismatic Qumran sect supply other explanations of the text, such as "an intramural pedagogical document" in which the "we" is used as a rhetorical collective that includes the "you" (Fraade) or as "a document-after-the-fact" that remembers the reasons for separation (Schiffman). In any case,

---

104. See von Weissenberg and Fraade, who both think that the text is modeled after Deuteronomy and argue that in Moses's speech "we" and "you" are inclusively used.

just like section B, section C does not provide us with any significant or concrete boundary markers that distinguishes a radical sectarian group like the Qumranites from the remainder of society, but rather it rhetorically exhorts the addressee to remember Israel's communal past, thereby stressing sociohistorical communalities rather than differences.

3.8.2. Turning Absence into Asset: Mild Polemics

The general scholarly opinion holds that 4QMMT demonstrates polemics but that the polemics are mild. This assessment of mild polemics commonly refers to perceptions of nonaggressiveness in the author's explication of the "we" group's halakic position in section B and the respectful manner in which the second-person singular "you" opponent is addressed in section C. As we saw above, some scholars have argued for the lack of polemics in both sections A and B, while others see in the use of a 364-day calendar a clear polemical reason for sectarian schism and in the halakah the early manifestation of the particular sectarian halakic position of the Qumranites and the topical reasons for the sect's segregation.

Several arguments are used to read section B polemically: (1) section B's polemics are clear when read in connection with section C's underlying principles, (2) section B's halakot lean towards stringency (and thus sectarian radicalism), (3) section B is preoccupied with matters of purity, and (4) section B is ostensibly critical with regard to the tasks and responsibilities of the contemporary priesthood. However, these observations are in themselves not enough reason and provide no clear textual evidence to justify the label polemical. With regard to section C, scholarly opinions can equally be placed on a continuum from polemical to nonpolemical. Against an evaluation of polemics speaks the courtesy that is expressed towards the epilogue's addressee. The epilogue most eye-catchingly praises the wisdom and knowledge of the "you" proponent and expresses concern for his well-being and the well-being of all Israel.

In short, the assessment of polemics in sections A and B is difficult to establish, while the respectfulness of section C's address toned down the scholarly evaluations of 4QMMT's polemical stance into the observation of mild polemics. This new term has taken on a matter-of-fact afterlife and is used in many scholarly articles without definition or critical assessment. More importantly, the notion of mild polemics has had its effect on the presumed provenance of the text. Because of its specific features (unfamiliar halakot, the famous separation clause in C 7–8), 4QMMT quickly became a blueprint for the study of sectarian halakah and a witness to the Qumranites' sectarian schism. The obvious tensions with such a *yahadic* provenance were explained from within the paradigm, so turning frictions into assets: the lack of Qumran terminology and the absence of Qumranic polemics became unique indicators for 4QMMT's position within the history of the Qumran sect. The perceived mild polemics were interpreted to reflect the nascent sect's formative years in which its ideas were not yet fully developed and they still sought reconciliation with their parent movement (and/or the Jerusalemite establishment). Hence, the obvious discrepancies with full-blown *yahadic* texts helped to provide the basis for 4QMMT's prominent and influential position of the foundational document within the Qumran corpus.

From a methodological point of view, a more fundamental question is in order: What is actually meant by *polemics*? More important, does the term *polemics* allow for it to become mild? Further, when do we consider oppositional views, discussion, disagreement, and so on to be polemical?

According to most dictionaries, the word *polemics* is used for the engagement in a controversial argument or dispute with rather strong and aggressive terminology. These are three current meanings: (1) a strong verbal or written attack on someone or something; (2) an aggressive attack on or refutation of the opinions or principles of another; or (3) a controversial argument, especially one refuting or attacking a specific opinion or doctrine.[105] Indeed, if we speak of a polemical text, normally we understand the text to comply with certain common denominators and criteria, such as the name-calling of opponents, assigning negative characteristics to one's opponent, and portraying his views as ridiculous, despicable, or wicked, or an aggressive rebuke and strong denunciations of the other. 4QMMT meets none of these criteria: the calendar (if originally part of 4QMMT) is rather descriptive, as is section B, which although critical of the temple cult and the Jerusalemite priesthood, nowhere renounces or aggressively rebukes these institutions. Of course, the author's critical stance towards the priesthood reflects tension with the established rule and execution of halakic practice, but discussion regarding halakah stood at the center of Jewish religious and sociopolitical life. As argued earlier in this chapter, the tasks and duties of the

---

105. *Oxford English Dictionary* (2012), *Collins Dictionary* (2013), and *van Dale Groot Woordenboek* (1986).

priests can be scrutinized as they carry a responsibility for the people's (socioreligious) well-being. Moreover, as we have seen, the supposedly oppositional views of the opponents can only be reached through a process of deduction. Bernstein is critical of many of the reconstructions that Qimron suggests in the halakic section, stating that "the impetus for the restoration seems to be the invariable position of the editors [of DJD X] that the author of 4QMMT must be polemicizing on all points to which he alludes, a posture which I believe is open to question."[106] If Bernstein is correct and the perception of polemics has influenced and thus made uncertain the restoration of the "we" group's halakic positions, then the insistence on a mild polemical outlook has not only had consequences for the document's dating, but also for our evaluations and understanding of its halakah. Finally, in section C the many features of concern, friendliness, and respect contradict the notion of polemics.

Hence, the function of an assessment of mild polemics can most likely be found in 4QMMT's assigned provenance in the Qumran paradigm. A nonpolemical text would simply be difficult to relate to the notion of Qumran sectarianism. However, the use of the term *polemics* denotes connotations of judgment, denunciation, rebuke, aggressiveness, and confrontation, and does not make use of the more subtle strategies like reasoning, persuasion, appeal to common knowledge, flattery, and expression of concern regarding the fate of others. By allowing a rather confrontational term like polemics to become mild, scholars have taken away much of its original meaning and subsequent explanatory power. Thus, it is my contention that there is no such thing as mild polemics and that the use of this terminology solely serves the objective to retrospectively maintain 4QMMT's (pre-)sectarian status.

3.8.3. The Absence of Sectarian Terminology

Part of the difficulty in connecting 4QMMT to the Qumran group lies in the fact that the text does not demonstrate any of the terminology that scholars have identified as sectarian or *yahadic*. Scholars have found various explanations for this absence, such as:

---

106. Bernstein, "Employment and Interpretation of Scripture," 43.

(1) The text is written for outsiders; therefore the Qumranites chose to write in the nonsectarian language that was contemporarily used in society.
(2) The text is a polemical document, written for outsider opponents, and therefore the Qumran author used the opponents' language.
(3) The document is an intramural pedagogical tool, to teach and reinforce the Qumranites' ideological foundations and self-understanding.
(4) 4QMMT is a sectarian document from the earliest stage in the Qumran sect's development, a time in which they were caught up in an intrapriestly halakic discussion but had not yet segregated from the temple worship and still hoped to be reconciled. Frustrated after 4QMMT's reception, they radicalized and developed a sectarian ideology of abandonment and rejection with its subsequent terminology.

These explanations more or less explicitly presume 4QMMT's Qumranic provenance, and they all stay well within the framework of the Qumran paradigm. Whichever explanation one chooses for the absence of sectarian terminology, it transforms an inconvenient friction into a functioning asset, thereby—in one way or another—preserving the (pre)sectarian classification of the text. Surprisingly, hitherto no Qumran scholar has openly argued for the most obvious and simplest explanation for the lack of sectarian features, namely, the distinct possibility that 4QMMT is not a (pre-)*yahadic* or sectarian or Qumranic text, but that its provenance needs to be found either elsewhere or in a much wider social setting. Instead, from its discovery onward, and later formalized in the DJD X edition in which Qimron placed 4QMMT "prior to or very early in the organized existence of the Qumran Movement,"[107] the text has kept its (pre-)sectarian function within the paradigm.

3.8.4. The Early Glimmers of Unique Halakah and Reasons for Separation

One of the most persistent arguments in all evaluations concerning 4QMMT's presumed provenance in the Qumran paradigm is the notion

---

107. DJD X, 113.

that its halakic section not only reflects those areas in which the Qumran sect differs from its opponents but also highlights the reasons for the Qumranites' schism from their parent movement. Therefore, 4QMMT's halakic section B is said to reflect the polemics between the sect and its opponents by focusing on their halakic differences. The contribution of section B and its halakah to the overall evaluation of 4QMMT as a foundational document consists of several arguments and observations, which are:

(1) 4QMMT is clearly related to 11QT^a, which reflects the same principles and concerns regarding ritual purity and the temple cult, calendar and festivals, and issues like tithes and marital status. Both texts are part of the presectarian formative period of the sect.
(2) Because developments can be observed from the positions expressed in 11QT^a, 4QMMT clearly reveals the topics of fundamental dispute and the sect's reasons for breaking away from its parent movement.
(3) The halakic section of 4QMMT demonstrates early traces of the Qumran sect's dualistic worldviews as the "we" group's halakic positions are polemically set over against the positions of its opponents.
(4) The halakic positions of the "we" group reflect the later halakic system of the Qumran sect, and its discrepancies can be explained by 4QMMT's early date.
(5) When read in conjunction, the halakic section B is supplemented by the hortatory section C, which provides its underlying principles. As such, 4QMMT is an early witness to the unique Qumranic halakah, which relies on the concepts of *nigleh* and *nistar* and characteristically consists of a combination of halakic views and particular Qumranic regulations.
(6) Finally, in the halakah of 4QMMT we find the early traces of Qumranic radical sectarianism as the "we" group's halakic position demonstrates a tendency towards stringency.

Together, these arguments have significantly contributed to 4QMMT's position in the paradigm. However, each of these convictions contains elements that need to be approached with scrutiny.

First, the relationship between 11QT^a and 4QMMT is far from straightforward. Because they are both notoriously hard to date and both lack clear historical information, scholars differ in their assessment of which document is earlier. This fact alone should caution us with regard to any theory that places these two texts in a chronological or developmental sequence or any attempts to use them in historical reconstructions. A related problem arises from Qimron's usage of 11QT^a to reconstruct halakic positions in 4QMMT. Based on a comparison of their halakah, Schiffman argued that both documents sprang from within a Sadducean tradition, but that they cannot be "linearly related."[108] Such evaluation is problematic in light of Qimron's reconstructions, many of which were recently challenged by Werrett.[109] One cannot help but wonder whether the fact that Qimron relies extensively on 11QT^a to reconstruct 4QMMT has contributed to the commonly presumed halakic resemblance between 11QT^a and 4QMMT.

Second, the specificity and presumed peculiar choice of the halakic topics needs to be reevaluated without the presupposition of a Qumranic context for 4QMMT, for—as already stressed by Strugnell and Qimron in DJD X—the text simply seems occupied with the most central topics of dispute between various fractions within Second Temple Judaism.[110] The lack of clarity with regard to the opponents' halakhic positions, together with the absence of polemics and the neutral and unidentifiable use of pronouns for the text's proponents, highly problematizes the view that 4QMMT reflects a (pre-)sectarian setting (or identifies specific disputes with another party). Moreover, Schiffman's contention that 11QT^a and 4QMMT reflect a common Sadducean past problematizes the uniqueness of Qumranic halakah and threatens a straightforward Essene identification. However, several scholars have recently challenged the Sadducean origin of the "we" group's halakic positions, as they only find two (out of twenty!) examples of known Sadducean halakic positions. Further, maybe most importantly, the absence of polemics in combination with the centrality of the topics as matters of debate in Second Temple Judaism and the text's central concern for all Israel do not point toward the notion of a schism.

Third, the contention that 4QMMT reflects the early developments of unique Qumranic halakah deserves a series of critical remarks. As we have seen above, most undisputed *yahadic* sectarian texts, like the so-

---

108. Schiffman, *Qumran and Jerusalem*, 121.
109. Werrett, *Ritual Purity*, 180–209.
110. DJD X, 131.

called Serakhim, or rule texts (1QS, 4QS fragments [4Q255–264], 1QSa [1Q28a], 1QSb [1Q28b]),[111] do not contain clear halakic material, as they are predominantly preoccupied with internal matters of organization and conduct. Therefore, scholars consider the *yahadic* texts less suitable for the establishment of a Qumranic halakah, which is commonly reconstructed and assessed from the following four building blocks: 11QT^a, 4QMMT, the Cave 4 fragments of CD and a disparate collection of Qumran fragments referred to by Schiffman as "remaining halakha" (i.e., DJD XXXV's Halakhic Texts, e.g., 4Q251, 4Q265, 4Q414). Interestingly, the presumed unique Qumranic sectarian halakic position is based upon documents, none of which can be designated *yahadic* beyond a reasonable doubt. Most interestingly, Schiffman's unique sectarian marker for Qumranic halakah, namely, the distinction between *nigleh* and *nistar* (or any other allusion to "secret revealed knowledge" regarding the correctness of the "we" group's halakic interpretations) is lacking in 4QMMT. On the contrary, the text presumes a certain openness and accessibility as to how it reaches its halakic positions, which is reflected in the fact that its addressee is supposed to have a certain awareness of common rules and practices. Moreover, the author of 4QMMT even appeals to the addressee's wisdom and knowledge of the torah. Also, Shemesh finds that, in contradistinction to the Qumranic lack of exegetical explanation for reaching its halakic positions, 4QMMT's author explains his exegetical considerations.[112] One cannot help thinking that the argument of uniqueness and not-yet-fully-developed halakic argumentation is quite seriously undermined by the amount of circular reasoning that is needed to construct Qumranic halakah in the first place.

Finally, scholars have argued that 4QMMT reflects early traces of the Qumranites' radical sectarian stance, as its halakah leans towards stringency. Hence, stringency is obviously—rightly or wrongly—associated with the notion of the Qumranites' sectarian radicalism and religious extremism. Yaakov Elman has objected to stringency as a criterion for the identification and positioning of halakic statements. He argues that "once we assert that Qumranic halakha represents a 'systematic and fully consistent' stringency, which applies 'to all details and aspects of any given halakha,' we are asserting that the *only* consistency is one of stringency,

---

111. I exclude the War Scroll (1QM), as I do not consider M an undisputed *yahadic* text.

112. Shemesh, *Halakhah in the Making*, 35 n. 31.

despite the direction in which the legal or ritualistic or exegetical logic may tend."[113] He warns against the presupposition of consistent stringency on the part of the perceived Qumranic "we" group, as it implicitly presupposes an equally consistent more lenient position on the part of its opponents, especially since 4QMMT is considered to reflect the polemics between both groups with regard to the text's specific topics. Finally, Elman finds several instances in Qimron's reconstruction of 4QMMT's halakic section that impress him as being driven by the conviction of systematic polemics in conjunction with this obligatory stringency, rather than by the most likely or closest physical reconstruction or parallel text.[114] If Elman is correct and these presumptions of polemics and stringency have influenced the text's reconstruction, they may equally have influenced the subsequent evaluation of 4QMMT's social world and relation to Qumran. As Bernstein has eloquently put it: "Theories about the legal system of the authors, about their attitude to Scripture and halakha, as well as the identity of their opponents have an effect on both the reconstruction and interpretation of the fragments."[115] No one will deny that Qimron has done a tremendous job in reconstructing a coherent text from such fragmentary manuscripts. However, Elman and Bernstein stress the importance of caution as to the possible discrepancies that are often found between what we have and what we wish, presume, or presuppose. By and large, these discrepancies are reflected in the story and the life of 4QMMT.

3.8.5. The Evidence of 4QpPsª: Written Communication of the Sect's Precepts of the Law

Another parameter for positioning 4QMMT in the early history of the Qumran sect is the suggestion that an undisputed Qumranic text, the pesher on Psalm 37 (4QpPsª [4Q171]), refers to the halakic letter. This suggestion is built upon two presumptions. First, in DJD X, Qimron connects sections B and C through the expression "Precepts of the Law" by interpreting the term מעשים of B 2, C 23, and C 27 as meaning "precepts" or "commandments." Moreover, for Qimron, מעשים signifies a Qumranic

---

113. Yaakov Elman, "4QMMT and the Rabbinic Tradition, or, When Is a Parallel Not a Parallel?" in Kampen and Bernstein, *Reading 4QMMT*, 99–128 (emphasis original).
114. Elman, "4QMMT and the Rabbinic Tradition," 102–3.
115. Bernstein, "Employment and Interpretation of Scripture," 30.

setting as he attributes this peculiar usage and meaning, that is, different from its traditional meaning "works" or "deeds," to the realm of the Qumran sect: "In MMT laws are not called halakhot, מצוות... but rather מעשים (B 2) and מעשי התורה (C 27), ... in this sense also found in some other Qumranic works (4Q174, 1–2 I 7, 1QS VI 18)."[116] Having established this inner-4QMMT connection, he suggests that a phrase in 4QpPs\u1d43 IV, 8c–9a, which speaks of the Teacher of Righteousness having sent to the Wicked Priest "a document of precepts and law,"[117] may be an inner-Qumranic reference to 4QMMT, which can establish its provenance. This very sentence, along with the harmonization of the term מעשים in 4QMMT itself, has thus significantly shaped the text's overall evaluation.

Qimron's evaluation of מעשים in the meaning of "precepts" as Qumranic has been criticized by García Martínez, who especially disagrees with the presumed implication of this observation, namely, that 4QMMT is a *yahadic* document. He argues that, not only in other Qumran writings, but also in 4QMMT itself, מעשים needs to be translated according to its traditional meaning of "works" or "deeds."[118] In B 2, the restoration of the text is difficult, but García Martínez seems correct in his evaluation that here the term מעשים needs to be connected with, but not necessarily taken as a synonym for B 1's "our rulings" (דברינו), as the use of both terms in one sentence clearly points to their different meaning. Moreover, in DJD's C 23, the term is translated traditionally: "Remember the Kings of Israel and contemplate their deeds" (מעשיהם). The employment of the same word, reflecting both its new distinctly sectarian semantic field and its traditional meaning within one document, seems rather unlikely. Moreover, García Martínez concludes that Qimron's other examples of the Qumranic usage of the term מעשים also need to be translated according to the traditional meaning of "deeds" or "works."[119] Interestingly, García Martínez demonstrates that the term can have its traditional meaning in C 27's מעשי התורה, which currently provides the manuscript with its title. Even though García Martínez's opinion is grounded in his investment to assign a pre-Qumranic, that is, a formative setting to 4QMMT, his pro-

---

116. DJD X, 139.
117. DJD X, 119.
118. Florentino García Martínez, "4QMMT in Qumran Context," in Kampen and Bernstein, *Reading 4QMMT*, 15–27.
119. Ibid., 24–25.

posal is convincing and has its implications for our evaluation of the perceived inner-Qumranic tradition pointed out by DJD X.

As we have seen, the proposed inner-Qumranic tradition refers to the phrase in 4QpPsᵃ IV, 8c–9a, which reflects a pesher on Ps 37:32–33 interpreted as follows: "the Wicked [Pri]est, who sp[ie]s on the ju[st man and wants to] kill him ... and the law [התורה] which he sent him."[120] The presumption that this passage refers to 4QMMT is probably partly based on the fact that the DJD edition constructs a lexical connection between the two texts by suggesting that the 4QpPsᵃ text reads "precepts and the law which the latter sent to the former."[121] As such, 4QpPsᵃ is thought to establish the identification of 4QMMT's author as the Teacher of Righteousness and its addressee as the Wicked Priest. Of course, such an identification would put 4QMMT firmly within the realm of the Qumran sect. However, even though the English translation in DJD X does not indicate restorations, its suggestion that the pesher reads "*precepts* and the law" is entirely based upon the text's reconstruction. Also, even the reconstructed text, which is abandoned in the *DSSSE*'s translation used above, does not use the connecting term מעשים but the more common term for "precepts" (דברים).[122] Hence, what we have in 4QpPsᵃ is a reference to the "torah" that the Teacher supposedly has sent, a term that, as Schiffman has correctly pointed out, 4QMMT employs frequently but never in reference to itself. According to Schiffman, the 4QMMT text itself demonstrates an awareness of distinction between the Mosaic torah and its own halakic writings, a point that would concur with García Martínez's evaluations concerning the meaning of מעשים. Furthermore, the term תורה is so frequently used that it can hardly function as a reference to a specific document. Moreover, the presumed identification of 4QMMT's proponents through the reference in 4QpPsᵃ is problematic as the former does not contain any historical data.[123] Nowadays, most scholars have abandoned the straightforward identification of the Psalm pesher passage with

---

120. *DSSSE*, 1:347.

121. DJD X, 120.

122. The reconstruction thus reads על דברי החו[ק והתורה אשר שלח אליו]; however, the *qof* is uncertain, and the simultaneous usage of תורה and חוק both indicating "law" seems odd.

123. Strugnell, "Second Thoughts," 70–71; von Weissenberg, *4QMMT*, 17; also Eyal Regev, *Sectarianism in Qumran: A Cross-Cultural Perspective*, RelSoc 45 (Berlin: de Gruyter, 2007), 107.

4QMMT, but some still maintain this view, a view that in the paradigm certainly has had its influence on the evaluations regarding 4QMMT's position within the Qumran corpus.[124]

3.8.6. The Evidence of Segregation and Separation from Society

The most important parameter for the evaluation of 4QMMT as the foundational document of the Qumran sect is its famous passage of separation in C 7–8 (4Q397 14–21, 7b–8c): "[And you know that] we have segregated ourselves [פרשנו] from the multitude [רוב] of the pe[ople and] [(ם)הע] from mingling in these affairs, and from associating wi[th them] in these things." Classically, this phrase is taken as evidence for the physical, social, and possibly even geographical separation of the Qumran sect. Before discussing the individual elements of the passage proper, a general observation must be made regarding this passage's overall evaluation. On the one hand, if we follow Strugnell and García Martínez in their conviction that 4QMMT is a pre-Qumranic text, how can we perceive their "segregation from the multitude of the people" at such an early stage? Moreover, if one places 4QMMT in García Martínez's formative period, would the group not first need to deal with the split-off from its parent movement and define its own identity while still struggling with the schism, before it would even consider a possible retreat to Qumran?[125] As such, a

---

124. Hanan Eshel, *The Dead Sea Scrolls and the Hasmonean State* (Grand Rapids: Eerdmans, 2008), 46–48.

125. In his Groningen hypothesis, García Martínez, seems to want to have his cake and eat it too. On the one hand, 4QMMT is used to prove his theory of a "discordant split-off" from the Essene parent movement over the halakic and calendar issues mentioned in the text, while at the same time the text is ascribed "as coming from the parent group of the Qumran Community." He states: "This pre-Qumranic group had already adopted the calendar, followed the halakha we know from other Qumran compositions." According to García Martínez, the Essenes had no calendrical issues, while halakic disputes and calendrical issues were the main reasons for the split-off. Moreover, according to Josephus, the Essenes lived everywhere and not "separated from the multitude of the people." Hence, García Martínez (*Qumranica Minora I*, 3–52) either conceives another, third sectarian group chronologically in between the Essene parent movement and the Qumran Sect, or he simply adjusts the parameters of his theory dependent on the question asked. In any case, who exactly separated from the multitude of the people, and how to interpret this separation—ideologically, physically, or even geographically—remains rather unclear; García Martínez.

physical and geographical separation from "the multitude of the people" seems unlikely. On the other hand, if we follow Qimron (and Dimant) and consider 4QMMT a document of the Qumran sect, the separation passage would make sense, but then an explanation needs to be found for all the discrepancies that the text demonstrates with what scholars consider *yahadic* texts.[126]

Recently, several scholars, while reinvestigating this important clause from various perspectives, have challenged the designated identification of C 7–8 as a witness to the Qumran sect's separation. The scholarly debate highlights several issues, which are more or less interconnected. These issues are discussed below (§3.8.6.1–3).

3.8.6.1. The Meaning of "These Things" (הדברים האלה) (C 8)

Miguel Perez Fernandez, Carolyn Sharp and, to a certain extent, Schiffman have argued that the C 7–8 passage still deals with the preceding subject of intermarriage.[127] An important indication as to whether they are right lies in scholars' ability to clarify the meaning of "these things" in C 8. The use of the plural (twice in C 8) indicates that the "things" from which the "we" group wishes to distance itself [מ]העם are plural, too, and hence extend beyond the issue of intermarriage. Recently, Hempel has suggested that 4QMMT's separation clause might indeed point to a separation between the "we" group and the people and their "inappropriate practices."[128] If she is correct, "these things" may refer to the halakic rules and corresponding practices in which the "we" group disagrees with the contemporary observance and practical execution of the law in Israel. Indeed, if read in conjunction with section B, as Hempel does, such a summary at the begin-

---

126. Also, and even though many linguistic features do not fit with the *yahadic* sectarian texts, Qimron seems to assess the text as "written by the Qumran sect" on purely linguistic grounds, without considering the implications of this evaluation for the other sociohistorical parameters assigned to the text.

127. Miguel Pérez Fernández, "4QMMT: Redactional Study," *RevQ* 18 (1997): 191–205; Carolyn Sharp, "Phinean Zeal and Rhetorical Strategy in 4QMMT," *RevQ* 18 (1997): 207–22; Lawrence Schiffman, "Prohibited Marriages in the Dead Sea Scrolls and Rabbinic Literature," in *Rabbinic Perspectives: Rabbinic Literature and the Dead Sea Scrolls, Proceedings of the Eight Symposium of the Orion Center for the Study of the Dead Sea Scrolls and Associated Literature (7–9 January 2003)*, ed. S. Fraade, A. Shemesh, and R. Clements, STDJ 62 (Leiden: Brill, 2006), 113–26 (121).

128. Hempel, "Comfortable Theories," 19.

ning of a new section would be conceivable. Unfortunately, the extreme fragmentary state of 4Q397 and the facts that (1) the junction between sections B and C is not preserved and (2) C 1–8 are only preserved in this one manuscript make it difficult to establish whether the lines preceding C 7–8 function as a bridge or summary of section B.[129]

In her reconstruction of 4QMMT's epilogue, von Weissenberg offers an alternative placement of the fragments, which places composite text C 7–8 in the middle of the epilogue (as lines C 14–15). Hence, in von Weissenberg's reconstruction, "these things" need not necessarily refer to or provide the bridge for the halakic issues discussed in section B. Moreover, it allows for an independent reading of section C in which case "these things" not only connects with the "we" group's historical awareness of what caused blessings and what caused curses in Israel's past but more precisely with their recognition of such causes for cursing in their contemporary social environment (and hence their conviction to separate themselves from such practices). Accordingly, von Weissenberg suggests reading C 7–8 more along these lines than as a declaration of segregation from wider society.

Read independently, section C can hardly shed light on the precise or detailed matters to which "these things" refer, as the candidates—deceit, violence, and fornication—are the prototypical accusations of transgressions known from numerous other biblical and nonbiblical texts. Hence, whether "these things" refers to the halakic concerns of section B or to it being an independent section C reference to the unspecified transgressions collected under "deceit," "violence," and "fornication" is hard to tell. Both options certainly seem possible and weaken the theory of C 7–8 being the declaration of the Qumran sect's total segregation from society.

3.8.6.2. The Use of פרש in C 7: פרשנו

Another important issue involves the use and meaning of the word פרש ("to separate oneself"). According to Qimron, 4QMMT attests to the earliest manifestation of this meaning of פרש.[130] In DJD X, Qimron notes

---

129. Also, there is considerable dispute regarding the correct placement of the fragments; see §3.8.1 above.

130. Interestingly Qimron openly demonstrates his surprise about 4QMMT's "neutral, or even positive, use of the verb פרש to describe the creation of sects," most notably its own group; DJD X, 111.

that the term does not occur in Biblical Hebrew but rather in Mishnaic Hebrew, where it can have several meanings, one of which is "the act of leaving the community because of differences of opinion over halakha."[131] More importantly, he notices that פרש is not used in other Qumran sectarian writings like CD/DD (which uses סור מדרך), when discussing the group's separation. Hence, he explains away this important disparity by suggesting an early date for 4QMMT or—in line with Dimant—the sectarians using their opponents' terminology. Both suggestions seem to denote Qimron's contention of the text's social location within the Qumran paradigm, rather than being comments based on textual evidence.[132]

Elitzur Bar-Ashur Siegal is critical of Qimron's assessment that the occurrence of פרש in 4QMMT is "the earliest attestation of the use of פרש for 'depart, secede.'"[133] Philologically, Siegal argues, such an evaluation on the basis of one occurrence of a lexical term is suspect, and more thorough investigation of the term's root and previous meanings is needed in order to establish whether a new meaning is justified. Moreover, he suggests that, if Qimron were correct and the term needs to be translated "to separate oneself," one would expect the term to be complemented by "path/way" (דרך).[134] Hempel also recently challenged the conclusions Qimron draws from his overall assessment of the usage of פרש in C 7, questioning whether the presupposition of a "discordant sectarian schism" concurs with 4QMMT's textual evidence.[135] Even though von Weissenberg's translation and reading of the epilogue still concurs with the traditional readings that a "separation from the multitude of the people" is indicated in C 7–8, she believes the passage to reflect the "we" group's need to dis-

---

131. DJD X, 99.

132. See DJD X, where Qimron notes that the Qumran sect uses the "biblicizing" סרי מדרך העם. Interestingly, if we would follow diachronic theories of evolutionary linguistic and semantic development with regard to the history of the Qumran sect, their characteristic biblicizing terminology seems rather in tension with an early date for 4QMMT, which seems to rely on the later MH terminology when it comes to describing the "we" group's separation.

133. DJD X, 58; Elitzur Bar-Asher Siegal, "Who Separated from Whom and Why? A Philological Study of 4QMMT," *RevQ* 25 (2011): 229–56; Interestingly, Siegal convincingly establishes connection between פרש and the biblical בדל, but his philological investigation does not find any relationship between פרש and the root סור, which is used in Qumran sectarian literature for the act of the sect's separation.

134. Siegal, "Who Separated from Whom," 245.

135. Hempel, "Comfortable Theories," 284–86.

tance themselves from what they perceive as "impure practices," rather than "signify an irrevocable and irreconcilable separation from all Jews or a complete abandonment of the Temple."[136] Moreover, she argues that the separation clause, which is so important for the Qumran paradigm, can hardly be seen as the central point of the epilogue, whose "main focus is on the repentance and reformation of the Jerusalem Cult."[137] If von Weissenberg is correct, 4QMMT's investment in the temple cult might reflect a genuine engagement with and deep concern for the fate of all Israel, rather than a move toward a radical exclusivist and separatist positioning on the part of its author's movement.

3.8.6.3. The Reconstruction of הע[ם]

An important and often overlooked issue is the restoration of העם ("the people"). In only some Hebrew reconstructions, the restoration of the *mem* is indicated, while no issue is taken over the fact that also the *ayin* is only partly visible.[138] Recently, Siegal has challenged the reconstruction of העם and suggests the reading רוב העמים, which would be a well-attested reference to the holiness of Israel and its separation from the nations. Moreover, Siegal finds references for his proposal in Deut 7, Ezra 9–10, and numerous examples in the targumic and rabbinic literature connecting the use of פרש to העמים. He thinks that the restoration of העמים also allows for an alternative reconstruction of the beginning of the sentence and a reflexive meaning of פרשנו as he translates: "And we were set off and apart from the multitude of the nations and we were prohibited from mingling with them."[139]

As we have seen above, some scholars have argued that the C 7–8 separation clause refers to 4QMMT's halakic position on intermarriage in section B. In favor of Siegal's reconstruction is the fact that the above-mentioned passages in Deuteronomy and Ezra also specifically address the prohibition of intermarriage between Israel and the nations.[140] If Siegal is correct, this leaves open the possibility that in 4QMMT, as in these scrip-

---

136. Von Weissenberg, *4QMMT*, 203.
137. Ibid., 235.
138. See Hempel, "Comfortable Theories," 17–18.
139. Siegal, "Who Separated from Whom," 244.
140. However, as we have seen, section C's reference of "these things" seems to involve other issues as well.

tural references, the separation-clause concerns all Israel and the nations, instead of reflecting a sectarian schismatic event. Recently, Hempel has pointed out another inconsistency with regard to the traditional opinion of a sectarian separation from "the multitude of the people." She suggests that the people (העם) cannot be the problem as they are not an active (or mentioned) party in the epilogue. Moreover, several passages (B 26–27, C 27, and C 31–32) seem genuinely concerned with their well-being.[141] If Siegal is correct and the C 7–8 clause is preoccupied with the preservation of Israel's holiness and purity over against the nations, we may see B 75–82 regarding the holiness of the seed of Israel in an entirely different light. In any case, his suggestions are intriguing and at times convincing enough to put warning signs on an all-too-convenient interpretation of this passage in light of the Qumran paradigm.

3.8.7. The Curious Case of the Sectarian Calendar

A less-highlighted but nevertheless important part of 4QMMT's (pre-)sectarian status involves scholarly assessments regarding the text's calendar. As we have seen, scholars early on have evaluated 4Q394 1–2 as not belonging to 4QMMT and hence were left with only three calendrical lines, which partly seem to reconstruct a 364-day calendar. Moreover, we have discussed how some scholars have even expressed their doubts about the originality of the calendrical section A to the text. Nevertheless, the fragmentary evidence of a sectarian 364-day calendar has been used as a valuable asset in 4QMMT's overall evaluation as a (pre-)sectarian Qumranic text.

While some scholars have argued that the presence of a calendar is rather unpolemical in nature, others have seen it as an important indicator of sectarianism and thus inherently polemical. Also, some scholars have argued that the fact that the calendar was preserved only in a single manuscript (4Q394) is an indication that a calendar is extraneous to 4QMMT, while at the same time claiming that the calendar clearly was an integral reason for the Qumran sect to segregate from "the multitude of the people."[142] Two more arguments are used to make the calendrical section A function within the Qumran paradigm: (1) the calendar is used to estab-

---

141. Hempel, "Comfortable Theories," 21–22.
142. For these various scholarly opinions, see §§3.3 and 3.8 above.

lish 4QMMT's connection to the Qumran sect solely on the basis of their presupposed usage of a 364-day calendar; and (2) the calendar is used to imply a textual *yahadic* characteristic, as the *yahad* is presumed to be quite familiar with the unusual attachment of a calendrical manuscript to their rulings, as the attachment of 4Q319 (4QOtot) to one of the copies of 4QS^e (4Q259) seems to indicate.[143] These often contradictory arguments demonstrate that the issue of a sectarian calendar has played an important role in the evaluation of 4QMMT's provenance.

No one will contest the fact that the calendar was an important topic in Second Temple Judaism as it regulated daily life in general and religious life in particular. Among the Qumran finds, many calendrical texts and texts containing calendrical sections have been found which attest to this affect.[144] However, the calendars found at Qumran are not identical; they do not have the same focus (priestly courses, festivals, days of the Sabbath, etc.). Some of them reflect a 364-day calendar, while others describe a schematic 354-day luni-solar calendar, which "was brought into alignment with the solar [i.e., 364-day] calendar by regular intercalations."[145] According to James VanderKam, none of the calendrical texts found at Qumran indicate that this luni-solar system was in any way considered inferior to a pure 364-day calendar. The variety of calendars found at Qumran therefore cannot be used as an indicator for 4QMMT's provenance. Moreover, even though the general opinion that the 364-day calendar was a sectarian calendar is taken over by most scholars without critical assessment, possibly on the basis that this calendar is attested for in Jubilees, 1 Enoch's Astronomical Book, and at Qumran, scholarly debate as to the common calendar used in the temple has not yet ceased.[146] Even if we presume that the 364-day calendar in general, and its occurrence in 4Q394 in particular, is sectarian, we still cannot use this assessment as evidence to establish 4QMMT's (pre-)Qumranic setting.[147] Similarly, Jubilees and 1

---

143. In §3.3.1, I have argued that these two instances of calendar-attachment are better not compared for material and textual reasons as well as with regard to their subject matter.

144. DJD X, 131: "MMT deals with the three topics [calendar, ritual purity with regard to the temple cult, and marital status] that stood at the centre of the controversy between the Jewish religious parties of the Second Temple Period."

145. James VanderKam, *Calendars in the Dead Sea Scrolls Scrolls: Measuring Time* (New York: Routledge, 1998), 110–12.

146. Ibid., 113–15.

147. More important, it is uncertain whether calendrical issues can at all be used

Enoch advocate strongly for a 364-day calendar, without being evaluated as Qumranic in origin. The fact is that the calendar in 4Q394 is only preserved in three highly reconstructed lines and gives us little secure information. Without the presumption of a Qumranic setting already in mind, the calendar cannot be attributed to the scholars' evidence kit to establish 4QMMT's provenance as a foundational document of the Qumran sect.

3.8.8. The Final Straw: Evidence of Presence

Of course, I am not the first one to notice the multitude of questions, uncertainties, and circular reasoning that has characterized scholarship with regard to 4QMMT. When all else fails, the sheer fact that many versions of 4QMMT are found among the Qumran manuscripts is often the only remaining argument to presume the text's (pre-)sectarian or (pre-)Qumranic provenance. This argument of presence, which reasons from the presupposition that the Dead Sea Scrolls reflect the religious library of the Qumran sect, regards the number of preserved 4QMMT manuscripts as evidence for the document being an authoritative text with near-canonical status at Qumran. This argument, which can be found in many scholarly publications as the last attempt to secure the text's pivotal position in the paradigm, inherently expresses the reluctance of scholarship to part with its original evaluation of 4QMMT's provenance and to open up the possibility of reevaluating this important text with fresh eyes. Instead, scholarship holds on to what Hempel has called the "relic" of a specific phase of research.[148] We find a good example of this last resort argumentation in von Weissenberg's thorough study of 4QMMT's epilogue and its relation to halakic section B in which she concludes that both sections have "nothing particular Qumranic or sectarian." Although she successfully deconstructs many of the pillars that hold up 4QMMT's firm position as a foundational document of the Qumran sect, she, like others,

---

to make a case for schisms. Both Goodman and Stern have argued that differences in calendar occurred throughout Jewish history and are in themselves no reason for separatism or sectarianism; see Sacha Stern, "Qumran Calendars and Sectarianism," in *The Oxford Handbook of the Dead Sea Scrolls*, ed. Timothy H. Lim and John J. Collins (Oxford: Oxford University Press, 2011), 232–53; Martin Goodman, "Josephus and Variety," 33–46; and Goodman, "A Note on Qumran Sectarians, the Essenes and Josephus," in Goodman, *Judaism in the Roman World*, 137–43.

148. Hempel, "Comfortable Theories," 285.

does not follow through on her own conclusions and firmly retreats into the comfort of the prevalent paradigm, as she states: "Several copies of 4QMMT found in Cave 4 at Qumran witness the importance of this document to those who compiled the Qumran library: the community living at Qumran. Therefore, even though 4QMMT could originally have been composed either at Qumran or elsewhere, it certainly was of considerable significance for the community."[149]

3.9. Conclusions

4QMMT is a difficult document to assess. The many peculiarities have made it one of the most fascinating documents among the Qumran texts. However, the many problems that we have encountered and laid bare in this chapter demonstrate that the straightforward identification of this document as the foundational document of the Qumran sect can no longer be maintained. In chapter 2 we have already unraveled the problems that are attached to classifications of presectarianism and the notion of a formative period. This chapter has attempted to demonstrate that, at least in the case of 4QMMT, these classifications are invested in sustaining the Qumran paradigm, rather than in evaluating the textual evidence on its own merits. As a test case, this reevaluation of 4QMMT has created awareness of the fact that if textual evidence does not fit, an all too stringent model of social reality might hold back new interpretations or different possible interpretive horizons. Thus, rather than pigeonholing 4QMMT in its paradigmatic position, we need to realize that there are simply too many unanswered difficulties at this point in time to proceed comfortably within the existing interpretative framework of the Qumran paradigm.

---

149. Von Weissenberg, *4QMMT*, 234–35.

4
Ideology as a Cohesive Strategy:
The Development of Qumran Dualism

The perception of the Qumran sect's antagonistic thought in rather radical forms has been part and parcel of Qumran scholarship from its inception. As we saw earlier in the case of 4QMMT, the presupposition of this text's provenance and the idea of sectarianism have dominated scholarly investigations in its perceived mildly polemical stance over against (the halakic positions of) the Qumran sect's perceived opponents. The characteristics of sectarianism as an assumed model, made to explain the Qumran community and library in general, and its main identifier of tension with or antagonism against the outside world in particular,[1] not only determined the way scholars evaluated texts with regard to style, language, and terminology; it also influenced scholarly evaluations with regard to the conceptualization of an overall uniquely Qumranite sectarian worldview and ideology, containing its own specific and identifiable characteristics.

A sectarian model presumes an irresolvable tension with the outside world of mainstream religion. Accordingly, the conceptualization of a Qumran community from the vantage point of a sectarian paradigm undergirds and reinforces a reading of texts as radical in language, style, thought, and practice. This perception of the Qumran sect's radicality is commonly reflected in (1) their specifically sectarian terminology, (2) applied in a concealed but for insiders recognizable web of meanings and

---

1. See, for instance, Rodney Stark and William Sims Bainbridge, *A Theory of Religion*, Toronto Studies in Religion 2 (New York: Lang, 1987), or, for Qumran studies, Jutta Jokiranta, "Identity on a Continuum: Constructing and Expressing Sectarian Social Identity in Qumran *Sekharim* and *Pesharim*" (PhD diss., University of Helsinki, 2005). Jokiranta's thesis is now revised and published as *Social Identity and Sectarianism in the Qumran Movement*, STDJ 105 (Leiden: Brill, 2013).

particular style (as for instance in the pesharim). These sectarian texts are thought (3) to reflect not only identifiable deviant ideological concepts and beliefs (such as a deterministic worldview and dualistic thinking) but also (4) the tendency towards stringency in their halakic positions and (5) a salvific self-understanding of being elected. This elected status is perceived to be (6) supplemented by the ideological creation of high boundaries between the group members themselves, the "good" insiders, and the "evil" outside world.

In short, the label of sectarianism provokes the search for textual evidence of such an irreducible oppositional framework and/or tempts us to read texts accordingly; it facilitates—rightly or wrongly—a tendency to evaluate and interpret opposition or difference in terms of antagonism, polemics, dualism, and Otherness. Thus, this and the next chapter will primarily focus on the ideological side of Qumran's sectarian purported radicality and will investigate the value and function of identifying the concept of dualism as a prime characteristic of the Qumran group's theology.

4.1. Dualism as a Qumran Characteristic

Dualistic thinking has long been perceived as one of the main characteristics of the Qumranites' theological outlook. For instance, in her essay on "Qumran Sectarian Literature," Dimant argues that the Qumran sectarian writings attest to a "system of strict predestination" in which "powerful dualistic notions are introduced."[2] In the Treatise of the Two Spirits (1QS III, 13–IV, 26), Dimant finds the "sect's dualistic ideology" at work in "all levels, in the world at large and 'in the heart of men.'"[3] Similarly, García Martínez identified dualistic thought as "one of the trademarks of the thought of the Qumran community" and also believes that the Treatise of the Two Spirits is "the most systematic exposition of the dualistic thinking of the community."[4]

---

2. Devorah Dimant, "Qumran Sectarian Literature" in *Jewish Writings of the Second Temple Period: Apocrypha, Pseudepigrapha, Qumran Sectarian Writings, Philo, Josephus*, ed. Michael E. Stone, CRINT 2 (Assen: Van Gorcum, 1984), 532–40.

3. Ibid., 535.

4. García Martínez, *Qumranica Minora I*, 202–6.

4.1.1. First Research into the Development of Qumran Dualism

Among the first scholars who investigated the perceived dualism in the Dead Sea Scrolls was Peter von der Osten-Sacken. Von der Osten-Sacken finds that "einen wesentlichen Bestandteil der Lehre der Gemeinde von Qumran bildet die dualistische Vorstellung, daß die Welt unter zwei einander befehdende Mächte geteilt ist."[5] Instead of merely presenting a phenomenological overview of dualistic elements in the Qumran manuscripts, von der Osten-Sacken attempts to lay bare a chronological development within the Qumran sect's dualistic thinking. Working from the hypothesis that 1QS III, 13–IV, 26 is the Qumran sect's most centralized and explicit representation of dualistic tradition, he presumes a diachronic element in its usage of specific sayings and imagery, consecutively supplementing the basic dualistic struggle of eschatological war (1QM) in representations of various levels of duality in the struggles between (1) God and Belial, (2) the Prince of Light and the Angel of Darkness, (3) the Spirits of Truth and Iniquity, and (4) The Spirits of Light and Darkness. Von der Osten-Sacken retraces the origins of such a Qumran dualism to the dualistic tradition not only of the motif of Israel and the nations and the book of Daniel but also in the early Maccabean period, during which he thinks the experience of war and oppression created the environment for the development of so-called *Endkampfdualismus* or eschatological-war dualism.[6] This *Endkampfdualismus* is supposedly reflected in the first Qumran phase of dualism, as represented by the eschatologically orientated 1QM. Eventually, it is thought to have developed into an ethical dualism for present-day conduct (as found in 1QH) and a more generalized anthropological dualism (as found in 4Q186).[7] According to von der Osten-Sacken, all three

---

5. Peter von der Osten-Sacken, *Gott und Belial: Traditionsgeschichtliche Untersuchungen zum Dualismus in den Texten aus Qumran*, SUNT 6 (Göttingen: Vandenhoeck & Ruprecht, 1969), 12.

6. Von der Osten-Sacken (*Gott und Belial*, 28–41, 239) also mentions the so-called "Jom-Jahwe" and holy war traditions in the Hebrew Bible as sources; see also Jörg Frey, "Different Patterns of Dualistic Thought in the Qumran Library: Reflections on Their Background and History," in *Legal Texts and Legal Issues: Proceedings of the Second Meeting of the International Organisation for Qumran Studies, Cambridge 1995; Published in Honour of Joseph M. Baumgarten*, ed. Moshe Bernstein, Florentino García Martínez, and John Kampen, STDJ 23 (Leiden: Brill, 1997), 285.

7. Von der Osten-Sacken, *Gott und Belial*, 28–41, 123–69, 185–89. On the comparison of the Treatise with 4Q186, see below and Mladen Popović, "Light and Dark-

stages of dualistic development correspond to three distinctive layers of textual development in the Treatise of the Two Spirits (1QS III, 13–IV, 14/ IV, 15–23a/ IV, 23b–26), which he holds to be representative of the most developed or end phase of the Qumran sect's dualistic thinking.[8]

In an important study published in 1987, Jean Duhaime strongly objects to von der Osten-Sacken's analysis, claiming that the latter's thesis depends "too heavily on the assumption that the earliest type of dualism is the eschatological dualism of 1QM I, and that any form of dualism which departs from it is the result of a later transformation."[9] In turning the developmental scheme around, Duhaime argues by contrast that the most original form of dualism found in the Qumran manuscripts is an ethical dualism, namely, the opposition between the two antagonistic groups of the righteous and the wicked, which he considers to have been a development from the late wisdom tradition. He furthers his argument by proposing that "dualistic reworking" has resulted in secondary additions to the original texts of, for instance, 1QM, 1QS, and CD, introducing cosmic dualism by the addition of two supernatural opponents (respectively, the Prince of Light and Belial, the Angel of Truth and the Angel of Darkness, and Michael and the Prince of the Domination of Ungodliness).[10] Hence, Duhaime argues against von der Osten-Sacken's unilinear chronological development, but he nevertheless likewise advocates one Ur-type of dualism, closely related to biblical wisdom literature, from which "various types of dualism have merged."[11]

In his important study into the Qumran sect's anthropology, Hermann Lichtenberger argues against the tendency to evaluate the variety of outlooks in the Qumran texts as an indication of a chronological development; he also does not encourage efforts to harmonize these varieties into one coherent cosmological and anthropological outlook.[12] Moreover,

---

ness in the Treatise on the Two Spirits (1QS III 13–IV 26) and in 4Q186," in *Dualism in Qumran*, ed. Géza Xeravits, LSTS 76 (New York: T&T Clark, 2010), 148–65.

8. In his conclusion, von der Osten-Sacken (*Gott und Belial*, 239–41) is unclear about other factors of influence on the development of his Qumran dualism, but mentions possible Persian/Zoroastrian influences on 1QS III, 13–IV 26.

9. Jean Duhaime, "Dualistic Reworking in the Scrolls from Qumran," *CBQ* 49 (1987): 32–56.

10. Ibid., 32.

11. Ibid., 36.

12. Hermann Lichtenberger, *Studien zum Menschenbild in Texten der Qumrangemeinde*, SUNT 15 (Göttingen: Vandenhoeck & Ruprecht, 1980), 174–75.

4. IDEOLOGY AS A COHESIVE STRATEGY 143

he warns against the centralization of 1QS III, 13–IV, 26 as the ultimate guideline for the establishment of Qumran's ideology and instead advises that one devote research to the Qumran manuscripts' various images and ideas concerning anthropology and cosmology in their own right. As such, he finds significant differences in the forms of dualism expressed in 1QS, 1QM, and 1QH. Moreover, Lichtenberger finds "nebeneinander eines dualistischen (1QM, 1QS) und eines undualistischen (1QH) Welt- und Menschenverständnisses, wobei auch die dualistische Vorstellungen untereinander verschiedene Ausformungen aufweisen und auf verschiedene Art dem theologischen Denken integriert sind und die anthropologischen Vorstellungen bestimmen."[13] Lichtenberger concludes that many of the Qumran manuscripts that reflect a dualistic outlook seemingly seek to overcome the discrepancy between the traditional belief in an omnipotent creator, on the one hand, and the dualistic worldview in which humanity is divided into two antagonistic groups of "righteous" and "wicked" ones, on the other hand. The various subtypes of dualism and their relations to one another are, according to Lichtenberger, reflections of how the Qumran authors attempted to solve this fundamental problem.

4.1.2. A Growing Variety of Types of Qumran Dualism

The diversity in dualism(s) to which Lichtenberger refers has not gone unnoticed in Qumran scholarship. Apart from attempts to uncover a chronological development or multiple textual layers in dualistic texts, many attempts have also been made simply to categorize and to classify the dualisms phenomenologically. Accordingly, James C. Charlesworth distinguishes seven Qumran-specific types of dualism: (1) psychological (two oppositional inclinations within man), (2) physical (matter/spirit), (3) metaphysical (God/Belial), (4) cosmic (two opposing celestial beings or a distinct division of the universe into two divisions), (5) ethical (division based upon virtues/vices), (6) eschatological (present-day versus future creation), and (7) soteriological (division of humanity according to faith or disbelief).[14] John Gammie adds two more to the list: (8) spatial

---

13. Ibid., 196.
14. James C. Charlesworth, "A Critical Comparison of the Dualism in 1QS 3:13–4:26 and the 'Dualism' contained in the Gospel of John," in *John and Qumran*, ed. James C. Charlesworth (London: Chapman, 1972), 76.

(heaven/earth or mundane/supramundane) and (9) theological (God/human or creator/creation) dualism.[15]

However, the question of dualism in Qumran has been most thoroughly addressed by Jörg Frey, who discusses and defines his variety of ten dimensions of dualism in light of Qumran:[16]

(1) Metaphysical dualism: The opposition of two dominating causal powers of equal rank as for instance in Zoroastrianism. Frey holds that in Judaism no such dualism exists.

(2) Cosmic dualism: According to Frey, this is Judaism's form of metaphysical dualism, which "denotes the division of the world (κόσμος) and of humanity into two opposing forces of good and evil, light and darkness."[17] This form of dualism Frey holds to be an umbrella for a variety of dualistic worldviews, expressed in varying language, terminology, and style.

(3) Spatial dualism: This form of dualism reflects the world being divided into two spatially divided parts such as heaven and earth. Frey stresses that the opposition of these realms does not necessarily always convey dualism; for example, in the biblical tradition the mentioning of these spatially divided realms might signify creation as a whole.

(4) Eschatological dualism: The rigid division of the world into two temporarily divided parts, for instance, this world and the next. However, Frey correctly denotes that the presence of eschatological expectations, a last judgment, a final annihilation of evil, or the perception of an eschatological war do not necessarily reflect dualism. Moreover, he states: "We should restrict our use of the term 'eschatological dualism' to the idea of two opposed עולמים or αἰῶνες."[18]

---

15. John Gammie, "Spatial and Ethical Dualism in Jewish Wisdom and Apocalyptic Literature," *JBL* 93 (1974): 356–59.

16. Frey, "Different Patterns," 283–85.

17. Frey states that in contrast to the earlier mentioned metaphysical dualism, these oppositional forces are neither causal nor coeternal, and thus this form of dualism cannot be seen as strictly dualistic.

18. Ibid., 284; as we will see in §4.3.1, this definition does not correspond with Udo Bianchi's definition of eschatological dualism, for whom the defining criterion is the final overcoming of one causal principle "at the end," not the division into two worlds.

(5) Ethical dualism: "The bifurcation of mankind into two mutually exclusive groups according to virtues and vices," which is often expressed in ethical terms such as good and evil, righteous and wicked.[19]
(6) Soteriological dualism: "The division of mankind caused by faith (acceptance) or disbelief (rejection) in a saviour" or by the participation or not in a certain salvific act.[20] Faith is the dividing principle, and the division between believers and nonbelievers equally causes the division between saved and lost.
(7) Theological dualism: Frey recognizes that others (i.e., Charlesworth, Gammie) have identified this type of dualism as the division between God and humanity or the creator and his creation, but since this division is "fundamentally present in biblical thought"[21] and does not deal with two causal principles, he wishes to avoid labeling this type of opposition dualistic.
(8) Physical dualism: The absolute division between matter and spirit.
(9) Anthropological dualism: The opposition between body and soul as distinct principles of being. Frey therefore relates this form of dualism to the former physical dualism.
(10) Psychological dualism: The internalized contrast between good and evil, which can be evaluated as the opposition between two principles or impulses waging battle within the human being, such as the good and bad *yetser* (inclination).

Even though Frey summarizes many of these earlier established dualistic categories, he is predominantly interested in uncovering the "different patterns in dualistic thought" in the Qumran manuscripts.[22] His seminal article on these "different patterns of dualism" has functioned as the background and starting point for many further investigations into Qumran dualism.[23] Because of its crucial influence on these later investigations into

---

19. Ibid., 284 n. 40.
20. Ibid., 284.
21. Ibid.
22. Ibid., 283–84.
23. Cf. the various essays mentioning Frey's work in *Dualism in Qumran*, ed. Géza G. Xeravits, LSTS 76 (London: T&T Clark, 2010).

the subject of Qumran dualism, Frey's main theses will be discussed at length below.[24]

4.1.3. A Synthesis: Frey's Systematic Analysis of Qumran Dualism

Next to evaluating the Qumran texts with regard to each of these ten types of dualism, Frey wishes to research them also in light of their possible combinations in order to "develop a more precise view of the differences and developments within the Qumran literature."[25] According to Frey, early research on Qumran dualism was primarily preoccupied with either the socioreligious origin of the dualistic phenomenon—possibly Persian/Zoroastrian—or how Qumran dualism related to the New Testament. Therefore, research into other aspects of Qumran dualism, such as its history and development, (conceptual) interrelatedness, similarities, and dissimilarities has been marginal. Hence, upon the final publication of the Cave 4 manuscripts, Frey recognizes the need for a renewed discussion on Qumran dualism based upon the following three observations.[26] (1) Dualistic thought and terminology can be detected in only a limited number of Qumran manuscripts. (2) The texts that scholars have evaluated to be dualistic demonstrate considerable differences in outlook and terminology. Moreover, the terminology is often not unique to Qumran, nor does it necessarily always need to be dualistic in its meaning, such as, for instance, the occurrence of "light" and "darkness." (3) Since scholarship has moved away from the view that all nonbiblical manuscripts from Qumran are sectarian and the origin of many important documents containing dualistic features (e.g., 1QM and the Aramaic corpus) is debatable, not all Qumran manuscripts containing dualistic thought can "actually be considered as a witness to the thought of the Qumran-people."[27]

In his evaluation, Frey is critical of both von der Osten-Sacken and Duhaime's approaches as he argues that "obviously the failure of the two theories lies in their presupposition of an entirely unilinear development of dualism in the Qumran documents."[28] Therefore, he proposes

---

24. This chapter will deal with Frey's theoretical framework, while in chap. 5 one of his "patterns of dualism" will be evaluated in detail.
25. Frey, "Different Patterns," 285.
26. Ibid., 277–80.
27. Ibid., 280.
28. Ibid., 288.

a more complex, nonlinear development and sets out to distinguish "different patterns of dualistic terminology and thought at the beginning of the Essene movement which subsequently conflate in the thought of the community and undergo further development."[29] His analysis of Qumran dualism recognizes at least two dimensions: "a sapiential type of multidimensional, ethically oriented cosmic dualism" (e.g., 1QS III, 13–IV, 14) and a "priestly type of sheer cosmic dualism dominated by the opposition of two angelic powers" (as in 1QM).[30] Moreover, to this second type of cosmic dualism as recognized in the War Scroll (1QM), an "originally pre-Essenic" nonpriestly strand of elaborated demonology is added. This third strand is thought to be observable in 1 Enoch's Book of the Watchers and the equally pre-Qumranic 11QApPs[a] (11Q11). Frey does not consider the two main strands of dualism (or the communities behind them) to be strictly separated. However, he holds that, even if interrelations between them might be detected, the two "different patterns of dualistic thought are clearly visible, especially in the pre-Essene texts."[31] Frey's hypothesis holds that "in the texts originating in the community, they [i.e., the two types of dualism] blend together, but traces of the formerly independent types are nevertheless discernible. So there is not one uniform type of Essene dualism, nor a unilinear development of thought, but a complicated web of different threads of dualistic thought," possibly originating "in the different precursor groups of the Essene movement" and "adopted in the texts of the community, mixed and modified according to the development and experiences of its sectarian existence."[32]

He tests this thesis first on the locus classicus of Qumran dualism, the Treatise of the Two Spirits (1QS III, 13–IV 26), which Frey considers to be the most impressive example of the multidimensional type of dualism originating from sapiential literature. Second, he tests it on the War Scroll (1QM and 4QM[a–g] [4Q491–497]), which he holds to be the most prominent example of cosmic dualism of which the earliest manifestations are not yet *yahadic*. Third, in light of his view that these documents not only demonstrate the prestage for the intermingling of dualistic ideas at

---

29. Ibid., 288–89.
30. Ibid., 287–88.
31. Ibid., 288; it is not entirely clear to which texts Frey specifically refers. On the confusing use of "Essene" and "sectarian" in, respectively, German and Anglo-Saxon scholarship, see Hempel, "Kriterien zur Bestimmung," 71–85.
32. Frey, "Different Patterns," 288.

Qumran but also reflect the subsequent patterns of development towards a particular Qumranite dualistic thinking, Frey attempts to rediscover those staged patterns with the help of other Qumran manuscripts, which he considers to contain dualistic thought. Frey's list of dualisms in Qumran (according to "different patterns") includes the following:[33]

- Parts of 1QS, mainly III, 13–IV, 26, but also I, 1–II, 18 and XI, 2b–22
- Parts of CD, chiefly II, 2–13 and IV, 12–VI, 11
- The War Scroll, not as a whole, but chiefly 1QM I, XIII, and XV–IXX
- A few passages of the Hodayot, perhaps 1QH^a XI, 20–37; XII, 6–13; VI; and VII
- A few passages of the Pesharim: 1QpHab IV, 17b–V, 12a and 4QpPs^a (4Q171) II, 1–IV, 18
- 4Q184, 4QInstruction (4Q418), 4QMysteries (1Q27 I, 2–II, 10 with textual parallels in 4Q299 and 4Q300) and a small fragment from 4Q413
- The Aramaic Testaments ascribed to Levi, Qahat, and Amram
- A Pseudo-Moses text documented in 4Q390
- The apotropaic incantation poems of 11QApPs^a (11Q11) and the exorcistic Songs of the Maskil of 4Q510 and 4Q511
- The pesher on the periods (4Q180) and the related text 4Q181
- The Melchizedek text from Cave 11 (11Q13)
- The so-called Midrash on Eschatology (4Q174 and 4Q177)
- Some of the blessings and curses from 4Q280, 4Q286, and 4Q287
- The physiognomic text 4Q186 with an Aramaic parallel in 4Q561
- Some passages in which Belial or another angelic figure appears; 4QMMT^e (4Q398) 14–17, II, 5; 11QT^a LV, 3; 4QpsEzek^b (4Q386 1, II, 3); 4QTestimonia (4Q175 23); 4QpGen^b (4Q253 3, 2)

The next three sections will address the patterns that Frey suggests have eventually formed the entirety of Qumran dualism (§4.1.3.1–3).

---

33. Ibid., 277–78.

4.1.3.1. Frey's Analysis of the Dualisms in 1QS III, 13–IV, 26

Frey holds that the Treatise demonstrates multidimensional dualism, but that the document is basically cosmic, with a strong ethical dimension and distinctive psychological aspects.[34] His starting point is that the Treatise has to be evaluated as an independent document that was later inserted into 1QS. As such, he argues against scholars who believe that the Treatise is the zenith of Qumran theology. Rather, he holds the Treatise to be pre-*yahadic* and thus takes its dualistic ideas to represent "the beginning of dualistic thought of the community."[35] Frey finds that the three levels of dualism (cosmic, ethical, and psychological) are interlinked. Even though he argues that the Treatise is basically cosmic, he also concludes that "the teaching of ethics and anthropology presumably reflects the most urgent problems of the group addressed." He argues that the "teaching of anthropological issues is presented in the framework of cosmological and eschatological thought."[36] This fundamental focus on urgent problems threatening the author's community, such as the occurrence of sin or evil among the pious, and the experience of affliction might thus have instigated solutions and reassurances on a cosmic and eschatological level. Frey thinks the tradition-historical background of the Treatise can be found within late wisdom literature, where similar oppositional thinking between "the righteous" and "the wicked" occurs. Moreover, he finds evidence for the Treatise's possible background in the wisdom tradition in Ben Sira, where the structure of oppositional pairs is connected to the order of creation and given an ethical dimension (e.g., Sir 42:24; 33:9, 14–15). He states that 1QS III, 13–IV, 26 reflects a further development in line with Ben Sira's teachings on the predestined order of creation, which can, in a slightly altered form, also be found in the "pre-Essene" Qumran documents 4Q417 (4QInstruction^c) and 1Q27 (1QMysteries).[37] Thus, Frey detects a development that originates from wisdom literature and its idea of a predestined order of being and history into a more cosmically expressed dual-

---

34. Ibid., 289.
35. The arguments for this evaluation will be discussed in ch. 5.
36. Frey, "Different Patterns," 291.
37. Frey's observation seems to be informed by Armin Lange's *Weisheit und Prädestination: Weisheitliche Urordnung und Prädestination in den Textfunden von Qumran*, STDJ 18 (Leiden: Brill, 1995), esp. 128–35, whose findings regarding the Treatise will be discussed in the next chapter.

ism in which metaphors like darkness and light and angelic beings make their entrance. Frey thinks that in the *yahadic* reception of the Treatise, the essentially ethical-oppositional line of thought not only serves to explain the occurrence of sin and evil in the community but that its cosmic dimension also reflects the group's fundamental interest in the concept of eternal election. Frey's analysis of some "other sectarian texts that cite or allude to the instruction on the two spirits" (1QH^a VI, 11–12; 4Q181 1, II, 5; CD II, 6–7; 4Q280 2, 4–5) finds that they lack the idea of two spirits and the concept of an internal struggle in the heart of man.[38] Therefore, Frey thinks that the multidimensional ideas in the (earlier) Treatise are modified and simplified in the later sectarian texts. Hence, Frey concludes that the Qumran community was probably less interested in the Treatise's dualistic terminology and the idea of two spirits than in a cosmic reassurance of eternal election.

4.1.3.2. Frey's Analysis of the Cosmic Dualism of the War Scroll

The second type of dualism from which Frey believes a pattern can be deduced is what he considers to be the "purely cosmic" dualism of the War Scroll (1QM). Recognizing two main layers in the 1QM/4QM manuscripts, Frey argues that the oldest layer is strongly nationalistic but has not yet any sectarian features and notably centralizes the leadership of the priests and ritual purity in eschatological wars.[39] 1QM I is the document's most dualistic part and still contains a pan-Israelite, nonsectarian outlook, as it not only describes the author's Jewish adversaries as "violators of the covenant," but also focuses on Israel's classical gentile enemies (1QM I, 2). Frey holds the War Scroll originally to be "a non-sectarian priestly rule of eschatological warfare."[40] He argues that the war dualism in the War Scroll needs to be distinguished from the sapiential type of dualism as expressed in the Treatise, even though it has common elements, such as the self-designation "sons of light," the idea of a struggle between two opposed spiritual beings (and their respective groups), characterized by light/darkness terminology, the expectation of the final extinction of evil, and the

---

38. Frey, "Different Patterns," 302.
39. Cf. Philip Davies, "Dualism in the Qumran War Texts," in Xeravits, *Dualism in Qumran*, 8–19.
40. Frey, "Different Patterns," 316.

occurrence of "angels of destruction."[41] He finds the following differences in the usage of terms and the pattern of dualistic thought:[42]

(1) The mutual relation between the opposed forces and their description is significantly different: in 1QM, the opposing forces are of equal strength, and the war is not easily won, while the Treatise is not mainly concerned with the struggle proper but is rather occupied with the explanation of the occurrence of sin and evil, while maintaining the conviction of a predestined, preordained order of creation.

(2) The concept of the angels of destruction is worked out very differently in each text: in the Treatise, the angels serve God voluntarily in executing punishment, while in 1QM they share Belial's devious plans.

(3) Belial is very prominent in 1QM but absent in the Treatise and in any of the other sapiential texts Frey connected to it.[43]

(4) The overall pattern of dualistic thought is different: 1QM's cosmic dualism lacks the multidimensionality of 1QS III, 13–IV, 26. Moreover, 1QM lacks ethical dualism, as a notion of virtues and vices, sin and justice is completely absent. Also, no psychological dimension can be detected.

(5) The eschatological extinction of evil is viewed as a complete annihilation of Belial and his lot, not as an act of purification as in 1QS.

Tradition-historically, Frey thinks 1QM has links to the book of Daniel, with which it shares the idea of holy war, the representation of human armies by heavenly leaders, the notion of Michael as a heavenly warrior, and the terminology of "violators of the covenant."[44] Moreover, Frey suggests that the basic structure of 1QM is possibly influenced by the Zoroastrian myth of Ahura Mazda and Ahriman, which might explain its thoroughly dualistic outlook. Finally, Frey thinks that this cosmic type of dualism springs from "pre-Essene" priestly circles, as he traces back the idea of opposed heavenly beings to Aramaic texts found at Qumran,

---

41. Ibid., 311.
42. Ibid., 311–12.
43. Hence, it is important for Frey to distinguish the Treatise from other parts of 1QS, which refer to Belial.
44. Frey, "Different Patterns," 313.

which may originate as early as the third century BCE (e.g., 4QTestament of Levi, 4QTestament of Qahat, 4QVisions of Amram). Particularly, 4QAmram^b (4Q544), dating to the first half of the second century BCE, describes Amram's vision of two angelic beings who belong to the Watchers and who hold a contest over him. Amram learns that these beings claim to rule over the world and every human being. Their rule is described in terms of light and darkness.

Hence, Frey describes the War Scroll's dualism as "a strongly expressed cosmic dualism with the notion of opposed heavenly powers and the strict division of humanity into two opposed groups dominated by their respective leaders and facing opposite eschatological fates."[45] He distinguishes this strand of dualism from the Treatise's dualistic thought, because it lacks ethical classifications and because its light/darkness—or truth/lie—terminologies are quite unspecified.

4.1.3.3. A Second Strand of Cosmic Dualism: Demonology in 11QApPs^a (11Q11), Jubilees, and 4Q390

Frey recognizes a second strand in the developmental pattern of cosmic dualism in Qumran, that is, an originally pre-Essenic strand which develops a rather elaborate demonology (and corresponding angelology). Especially the "apotropaic songs of 11QApPs^a" (11Q11 V, 3–14) are mentioned, since they reflect an elaborate demonology, seemingly dependent upon the Book of Watchers and a thoroughly dualistic outlook with angel/demon terminology. These occurrences reflect (1) Belial and his host of evil spirits and demons against God and a powerful angel, (2) evil spirits that cause illness versus Raphael who heals them, (3) Satan as the accuser at the time of judgment versus the angel who supports the just, and finally (4) God who judges the demons and incarcerates Belial.[46] However, Frey notes that the text lacks a priestly outlook.

Frey recognizes a further development of demonology in the "pre-Essene priestly thought" in Jubilees, which—even though its dualistic outlook is disputable—reflects a division within the angelic world and a corresponding division within humanity (between Israel and the gentiles). Moreover, the book of Jubilees contains terminology that reflects a con-

---

45. Ibid., 321.
46. Ibid., 323.

nection to later dualistic thought, such as (the spirit of) Belial and (the spirit of) Mastema. Hence, Frey concludes that "even if there is no mention of an eschatological war (as in 1QM) or of directly opposed heavenly leaders (as in 4QAmram), the book [Jubilees] attests to the basic elements of a growing cosmic dualism and the reception of an elaborate demonology (depending on the Book of Watchers and related to 11QApPs^a) within the context of pre-Essene priestly thought."[47] Finally 4Q390, which Frey believes is dependent on Jubilees, uses the term "angels of Mastemot," angelic beings that apparently mislead the Israelites and make them violate the covenant. Dimant, who has worked extensively on this text, considers it to have originated out of a priestly parent group of the Qumran community, which "did not yet have the peculiar community-ideology, or the specific ideas about dualism."[48] Frey takes 4Q390 as a document that reflects an early stage in the development of Qumranite ideas regarding dualism and demonology.

Moreover, Frey finds evidence for such a development in "sectarian" texts such as 4Q280 2, 2; 1QS II, 4–25; 4Q286 7, II, 1–13; 4Q510 1, 4–6; 11Q13; and 4Q174/4Q177's Midrash on Eschatology, which, according to Frey, not only reflect the reception of certain names and other related terminology, but also the reinforcement of strict cosmic dualism.

These three sections (§§4.1.3.1–3) together are intended to reflect Frey's idea of the development of dualism at Qumran. The next section addresses his conclusions, which attempt to lay bare the detectable patterns in the various texts we have discussed above.

4.1.3.4. Frey's Conclusions and Their Implicit Model of Development

As we have seen, Frey concludes from his analysis that Qumran dualism basically developed out of two major strands of dualistic thinking, which can be observed within the Qumran manuscripts, "a sapiential type of multi-dimensional, ethically oriented cosmic dualism," which is mainly represented by the Treatise of the Two Spirits, and a "priestly type of sheer cosmic dualism dominated by the opposition of two angelic

---

47. Ibid., 325.
48. See ibid., 326; Devorah Dimant, "New Light on Jewish Pseudepigrapha— 4Q390," in *The Madrid Qumran Congress: Proceedings of the International Congress on the Dead Sea Scrolls, Madrid, 18–21 March, 1991*, ed. Julio Trebolle Barrera and Luis Vegas Montaner, STDJ 11 (Leiden: Brill, 1992), 405–48.

powers,"[49] whose main representative is the War Scroll. Moreover, to the cosmic dualism of the War Scroll, an elaborated demonology is added, as can already be observed in 1 Enoch's Book of the Watchers and the equally pre-Qumranic 11QApPs[a]. These strands influenced one another, mixed and mingled, and developed further within the *yahad*, where they became an intrinsic and recognizable part of the Qumranites' ideology. Importantly, Frey characterizes the Qumranic reception of these strands of dualistic tradition as "the radicalization process of the *yahad*." During this process, the *yahad* supposedly adopted the sheer cosmic dualism of 1QM without any specific ethical precepts, while at the same time it modified and simplified the complex dualistic outlook of the Treatise without the notion of two spirits or an internal struggle in man's heart. Hence, while the strand of cosmic dualism is strengthened, the *yahadic* reception of the sapiential strand of dualism reflects a development from complex to simple, from multilayered dualism to radical good/evil categories in which a clear sociological conceptualization of insiders and outsiders can be observed.

Before returning to Frey's evaluation of Qumran dualism in §4.5, we need to address the milieu in which the concept of dualism arose. The next section deals with dualism as part of larger socioreligious conceptualizations.

4.2. Dualism as an Aspect of Larger Socioreligious Phenomena

The term *dualism* is traditionally used to describe the phenomenon of fundamental oppositions in ancient Persian Zoroastrianism, which perceives existence and history "to be a struggle between the forces of good and evil, between the powers of light and darkness."[50] Hence, the study of dualism as a concept in the religious development of Judaism predominantly consisted of heated scholarly debates about whether or not, and to what extent, Jewish thought was influenced by Zoroastrianism.[51] For the purpose of this chapter however, not the search for the origins and (pre-)history of

---

49. Frey, "Different Patterns," 287–88.

50. Eric M. Meyers, "From Myth to Apocalyptic: Dualism in the Hebrew Bible," in *Light against Darkness: Dualism in Ancient Mediterranean Religion and the Contemporary World*, ed. Armin Lange et al., JAJSup 2 (Göttingen: Vandenhoeck & Ruprecht, 2011), 92–106.

51. This discussion falls outside of the scope of this chapter and is rather avoided,

dualism is of interest in itself, but rather the implications of this search, that is, how the concept of Jewish dualism is perceived to be part of or tied to other—related—concepts and ideas, and as such functions within a web of relations, which influences and determines not only the boundaries of its semantic field but also scholarly evaluations of its social background and milieu. In other words, is the perceived dualism at Qumran indeed a core characteristic of the Qumran sect, the development of which can be traced in the manner suggested by Frey, or does dualism function as an aspect of larger socioreligious phenomena[52] and as such cover a much broader Jewish spectrum than just the Qumran situation?

4.2.1. A Conglomerate of Influences?

Many scholars have argued that the development of Jewish dualism most probably needs to be seen against the background of a multitude of internal and external sociohistorical, religious, and political influences and events. For instance, Eric M. Meyers argues that the beginnings of Jewish dualism ought not to be ascribed to influences from either the Persian tradition or more exclusively from within the Jewish tradition, but rather in a combination of various sources. He argues that, already in the Hebrew Bible, dualism's early development can be detected within "early modes of Israelite thinking."[53] Meyers calls these early influencing factors "incipient dualism," early myths in biblical literature in which God finds worthy foes.[54] Meyers argues that the development of Jewish dualism can be retraced through specific elements in the creation myth of Gen 1; the influence of the Canaanite myth on biblical literature; a transformation of prophecy (Isa 24–27, Ezekiel, Zechariah); ideas about good, evil, sin, and suffering in wisdom literature (e.g., Qoh 3:1–8, Ps 44); and apocalyptic literature (1 Enoch and Daniel), which brings in Zoroastrian elements (Avesta) such as light/darkness terminology and the presence of angels,

---

as it often seems to reflect political and ideological elements, especially of those scholars who wish to keep Judaism devoid of foreign influences.

52. This seems to be suggested by Jacob Licht, "An Analysis of the Treatise on the Two Spirits in DSD," in *Aspects of the Dead Sea Scrolls*, ed. Chaim Rabin and Yigael Yadin, ScrHier 4 (Jerusalem: Magnes, 1958), 88–100.

53. Meyers, "From Myth to Apocalyptic," 93.

54. Ibid., 92, 95–99, 105–6.

demons, and other forces that challenge God's order of creation.[55] Schematically, Meyers's proposal can be sketched as follows:

Figure 6. Overview of Meyers's Assessment of Influences on Jewish Dualism.

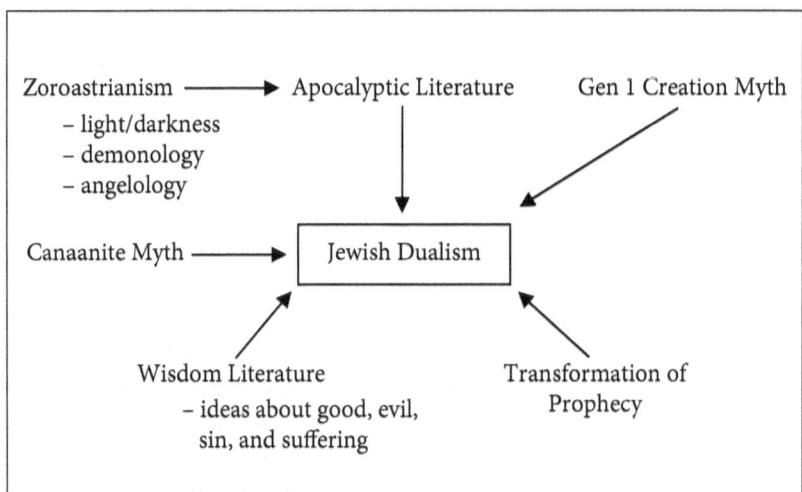

According to Meyers, all these elements had the chance to develop in a socioreligious milieu that was characterized by oppression, trauma, and human tragedy. Against this background, dualism might be seen as a characteristic aspect of larger contemporary phenomena that developed as a result of sociohistorical circumstances.

4.2.2. The Power of the Semantic Web: Apocalypticism, Dualism, and Determinism

The retracing of the complex development of dualism as a concept seems rather closely associated with the development and rise of apocalypticism. Just as in the case of the concept of dualism, the study of apocalyptic literature and the phenomenon of apocalypticism are characterized by heated debates regarding its origins: early scholarly opinions have viewed apocalypticism as a development of prophecy or of wisdom, as a mixture

---

55. Meyers (ibid., 99–103) thinks that already Deutero- and Trito-Isaiah (Isa 40–55 and 55–66) demonstrate Persian influences, especially in introducing the ideas of messianism and eschatology.

of (Canaanite) Near Eastern mythology and prophecy, or as derived from Persian dualism. Collins has pointed out that, even though the question of sources is important, most apocalypses seem to draw from a diversified and wide-ranging set of sources. Moreover, he attacks the idea of apocalypticism as a derivative phenomenon as "theological prejudice," since such evaluations are often made to undermine its inherent value and authenticity as a phenomenon in Judaism.[56] Furthermore, he distinguishes between "the apocalypse as a literary genre, the phenomenon of apocalypticism as a social ideology and apocalyptic eschatology as a set of ideas and motifs that may also be found in other literary genres and social settings."[57] Thus, the term *apocalypse* does not need to reflect a sociological entity, but rather gives information about and sets criteria with regard to literary style, language, terminology, and narrative form and content. Of major importance is the revelatory character of the apocalypse, either through visions or otherworldly journeys that are interpreted or guided by an angelic figure and often "supplemented by discourse or dialogue and occasionally a heavenly book."[58] Other characteristics of the apocalypse are a final judgment, the destruction of the wicked, and some form of retribution beyond death, in other words, some form of eschatology. Literary aspects of the genre are authorial pseudonimity, more or less elaborate exhortations and admonitions, and allusive language adding to the mystery. Generally, one can distinguish between historical apocalypses, which contain visions, and otherworldly journeys and which seem to engage in "cosmological speculation."[59] Collins stresses that the genre apocalypse reflects a specific worldview as "it provides a framework for viewing the problems of life."[60]

Therefore, apocalypticism as a sociological phenomenon may go beyond the literary criteria of the apocalypse, since apocalyptic ideas about cosmology and anthropology are also found outside the strict literary genre of the apocalypse.[61] In fact, Collins points out that in the case

---

56. John J. Collins, *The Apocalyptic Imagination: An Introduction to Jewish Apocalyptic Literature*, 2nd ed. (Grand Rapids: Eerdmans, 1998), 20.
57. Ibid., 2.
58. Ibid., 5.
59. John J. Collins, "Introduction: Towards the Morphology of a Genre," *Semeia* 14 (1979): 1–20.
60. Collins, *Apocalyptic Imagination*, 8.
61. For instance in oracles and testaments; see ibid., 9.

of Qumran, only a small number of texts can be labeled apocalypse, even though scholars generally agree that the Qumran sectarian writings demonstrate an underlying apocalyptic worldview in which the opposition between good and evil is worked out in a wider dualistic scheme.[62] Hence, "a movement might reasonably be called apocalyptic if it shared the conceptual framework of the genre [apocalypse], endorsing a worldview in which supernatural revelation, the heavenly world, and eschatological judgment played essential parts."[63] Moreover, even though this definition sets the basic conceptual structure, the social reality might be that social groups with an apocalyptic worldview may differ quite considerably, just like the exponents of the literary genre do. As its literary and social matrix is complex, Collins has attempted to trace the various signifiers of apocalypticism back to their sources. In part, he is able to make a convincing case in tracing various culturally specific elements that, under the influence of the contemporary sociopolitical reality, merge into the apocalyptic imagination. However, it remains difficult to distinctly separate or clearly distinguish between the various influences and backgrounds that gave rise to the ideas, which we now recognize as characteristics of apocalypticism. In his attempt to do so, Collins recognizes the following strands of development that make up what he calls "the matrix of apocalypticism" (which in the table below I have organized schematically, with "Ideas" on the left and "Texts and Social Setting" on the right):

Table 4: Overview of Collins's Assessment of Influences on the Development of Apocalypticism	
Ideas	Texts and Social Setting
Traditional (Ugaritic-Canaanite) Mythology	
<ul><li>various Near Eastern mythological imagery</li><li>Canaanite myth: Baal versus Mot (Death)</li></ul>	

---

62. Collins, *Apocalypticism in the Dead Sea Scrolls*, 30–51, 150–53; *Apocalyptic Imagination*, 153–55; García Martínez, *Qumranica Minora I*, 195. Of course, such an evaluation depends upon the presupposition that the Qumran texts are to be taken as the coherent library of a sectarian movement and, as such, reflect a sociological entity and its comprehensive ideology.

63. Collins, *Apocalyptic Imagination*, 13.

Wisdom Literature

- idea of "inclination"
- good and evil expressed in "paths"
- double-heartedness
- early tones of determinism; "the order of God's creation"

- Sir 11:16; 15:11, 14; 16:16; 33:11–15; 42:24–25
- Qoh 3:1–8
- Ps 44:24–25
- Prov 1–9

Postexilic Prophecy

- a new creation, new heavens, and a new earth
- biblical antecedents to, and use of, mythological language:
   "death swallowed up"
   "punish Leviathan"
   "slay the dragon that is in the sea"
- metaphorical use of "destruction of death" and "resurrection of the dead" in Isa 25–26
- increasing use of cosmic imagery to express the hope for social change

- Haggai: Presentation of the hierocratic party
- Zechariah: Visions interpreted by an angel
- Ezek 40–48
- Isa 24–27; 56–66

But lacking:
- interest in the heavenly world
- eschatology is not presented as "other-worldly," but rather distinctly "this-worldly"

Babylonian Influences

Similarities to divination:
- interpretation of mysterious signs and symbols
- overtones of determinism

Akkadian prophetic influence:
- "predictions of the past"
- "the cryptic manner of presenting these predictions"

Akkadian dream visions:
- ascent of a visionary to the divine throne

But lacking:
- revelation in form of a heavenly tour
- indications of eschatology

- affinities with the "Mantic wisdom" of the Chaldeans
- "Enmeduranki," Babylonian guild of barus, diviners
- Marduk and Shulgi prophetic speeches
- Akkadian dream visions: "Vision of the Netherworld"
- similarities with divination techniques

Persian Influences	
• dualism of light and darkness • eschatological woes • wisdom of all-knowledge: divine revelation to an authoritative human being (Zoroaster) • sequence of the four kingdoms (cf. Daniel) • idea of the final renewal of the world • periodization of history • determinism • ongoing dualistic supernatural struggle between the forces of good and evil • in the end, good conquers evil, which will perish forever • idea of resurrection • destruction of the world by fire • ascent of the soul • possibly: visions of hell and heaven, attended by interpreting angels	• Avesta, Gathas, Stutkar Nask • Pahlavi literature: Zand-I Vohuman Yasn, Vohuman Yast, Bahman Yast • Oracle of Hystaspes • Bundahisn • a brief early account of Persian religion in Plutarch's *On Isis and Osiris*
Hellenistic Milieu	
• Influences from widespread Hellenistic ideas, which can be detected in two clusters of texts: (1) Otherwordly journeys, which deal with personal eschatology of life after death; (2) eschatological prophecy: "ex eventu prophecy" provides a base for politically based apocalyptic texts narrating a state of oppression followed by cosmic renewal and national restoration.	• Hellenistic culture inspired not only the easy "floating around" of ideas; it also set similar political and social circumstances in the cultures that developed the ideas that developed into apocalyticism as a social ideology.

Collins concludes that the rise of apocalypticism can best be explained by the "globalizing effect" of Hellenism, which "changed the political and social circumstances of the Near East" and an overarching "sense of a *Zeitgeist*, of a common atmosphere of ideas and attitudes" in which "similar circumstances produced similar effects in traditions that had considerable similarity to begin with."[64]

---

64. Ibid., 37.

For our purposes, the retracing of sources is of particular interest as it demonstrates sociocultural clusters of themes, ideological concepts, and ideas, which give content to the semantic field in which the concept of dualism functions. In fact, it provides us with the hypothesis that certain concepts and ideas might inherently contain the roots for the formation of a seemingly dualistic worldview but are in themselves not dualistic in nature. These ideas and themes, which provoke division, are predominantly preoccupied with the origin and experience of evil, the reality of oppression, and the hope for relief and salvation from this oppression. Therefore, dualism as a concept might prove to be an ancillary factor to the essential preoccupation of apocalypticism to find an eschatological solution to evil, rather than functioning as a concept or ideology in itself. Moreover, closely related concepts such as determinism and eschatological expectations of the "end" in which evil and the wicked will perish are not necessarily dualistic, even though they might provoke oppositional imagery.

If this hypothesis has merit and dualism—or at least the tendency to view the world in oppositional forces—might be seen as the by-product of apocalypticism or of its related concepts, the independence of dualistic thinking as a characteristic ideology must be reevaluated. Moreover, then, the concept of dualism cannot be seen as simply or exclusively Qumranic, nor as a characteristic solely of the social groups associated with the Qumran sect. Rather, and in line with Collins's investigation, the umbrella term of apocalypticism, under which dualistic thinking often might shelter and in which many concepts related to dualism fall together, reflects trends and tendencies of socioreligious thought within a large, complex, geographically dispersed, but socioculturally connected web of relations built over an extended span of time.

4.2.3. Opposites Attract: Dualism as the Radicalized Wisdom of Appointed Time

A second and similar sort of argument can be made for the influence of wisdom literature on the development of Qumran dualism. Early research, such as von der Osten-Sacken's *Gott und Belial*, Duhaime's "Le dualisme de Qumrân," and, to a certain extent, Frey's synthesis of these theories into various "patterns of dualism," has placed a variety of building blocks of the Qumran sect's dualistic thinking within the biblical wisdom tradition.[65]

Frey mainly identifies Proverbs and Ben Sira as the tradition-historical background to the sapiential type of Qumran dualism (e.g., Prov 29:27; Sir 33:14–15; 39:16, 24–34; 42:22–25). He argues that these sapiential texts further develop the concept of God's created order and its organization, reflected in pairs of opposites. Furthermore, Frey thinks that within Qumran, the dualistic outlook of the originally non-*yahadic* Treatise is further developed within the early 4QInstruction (cf. 4Q417 2, I, 15–18) and 1QMysteries (1Q27) and is cited, recognized, and reworked in *yahadic* texts such as 1QH[a], 4Q181, CD, and 4Q280.[66]

For our purposes, it is of interest to investigate whether dualism can be seen as an ancillary aspect of developing concepts within the wisdom tradition. The most exhaustive study into the perceived sapiential background of Qumran dualism was undertaken by Lange, who argues that the sapiential idea of "eine präexistenten Seins- und Geschichtsordnung … wird in den Texten des *yahad* auf unterschiedliche Weise funktionalisiert und weiterentwickelt."[67] Lange's most important presupposition is that the "Qumran library" certainly reflects a heterogeneous, but at the same time complete and coherent collection of documents, which demonstrate literary dependencies among the nonbiblical texts. Moreover, he thinks that the "library" can, by the confined context of its location, shed an undisturbed light on a sociologically and culturally separable phenomenon (i.e., the Qumran sect), whose documents build upon, develop in light of, and are dependent upon one another.[68] Thus, the developmental model, so characteristic for the explanation of differences between documents or/and ideologies at Qumran, is firmly established within Lange's conceptualization: "Dabei werden nicht in jedem Text alle mit diesem Theologumenon [i.e., eine präexistenten Seins—und Geschichtsordnung]

---

65. Some scholars remain of the opinion that the origins of apocalypticism must be sought in the wisdom tradition. As such, the semantic fields of apocalypticism and wisdom text might demonstrate considerable overlap. My objective is not to solve the puzzle of origins, but rather to demonstrate that dualism as a concept does not function in total segregation from related ideological concepts.

66. Frey, "Different Patterns," 296–300; this theory will be evaluated in more detail in ch. 5.

67. Lange, *Weisheit und Prädestination*, 297.

68. Ibid., 305.

4. IDEOLOGY AS A COHESIVE STRATEGY 163

verbundenen Vorstellungen adaptiert. Es läßt sich vielmehr eine schrittweise Integration des Gedankengebäudes feststellen."[69] Hence, Lange suggests that a variety of imagery and concepts is attached to the umbrella concept of a preexistent divine order of creation and existence and that different individual Qumran texts might provoke and address a different combination of concepts and imagery. For instance, 1QH[a] uses wisdom imagery and terminology and reflects the concepts (related to the concept of God's preexistent order of creation) of (1) human humbleness in the face of God's omnipotence and (2) divine revelation as the only possibility for humans to gain knowledge of God's created order. In CD, which Lange thinks is directly influenced by the Treatise, the umbrella concept of a predestined order of creation provokes an ethical dualism, which develops cosmic overtones when the text discusses eschatological matters, such as the annihilation of evil at the end of time. Moreover, in CD Lange finds not only this dualistic framework of creation divided into righteous and wicked but also the related principles of predetermined election, periodization of time, the idea of secret knowledge and divine revelation, and the imagery of heavenly tablets. Thus, Lange retraces CD's roots within the wisdom tradition "an der weisheitlichen Form von CD II$_{2-13}$ (weisheitliche Lehrrede), dem Zitat eines Spruches in CD II$_{3f.}$ und der spruchartigen Struktur des ersten Teil dieses Textes (CD II$_{3-7}$)."[70] Finally, in 1QpHab, Lange sees the idea of a predestined order reflected in the eschatological expectations of the last days, the obvious periodization of time, and its recounting of history on heavenly tablets. He argues for a background in the wisdom tradition on the basis of the text's esteem for the רזי ערמתו ("the mysteries of his wisdom"; 1QpHab VII, 14) reflecting the "wunderbaren, dem Menschen verborgenen, Ordnung Gottes."[71]

Interestingly, many of Lange's recognized wisdom elements under the umbrella of *präexistente Seins- und Geschichtsordnung* can equally be recognized as indicators of apocalypticism. However, Lange argues that the Qumran sect cannot be defined as an apocalyptic movement, because its literature not only lacks the typical apocalyptic imageries of visions, heavenly journeys, and dreams but also their interpretation by an angelic figure. Furthermore, Lange argues that no documents of the genre apocalypse can be detected among the *yahadic* writings (cf. Collins). Hence,

---

69. Ibid., 297.
70. Ibid., 298.
71. Ibid., 299.

Lange places the development of dualism within the development from a biblical *Urordnung* into a cloaked preexistent order of creation, which was only penetrable through divine revelation.[72] In the preexistent order of creation, human deeds are fixed and run their course in history, according to the dualistic nature of existence. Even the occurrence of cosmic dualism (as for instance in the Treatise) is grounded, experienced, and realized in the ethical aspects of life, in humans as well as in history itself.[73]

Without subscribing to Lange's predestination theory of an airtight linear development of wisdom principles, which inherently carry the notion of a dualistic worldview, one can clearly observe certain concepts and ideas within the wisdom tradition, which might in some way relate to the ideas reflected in the Qumran manuscripts. Also, others have reflected on the similarities between known wisdom texts and the perceived dualistic thought at Qumran.

In his research on the interiorization of dualistic thought in the Treatise of the Two Spirits, Loren Stuckenbruck chooses to focus on similar language of oppositions in other texts, without presuming dualistic thought.[74] In Ben Sira, Stuckenbruck finds the categorical division of humanity, which sits in a framework that reflects the basic conviction that God created a cosmos consisting of "a principled opposition" between the "righteous" and the "sinners":

> All things are twofold, each over against one another; and he has not made anything lacking. (42:24)[75]

---

72. As such, Lange sees cosmic dualism, the idea of a preexistent order, and the necessity of divine revelation to gain knowledge of God's order as primary wisdom elements in the build-up towards apocalypticism. Interestingly, however, Lange not only ignores the significance of the presence of multiple manuscripts of 1 Enoch, Jubilees, and Daniel (and also the Aramaic corpus) among the Dead Sea Scrolls but also the occurrence of many apocalyptic elements within the very texts he studies, possibly because he defines them as subsidiary to his central concept of the preexistent order of creation as the primary driver in these texts; Frey, "Different Patterns," 303–6.

73. Lange, *Weisheit und Prädestination*, 169.

74. Loren T. Stuckenbruck, "The Interiorization of Dualism within the Human Being in Second Temple Judaism: *The Treatise of the Two Spirits* (1QS iii 13–iv 26) in Its Tradition-Historical Context," in Lange et al., *Light against Darkness*, 145–68.

75. Ibid., 148. Translation from Pancratius C. Beentjes, *The Book of Ben Sira: A Text Edition of All Extant Hebrew Manuscripts and a Synopsis of All Parallel Hebrew Ben Sira Texts*, VTSup 68 (Leiden: Brill, 1997).

Humanity is clearly part of God's order of creation, and as such human beings are intended to function according to their appointed ways (Sir 33:10–15):

> All human beings come from the ground, and humankind was created out of the dust. In the fullness of his knowledge the Lord distinguished them and appointed their different ways. Some he blessed and exalted, and some he made holy and brought near to himself; but some he cursed and brought low, and turned them out of their place. Like clay in the hand of the potter, to be moulded as he pleases, so all are in the hand of their Maker, to be given whatever he decides. Good is the opposite of evil, and life the opposite of death; so the sinner is the opposite of the godly. Look at all the works of the Most High; they come in pairs, one the opposite of the other.[76]

Interestingly, Ben Sira's conception of humanity's natural division is not as clear-cut as these words assume. Rather, the text demonstrates numerous tensions with regard to human agency and responsibility, free will, and ethical behavior. So, for example: "From the beginning He made man, and left him in the power of his freedom of choice" (Sir 15:14). Moreover, while the text allows for sinners to repent and be forgiven (Sir 21:6), the godly are capable of sin (Sir 23:2–3). The behavior of the sinners is described in moral categories: they ignore the torah, lack wisdom, and misuse wealth. In contrast, the godly seek forgiveness for their sins and the removal of evil from their lives. Interestingly, Ben Sira acknowledges the possibility of man walking "on two paths" (Sir 2:12) or being "double-hearted" (Sir 1:28), but both are seen as characteristic behavior of sinners. Ben Sira's wisdom is set in overtones of ethical behavior (some in the form of virtues and vices) and advice for daily life, which Stuckenbruck calls socioethical dualism. Moreover, he thinks that in Ben Sira conceptual tensions (derived from the notion that sinners can do good) eventually are harmonized by perceiving such good behavior to be hypocrisy. These fundamental sapiential ideas might have influenced the evaluation of ethical dualism in the Treatise in which humans and their behavior are viewed less dualistically. That is, in the Treatise, double-heartedness and "being in two paths" are no longer seen as uniquely characteristic of sinners, as in Ben Sira. Rather, "the Trea-

---

76. Translation from John G. Snaith, *Ecclecsiasticus, or The Wisdom of Jesus Son of Sirach*, CBC (Cambridge: Cambridge University Press, 1974).

tise ... has given way to a polarizing framework that explains inconsistent behaviour as an inevitability for human beings."[77] Moreover, in 4QInstruction, Stuckenbruck finds that good/evil are connected to the concept of the righteous/the wicked but without entertaining the possibility that the righteous only engage in good deeds, while the wicked only display bad deeds. This idea, along with the text's ethical advice to "be humble" and "not to overlook transgressions" comes close to Ben Sira's ideas of human ambiguity, conduct, and experience.[78] Thus, Stuckenbruck, who is careful not to label all oppositions dualistic, finds that the late wisdom literature demonstrates "a wide variety of approaches to antitheses" and, hence, might have been a source for the polarized conceptualizations of human behavior as reflected in some of the Qumran manuscripts.[79]

In his search for a sapiential source for the dualism in the Treatise (and 4QInstruction), Matthew Goff attacks the idea of a perceived development from certain oppositional concepts in the wisdom tradition to a full-blown dualism in the Qumran sectarian writings. Although he recognizes the explicit and rigid division between right and wrong in Proverbs, he argues that this basic polarity is frequently found in numerous other biblical and nonbiblical texts, and, therefore, it seems "gratuitous, if not impossible, to distinguish a purely ethical dualism rooted in the Wisdom tradition from the ... conception of the natural order."[80] He stresses that Proverbs encourages the reader to "perceive the natural and social order and act accordingly."[81] As such, Proverbs draws sharps distinctions between right/wrong, righteous/wicked, and wise/foolish, each ethically correlated with its corresponding results in daily human life. These ideas feed into a deterministic ideology closely related to man's understanding of the created order. However, Goff argues that presuming a direct influence of Proverbs (or even Ben Sira) on Qumran dualism in general and its "core document" 1QS III, 13–IV, 26 in particular is highly problematic, since moral dualism is in itself not distinctively or exclusively sapiential. Therefore, Goff investigates the deeper characteristics of sapiential texts in relation to dualistic thinking. In the case of Proverbs, he studies the

---

77. Stuckenbruck, "Interiorization," 165.
78. Ibid., 159.
79. Ibid., 168.
80. Matthew Goff, "Looking for Sapiential Dualism at Qumran," in Xeravits, *Dualism in Qumran*, 24.
81. Ibid., 25.

specific characteristics of dualism, such as the representation of Wisdom and Folly as female figures, a theme with which several Qumran manuscripts seem familiar (4Q184, 4Q185, 4Q525, and 11Q5 XVIII and XXI). As a result, Goff finds that "the dualistic opposition of personified wisdom and folly is not found in any text from the Dead Sea Scrolls."[82] Moreover, Goff argues that, even though, for instance, the Treatise uses language reminiscent of the sapiential tradition and 1QS IV, 23–24 narrates about the "spirits of truth and injustice feuding in man's heart as they walk in *wisdom* and in *folly*," the text lacks both the linguistic characteristic of Proverbs and "the practical advice regarding specific areas of ordinary life."[83] Finally, Goff regards the wisdom tradition (as well as apocalypticism) as a potential source of influence on the development of Qumran texts such as the Treatise, 4QInstruction (4Q415–418, 4Q423, 1Q26) and 4QMysteries (4Q299–301, 1Q27). This possible influence he regards predominantly to be reflected in connected themes/terminology and the presence of eschatological dualism that developed within the wisdom tradition from the second century BCE. However, he concludes that since these features are widespread in early Jewish literature and dualism is neither prominent in, nor characteristic of, the Qumran wisdom texts, the presumption of the sapiential tradition being an important source for Qumran dualism in general and for the Treatise of the Two Spirits in particular, is rather unwarranted for lack of evidence.

4.3. Dualism as a Concept in Religious Systems

From the preceding sections, the complexity with regard to the concept of dualism in Qumran seems rather clear. The cause of this complexity is partly methodological: The label dualistic language carries a variety of different meanings and appearances with regard to the Qumran texts, and not all recognized instances of dualism seem equally dualistic. This variety in outlook among individual texts and the eagerness among scholars to employ a seemingly univocal term like dualism have implicitly led to the identification of a seemingly inexhaustible number of different sorts of dualism. Thus, in order to meaningfully evaluate the question of dualism at Qumran, we need to revisit the definition of dualism as a concept in

---

82. Ibid., 29.
83. Ibid., 33, emphasis added.

religious systems. Subsequently, and in light of this definition, its meaning and usage at Qumran needs to be investigated in order to establish to what extent the concept of dualism is used within the boundaries of its definition and to what extent it is used as a synonym or substitute for related concepts and terminology, such as antagonism, opposition, polemics, alterity, exclusivism, the occurrence of insider/outsider strategies, and so on. Before turning to the evaluation of Qumran's types of dualism in §4.4, the remainder of this section (§4.3.1 and §4.3.2) will deal with matters of definition.

4.3.1 Dualism: A Flexible Concept? Or Not?

As we have seen above, within Qumran scholarship no less than ten types of dualism have been developed and discussed, not all of them exclusive to but some of them distinctive for the Qumran situation. The dualisms as defined by Gammie, Charlesworth, and Frey at times demonstrate overlap, inclusiveness, and partial fit, while some of them are not conceived to be problematic but rather programmatic for the nature of the Jewish religion in general and the Qumran situation in particular.[84] This sheer amount of types of dualism in Qumran scholarship has caused some confusion and at times creates the impression that for every occurrence of opposition a new dualism type is used. As such, the various types of dualism perceived in the Qumran manuscripts might have departed quite substantially from the initial meaning of the term *dualism*, as first used by Thomas Hyde in 1700 CE to describe the ancient Persian religion and later fine-tuned by Udo Bianchi, whose definition of and work on religious dualism set the stage for all research on this phenomenon.[85]

Bianchi observed that the term *dualism* was used interchangeably with related but differing concepts like duality, polarity, pairs, and oppositions. In order to prevent further dilution of the term and restricting himself to dualism understood as "a category within the history and phenomenology

---

84. See Jutta Leonhardt-Balzer, "Dualism," in *The Eerdmans Dictionary of Early Judaism*, ed. John J. Collins and Daniel C. Harlow (Grand Rapids: Eerdmans, 2010), 553–56.

85. Cited in Udo Bianchi, "Dualism," in *The Encyclopedia of Religion*, ed. Mircea Eliade (New York: MacMillan, 1987), 4:4506–12; or, in the new edition coauthored with Yuri Stoyanov, *Encylopedia of Religion*, ed. Mircea Eliade (New York: MacMillan, 2005), 4:2504–17.

of religion,"[86] Bianchi defines dualism as "the doctrine of the two principles"; that is, "dualistic are all those religions, systems, conceptions of life according to which two principles, coeternal or not, cause the existence, real or apparent, of that which exists or is manifest in the world."[87] Bianchi distinguishes between three pairs of dualism.

(1) Radical versus moderate dualism. In radical dualism, the two fundamental principles are thought to be coeternal and coequal, that is, both principles "exist and act from the very beginning" without hierarchy or final destiny. Moderate dualism recognizes only one primordial principle, while the second principle is a derivative from the first, coming into existence "under particular circumstances at a particular moment in time."[88] "The second principle is usually negative and caused by an incident on a metaphysical level, on the margins of the heavenly realm."[89] Importantly, a creator is responsible for the totality of existence.

(2) Dialectical versus eschatological dualism. The difference between dialectical and eschatological dualism is that in the former the two fundamental principles function eternally and often in recurrent cycles, while in the case of eschatological dualism one principle (the evil one) will be overcome at the end of history. Dialectical and eschatological dualism conceive the two principles as good and evil, "both in the ethical and metaphysical sense."[90] Bianchi stresses that, while dialectical dualism is always also radical dualism (both principles exist coeternally), not all radical dualism necessarily has to be dialectical.[91] For example, Zoroastrianism reflects a radical dualism, but the evil principle will be eliminated in the end, which reflects eschatological dualism.

(3) Procosmic versus anticosmic dualism. Procosmic dualism is recognized by a positive evaluation of the cosmos that welcomes creation and the visible world. Anticosmic dualism reflects the opposite: the cosmos

---

86. Udo Bianchi, *Selected Essays on Gnosticism, Dualism and Mysteriosophy*, SHR 38 (Leiden: Brill, 1978), 49–64.

87. My translation. "Sono dualistiche quelle concezioni che ammettono una dottrina dei due principia.... Sono dualistiche le religioni e le concezioni della vita secondo le quali due principii—concepiti o meno come coeterni—fondano l'esistenza, reale o 'apparente,' di cio che esiste e si manifesta nel mondo" (Bianchi, *Selected Essays*, 50; cf. Frey, "Different Patterns," 281).

88. Bianchi, *Selected Essays*, 50.

89. Ibid., 59.

90. Bianchi and Stoyanov, "Dualism," 4:2508.

91. Bianchi, *Selected Essays*, 60.

and creation are perceived to be intrinsically evil. Therefore, created matter, such as the earth or the human body, is thought to be essentially negative or delusive.[92]

Bianchi argues that rather than the first category (radical versus moderate dualism), the second is the most important, that is, the distinction between dialectical and eschatological dualism, since these types of dualism function on a metaphysical level and conceptualize a religion's cosmology and anthropology. The third category, procosmic and anticosmic dualism, comes second, as it plays a key role in how we conceptualize life and life experience.[93]

Moreover, Bianchi stresses the fact that

> Dualism is more specific than either simple duality or polarity. Not every duality or polarity is dualistic—only those that involve the duality or polarity of causal principles. Thus, not every pair of opposites (such as male and female, right and left, light and darkness, good and bad, spirit and matter, and sacred and profane) can be labeled as dualistic, even when their opposition is emphasized. They are dualistic *only when they are understood as principles or causes of the world and its constitutive elements*.[94]

Thus, according to Bianchi and Stoyanov, there is no dualism "where there is no account of the principles responsible for bringing the world and humans into existence."[95] In fact, they argue that "the simple contrasting of good and evil, life and death, light and darkness, and so on is in fact coextensive with religion itself and cannot be equated with the much more specific phenomenon of dualism."[96]

4.3.2 Sociological Strategies: Dualism as a Means of Social Stratification

In different research fields within the social sciences and humanities, predominantly in sociology, psychology, and anthropology, the term *dualism* is often used in a much broader sense, for the simple reason that outside

---

92. Bianchi and Stoyanov, "Dualism," 4:2509.
93. Bianchi, *Selected Essays*, 61–62.
94. Bianchi and Stoyanov, "Dualism," 4:2505, emphasis added.
95. Ibid.
96. Ibid.

the religiohistorical realm, dualistic thinking is described as less conceptual but more as a socioculturally based human strategy of social stratification. In short, in these disciplines language and praxis reflecting dualism, opposition, dichotomy, antagonism, alterity, and more are often simply seen as human strategies that help groups build their social identity and distinct self-definition.

The social anthropologist Rodney Needham, who investigated social classification and the functions of dual or oppositional language, argues that such language must be seen in light of the need for humans to classify and categorize their existence. He finds that the need for order, and additionally the need for clarity about rights and duties, drives people towards a system of categorization. Also, he argues that metaphysical speculation can urge people to divide the existing world into different spherical and spatial categories, thereby symbolically classifying seemingly different ontological principles into the same category. In an encompassing way in which the symbolic classification of ontological principles plays a major part, he identifies two major types of dualism that function to establish a system of classification.[97] According to Needham, one way of dualistic classification establishes two major categories under which everything is divided. His description of this first type of dualism, which often extrapolates into a cosmic or metaphysical level and defines existence into two mutually exclusive categories or principles, is much in line with Bianchi's strict definition of dualism. However, in Needham's other type of dualism, which is distinctively different from the former type, "classification is seen not in two great classes, whether metaphysical or social, but in the symbolic linking of categories by pairs. This does not mean that each individual category is in an absolute sense of either one type or another, i.e., what is right in relation to one category can be left in relation to another."[98] In this second form of dualism, in which categorization is flexible according to context, each pair consists of one category that in some respect is considered superior to the other. Needham concludes that this second type of dualism is the most common form of human categorization, which he calls "classification by partition," and which he believes inherently creates hierarchy and separation, even though the basis of its distinction is not absolute. Hence, viewed on a sociological or anthropological level, not all dualisms

---

97. Rodney Needham, *Symbolic Classification*, Goodyear Perspectives in Anthropology (Santa Monica: Goodyear, 1979), 7–9.
98. Ibid., 8.

are equally dualistic, and categorizations must be investigated carefully in order to establish which type of dualism they reflect and/or which function they serve. As such, anthropological or sociological research is interested in all categorizations of human life, whether language reflects dualism proper or merely paradoxes, tensions, or oppositions without being strictly dualistic. In other words, the different forms of dualistic or oppositional thinking are of interest in order to help analyze the strategies of self-identification of those who use it. As categorizations of difference and similarity are intrinsic to human life and oppositions and affinities are used all the time to establish identity and self-designation over against others, the mere occurrence of dual or oppositional concepts can, however sociologically interesting, not be seen as evidence for dualistic thinking.[99] As Petrus Fontaine has stated, "in cases of dualism, it is no longer possible to reduce the terms of the opposition more or less to each other; there are no longer intermediate terms. The opposition has become unsolvable."[100] Therefore, Needham's second type of dualism cannot be identified as dualism but merely as a categorization tool for sociological research into social stratifications and social processes of identification and alterity. What dualism has in common with other notions of oppositionality and duality is its inherent implications of disruption and division, which makes dualistic thought ideally suited as a characteristic of a radicalized sectarian group, thought to self-identify as the only righteous element in a world of evil. However, if one wants to determine whether a wide variety of written expressions have a specifically sectarian ideology of dualistic thinking in common or at least reflect a diachronic development towards such a recognizable dualistic ideology, dualism as a concept needs to be strictly defined and cannot be used in the sociological sense of a social stratification tool.

4.4. Revisiting Types of Dualism at Qumran

In the preceding sections, the boundaries and environment of dualism have been explored. In the search for coherence in the Qumran library, scholars have long identified a tendency towards dualistic thinking as part

---

99. Such sociological perceptions of the various strategies of self-designation and the problem of discrepancy between we/other language in texts and Otherness in social reality falls outside the scope of this chapter.

100. Petrus Fontaine, "What Is Dualism, and What Is It Not?" in Lange et al., *Light against Darkness*, 266–76.

4. IDEOLOGY AS A COHESIVE STRATEGY

of the theological ideology of the Qumran sect, which is believed to have gathered precursory material that fitted their contemporary ideology as well as documents that reflect their own ideas and beliefs. Thus, dualism at Qumran has long been seen as a core principle of the Qumran sect and as such—to an extent—holds an important subset of Qumran manuscripts meaningfully and coherently together. However, the sheer amount of dualisms that scholars have identified in these manuscripts seems somewhat bewildering and has taken us away from the original definition and meaning of the term as defined by Bianchi. Bianchi distinguishes between radical and moderate, dialectical and eschatological, and procosmic and anticosmic dualism. Dualism in the strictest sense, that is, radical dualism, according to which two causal principles function in opposition coeternally and coequally without hierarchy, does not occur in Judaism, as God is thought to be the omnipotent creator, who is responsible for the totality of existence. Several Qumran texts have clear statements to this effect, for example, 1QS III, 15: "From the God of knowledge stems all there is and all that shall exist"; or 1QS XI, 11, "By his knowledge everything comes into existence, and all that does exist he establishes with his calculations and nothing is done outside of him." In 1QM, certain passages seem to place God against Belial (e.g., 1QM I, 5; 1QM VIII, 1b–7), but in its context God's omnipotence becomes clear: he "aids the righteous" by appointing "the Prince of Light to assist" and apparently he "made Belial for the pit" (1QM XIII, 10b–12b). Hence, all possible instances of dualism in Judaism in general and Qumran in particular should be evaluated as moderate dualism.

Bianchi's second distinction of dualism, which he considers the most important one, is between dialectical and eschatological dualism. Even though some of the Qumran texts recall other instances in Israel's history in which evil and iniquity occurred, none of them perceive two causal principles in opposition in recurrent cycles for eternity. Rather, most of them, with the exception of texts that narrate a different theme like 4Q184, portray their contemporary time and age as a period of wickedness leading up to the end times, often envisioned as a final battle or an intervention of God, destroying all evil. Thus, the Qumran texts, in as far as we would evaluate them as dualistic, would reflect Bianchi's eschatological dualism.[101]

---

101. Importantly, Bianchi stresses that this level of dualism is the most important level as it functions on a metaphysical as well as an ethical level, thereby conceptualizing a religion's cosmology and anthropology.

Third, Bianchi distinguishes between procosmic and anticosmic dualism, which is thought to establish a religion's basic conceptualizations of life and life experience. It seems rather difficult to establish whether the Qumran texts convey a procosmic or anticosmic outlook. Obviously, most texts reflect a negative view of the contemporary era and are concerned with the level of perceived evil, wickedness, and iniquity in their socio-religious environment. However, many texts also marvel at the greatness and mercy of God, his mysteries, and the wonder of his creation, which is thought to be exactly as he intended but beyond human comprehension. Moreover, they reflect confidence in the future as they believe God will bring an end to all that is evil. In fact, many texts seem to struggle with this exact question of evil and hardship, a question that seems hardly related to the more fundamental question of whether creation is intrinsically good or intrinsically evil. Therefore, since God created the world, why would man doubt his provenance?

In sum, if dualism can be found among the Qumran texts, it has to be moderate, eschatological dualism. Importantly, Bianchi has stressed that not all forms of duality or opposition can be evaluated as dualistic, only those that involve the duality or polarity of causal principles. In other words, there is no dualism "where there is no account of the principles for bringing the world and humans into existence."[102] Hence, in order to evaluate dualism at Qumran, we now need to evaluate the ten types of dualism identified by Frey in light of Bianchi's understanding of dualism. As we have seen, Frey himself has already excluded two types of dualism (metaphysical and theological) from his list. Metaphysical dualism is excluded, because this strict type of dualism does not occur in Judaism, and theological dualism is excluded, because it does not deal with two causal principles and therefore cannot be evaluated as dualistic. This leaves eight types of dualism to evaluate: cosmic, spatial, eschatological, ethical, soteriological, physical, anthropological, and psychological dualism.

4.4.1. Cosmic Dualism

According to Frey, cosmic dualism "denotes the division of the world and of humanity into two opposing forces of good and evil, darkness and

---

102. Bianchi and Stoyanov, "Dualism," 4:2505.

light."[103] Frey states that "in contrast to metaphysical dualism, these forces are viewed as neither coeternal nor strictly causal," the latter of which would make this category an unsuitable candidate to be called dualistic.[104] However, Frey's description makes clear that his cosmic dualism category is rather an umbrella-category for all sorts of oppositional constructions from the "metaphorical use of light/darkness terminology" to the mentioning of "hosts of human or spiritual beings," while "in some texts we find heavenly leader figures such as Michael, Belial, the Prince of Light and the Angel of Darkness, and so on."[105] Frey seems to be aware of the fact that his cosmic dualism category contains a variety of rather different concepts and suggests that it "may allow for further distinction."[106] However, the assembly of rather different concepts under the one category of cosmic dualism not only obscures the category; it also might falsely establish a sense of coherence among texts that in their content and outlook are rather different. If we assume that Frey's cosmic dualism implicitly recognizes the one primordial principle of God (even though this is not mentioned in his definition), we might hold on to its category as long as and to the extent of cosmic dualism equaling Bianchi's moderate dualism. This way, the opposition between heavenly leaders and hosts of spiritual beings (possibly reflected by their human counterparts) can be maintained under this category. However, noncausal or ethical oppositions, such as the use of light/darkness terminology in a text, ought not to be part of this category and, moreover, are in principle not dualistic in nature. Therefore, in the evaluation of Frey's analysis of dualism at Qumran, one should be aware that his important category of cosmic dualism is actually a nonuniform container for a multitude of quite different forms of opposition, not all of them dualistic in nature.

4.4.2 Spatial Dualism

The division of the world into two spatially divided parts, such as heaven and earth, below and above, and so on. Frey himself is quite aware of the awkwardness of the category as these spatially divided spheres in general do not oppose one another dualistically but together form the totality of

---

103. Frey, "Different Patterns," 283.
104. Ibid.
105. Ibid.
106. Ibid.

creation. Moreover, the spatial categories are not causal to existence but merely representatives of the same system with assigned (not opposing) purposes. In fact, Frey himself notes that there are many correspondences and mutual influences between these spatial spheres, and often they are used to express the wholeness of God's creation. Texts like 1 Enoch seem especially interested in geography and spatial divisions of creation but always in order to demonstrate the deliberate appointment of their function and purpose by God. Hence, Frey's spatial dualism is not causal and often not oppositional either; therefore, it cannot be evaluated as dualism.

4.4.3. Eschatological Dualism

Frey's definition of eschatological dualism does not equate to Bianchi's eschatological dualism of two causal principles of which one (i.e., evil) will be overcome at the end of history. In Frey's definition, eschatological dualism, for which he finds the term *temporal dualism* more fitting, denotes the division of the world into two temporally divided parts, that is, "the rigid division of time between the present aeon and the future one."[107] In contradistinction to Bianchi's definition of eschatological dualism, Frey states that "not every expectation of last judgment or of a final extinction of evil can rightly be called 'eschatological dualism,' nor can we speak of an 'eschatological dualism' if the opposition of (cosmic) powers is only thought to be manifest or acted out in an eschatological struggle (e.g., in 1QM)."[108] Instead, Frey considers only those occurrences eschatological dualism that reflect two opposing עולמים or αἰῶνες, in the sense of 4 Ezra 7:50 ("The Most High has not made one world but two").[109] Apart from the difficulties surrounding the complexity of eschatological visions in 4 Ezra and the uncertain meaning of the passage mentioned by Frey, the two spheres, this age and the age to come, are not conceived as causal principles. Moreover, they do not oppose one another as they do not exist within the same time frame but are following upon one another. Thus, as Frey removes the eschatological struggle, the final judgment and the extinction of evil from his definition and chooses to focus on two different perceptions of the world

---

107. Ibid., esp. n. 39.
108. Ibid., 284.
109. Translation from Bruce M. Metzger, "The Fourth Book of Ezra: A New Translation and Introduction," in *The Old Testament Pseudepigrapha*, ed. James C. Charlesworth (New York: Doubleday, 1985), 1:538.

4. IDEOLOGY AS A COHESIVE STRATEGY

that chronologically are following upon one another but in themselves are not causal to existence, his eschatological dualism cannot be seen as dualistic. Therefore, in evaluating Frey's analysis of the Qumran texts, one should be aware that his eschatological dualism differs from Bianchi's, and, accordingly, some texts might reflect Bianchi's eschatological dualism while they do not reflect Frey's. As dialectical and eschatological dualism are Bianchi's most important pair for the ideological conceptualization of a religion's cosmology and anthropology, the sheer difference in definition might have consequences for our overall evaluation of this type of dualism at Qumran.

4.4.4. Ethical Dualism

Frey quotes Charlesworth as he defines ethical dualism as "the bifurcation of mankind into two mutually exclusive groups according to virtues and vices."[110] Frey adds that this division between groups is usually expressed in ethical terms like good and evil, righteous and wicked. As already can be deduced from Bianchi's definition of dualism, the mere existence of good and evil opposition in the world does not equal the concept of dualism. In his work on dualism in 1QS III, 13–IV 26, Stuckenbruck reads the text's multidimensional oppositional character as symbolic classifications of day-to-day experiences.[111] Like Bianchi, who holds that "the simple contrasting of good and evil, life and death, light and darkness, and so on is in fact coextensive with religion itself and cannot be equated with the much more specific phenomenon of dualism,"[112] he argues that opposition, tension, and paradoxes are part of the human experience and as such can be evaluated as intrinsic to human life. If the Qumran texts reflect a strict irreducible division between two oppositional groups, which not only reflect a strict division in ethical terms, but also in metaphysical terms, then they need to be considered as expressions of Bianchi's eschatological and/or moderate dualism.[113] This is also the case if, as Frey suggests, "it may be combined with a supreme cosmic dualism" (see cosmic dualism, §4.4.1., above). However, if the opposition is purely expressed in ethical terms (as through a list of virtues and vices), the label dualism should not be used as

---

110. Frey, "Different Patterns," 284 n. 40.
111. Stuckenbruck, "Interiorization," 145–68.
112. Ibid.
113. As we have already established that dialectical dualism does not occur at Qumran.

its usage with regard to ethical categories is problematic: the "mere ethical dualism, stressing the moral opposition between good and evil is not properly dualistic in the religio-historical and phenomenological sense."[114]

4.4.5. Soteriological Dualism

Frey again quotes Charlesworth, who defines this type of dualism as "the division of mankind caused by faith (acceptance), or disbelief (rejection) in a 'savior,' or by participation or not in a certain salvific act."[115] First, this category is not concerned with the opposition of two irreducible causal principles and is therefore not to be considered dualistic. Second, this category is only concerned with human behavior and does not convey any metaphysical and/or ethical cosmology or overarching anthropology. Moreover, the division of the world according to believers or nonbelievers depends upon one's standpoint, is not exhaustive, exclusive, irreducible, or unchangeable, nor is the mere notion of faith a substantial criterion that in itself causes the world or brings human beings into existence. Moreover, it does not in itself provoke dualism: the opposition believers/nonbelievers might, from the emic point of view of the believers, subsequently develop or go together with dualistic tendencies, which naturally do not come forth from faith in itself, but from the components with which a religion is built, such as dogmas, doctrines, and systemic connotations of election, ethical behavior, and salvation. Hence, faith as a signifier for dualism needs to be discarded, and the category of soteriological dualism needs to be abandoned.

4.4.6. Physical Dualism

Frey defines this type of dualism as the division between matter and spirit. He does not elaborate on this type of dualism, but he relates, though not equates, this category to the following one.

4.4.7. Anthropological Dualism

Frey considers this to be "the opposition between body and soul as distinct principles of being."[116] In the cases of both physical and anthropological

---

114. See Goff, "Sapiential Dualism," 24; Bianchi and Stoyanov, "Dualism," 4:2506.
115. Frey, "Different Patterns," 284 n. 41.
116. Ibid., 284–85.

dualism, the label dualism seems difficult to maintain. Even within those philosophical strands in which matter/spirit and body/soul are oppositional, they do not reflect two fundamental and causal principles that bring the world into being. Perhaps exceptions can be made with regard to the notions of *atman* and *maya* in Hinduism, which possibly reflect a radical, dialectical dualism, or to Plato's ideas of the cave. However, in the Judaism of Qumran, such notions are not found, and it is uncertain whether creation and mankind could even be divided as such. Moreover, elsewhere Frey investigates the Pauline opposition of spirit and flesh, and he concludes that even though flesh does occur in a negative connotation within some of the wisdom texts of Qumran (e.g., 4QInstruction and 4QMysteries), "there is no fixed antithesis between 'flesh' and 'spirit' in early Jewish thought, neither ... nor in Qumran."[117]

4.4.8. Psychological Dualism

In this type of dualism, "the contrast between good and evil is internalized and seen to be an opposition not between two groups of people, but between principles or impulses waging battle within man," "e.g., the opposition of יצר הטוב and יצר הרע."[118] Thus, Frey himself already mentions the idea of good and bad inclination (*yetser*) as can be found in Ben Sira and later in the rabbinic two impulses theory. Hence, the idea of two impulses or inclinations within human beings does not reflect two irreducible causal principles, nor do they bring the world or mankind into existence. Moreover, since the locus of conflict is the human being, one can hardly deduce a cosmology or anthropology from it. Moreover, the only Qumran text that reflects such a "battle in the heart of man" is the Treatise of the Two Spirits (1QS III, 13–IV, 26), and, as such, this psychological dualism seems to be modeled upon this one text, rather than being a distinct, objective and recognizable category. Finally, as the Treatise perceives that the two spirits "walk to and fro" in the heart of man according to God's mysterious plan, we might perceive this battle a unifying rather than a dividing characteristic of human life. Hence, Frey's psychological dualism does not meet the criteria of dualism and needs to be treated as

---

117. Jörg Frey, "Flesh and Spirit in the Palestinian Jewish Sapiential Tradition and in the Qumran Texts: An Inquiry into the Background of Pauline Usage," in Hempel, Lange, and Lichtenberger, *Wisdom Texts from Qumran*, 367–404.

118. Frey, "Different Patterns," 285.

simply recognizable oppositional forces congruent to the everyday experiences of human life.

4.4.9. Conclusion

Before evaluating the Qumran texts that Frey has identified as dualistic, we have considered the definitions and criteria of dualism and compared those to Frey's dualistic categories. The above-mentioned enquiry into the definition of dualism has not only revealed that the term is often used rather loosely but also has raised awareness with regard to the different meanings behind similar terminology. Moreover, our evaluation of the classification system that has become commonplace within Qumran studies has demonstrated that not all categories can be considered dualistic and that some categories contain a variety of different appearances, which cannot be compared.

First, Bianchi's definition establishes that any form of dualism within Judaism is not radical, but moderate dualism. Moreover, most Qumran texts reflect a notion of the end and/or of eschatology, which makes them more likely to reflect Bianchi's eschatological dualism, than his dialectical dualism, in which the dualities are eternal. Finally, because of the ostensible hardship of the end times and in combination with the notion that God has created everything there is and will be, the question of procosmic or anticosmic dualism seems impossible to answer, simply because the texts do not seem to have an opinion on the matter.

With regard to Frey's categories of dualism, we find that spatial, soteriological, physical, anthropological, and psychological dualism as categories do not reflect irreducible oppositional causal principles and do not meet Bianchi's criteria. Therefore, these categories need to be abandoned as dualistic. Frey's cosmic dualism is an umbrella term for various, very different terms and ideas, some of which cannot be considered cosmic or dualistic. Assuming Frey's definition of cosmic dualism perceives the one primordial principle of God, those varieties of opposition that coincide with Bianchi's moderate dualism can be maintained within this category, that is, the opposition between heavenly leaders and hosts of spiritual beings (possibly reflected by their human counterparts). However, Frey's evaluation of cosmic dualism, which importantly builds his case for the chronological development of Qumran dualism, needs to be approached with caution as it contains elements that do not meet the criteria of this category and/or are not properly dualistic. As such, Frey's umbrella-term of cosmic dualism might create a false sense of unity and development among the various Qumran manuscripts. Frey's eschatological dualism does not equate to Bianchi's understanding of eschatological dualism, and since it also does not meet the criteria of dualism as the opposition of causal principles, it must be dismissed as not dualistic. There is cause to reevaluate the Qumran texts with regard to Bianchi's definition of eschatological dualism, which can be seen as much more suitable. However, in reevaluating Frey's analysis, we need to take into account that his eschatological dualism is in fact not dualistic at all. Finally, and most problematically, Frey's category of ethical dualism cannot be considered dualistic if it only describes opposition in ethical terms or behaviors. If, however, the Qumran texts reflect a strict irreducible division between two oppositional groups, which not only reflect a strict division in ethical terms, but also in metaphysical terms and/or perceive an eschatological end of history, they might be considered as expressions of Bianchi's moderate and/or eschatological dualism.[119] Schematically, we can now reduce the types of dualism and recombine some of Frey's loose subcategories into Bianchi's scheme:

Table 5: Frey's versus Bianchi's Definition of Dualism(s)			
Frey	Prerequisite	Subtype that fits criteria	Bianchi
Cosmic dualism	The one primordial principle of God	The opposition between heavenly leaders and hosts of spiritual beings (possibly reflected by human counterparts)	Moderate dualism
Eschatological dualism	Redefinition according to Bianchi		Eschatological dualism

---

119. Frey suggests that certain texts reflect ethical dualism combined with "supreme cosmic dualism." Since both categories are problematic in Frey's definition, the instances in which this combination occurs needs to be reevaluated as they might fit the criteria of Bianchi's eschatological dualism.

Ethical dualism in combination with supreme cosmic dualism	Reevaluation of those texts that combine these two forms, providing they meet the criteria of Bianchi's moderate and/or eschatological dualism		Moderate and/or eschatological dualism

Interestingly, this reshuffling of categories demonstrates that only two types of Frey's dualistic categories (cosmic and ethical dualism) contain elements that might be considered dualistic, while a third category (eschatological dualism) needs to be redefined altogether. Even more importantly, it demonstrates that the elements within these three categories can be more easily defined within Bianchi's clear categorization of moderate, eschatological dualism, which is often characterized by overtones of a principal and hierarchical distinction between good and evil, both in a metaphysical and in an ethical sense. With these methodological conclusions in mind, §4.5 returns to Frey's patterns of dualistic thought.

4.5. Revisiting Frey's Patterns of Dualistic Thought and Their Developments

Frey's analysis of Qumran dualism has proven to be rather influential in its afterlife and is often taken as a roadmap into the scholarly evaluations of dualism as a Qumranite phenomenon. The preceding section has made clear that not only the majority of the ten types of dualism as identified by Frey cannot be evaluated as dualistic, but more importantly, the three remaining types (cosmic, eschatological, and ethical) need to be reshuffled, redefined according to Bianchi's standards, and reevaluated with regard to the dualistic value of their subtypes. Moreover, since these three types of dualism play an important part in Frey's overall analysis of the Qumran texts in general and his establishment of patterns of dualistic thought in particular, such reevaluation might have an important impact on Frey's overall assessment of Qumranic dualism. Most importantly, a reevaluation of Qumran dualism in light of our findings regarding the definition of dualism certainly will affect Frey's idea of two patterns of dualistic thought, which in a complex, nonlinear development mix and mingle into Qumran dualism as both patterns consist of cosmic and ethical dualisms, the very categories that need reshuffling and redefining.

If many of the dualistic categories need to be discarded as not dualistic, the impact on Frey's conceptualization of a cohesive model of dualistic development from multiplex/complex to simple might be considerable. However, even before such evaluations can be made, another rather important point of caution needs to be addressed with regard to Frey's original analysis. Even though Frey did not intend to create a developmental model of dualistic thought, the fact that he places all non-*yahadic* texts in the Qumran sect's historical past implicitly presupposes such a diachronic and developmental model. The table below demonstrates schematically Frey's analysis of the various sources of influence and the developmental stages of his perceived two major strands of dualism:[120]

Table 6: Frey's Two Patterns of Dualism Schematically Described		
Development of Sapiential Type of Dualism		
Early Influences	Pre-*Yahadic*/Early *Yahadic*	*Yahadic*
Prov 29:27 Sir 42:24; 33:14–15; 39:16, 24–34; 42:22–25	1QS III, 13–IV, 26 4Q417 2, I, 15–18 1Q27	1QH^a VI, 11–12 4Q181 1, II, 5 CD II, 6–7 4Q280 2, 4–5 4Q502??

---

120. The next chapter will address Frey's analysis of these strands of development in more detail.

Development of Priestly, Cosmic Dualism		
Early Influences	Pre-*Yahadic*/Early-*Yahadic*	*Yahadic*
Sapiential/Laic influences: Book of Daniel Zoroastrian Influences	1QM 4Q390	4Q280 2, 2 1QS II, 4–25 4Q286 7, II, 1–13 CD XVI, 3–4
Priestly Influences: 4QTestament of Levi 4QTestament of Qahat 4QVisions of Amram		4Q510 1, 4–6 11Q13 4Q174/4Q177
Demonology: Book of the Watchers 11Q11 Jubilees		

Such an implicit diachronic framework not only creates the opportunity to explain linguistic and ideological differences between texts in terms of developmental stages in the sect's theological formation; it also provides the opportunity to interpret different texts in light of one another.[121] Frey's patterns of dualism thus implicitly take the presumptions of the Qumran paradigm (a Qumran sect and its library) as their starting point and attempt meaningfully to relate Qumran manuscripts that are thought to reflect opposition or dualistic terminology into a cohesive whole. Thus, Frey's conclusion that the dualistic texts from Qumran demonstrate "the radicalization of the Qumran sect" might reflect no more than a tendency to interpret differences in and the absence of dualistic thinking as indicators for the dating and ideological positioning of individual documents within their presumed chronological order. As such, developmental explanations can become powerful tools to harmonize tensions in the paradigm. As many of the Qumran manuscripts are notoriously hard to date, give little information regarding their social background, and have multilayered, multifaceted redaction levels, the invocation of inherent tendencies to interlink documents chronologically on the presupposition of thematic or ideological relatedness (and development) might not be the

---

121. Frey's patterns of dualism will be discussed and analyzed in ch. 5.

best way to analyze the variety of dualistic outlooks at Qumran. Moreover, if Frey's analysis of Qumran dualism is correct in its identification of the many above mentioned precursory influences that, put together over time, developed into a "uniquely and recognizably Qumranite ideological outlook of rather specific dualistic thinking," this very analysis undermines the idea of the sect's radicality over against other groups as it recognizes threads of dualistic thought in many contemporary writings, thereby proposing dualism to be a more widespread phenomenon in the Second Temple period prior to the Qumran sect.

4.6. Revisiting Dualism in its Socioreligious Milieu: Aspect or Core?

The concept of dualism seems to be an aspect of larger socioreligious phenomena, which developed within specific politicohistorical circumstances, like apocalypticism and a *weisheitliche* preoccupation with God's order of creation. The two Qumran manuscripts that Frey identified as the core documents from which his two patterns of dualistic thought develop, 1QM and 1QS III, 13–IV, 26, both in their own specific way seem to be interested in eschatological expectations of the end and the preexistent divine order of history and being. As such, dualism might be an indicator for the detection of these larger socioreligious phenomena being thematized in certain texts. If this view has merit, dualism can be seen as merely an aspect of these larger phenomena and cannot be seen as an isolated and independent ideology in itself.

Interestingly, in his evaluation of apocalypticism in the Dead Sea Scrolls, García Martínez makes use of the same textual evidence to make his case as Frey does to prove dualism at Qumran.[122] This feeds into the above mentioned observations that related elements of apocalypticism, such as a deterministic idea of God's order of creation, the problem of evil therein, and its eschatological solution, but also linguistic features such as light/darkness terminology, mythological/cosmic imagery, and the use of allusive and symbolic language might implicitly—but not necessarily correctly—be taken as indicators of dualistic thinking. Moreover, many scholars have recognized the good/evil, virtues/vices, and

---

122. Frey, "Different Patterns," 277–78 and further explanations of the two strands of dualism throughout the article; García Martínez, *Qumranica Minora I*, 195–226.

appointed time concepts in late wisdom literature as an influence on the perceived dualistic tendencies in the Qumran manuscripts. As apocalypticism might partly have its roots in the wisdom tradition as well, the perceived concept of dualism at Qumran does not necessarily need to have developed out of one or the other, but might demonstrate a complex synthesis of both traditions. Such an evaluation would be in line with Lange's theory of *weisheitliche Prädestination*, according to which the ethical aspects of Qumran dualism relate closely to late biblical wisdom texts, which grapple with the realization that, in the sociopolitical reality of Israel, good conduct does not always lead to a good life. These texts often reflect the idea of a predestined order of creation, which, according to Lange, under the influence of apocalyptic elements is creatively further developed in the wisdom-related Qumran sectarian texts (such as the Treatise, 4QInstruction, and 1QMysteries) and possibly inspired their dualistic outlook.[123]

Apart from dualism possibly being an integral part of larger socioreligious phenomena, the core concepts within these phenomena might linguistically provoke the style and imagery of opposition. The idea of eschatological expectations of the end, end-time war, and ethically expressed ideas of God's predestined world order are likely to create imagery of opposition, which do not necessarily need to be dualistic. Moreover, from a sociological point of view of social stratification, authorial sociological strategies to define one's group identity over against others, such as antagonism, opposition, polemics, alterity, exclusivism, the occurrence of insider/outsider language, and so on, are quite common. As these strategies do not necessarily negotiate irreducible causal oppositions but are mere human strategies to classify and categorize existence, they cannot be taken to be synonymous with dualism in a religiohistorical sense. In return, the occurrence of larger socioreligious phenomena such as *weisheitliche Prädestination* or apocalypticism should not be taken indiscriminately as evidence for the presence of an underlying dualistic worldview in the Qumran documents.

---

123. Lange, *Weisheit und Prädestination*, 296–99.

4.7. The Cohesive Ideology of Dualism: Building Block of the Qumran Paradigm?

This chapter has occupied itself with the concept of dualism in general and the perception of dualistic thinking as a characteristic of the Qumran community in particular. We have established that the growth of typologies of dualism in Qumran has obscured the concept of dualism, and we have reevaluated them in light of Bianchi's understanding of religious dualism. This reevaluation has led to the conclusion that only two types of Frey's dualism categories can be maintained partially, while a third one needs to be thoroughly redefined and Frey's analysis of its occurrences reanalyzed.

These findings might also have an impact on Frey's overall analysis of dualism at Qumran and in particular on his evaluation of patterns of dualistic thinking. Moreover, we have detected that Frey implicitly created a model of chronological development, which is based upon the paradigmatic assumption of a coherent Qumran library and a Qumran sect. That is, Frey's evaluation of the patterns of dualistic thinking presents a model in which 1QS III, 13–IV, 26 and 1QM are the pre-*yahadic* chronological linchpins that bind assumed precursory documents (containing various forms of early indicators to dualism) together through elements of dualism and which set the stage for a *yahadic* radicalization process, combining and mingling various of their dualistic elements. Because of our reevaluation of the boundaries of dualism's definition and in light of our question of whether the notion of dualism might function as an ideological building block for the Qumran paradigm in which perceived dualistic variety and differences are thought to reflect chronology, a new evaluation of the texts that Frey has identified as dualistic is needed.

Moreover, we have suggested that dualism might not function as an independent ideological concept but might merely be an aspect of a larger phenomenon, which found a wide audience within Second Temple Judaism and, hence, might have provoked many textual witnesses negotiating human history and existence.

In conclusion, there seems to be a tendency in Qumran studies to evaluate all sorts of perceived oppositions as dualistic, thereby creating new types of dualism many of which do not in fact meet the criteria of religious dualism. Moreover, the perception of patterns of dualistic thought implicitly creates a model of chronological development, placing very different texts in a cohesive and coherent chronological order, thereby sustaining the underlying Qumran paradigm, this time on the basis of a perceived ideological development. If, however, many identified instances of dualism might not meet the criteria of its definition or need to be evaluated differently, the parameters of this model consisting of patterns might shift.

The concept of dualism sits well in the perception of the Qumran paradigm as dualism fits well with the notions of radicality and sectarianism. However, we have seen that there are good reasons to assume that dualism might not function as an independent ideology, but rather as an integral aspect of larger—and widespread—socioreligious phenomena, such as apocalypticism and wisdom traditions.

The next chapter will come back to these issues as it investigates the chronological development of dualism in one of Frey's core patterns of dualistic thought, the multidimensional sapiential dualism strand. To do so, chapter 5 is constructed as a test case that focuses on the dualistic coretext of this pattern, the Treatise of the Two Spirits (1QS III, 13–IV, 26). Not only will this chapter reevaluate the various types of dualism that scholars have identified in the Treatise but also the idea of its growth and chronological development within the sectarian realm. Underlying this investigation is not only the question of the possible presence or absence of dualistic thought in light of the stricter definitions of dualism but also whether and to what extent the notion of dualism functions as a cohesive ideological concept that is read into certain texts, thereby creating the social reality of a radical Qumran sect.

5

THE ZENITH OF QUMRAN THOUGHT:
THE CASE OF DUALISM AND 1QS III, 13–IV, 26

In the preceding chapter, we discussed the concept of dualism as a perceived characteristic of the Qumran *yahad*. We saw that the insistence on the dualistic outlook of the Qumran sect has burdened us with a bewildering amount and variety of dualisms in the various Qumran texts, which often seem to obscure and divert from the principle definition of dualism (i.e., the doctrine of two irresolvable principles that cause existence). Also, and most importantly, we have seen that these perceived examples of dualism have implicitly opened the backdoor to enforce well-known models of chronological development of the Qumran sect and its theology based upon the coherence and representativeness of its library, as scholars have attempted to trace back the various stages of development within and between those Qumran manuscripts that are thought to express a dualistic worldview. Whereas 4QMMT seems to have a crucial function in the paradigm as the linchpin for the categorization of texts as presectarian or *yahadic*, even though the text itself seems to successfully escape all categories, the Treatise of the Two Spirits (1QS III, 13–IV, 26) seems similarly to have played a crucial role in models attempting to trace a chronological sectarian development on the basis of assumed ideological coherence in the form of dualistic thought.[1] Moreover, like 4QMMT, the Treatise is nowadays recognized by many as a virtually unique document at Qumran, with the following points regarded as distinctive: (1) its combination of three perceived dualisms (cosmic, ethical, and psychological) is found nowhere else among the Qumran manuscripts; (2) it demonstrates some unique linguistic features and themes; and (3) it also lacks some of what schol-

---

1. Whether it be unilinear models such as von der Osten-Sacken's or a "web of relations" à la Frey.

ars have identified as specific Qumranite terminology. Hence, whether we agree with Frey that "the dualistic section 1QS 3:13–4:26" can no "longer be considered the definite summary of the community's ideology"[2] or we take Dimant's view that the presence of the Treatise in 4QpapS^a (4Q255, the oldest copy of the Community Rule) proves that "dualism seems to have been part of the Qumran community's outlook from the initial phases of its existence"[3] and that the text reflects the "most systematic exposition of the dualistic thinking of the community,"[4] one thing seems to be certain: the Treatise holds a central position in all scholarly discussions on the topic of Qumran dualism. This chapter, in taking the Treatise as its point of departure, investigates the degree to which the function of ideology as a cohesive strategy can sustain the Qumran paradigm. It will be argued here that the perception of dualism in various Qumran texts not only creates a false sense of cohesion and coherence between these texts but also implicitly generates the same developmental literary models and their subsequent (and/or underlying) sociological presumptions of reality that we have already seen in the case of 4QMMT. Thus, while cohesion creates coalescent forces, developmental models tend to be more or less linear in character; nevertheless, either way, at the center of the question of the function of Qumran dualism we find the Treatise of the Two Spirits (1QS III, 13–IV, 26), which makes this text the natural starting point of this chapter.

5.1. The Text: The Treatise of the Two Spirits

In its current form, the Treatise of the Two Spirits (1QS III, 13–IV, 26) is part of 1QS (1Q28) or the Rule of the Community, which is taken to provide much information about the Qumran sect's ideology and praxis. Other copies of (parts of) the Serekh (S) are found in eleven further manu-

---

2. Jörg Frey, "Different Patterns of Dualistic Thought in the Qumran Library: Reflections on Their Background and History," in *Legal Texts and Legal Issues: Proceedings of the Second Meeting of the International Organization for Qumran Studies, Cambridge, 1995; Published in Honour of Joseph M. Baumgarten*, ed. Moshe J. Bernstein, Florentino García Martínez, and John Kampen, STDJ 23 (Leiden: Brill, 1997), 290.

3. Devorah Dimant, "The Composite Character of the Qumran Sectarian Literature as an Indication of Its Date and Provenance," *RevQ* 22 (2006): 615–30.

4. García Martínez, *Qumranica Minora I*, 202.

scripts, namely, 4Q255–264 (4QS^{a-j}) and 5Q11. The Treatise is preserved in its entirety in 1QS, while the 4QS manuscripts demonstrate only sporadic evidence of the Treatise's presence. According to Frey and Lange, 4QS^c (4Q257) is the only text which undoubtedly preserves parts of the Treatise (i.e., parallels to 1QS IV, 4–10; 12–15; 23–25).[5] Recently, however, Tigchelaar has proposed that two fragments, which were previously ascribed to other compositions, 4Q502 16 and 4Q487 37, might also belong to the manuscript of 4QS^c.[6] Moreover, Metso has argued that 4QS^a (4Q255) also contains a fragment that "has no direct parallel in 1QS but which forms a part of the doctrine."[7] Accordingly, Dimant regards this manuscript of S as evidence for the originality of Qumran dualism.[8] In order to avoid basing observations on too much speculation, Charlotte Hempel warns that the fragmentary preservation of this text does not "allow for any firm conclusions."[9] Metso also suggests that the content of the reconstructed text of 4QS^b, as well as a fragment in 4QS^h, might indicate that the Treatise was included in these manuscripts.[10] No other scholar, however, seems to have provided evidence or support for this suggestion. On the contrary, Lange considers the Treatise to be lacking in 4QS^b, which he conceives to be particularly significant as he holds it to be the only S manuscript that contains parts of both 1QS I, 1–III, 13 and 1QS V–XI.[11] Lange's observation is informed by evidence provided in 4QS^{d-e} (4QS 258–259): in these two manuscripts of the Community Rule not only the Treatise is lacking but also the entire first four columns (1QS I–IV), an absence of material that has strengthened scholarly arguments that these first four columns of S were attached to columns V–XI at a later stage.[12] This discussion regarding the textual development of S is particularly relevant in light of schol-

---

5. Frey, "Different Patterns," 289–99; Lange, *Weisheit und Prädestination*, 120–26.
6. Eibert J. C. Tigchelaar, "'These Are the Names of the Spirits of...': A Preliminary Edition of *4QCatalogue of Spirits* (4Q230) and New Manuscript Evidence for the Two Spirits Treatise (4Q257 and 1Q29a)," *RevQ* 21 (2004): 529–47.
7. Sarianna Metso, *The Textual Development of the Community Rule*, STDJ 21 (Leiden: Brill, 1997), 135.
8. Ibid., 106.
9. Charlotte Hempel, "The *Treatise on the Two Spirits* and the Literary History of the *Rule of the Community*," in *Dualism in Qumran*, ed. Géza G. Xeravits, LSTS 76 (London: T&T Clark, 2010), 108.
10. Metso, *Textual Development*, 106, 135.
11. Lange, *Weisheit und Prädestination*, 126.
12. See §§5.1.2–3 below.

arly discussions about the origin and provenance of the Treatise, discussions which in turn have an impact on overall scholarly opinions on the topic of dualism and its perceived Qumranic development. Indeed, scholarly opinions are rather varied in regard not only to the incorporation of the Treatise into S but also the issue of the possible growth and redaction of both the Community Rule and the Treatise. In addition to the consideration of evidence from the manuscripts, the tradition-historical theories regarding the Treatise as an independent text and the possible direction of its development are being researched. Also, the background and timing of the Treatise's incorporation into S, its redaction history, and the perceptions regarding the Treatise's *yahadic* reception are being considered. Various scholarly views on these matters, which are relevant to our central question of dualism, will be discussed below.

5.1.1. An Independent Document?

Over time and based on its terminology and linguistics, an increasing number of scholars have become convinced that the Treatise used to be an independent document that at some stage was incorporated into the Rule of the Community. While some specialists remain convinced that the Treatise reflects the community's main theology, Metso, for example, has advocated that the Treatise should rather be evaluated as a document in its own right, as it is likely to have had an independent existence.[13] At the same time, Metso argues that the Treatise has undergone some degree of redaction as it demonstrates certain assimilations, possibly in order to "provide a better context for the insertion" into the Community Rule. Moreover, she argues that this insertion took place at a relatively late stage.[14]

---

13. For instance, García Martínez (*Qumranica Minora I*, 202) calls the Treatise "the most systematic exposition of the dualistic thinking of the community." For arguments to treat the text as a document in its own right, see Metso, *Textual Development*, 90–91, 135–40, 145. Metso (107 n. 1) also points to preliminary research by Jerome Murphy O'Connor and Hartmut Stegemann; see also Stuckenbruck, "Interiorization," 145–68. Stuckenbruck holds that the fragmentary remnants of 4Q255/257 are not enough to demonstrate the Treatise's prominence for the Qumran community.

14. Metso, *Textual Development*, 19, 113–14, 145. Interestingly, although Metso holds the Treatise to be best evaluated as an originally independent document, she rejects the suggestion that in its incorporated form, the Treatise is a literary unity; see §5.1.2. For her evaluation about the text's redaction process, see §§5.1.3–4.

Stuckenbruck also proposes a separate, independent evaluation of the Treatise. He finds that certain vocabulary and essential features of the Treatise relate better to other sapiential compositions of the Second Temple period than to the unambiguous *yahadic* texts. This argument is most elaborately studied by Lange, who argues that "es sich 1QS III13–IV26 um einen eigenständigen Text handelt, der an die liturgische Bestimmung von 1QS I1–III13 angehängt wurde.... Das Verknüpfen der Zwei-Geister-Lehre mit dieser Liturgie ... läßt es möglich erscheinen daß es sich bei ihr um einen nicht vom *yahad* verfaßten Text handelt, der gleichwohl für Essener von großer Bedeutung war."[15] Lange finds evidence for the non-*yahadic*, independent origin of the Treatise as he lists a series of differences between the Two Spirit Treatise and texts "more evidently produced by the Qumran community":[16]

(1) Lack of community terminology: words such as עצה, יחד, תורה, and חוק, which are considered to be typical *yahadic* words, are missing from the text. Also, the self-identifying word יחד occurs sporadically but is only used adverbially.
(2) In 1QS III, 24, the divine name אל ישראל is used: this name is used almost exclusively in nonsectarian texts.
(3) In other parts of 1QS, Belial (בליעל) is used as the name for the evil power, but this name is lacking in the Treatise, which uses names such as "spirit of deceit," "spirit of injustice," and "angel of darkness."
(4) The Treatise does not focus on the correct interpretation and observance of the torah, a central theme for the *yahad*.
(5) The covenant is central in the theology of the *yahad* and much is concerned with its entry requirements. However, in the Treatise, ברית only occurs once (IV, 22) and is not used in a "sectarian manner."[17] Moreover, in the Treatise, being part of the covenant seems a matter of predestination and will become clear in the eschaton.
(6) The sectioning and structure of the Treatise is different from the structure (indicated by ____ and *vacat*) of 1QS, which Lange

---

15. Lange, *Weisheit und Prädestination*, 126–27, also n. 35.
16. Ibid., 127–28.
17. Frey, "Different Patterns," 296.

holds to be an indication that the Treatise is redacted to fit in with the purpose and meaning of 1QS.

(7) Moreover, and possibly in addition to Lange's list, Popović, Tigchelaar, and Hempel have pointed out that there is a remarkable absence of light and darkness terminology in the remainder of 1QS/4QS.[18]

Hence, as the Treatise is considered to be rather unique, both in content and form, most scholars who have studied the text closely now hold the view that the Treatise should be treated as a formerly independent document that at some stage was incorporated into the compilation of the Community Rule. As a result, the Treatise is often studied as if it were an independent document.[19] However, the matter of its incorporation into S has caused many debates and has raised questions regarding the veracity of the text's literary unity, the process of insertion, and the level of inner-Treatise and outer-Treatise redaction.

5.1.2. A Literary Unity or a Layered Composition?

Many scholars regard the Treatise as a literary unity, and some even tend to treat it as if it were an untouched independent text. In his 1958 article, Jacob Licht describes the Treatise as a "harmonious whole," which sets forth "a continuous and logically constructed argument, combining several notions and ideas into a single chain of reasoning." Accordingly, he expresses his admiration for the text's "continuity of thought" and "unity of structure."[20] According to Licht, this unity of structure is demonstrated by the central theme of a preordained existence and history of mankind, subdivided in three logically interwoven main themes: predestination, dualism, and eschatology.[21] Licht further based this conclusion of literary

---

18. Popović, "Light and Darkness," 148–65; Hempel, "*Treatise of the Two Spirits*," 102–20; cf. Eibert J.C. Tigchelaar, *To Increase Learning for the Understanding Ones: Reading and Reconstructing the Fragmentary Early Jewish Sapiential Text 4QInstruction*, STDJ 44 (Leiden: Brill 2001), 194–207.

19. A good example is Donald W. Parry and Emanuel Tov, eds., *The Dead Sea Scrolls Reader*, 6 vols. (Leiden: Brill, 2004), in which the Treatise is divorced from the Community Rule and placed in a separate volume: vol. 1, *Texts Concerned with Religious Law*; and vol. 4, *Calendrical and Sapiential Texts*.

20. Licht, "Analysis of the Treatise," 88–89, 99.

21. Ibid., 88–89.

5. THE ZENITH OF QUMRAN THOUGHT

unity on his perception of the Treatise's chiastic form, a conclusion that subsequently was adopted by Dimant.[22] Lange also seems to subscribe to the Treatise's literary unity as he calls it "ein kunstvoll komponierter Text" with its own literary structure and sectioning.[23] In his tractate on Qumran dualism, Frey equally argues for the literary unity of the Treatise, based on his evaluation of a clear correspondence between the Treatise's heading and its overall structure.[24] In DJD XXVI, Philip Alexander and Vermes state even more boldly: "The Sermon on the Two Spirits (III 13–IV 25) is indubitably an autonomous unit with no internal links either with what precedes or with 1QS Vff."[25]

Despite this bold evaluation, there is reason to believe that the Treatise cannot be straightforwardly regarded as a complete independent and discernable literary unit, especially in light of its relation to and incorporation in 1QS. The following sections, which mainly deal with tradition-historical and redaction-critical issues, will attempt to evaluate whether and to what extent the hypothesis of the Treatise's coherence and independence can be sustained.

5.1.2.1. Source-Critical Evaluations of the Treatise

On literary grounds, the Treatise is generally subdivided in various sections, the boundaries of which are, more or less, commonly accepted by scholarly consensus. The basic structure of the Treatise in 1QS—even though subdivided into smaller sections—reflects a basic threefold scheme: (1) introduction, (2) main body (containing three subsections), and (3) summary and conclusion. In more elaborate form, scholars more or less recognize the following subsections:

III, 13–15: Introduction (and overview)
III, 15–18: Introductory paragraph, which in hymnic form praises creation and the preexistent order of history
III, 18–IV, 1: Explanation of the nature of the spirits

---

22. Ibid.; also see his schema on page 100; Dimant, "Qumran Sectarian Literature," 501.
23. Lange, *Weisheit und Prädestination*, 140.
24. Frey, "Different Patterns," 290.
25. Philip Alexander and Géza Vermes, eds., *Qumran Cave 4.XIX: Serekh ha-Yahad and Two Related Texts*, DJD XXVI (Oxford: Clarendon, 1998), 10.

IV, 2–14: Passage on their respective virtues and vices
IV, 15–23a (or IV, 15–18, 18–23a): Human actions according to their divisions and current and future visitations
IV, 23b–26: Résumé of the main topics and conclusions

In their source-critical research of the Treatise, scholars have identified different sections within the text, the differences of which were explained in various ways. For instance, von der Osten-Sacken distinguishes between 1QS III, 13–IV, 14 and IV, 15–26 on the basis of differentiating terminology and stylistic-syntactical differences.[26] The latter (IV, 15–26) is seen as a development of the Treatise's primary cosmic dualism (in III, 13–IV, 14) into a more ethical dualism, which is subsequently subdivided into an eschatological part (IV, 15–23a) and an anthropological part (IV, 23b–26), both of which von der Osten-Sacken considers to be later additions to the Treatise.[27] The basis of von der Osten-Sacken's theory lies in his perception that the Treatise combines the earliest form of cosmic dualism as presented by the War Scroll (1QM) with the ethical teachings of the Hodayot (1QH^a). Lange has argued against this evaluation, as section IV, 15–23a seems to correspond very well with the introduction (III, 13–15). Moreover, he argues that IV, 23b–26 cannot be evaluated as secondary, since III, 15 is discussed and taken up in IV, 25.[28]

Duhaime subdivides the Treatise into a five-fold scheme: (1) III, 13–18a; (2) III, 25b–26a; and (3) IV 1–14, which are thought to form the earliest stages of the document; while (4) III, 18b–23a and (5) III, 23b–25a represent a secondary layer. In contradistinction to von der Osten-Sacken, who considers cosmic dualism (related to 1QM) as forming the Treatise's primary structure, Duhaime believes that the "ethical dualism" between the righteous and the wicked forms the basis of the Treatise's dualistic thinking, while every mention of the two spirits needs to be assessed as secondary.[29]

---

26. Von der Osten-Sacken, *Gott und Belial*, 17–18.
27. Ibid., 17–27.
28. Lange, *Weisheit und Prädestination*, 131; it remains unclear from Lange's work whether he argues against a source-critical division of sections in the Treatise in general (as he does indeed advocate for the Treatise being a literary unit) or whether he simply disagrees with von der Osten-Sacken's evaluation.
29. Duhaime, "Dualistic Reworking in the Scrolls from Qumran," 32–56.

Tigchelaar, whose source-critical evaluation reveals a common source between 4QInstruction (4Q415–418, 4Q423, 1Q26) and the Treatise, holds that the latter consists of two groups of texts: (1) III, 18–IV, 14 and (2) III, 13–18 and IV, 15–26. Moreover, Tigchelaar argues that within the first group (III, 18–IV, 14), III, 18–IV, 1 can be discerned as the first layer of text to which a list of virtues and vices (IV, 2–14) is added. According to Tigchelaar, these two pieces of text were later put into a new framework (IV, 15–23a; III, 13–18; and the résumé IV, 23b–26). Also, even though Tigchelaar conceives that redaction and editing took place in a more complex manner, he basically holds on to the two groups of text, which can be discerned by different vocabulary and terminology. For instance, he finds that the text's "later additions" lack the eye-catching "light and darkness" terminology.[30]

Next to these source-critical remarks that question the unity of the Treatise's composition and the possible developments within the text, scholars have lately asked redaction-critical questions about the Treatise's internal development process and its insertion into S.

5.1.2.2. The Redactional Process of S and Outer-Treatise Redaction

The above-mentioned earlier research in the Treatise's unity consisted of attempts to retrace sources and reveal the text's history of traditions. Recently, Hempel has suggested looking more closely at the redaction process that might have taken place when the Treatise was incorporated into 1QS.[31] She has pointed out that next to the Treatise's distinctiveness in content and language, a remarkable continuity can be observed between the Treatise and the remainder of S. She proposes that this ostensible contradiction between distinctiveness and commonality might be explained as the work of a redactor, who created an editorial framework that encompasses both texts.[32] She also thinks that such a redactor not merely incorporated the Treatise into the Community Rule (both 1QS and 4QS materi-

---

30. Tigchelaar, *To Increase Learning*, 194–207.
31. Hempel, *"Treatise of the Two Spirits,"* 102–20.
32. Hempel holds the typical *maskil* headings to be an example of the presence of such an editorial framework. Cf. Metso, *Textual Development*, 112, who thinks the *maskil* heading of III, 13 is a secondary addition in order to help insert the Treatise into the Rule. See also Duhaime, "Dualistic Reworking," 32–56.

als) but also must have given both texts their final integrating redaction.³³ Based on the peculiar absence of light and darkness terminology in 1QS, V–XI, Hempel suggests that the Treatise might not have been important or even known to the authors of the 1QS V–XI/4QS.³⁴ She suggests that a redactor might have been struck by the Treatise's suitability for the Rule and that he, therefore, compiled, redacted, and "artfully connected forwards" both texts into one document that suited the author's contemporary community.³⁵ If Hempel is right and the Treatise was "certainly not incorporated wholesale, but adjusted at the point of its inclusion into S,"³⁶ it might be difficult to establish what exactly can be ascribed to this redactor and what are the Treatise's original ideas and ideology.³⁷

5.1.2.3. Inner-Treatise Developments and Redaction

Another redaction-critical argument to consider with regard to the question of the Treatise's literary unity is advanced by Metso and concerns the evidence from the 4QS manuscripts. Metso argues that the 4QS manuscripts not only demonstrate textual differences but also contain fragments of the Treatise that have no parallel in 1QS.³⁸ Hence, she not only suggests that the Treatise has undergone redaction due to its incorporation into S (cf. Hempel) but also that these issues possibly are evidence of inner-Treatise redaction. Hence, Metso argues that "the scribe of 4QSᵃ is hardly likely" to be responsible for creating the Treatise, so the textual differences between this fragmentary manuscript and 1QS III, 13–IV, 26 might best be explained if "the text has undergone redaction."³⁹ That is, if one discerns between different layers of textual development within the Treatise itself.

---

33. Hempel, "*Treatise of the Two Spirits*," 102–20; the idea of a final redaction of S is supported by Metso, who on this basis argues that the Treatise cannot be treated as a literary unit; see §§5.1.1 and 5.1.2.2.
34. Hempel, "*Treatise of the Two Spirits*," 118.
35. Ibid., 119.
36. Ibid., 120.
37. For a good example of such difficulty, see the discussions regarding the originality of the occurrence of the *maskil* in III, 13: Hempel, "*Treatise of the Two Spirits*," 114; von der Osten-Sacken, *Gott und Belial*, 18–21.
38. Metso, *Textual Development*, 137. Metso bases this idea of redaction on her conviction that 4QSᵃ and 4QSʰ contain textual material without direct parallels with, but clearly related to, the Treatise.
39. Ibid.

5. THE ZENITH OF QUMRAN THOUGHT

Metso's proposal is difficult to evaluate as it is unclear whether she indeed points to redaction within the Treatise or whether she merely wants to make a source-critical observation, as Metso seamlessly involves the source-critical evaluations of Licht and von der Osten-Sacken into her argument for redaction within the Treatise's early manuscripts. Metso's theory works from the assumption of an original text, which through editing and redaction has gone through various stages (4QS), of which the Treatise in 1QS is the end-form. Therefore, she needs to deal with the fact that these 4QS older "hold-over forms" are paleographically often later than the 1QS "end-form." She somehow does not address the question of why the Qumran community would continue copying archaic text forms. Moreover, if one entertains the possibility that earlier forms of the Treatise are contained in later manuscripts, it becomes problematic to sustain the idea of a fairly coherent social unity like the construct of the Qumran paradigm.[40]

However, if Metso is correct and at least one more layer of redactional activity can be detected within the Treatise before it was incorporated into 1QS, the text would be more difficult to evaluate with regard to its basic ideas and peculiarities. Moreover, it would make an evaluation of textual unity difficult to sustain.

In conclusion, the questions of outer- and inner-Treatise redaction and the process of incorporation into S are part of a careful and complex evaluation of the literary status and perceived (pre-)*yahadic* ideology that the Treatise might represent. Even though the Treatise might have undergone some development (tradition-historically or redaction-critically), scholars have noticed the impossibility of clinically dissecting the various sections of the current text (1QS III, 13–IV, 26) source-critically. For instance, Tigchelaar denotes that, even though he might be able to distinguish between sections on the basis of their form and content, at the same time these sections cannot be separated or isolated, as 1QS III, 17–19 makes clear.[41] Von der Osten-Sacken has also recognized this entanglement, as he calls III, 19 "eine wohlüberlegte Verklammerung," designed to connect the two oppositional pairs עול/אמת and חושך/אור.[42]

---

40. Schofield, *From Qumran to the Yaḥad*, solves this problem in her radial-dialogical model; however, the model does not explain the copying of various forms within a supposedly sectarian, i.e., ideologically stringent, organization.

41. Tigchelaar, *To Increase Learning*, 202.

42. Von der Osten-Sacken, *Gott und Belial*, 144.

Also, Hempel suggests that even though "some of the distinctive cosmic and ethical elements may well have originated separately," in their present state these elements cannot be disentangled.[43] Finally, Stuckenbruck has focused more specifically on the various forms of dualism in the Treatise and concludes similarly that apart from the ethical antitheses in IV, 2–14, the additional oppositional structures are not able to stand on their own without them mutually contextualizing and modifying each other.[44] Hence, even though clear indications can be given for the assumption of different sources behind the text and/or even inner-Treatise redaction, these arguments of entanglement advocate for treating the Treatise as a literary unity, while at the same time cautiously realizing that the process of incorporation possibly provoked a certain level of redaction in both the Rule and the Treatise.

5.1.3. The Relationship with S: The Direction of Growth and the Question of Insertion

The evaluation of the Treatise's independent origin and the process of editing and redaction in both 1QS/4QS and the Treatise are closely related to the question of the direction of literary development and the moment of the Treatise's insertion into the Rule. The preceding sections demonstrate that both texts and their integration were still fluid. The question of insertion is closely related to the dating of the original version of the Community Rule, its direction of growth/shrinking, and the positioning of the Treatise as an originally independent document within this process. The fact that not all the 4QS documents, in their preserved form, contain the Treatise or even 1QS I–IV, has been reason for debate about the direction of the textual development of S. Some scholars argue that the Community Rule was originally shorter than 1QS (i.e., without 1QS I–IV), while others argue that some 4QS manuscripts are shorter versions of an originally longer document.[45]

---

43. Hempel, "*Treatise of the Two Spirits*," 107.

44. Stuckenbruck ("Interiorization," 162) considers the three conceptualizations of dualism—cosmic, ethical and psychological—as progressions, bound up in the Treatise's antitheses.

45. Cf. Metso, *Textual Development*, 147; Philip Alexander, "The Redaction-History of the Serekh ha-Yahad: A Proposal," *RevQ* 17 (1996): 437–53; Géza Vermes,

The point of insertion not only has consequences for our overall evaluation of the Treatise's provenance; it also has an impact on the conceptual and ideological framework it came to represent—that of a crucial witness to and linchpin of sociohistorical models that attempt to trace a chronological sectarian development on the basis of perceived dualistic thought. As such, evaluations regarding the Treatise's point of insertion in 1QS contribute to scholarly conceptualizations of the *yahad*'s ideological foundations and development (and vice versa). Thus, the problem of insertion is closely related to the question of date, which is an important building block in models that sustain the Qumran paradigm. Therefore, the problem of insertion and the problem of date will be discussed together in the next section.

5.2. Dating the Treatise

The dating of the Treatise is often connected to the paleographical dating of the manuscript of which it is now a part: the Community Rule. This manuscript (1QS) is generally dated to 100–75 BCE.[46] Lange holds that the incorporation of the Treatise into the Community Rule must have taken place a while after the independent text was created, and, therefore, he establishes as *terminus ante quem* for 1QS III, 13–IV, 26 the middle or end of the second century BCE. Moreover, Lange establishes as *terminus post quem* the end of the third or the beginning of the second century BCE based on linguistic criteria, such as the use of Persian loanwords.[47] Hence, Lange believes the original independent document of the Treatise was created between approximately 200 and 150 BCE.

Metso argues, however, that 1QS is the result of a compilation of an original Rule document that is not attested to in the Scrolls with two

---

"Preliminary Remarks on Unpublished Fragments of the Community Rule from Cave 4," *JJS* 42 (1991): 250–55.

46. DJD XXVI. Two related texts, 4Q255 and 4Q257, possibly contain parts of (earlier?) versions of the Treatise, but due to their fragmentary nature nothing can be stated with certainty. Moreover, Tigchelaar suggests that 1Q29a might preserve an alternative version of the Treatise. If he is right, 1Q29a and 4Q257 preserve alternative lists in the Treatise's section on the two ways (1QS IV, 2–11); "These are the Names," 529–47.

47. These linguistic criteria are based upon the linguistic criteria that were used to help date two related Qumran texts: 4QInstruction and 4QMysteries; Lange, *Weisheit und Prädestination*, 130–31.

additional traditions, represented by 4QS^d and 4QS^e, respectively, in which the former in a later stage (represented by 4QS^b) took up the material we now know as 1QS I–IV, including the Treatise.⁴⁸ Hence, Metso believes that the original version of the Rule lacked columns I–IV. She can only reach the conclusion of 1QS being a compilation of earlier (b, d, e) traditions if she establishes these documents to be earlier than 1QS. While acknowledging that 4QS^b and 4QS^d are paleographically later than 1QS, Metso follows Milik, who believed that 4QS^{b-d} preserve an earlier version of the Community Rule. In the case of 4QS^e, she adheres to Milik's judgment and dates it as the paleographically oldest document (150–100 BCE). However, the editors of DJD XXVI point out that due to the renaming of several of the documents, Milik's 4QS^e is actually 4QS^a, which they indeed acknowledge as the oldest version of S among the scrolls (125–100 BCE).⁴⁹ Moreover, the editors contest Metso's theory that 4QS^d and 4QS^b can be viewed as unilinearly developed copies within the same traditional line. They argue that, based on the orthography of both documents "it is not easy, therefore, to postulate a direct stemmatic relationship" between the two.⁵⁰ If these observations are correct, Metso's theory regarding the textual development of S is highly questionable.⁵¹ Moreover, such an evaluation has severe consequences for our evaluation of the origin, insertion, and date of the Treatise, since 4QS^a is thought to contain parts of the Treatise.

In table 7 I have attempted to give an overview of the S manuscripts according to their date, with special attention to the presence of columns I–IV and more specifically to the presence of (parts of) the Treatise.⁵²

---

48. Metso, *Textual Development*, 147.
49. DJD XXVI, 23.
50. Ibid., 11.
51. Recently, Schofield has argued that the complex textual development of S is better explained by multiple scribal circles and different sociohistorical backgrounds, which together are responsible for the "semi-independent radial-dialogic" development of S; *From Qumran to the Yahad*, 274–75.
52. The table is my assessment of the dating section in DJD XXVI.

5. THE ZENITH OF QUMRAN THOUGHT   203

Table 7: Overview of S Documents and Their Dates (according to DJD XXVI)

Document	Date	Treatise?	Columns I–IV?
4QS^a (4Q255)	125–100 BCE	unparalleled parts	I, 1–5; III, 7–12
1QS (1Q28)	100–75 BCE	Yes	Yes
4QS^c (4Q257)*	100–75 BCE	IV, 4–10, 13–15, 23–25	I, 2–3; II, 4–11, 26; III, 1–10 Perhaps: 4Q502 16 and 4Q487 37
4QS^e (4Q259)†	50–25 BCE	No	No
4QS^j (4Q264)	50–25 BCE	No	No
4QS^g (4Q261)	50–1 BCE	No	III, 4–5
4QS^b (4Q256)	30–1 BCE	No	I, 10 (?), 15–19, 21–23; II, 4–5, 6–11
4QS^d (4Q258)†	30–1 BCE	No	No
4QS^f (4Q260)	30–1 BCE	No	No
4QS^i (4Q263)	30–1 BCE	No	No
4QS^h (4Q262)‡	1–50 CE	No	III, 4–5

* 4Q257 only has material from 1QS I–IV and some scholars believe it never contained columns V–XI.

† Metso argues that, despite the later dating, 4Q258–259(4QS^{d-e}) are more original than 1QS, and they both do not contain the Treatise. Metso argues that b, d, and e represent two older traditions that were brought together in 1QS by a compiler (*Textual Development*, 147).

‡ Metso argues that 4Q262 might not be a copy of the Rule but rather contains material that might be reminiscent of the Treatise. Hempel states that the fragmentariness of the text (five words) does not allow for firm conclusions ("*Treatise of the Two Spirits*," 109).

As table 7 makes clear, on the basis of all the available information and with the restriction in mind that the 4QS texts are often so fragmentary that solid conclusions regarding the presence or absence of certain elements are difficult to draw, Lange's estimate of the Treatise's date would thus appear to be rather accurate. However, Lange does not take the evidence of the 4QS fragments into account as he bases his date entirely on 1QS itself. Moreover, Lange's evaluation seems to have a high investment in proving that the Treatise has a specific place in the development of *yahadic* ideology. He holds the Treatise to be of a "proto-Essenisch" (i.e., pre-*yahadic*) character, closely linked to but further developed in its dualism than 4QInstruction and 4QMysteries (4Q299–301, 1Q27). Moreover, he considers the Treatise a main influence on later *yahadic* thought, as he observes in 1QH^a and CD.[53]

Interestingly, one needs to rethink the insertion and positioning of the Treatise in light of the paleographically latest document of the 4QS fragments, 4QS^h: its highly fragmentary state leaves no material evidence for the presence of the Treatise in this document, but the small amount of material of column III obliges us to reckon with at least the possibility of the Treatise's presence in this document. Moreover, table 7 demonstrates that (1) both early and late Qumran S documents might have either contained or lacked the Treatise, (2) that identification is extremely difficult due to the fragmentariness of the evidence, and (3) that, since earlier versions of S than 1QS have existed, the evaluation of a date of origin is extremely speculative and often tied to socio-historical perceptions of Qumran. These sociohistorical perceptions are subsequently connected to the evaluation of the Treatise's position and relation to other Qumran manuscripts, which will be discussed below.

5.3. Textual Correspondences and Sociohistorical Setting

The original setting and sociohistorical background of the Treatise is often evaluated from the perspective of its position within the development of the Qumran *yahad*. Naturally, once the Treatise is incorporated into 1QS, the document has become a part of a bigger whole and as such it contributes to the overall representation of the outlook and practice of the authors and audience of the Community Rule. As we have seen above, most scholars believe the Treatise to be a presectarian, that is, pre-*yahadic*, document. As for this contemporary pre-*yahadic* setting, Lange has suggested that the Treatise (1) has close ties to two other documents found among the Dead Sea Scrolls: 4QInstruction (4Q415–418, 4Q423, 1Q26) and 4QMysteries (4Q299–301, 1Q27), and (2) subsequently has had a tremendous influence

---

53. Lange, *Weisheit und Prädestination*, 131–34; see also Frey, "Different Patterns," 301–8.

on the theology of the *yahad*, as he thinks can be demonstrated in 1QH^a VI, 22–23; CD II, 6–7; II 7–8; 4Q181; 4Q511; and 4Q280.[54]

Indeed, 4QInstruction and 4QMysteries contain various similarities with the Treatise, predominantly in certain specific terminology and themes. However, whether the Treatise originated in the same community that was responsible for 4QInstruction and 4QMysteries is an entirely different matter and is very difficult to establish, especially since all three texts tell us little about the social world in which they originated. Moreover, various communities that exist in a relatively small geographical area may share common thoughts and ideas and have knowledge of the same traditions, but they might nevertheless have as many differences as similarities. The question of social background is only vaguely answered by the Treatise itself, as the text states that it provides insight "into the history of all the sons of man, concerning all the ranks of their spirits, in accordance with their signs (cf. III 18–IV 1), concerning their deeds in their generations (cf. IV 2–14 and IV 15–18) and concerning the visitation of their punishment and the periods of their salvation (cf. IV 18–23)."[55] Hence, the viewpoint of the Treatise is thereby mostly defined in anthropological terms: human beings are the subjects of concern. Frey considers the Treatise to be written to address the most "urgent questions and troubles in the circles of addressees":[56] "the occurrence of sin even within the community of the pious (3:21–22), the experience of present affliction and hostility (4:6–8) and the reality of struggle in the world, even in the heart of every human being."[57] According to Frey, the inherent tension of the text lies in its wish to balance "the fundamental thought of the unity of God and his sole responsibility for creation" with the ostensible presence of evil.[58] Frey argues that the community behind the Treatise clearly perceives that the explanation for their contemporary troubles needs to be found in God's plan for creation. Therefore, Frey seems to argue that the Treatise functioned as a soothing and pastoral device to encourage its readers not to despair but to obey and uphold the precepts of God. Also, he considers

---

54. Lange, *Weisheit und Prädestination*, 127–35. This chronological developmental idea is consistent with Frey's "patterns of dualism" and will be further discussed in §5.5 below.
55. Frey, "Different Patterns," 290.
56. Ibid., 295.
57. Ibid., 291.
58. Ibid., 295.

the text's dualistic tendencies as an elaboration of Ben Sira's emphasis on the perfection of creation (see 39:16, 24–34; 42:22–25), which he thinks is characterized by a certain determinism in the idea of a predestined order of being and history. Frey also argued that the Treatise combines and develops this theological interest in creation by attaching the ethical oppositions of the wisdom tradition with the ontological principles of light and darkness, thus creating a clear connection to Gen 1 (cf. Newsom below). Even though Frey believes the Treatise to have originated in a pre-Essene environment, his analysis does not elaborate upon its recipients' social location, which he inherently interprets intracommunally; that is, the text is thought to be mostly concerned with the pressing problem of sin and apostasy within the community of addressees itself. Therefore, Frey's analysis presupposes some sort of sectarian background as it presumably addresses the possibility of leaving or sinning against (the rules of) a recognizable community. Even though this interpretation is certainly valid in light of the Treatise's current incorporated occurrence in S, it does not reckon with the possibility that this text originally might have been non-sectarian or even written for all Israel.

In her study of the conception of knowledge in the Treatise, Newsom clearly reckons with this possibility.[59] Newsom argues that the Treatise might have a political subtext that is concerned with "concrete historical and political realities." Interestingly, she ascribes a significant function to the Treatise's use of "balanced pairs, especially antonyms"[60]; in a sense, they simplify complexity. In other words, they enhance one's understanding or knowledge of the totality of things, because they categorize everything imaginable into two opposed categories.[61] In this respect, Newsom also points to the frequent use of כול ("all") and the use of temporal expres-

---

59. Carol Newsom, *The Self as Symbolic Space: Constructing Identity and Community at Qumran*, STDJ 52 (Leiden: Brill, 2004), more specifically ch. 3, "Knowing as Doing," 77–90.

60. Ibid., 80–81.

61. Cf. Needham, *Symbolic Stratifications*, 7–9. Needham holds that this dualistic division simply reflects a human strategy of categorization. Even though the pairs are oppositional and exclude "shades of gray," their "classification by partition" is not absolute. Moreover, the symbolic linking of categories by pairs is flexible by context and helps to build social identity. Cf. Lawrence Wills, *Not God's People: Insiders and Outsiders in the Biblical World* (Lanham, MD: Rowman & Littlefield, 2008), who argues that such categorization of the world enhances the constructs of we/they by what he calls "the Law of the Excluded Middle," i.e., every individual, group, behavior,

sions for great quantities of time (עוֹלָם, נֶצַח, עַד) as devices to make the incomprehensible and ungraspable understood and known.[62] Moreover, Newsom argues that this need for knowledge and understanding (of God's plan and creation) is syntactically signified by the creation of a web of meaning: in order to understand one thing on one level, one also needs to develop knowledge of other things on other levels and of the relationships between these levels. Newsom demonstrates that the Treatise is not only interested in God's plan (atemporal divine level) but also in Israel's genealogy and history (temporal human level). Moreover, she reads the Treatise as a pretext to Gen 1. In doing so, she finds that "the allusions, echoes and parallels between 1QS III–IV and Gen 1 ... often link different levels or aspects of reality (e.g., luminaries/humankind) by associating each with the same keyword."[63] In short, these different levels or aspects of reality make clear that temporal and atemporal levels of knowledge both stem from the same source: God's plan for creation. It is precisely in this "field of tension" that Newsom finds the grounds to read the Treatise as a political text.[64] The explanation of history and genealogy, the periodization of history, predetermination, opposing angelic powers, the reflection of those powers in human behavior and eschatological resolutions; all are elements of this alleged political subtext. Read or positioned as a pretext to Gen 1, the Treatise adds a dimension to the creation account; it is no longer a mere account of the organization of creation, but it now reveals God's plan for creation, and it teaches reading the physical world as a sign of this plan.[65] Hence, Newsom reads the Treatise as a symbolic narrative of self, underneath which lies the concern about the ideological incomprehension of the historical fact of Israel's suppression by gentile powers. According to Newsom, the Treatise thus moves out of the "priestly/scribal mode of knowledge" and explains Israel's history of observance and transgression in a more intellectual mode of knowledge, expressing a funda-

---

or belief, that does not belong to the Self or Other needs to be categorized and allocated to one or the other.

62. Newsom, *Symbolic Space*, 81.

63. For how this works exactly, see ibid., 87.

64. Cf. the idea of hidden transcripts, i.e., the possibility of the repressed to protest in a hidden, yet for insiders recognizable, manner through the use of certain subtexts; see James C. Scott, *Domination and the Arts of Resistance: Hidden Transcripts* (New Haven: Yale University Press, 1990).

65. Newsom, *Symbolic Space*, 86–87.

mental understanding of human nature. This intellectual exercise attempts to resolve problems of sin, evil, and subjugation in the temporal reality by explaining Israel's conflict situation with imperial powers in light of the atemporal plan of God.

According to Newsom, the text's strategy to transform its political and historical subtext into a text about anthropology serves to provide "imaginary solutions for irresolvable social contradictions."[66] If Newsom is right and the text is concerned with the reality of Israel's subjugation to foreign powers, she thereby implicitly argues that its concern is for all Israel. Such a conclusion would invite the interpretative possibility that the recipients of the Treatise originally also might have been all Israel.[67] At least, Newsom reckons with the fact that the text universalizes the nature of the conflict into a conflict between Israel and gentile powers, which might indicate a nonsectarian background. Moreover, Newsom thinks the text provides its audience with a reason not to act politically (e.g., in uprising), but—by its use of special language and special knowledge—helps to postpone direct action in favor of the symbolic construction of self as the "sons of light."[68] Logically, such a stance will only be taken by a group or a people that is powerless over against its opponents. Hence, both a small nation (Israel) and a sectarian group (the Qumran community) would recognize the text's ability to make sense of their suppressed position and might be helped by its explanation of God's plan regarding life and human nature.

In contradistinction to Newsom's evaluation of an oppressed and powerless audience, Stuckenbruck thinks that the socioreligious background against which the Treatise was written was not necessarily one of instability or poverty. Sociologically, so he argues, a document like the Treatise "presupposes an established, though not necessarily 'sectarian' community and takes the luxury of indulging in the sort of reflection that takes a certain degree of vulnerability for granted."[69] Moreover, Stuckenbruck perceives that the Treatise has a hortatory function, while at the same time demonstrating a level of realism in explaining "inconsistent behavior as

---

66. Ibid., 90.
67. The Treatise itself mentions Israel once: the God of Israel, 1QS III, 24.
68. However, since Newsom reads the Treatise in light of 1QS and the Qumran community, her interpretation of this obtaining of special knowledge through language establishes a sectarian realm to her analysis; I will come back to this.
69. Stuckenbruck, "Interiorization," 166.

an inevitability for human beings."[70] He proposes that, rather than in an unstable sectarian setting, the text might have originated within "a community that has had a history of ups and downs, that has had the sort of longevity and social stability as a group that can contemplate such tough questions."[71] In its contemporary 1QS setting, Stuckenbruck thinks the Treatise, which is best read in proximity to 1QS I, 1–III, 12, functioned similarly as in its original environment: to explain the experience of sin (or hypocrisy) within the righteous group of addressees and exhort them to walk on righteous paths.

The evaluations of these various scholars demonstrate a range of possible social settings. This ambiguity with regard to the text's social world can be seen as an indication that the sociohistorical information of the Treatise is rather scarce. Nevertheless, it is interesting to observe that scholarly opinions do not unanimously perceive a sectarian setting with regard to this text. Even though Lange and Frey seem to take a sectarian setting as their point of departure without much consideration, Newsom and Stuckenbruck clearly seem to reckon with the possibility that the Treatise did not originate in nor was it written for a segregated sectarian group.

The next section, which deals with the perceived dualism(s) in the Treatise, will therefore approach the text without any presupposition of a sectarian social setting. Our point of departure is the evaluation of the Treatise's "multidimensional pattern of dualism" as advanced by Frey and already briefly discussed in chapter 4. First, we return to Frey's conceptual framework of development as it has proven to be extremely influential in scholarly evaluations of Qumran dualism. In fact, some of the arguments that Frey advanced and which will be reconsidered here have been taken for granted and are uncritically used as points of departure. The next section will look at these arguments with regard to the Treatise in more detail.

5.4. Dualism in the Treatise

As mentioned in chapter 4, Frey distinguishes three levels of dualism in the Treatise: cosmic, ethical, and psychological dualism. The cosmic dualism is thought to consist of the opposition between two spiritual beings, as well

---

70. Ibid.
71. Ibid., 165–67.

as their linkage to truth/light and wickedness/darkness, especially signified by, respectively, the Prince of Lights and the Angel of Darkness. Also, human beings are brought into this realm as they are thought to be under the influence of either cosmic spirit. The ethical dualism is represented by the virtues and vices, which seem to divide the deeds and actions (and nature) of human beings into two groups. In this form of dualism, Frey thinks "all humanity is divided up."[72] Finally, Frey argues that on the level of psychological dualism, the author of the Treatise arrives at the pivotal question that he wants to have answered: why evil and sin occur among the righteous. Hence, the "psychological level of dualism" portrays both of the two spirits to be present within the heart of humans. The table below is a schematic overview of the three levels of dualism that Frey recognizes in the Treatise and the elements he distinguishes as dualistic.

Table 8: Frey's Three Levels of Dualism in the Treatise		
Central Element	+	−
Cosmic Dualism		
Two spiritual beings	• Spirit of Truth • Prince of Lights • Angel of His Truth • light terminology • humans share in their lot	• Spirit of Wickedness • Angel of Darkness • Darkness terminology • Spirits of His Lot • dominion of his enmity • humans share in their lot
Ethical Dualism		
Two classes of human beings Participation in the two spirits	• virtues • truth/justice • metaphor of source • term dominion • Sspatial: "Walk in"	• vices • wickedness • metaphor of foundation • term dominion • spatial: "Walk in"
Psychological Dualism		
Central question of the commitment of sin among the pious	• God assigns fate • humans share in both spirits "in their heart"	• God assigns fate • humans share in both spirits "in their heart"

---

72. Frey, "Different Patterns," 293. The text seems to contradict this statement of total division as it envisions the possibility that the "sons of light" may "stumble" (1QS III, 24).

Frey's analysis of the Treatise does not seem to be entirely coherent. On the one hand, he states that its pattern of dualism "though basically cosmic ... includes a strong ethical dimension and distinctive psychological aspects,"[73] while on the other hand, he holds that "the teaching of ethics and anthropology presumably reflects the most urgent problems of the group addressed."[74] Frey believes this teaching of anthropological issues to be "presented in the framework of cosmological and eschatological thought."[75] Thus, if we are to understand from Frey's analysis that the core of the Treatise teaches us about ethics and anthropology, which merely presents itself in a cosmological frame, how can he at the same time advocate the centrality of cosmic dualism?

Part of the answer to this question is found in Frey's definitions of dualism, as we saw in the previous chapter. First, his cosmic dualism is an umbrella term for various dualistic and nondualistic terms and ideas and needs to be maintained only if it reflects Bianchi's moderate dualism. Second, Frey's ethical dualism cannot be considered dualistic if it only negotiates oppositions in ethical terms or behaviors but might be considered dualistic if these ethical oppositions are expressed as a part of Bianchi's moderate or eschatological dualism. Third, even though the "struggle in the heart of man" is an interesting and unique element of the Treatise, Frey's conception of its psychological dualism has to be dismissed, as they unite rather than irreducibly divide creation and humanity and are therefore nondualistic expressions of human nature and experience.

Therefore, before turning to the question of the development of Qumran dualism, which will be discussed in §5.5, we need to reevaluate carefully the question of dualism with regard to the Treatise. According to the text, the Treatise is a teaching for the Sons of Light:[76]

> about the *natures* [תולדות] of all the sons of man, concerning all sorts of their spirits by means of their (astronomical) signs, and concerning the works in their *generations* [דורתם], and concerning the visitation of their plagues and the times of their peace. (1QS III, 13–15a)

---

73. Ibid., 289.
74. Ibid., 291.
75. Ibid.
76. The translations of the Treatise used in this section are mine.

In short, the Treatise is an attempt to explain human history and human conduct. The text seemingly embraces the entirety of (the nature of) humankind and envisions "all the sons of man" to be characterized by a variety of "spirits," which apparently are in accordance with their astronomical signs.[77] So far, this variety of "spirits," as indicated in the text, does not point to a dualistic division of humanity into two opposing groups but rather envisions the various astronomical signs playing an important part in the make-up and subsequent behavior of humans. Moreover, the text indicates that it explains humanity's history in terms of this astronomically assigned human behavior and envisions the consequences of this behavior as periodically visible through bad times ("visitation of their plagues") and good times ("times of their peace"). As such, the text offers a complete cosmology with an inherent and implicit anthropology.

The totality of its explanation becomes clear as the Treatise now introduces the reason why human history and human conduct can be explained exhaustively and recognizably: because of the existence of an omnipotent and wise creator with an overarching preordained design/plan of creation (1QS III, 15–17).

> From the God of knowledge all exists and shall exist. Before they existed he ordained all of their plans/thoughts/designs. And when they come into being at their appointed times according to the plan of his glory, they shall fulfill their work and there is no change/perversion. In his hand are the laws/judgments of all and he provides them with all their pleasures.

This background information corresponds neatly with 1QS III, 13–14. Therefore, it becomes clear that even though human actions coming forth from natural behavior according to the various spiritual-astronomically influenced human inclinations might result in and become visible through good and bad periods throughout human history, God has not only created the world and humans this way, but even these good and bad periods in history are the result of God's ongoing interference in and control

---

77. P. Wernberg-Møller, "A Reconsideration of the Two Spirits in the Rule of the Community (1Q Serek III, 13–IV, 26)," *RevQ* 3 (1961): 419, has argued that תולדות in III, 13 is likely to mean "natures" instead of generations and hence the variety of spirits ought to be seen as its further explanation; see also Tigchelaar, *To Increase Learning*, 197.

over his creation. As such, these lines do not necessarily stress the idea of predestination or determinism. Rather, they might glorify God's ongoing interest in and control over the world as they attempt to reassure as well as explain that times of affliction and hardship are also part of God's plan of creation.[78] Moreover, these first sentences seem to embrace the tension between God's providence and humanity's free will, while ultimately stating God's supremacy over the entirety of his creation.

Once the author of the Treatise has established God's omnipotence, knowledge of, and control over the whole of creation, he turns to the creation of humans, reminding his audience of man's biblical task to "rule over the earth" (Gen 1:26–28; cf. Ps 8:7). As Newsom has convincingly shown, the Treatise has a clearly marked intertextual relation to Gen 1. Newsom thinks that, whereas Gen 1 is concerned with creation, the Treatise is interested in God's מחשבה (plan/design) that "grounds creation."[79] If Newsom is right and the Treatise sees itself as an explication or pretext to the biblical creation story of Gen 1 and intends to transform this rather organizational account of the cosmic creation in order to create the possibility of a "hidden reality" (warranting a sense of mystery and secret knowledge), according to which the physical world is informed by spiritual structures and their signs, then the complexity and difficulty that humankind experiences in the execution of its biblical task to "rule the world" can confidently be explained by such a subtext:

> And he created mankind for the domination of the world/earth and he made for him two spirits in order to walk to and fro in them until the appointed time of his visitation. (1QS III, 17c–18)

Many scholars think that these introductory sentences (III, 13–18) function as forming an eschatological framework in which the author of the Treatise introduces a deterministic worldview that culminates in a cosmic dualism through the introduction of "two spiritual beings."[80] However, the actual text of the Treatise does not provide such a straightforward explanation. First, as Lichtenberger has correctly noted, the text restricts the influence of the spirits, partly through its statement that both spirits are

---

78. As Frey has noted, the Treatise seems importantly concerned with the question of sin, affliction, and apostasy among the pious.
79. Newsom, *Symbolic Space*, 86–87.
80. E.g., Frey, "Different Patterns," 291.

created by God and partly by placing them in a time-restricted eschatological setting.[81] Hence, if the spirits would reflect a form of dualism, this can only be a moderate one as God remains in control. Second, our evaluation of the nature of the two spirits influences not only our understanding of the text's perceived dualistic worldview but also its presumed outlook of determinism or predestination. In fact, the text gives little useful information in regard to these ideologies, and it does not indicate whether or not humans can choose in which of the two spirits they might walk or whether human beings are influenced by either one of the spirits or by both spirits simultaneously. The verb הלך (HtD), which is often used in scripture to accompany ethical behavior, provides no indication as to a person's capability to choose or free will to act with regard to both spirits placed before one.[82] Such a tension between divine providence (or a predestined order of creation) and human free will is part and parcel in many theological writings that deal with theodicy and evil and thematically not necessarily attached to a deterministic or dualistic outlook or a concept of rigid predestination (cf., for instance, Augustinian and Lutheran contemplations regarding these themes: Augustine, *On Free Choice of the Will*; Luther, *On the Bondage of the Will*).

Due to their closeness to the scriptural reminder that "man's task is to rule the world," we might consider the introduction of the spirits to function as a specific and purposeful elaboration upon God's intention with regard to man's rule and the author's subsequent solution to the problematic social reality of the occurrence of sin and evil in the world. As such, the "spirits set before man" cannot be seen as separate cosmic entities but rather resemble the idea of good and evil inclinations or dispositions (cf. Sir 15:11–20; 21:10–11; 33:10–15). Thus, their place and function in the text seems likely to be more psychological and anthropological in nature. A similar argument has been made by P. Wernberg-Møller, who perceives the text as envisioning the "dual nature in which humans were created," a nature that obviously has an impact upon their manner and capacity to rule the world. Wernberg-Møller suggests that the conceptualized dual nature of humans functions to answer the question of theodicy and the apparent social reality of hardship and evil that lie behind the text.[83] As a result, the text finds an explanation in the fact that humans were given

---

81. Lichtenberger, *Menschenbild*, 127.
82. Cf. Wernberg-Møller, "Reconsideration of the Two Spirits," 423.
83. Ibid., 422.

a dual nature and thus were placed under the influence of oppositional forces: "They are spirits of truth and iniquity" (III, 19).[84]

The concepts of truth (אמת) and iniquity (עול) are closely linked to the observance and/or transgression of the law, visible in human conduct and behavior, but in Second Temple Judaism equally disputable with regard to its perceived correct interpretation. Consequently, the fact that the two "spirits of truth and iniquity" are described in ethical overtones makes the evaluation of dualism rather problematic. As we have argued in the preceding chapter and in concurrence with Bianchi's framework of dualism, the mere contrasting of ethical terms is an inherent characteristic of religion or, even more so, an inherent and common way to describe human experiences and human understanding of selfhood and alterity. Therefore, this ethical oppositionality cannot be equated with the much more specific cosmological conceptualization of dualism. Hence, with regard to the character and function of the two introduced spirits, there is no reason to presume that they exist as independent entities inside or outside the human body. Rather, as Paul Heger has correctly stated, the focus is predominantly anthropological, as the texts prove to be "relevant to humans, instructing them about human nature, not about the cosmos." As such, the oppositional forces described as "spirits of truth and iniquity" reflect, "rather than dualism," "the rational idea that every concept in human life has its opposite."[85]

However, scholarly evaluations of the Treatise's dualism are possibly not only reached by the interpretation of the two spirits in III, 18–19 as independent spiritual beings but also by the translation of תולדות in III, 19 as "generations," which, together with the notion of the two spirits, thus provokes the idea of strictly oppositional groups of people. Hence, much depends on the meaning and reference of תולדות in III, 19 and how the use of the term here corresponds to its usage in III, 13 and IV, 15. Fierce scholarly debates have taken place regarding the correct translation of תולדות in the Treatise. Licht has argued that the use of two very dissimilar or even oppositional translations of תולדות in one textual unity is "unadvisable."[86]

---

84. If Wernberg-Møller is right, III, 17c–18 and III, 19 (which defines the two spirits as "the spirits of truth and iniquity") correspond with IV, 23, which states that, "the spirits of truth and iniquity will strive in the heart of man."

85. Paul Heger, "Another Look at Dualism in Qumran Writings," in Xeravits, *Dualism in Qumran*, 51, 55.

86. Licht, "Analysis of the Treatise," 90 n. 5.

However, most scholars use two or sometimes even three variant translations for the occurrences of this term in III, 13, 19, and IV 15.

In 1QS III, 13, Licht, Wernberg-Møller, Tigchelaar, and others have translated תולדות as "natures" or "characteristics," which is a significant alteration of its traditional meaning. Licht has pointed out that the root meaning of תולדות must be "things originated," and from there translations such as "generations," "secondary rulings," "development," "chain of preordained events," "characteristics," and even "natures" can be derived.[87] In Biblical Hebrew, the term is almost exclusively used in genealogical accounts, where it fittingly translates as "generations." Licht has suggested that the Treatise might refer to זה ספר תולדת אדם of Gen 5:1, which would simply translate traditionally as "generations," but which in rabbinic midrashim demonstrates "a wealth of speculation about the book in which the destiny of all human generations is written beforehand."[88] He even finds evidence in early medieval treatises on physiognomy, in which the phrase from Gen 5:1 needs to be translated as "natures." Of course, these later meanings of תולדות might indicate that the term had the potentiality for the widening of its original meaning, but it remains rather uncertain whether reasoning backwards in time can be sufficiently legitimized.[89]

Another, possibly closer connection might be found in Gen 2:4, which demonstrates a more metaphorical usage of the term: תולדות השמים והארץ (lit. "the begetting of heaven and earth"), introducing "the account of heaven and earth and which proceeded from them."[90] This passage introduces, in a similar manner to 1QS III, 13–15, the account of creation and humankind's place in it. Next to its usage of תולדות, Gen 2:4–9 reflects, just like the Treatise, God's activities in a combination of ברא (to create) and שים (to place).[91] Ultimately, God "put" (וישם) the man he formed in the same space with "the tree of knowledge of good and evil" (Gen 2:8–9) in a very similar manner as he puts in front of man "two spirits to walk in" (III, 18). If the assumption that Gen 2:4–9 plays a role in the background

---

87. Ibid.
88. Ibid.
89. Interestingly, 1QS III, 18 perhaps intentionally avoids this connection as it uses אנוש instead of אדם.
90. BDB (11th edition; 2007), 410.
91. Contra von der Osten-Sacken (*Gott und Belial*, 142–43), who sees the Treatise's use of שים instead of יצר as key evidence that the spirits should not be considered to be "inclinations" in the rabbinic sense, but rather independent spiritual entities.

in the Treatise is correct and the text indeed intends to shift from the overarching cosmological focus of the creation account toward its own more anthropologically urgent questions of theodicy and the presence of evil, תולדות might need to be translated in close proximity to its more metaphorical usage in Gen 2:4.

The argument that תולדות, at least in III, 13, ought to be translated differently from its original meaning of "generations" is furthermore strengthened by the observation that in III, 14 another term for "their generations," namely, דורותם is used. A similar contrasting of תולדות and דורות occurs in another instance in which תולדות seems hard to translate, namely 1QS IV, 15. Here many scholars resolve the difficulty by translating "history," which might equally cover the expansion of its meaning, embracing its larger context as "an account of humankind." Hence, if we agree with the scholarly consensus that the traditional meaning of תולדות, that is, "generations," does not apply in 1QS III, 13 or in IV, 15, but that its translation rather needs to reflect "an account of the creation of humankind and what proceeds from them," the translation "natures" seems rather accurate and certainly within the scope of its larger semantic field. However, in 1QS III, 19, recent scholars have resisted alternative translations of תולדות, generally translating it "generations." In light of the other occurrences of the term in the Treatise, there is, however, no compelling reason to assume that such traditional translation is accurate. Earlier scholars, like von der Osten-Sacken and Lichtenberger used translations like *Herkunft* and *Ursprung*, which are well in line with the translation of תולדות in III, 13 and IV, 15: "Ging es dort [1QS III, 13] um die Herkunft der Menschen, so hier um den Ursprung von Wahrheit und Frevel."[92] Hence, a traditional translation might mostly be informed by the scholarly presupposition of the Treatise's dualistic outlook, rather than by the more logical proposition that such a small text is unlikely to use three variant meanings for one word *and* two variant terms for "generations" twice in one sentence. Thus, it seems conceivable to translate תולדות in 1QS III, 19 in line with III, 13 and IV, 15:

> In the source of light [מעין אור] lie the originated things/natures of the truth, and from the source of darkness [מקור חושך] are the originated things/natures of the iniquity.

---

92. Von der Osten-Sacken, *Gott und Belial*, 19, 142; Lichtenberger, *Menschenbild*, 127–28.

As von der Osten-Sacken has already noted, 1QS III, 19 is "eine wohlüberlegte Verklammerung" of many elements, which have played a crucial role in scholarly assessments of the text's dualistic outlook. First, the text cleverly builds a bridge between the notions of "truth-iniquity" and "light-darkness." Second, by using two variant terms for "source" or "fountain," that is, מעין and מקור, III, 19 contrasts the "natures" or "beginnings" (תולדות) of truth and iniquity. Subsequently combined with a traditional translation of תולדות as "generations," thus provoking the interpretation of a strict division between two human groups, many scholars have evaluated these two linguistic strategies as evidence for the strict cosmic dualism of the text, interpreting the light/darkness terminology as a metaphorical cosmic expansion of the human dualistic realm.

Perhaps the variant usage of "source" (מעין and מקור [lit. "spring"]) has a further function and might provide us with information regarding the author's intention in contrasting them. In only two instances in the Hebrew Bible do we find the two terms mentioned together. First, they appear in Prov 25:26, where it negotiates the theme of good and evil: "A righteous man tottering before the wicked is as a troubled fountain [מעין] and a corrupt spring [מקור]." Second, they occur in the more eschatological context of Hos 13:15, which indicates that Israel has fallen through its iniquity: "An Eastwind from the Lord will come, blowing in from the desert; his spring [מקורו] will be dry, his well [מעינו] will dry up." Whereas מעין is generally used in its literal meaning of "spring," the biblical use of מקור is often metaphorical (e.g., the Lord is called "fountain of living waters" in Jer 2:13; 17:13; God possesses "the fountain of life" in Ps 36:9). Elsewhere, this fountain is recognized as Israel (Ps 68:26), while Proverbs states that the "fountain of life" is "the mouth of the righteous" (Prov 10:11), "the law of the wise" (Prov 13:14), "wisdom and understanding" (Prov 16:22, 18:4), and finally the "fear of the Lord" (Prov 14:27). At Qumran, both terms are predominantly used metaphorically. Von der Osten-Sacken finds that in the Serekh and the Hodayot, both terms are used to describe qualities of God. In 1QS X, 12, God is a "source of knowledge" (מקור דעת) and a "fountain of holiness" (מעין קודש). Also, God is considered a "source of righteousness" (מקור צדקה, 1QS XI, 3–6), a "spring of life" (מקור חיים, 1QHª XVI, 15), an "eternal spring" (מקור עולם, 1QHª X, 31, cf. 4Q418 81/81a, 1) and finally a "source of light" (מעין אור, 1QHª VI, 17). Von der Osten-Sacken concludes that this usage of both "sources" indicates that in 1QS III, 19 "Gott selbst ist als Quelle des Lichts Ursprung der Macht der Wahrheit," a conclusion that poses him with a problem of finding a suitable origin for the "source of darkness." He finds the solution to this problem in the *Urzeitliche Chaos* of תהום. He proposes that God's creation of the light out of the darkness over the תהום in Gen 1 connects not only the discernment of both sources but also explains their connection to the light/darkness terminology.[93] The function of 1QS III, 19 would thus be to establish an ethical connection between God's discernment of light/darkness in Gen 1 and the human conducts of truth/iniquity. However, although von der Osten-Sacken's argument might have some merit in the discussions regarding the background, meaning, and function of the light/darkness terminology, it hardly explains the variant terms that are used for "source." In fact, the indiscriminate usage of both terms מעין and מקור in scripture and in other Qumran texts and their close connection to or even synonymity with God not only reinforce the Treatise's earlier statements that "from the God of knowledge all exists and shall exist" but also creates an interpretative context in which the creation story of Gen 1 can be connected to human ethical behavior. Hence, rather than the concept of dualism, the usage of מעין and מקור creates a bridge of unity in which God is the source of creation of all.[94]

This conclusion might be slightly in tension with what we find in 1QS III, 20–21 in which we finally encounter the first notions indicating that the Treatise might convey a layer of moderate dualism:

> In the hand of the Prince of Lights is the dominion over/of all the sons of righteousness; in the paths of light they shall walk to and fro. And in the hand of the Angel of Darkness is all dominion of the sons of iniquity and in the paths of darkness they shall walk to and fro.

Many scholars have evaluated this passage as thoroughly cosmic-dualistic. However, as seen above, most studies of the Treatise regard this part of the text (III, 18b–23a and possibly III, 23b–25a) as representing a secondary layer to the text.[95] Indeed, the eye-catching light/darkness terminology of this section is absent from the rest of the Treatise.[96] Nevertheless, this cosmic

---

93. For a fuller account, see von der Osten-Sacken, *Gott und Belial*, 143–47.

94. Cf. Isa 45:7: "I form the light and create darkness, I make peace and create evil; I the Lord create all these things."

95. E.g., Duhaime, Frey, and maybe Hempel; contra Tigchelaar, but see also von der Osten-Sacken, who emphasizes the Treatise's ethical concerns but on a structural level holds the cosmic part of the Treatise to be the oldest.

96. Hempel (*"Treatise of the Two Spirits,"* 119) points out that the light/darkness terminology is entirely absent from the legal and organizational material in 1QS V–IX.

layer seems to convey a certain investment in extrapolating the human/ethical division into a supportive cosmic layer, thereby perhaps creating a limited human responsibility for sinful behavior. In contradistinction to the preceding notion of two spirits or inclinations with which humans need to reckon in their daily conduct and behavior, these lines seem to envision a cosmic division between two angelic beings that rule over two respective groups of humans, the "sons of righteousness" and the "sons of iniquity."[97] Even though God has created all and therefore radical dualism does not exist, this rather thorough division of creation into two opposed realms certainly provokes the impression of a moderate dualistic scheme.

However, some scholars have pointed out that these lines of perceived cosmic opposition need not necessarily be interpreted dualistically. For instance, Wernberg-Møller, who has analyzed these lines together with 1QS III, 19, argued against a strict dualistic interpretation of this passage, as he perceived an inherent hierarchy in the terms שר and מלאך. On this basis, he also argued that the contrasting terms of light and darkness cannot be interpreted in such a way that they would function as representatives of two cosmic equally powerful principles. Wernberg-Møller's argument is fourfold:

(1) The fact that the text contrasts מעין and מקור, the former of which he translates as "dwelling" and the latter as "well," is thought to demonstrate their inequality, presumably even geographically representing a divine force (high up in the light) and a wicked force (down in the dark ground).[98]
(2) The use of שר (prince) over against מלאך (angel) demonstrates the former one's superiority over the latter.

---

97. See Charlotte Hempel, "The Community and Its Rivals according to the Community Rule from Cave 1 and 4," *RevQ* 21 (2003): 47–81; Hempel regards the "sons of injustice" as opponents to the author's community.

98. The mere fact that מעין mostly means "spring of water" and only translates as "dwelling" in Isa 12:3 weakens this part of Wernberg-Møller's argument; "Reconsideration of the Two Spirits," 423. Von der Osten-Sacken's insistence on contrasting these two terms might be informed by him reading מעון (dwelling) instead of מעין. The former term is rather rare in scripture, where it is not used in connection to "light" but on occasion in reference to God's dwelling; e.g., מעון קדשך (Deut 26:15) and מעון קדשו (Jer 25:30). However, the term מעין can be found in equally negative imagery in Jer 9:10; 10:22; 49:33; and 51:37, where מעין תנים ("lair of jackals") refers to desolate cities.

(3) The fact that the Angel of Darkness and the spirits of his lot are paralleled by God and his Angel of Truth (III, 23–25) equally demonstrates the presence of a hierarchy. (No "host of spirits" seems to be accompanying God and his true angel.)

(4) The position of כל. Not only does the Angel of Darkness guide the wicked, he also influences the righteous, being responsible for their sins and iniquities. This demonstrates that the domains are fluid and not strictly and irreducibly divided.

Indeed, the scheme as laid out in 1QS III, 20–21 turns out not to be thoroughly antithetical or symmetrically oppositional. On further reading, the text narrates a less straightforward dualistic image of creation as the sphere of influence of only one of the angelic beings, the Angel of Darkness, extends beyond its clear-cut division line:

> And with the Angel of Darkness is the error of all the Sons of Righteousness, and all their sins and their iniquities and their offences and the transgressions of their deeds are in his dominion in accordance with the mysteries of God until its/his appointed time. And all their afflictions and the periods of their distresses are within the dominion of his hatred. And all the spirits of his lot make the Sons of Light stumble. And the God of Israel and the Angel of his Truth is/are a help to all the Sons of Light. (1QS III, 21c–25a)

Obviously, the text is not interested in the "sons of iniquity" doing good deeds, but rather wants to explain the occurrence of sin and evil in the world and especially when it happens among the righteous. Therefore, we do not learn whether the Prince of Lights attempts to influence the wicked to do good. However, the asymmetrical schema of the Treatise demonstrates that this section of the text cannot be evaluated as thoroughly dualistic as the two oppositional realms have contact and do not seem to be stuck in irreducible oppositions: The sons of righteousness experience the influence of the Angel of Darkness and "all their sins, their iniquities, their offences and the transgressions of their deeds are in his authority." Moreover, they apparently experience "afflictions and periods of distress" while being subjected to the dominion of the Angel of Darkness.

Finally, the cosmic division of these forces might be part of the author's strategy. The author might extrapolate into the cosmic realm such a division, because on a human level he cannot control sin and iniquity among righteous people, and, thus, in his experience a clear-cut division is not perceived to be existent. As such, the sublimation of human difficulties into a much clearer division of right/wrong on a divine level demonstrates the author's wish to divide things that in reality are not so easily separated.

The next section seems to function as a summary of the former statements. Licht has denoted that lines III, 25–IV, 1 "restate the main focus" of the Treatise of the Two Spirits, while at the same time drawing in the newly obtained detailed information from the preceding section.[99] As such, these lines seem to create a conscious analogy with III, 18, simultaneously connecting (yet another time) the notions of light/darkness with truth/iniquity:

> And he created the spirits of light and darkness and upon them he established every deed and on their [path/foundation] is every deed and on their path is every [deed/visitation].[100] One God loves for all eternal ages and with all her deeds He will be pleased until forever. One He abhors, her secret counsel and all her paths He hates forever. (III, 25–IV, 1)

For Wernberg-Møller, the reenactment of III, 18 in III, 25 is an indication that the author is still addressing ethical issues without the usual evaluation of this section in terms of dualism and predestination. Indeed, the contrasting of righteousness and injustice is a rather common theme in wisdom literature and Jewish writings from the Second Temple period, without necessarily invoking connotations of either ideological concept (e.g., Prov 29:27; Sir 15:11–20; 33:14–15; 1 En. 91:3–4; 18–19; 94:1–5 [the Exhortation and Epistle of Enoch]; and underlying the Apocalypse of Weeks in 1 En. 93:1–10; 91:11–17).[101] Furthermore, the passage also functions to reinforce earlier statements that God has created all.[102] Finally, this passage functions as a bridge to the next section (IV, 2–14) in which the realms of light/darkness (resp. truth/iniquity) are further described

---

99. Licht, "Analysis of the Treatise," 93; cf. Wernberg-Møller, "Reconsideration of the Two Spirits," 428.

100. The brackets indicate that the text is reconstructed at this instance. Here, the two alternative readings follow García Martínez/Tigchelaar and Accordance (Abegg). Eye-catchingly, the reconstruction of the former demonstrates a repetition.

101. Such connotations are also found in other parts of the Community Rule, see 1QS I, 1–II, 18. As to the evaluation of dualism in these instances, see §5.5 below.

102. See Wernberg-Møller, who compares ברא in III, 18 with יסד in III, 25; see also von der Osten-Sacken, Gott und Belial, 149 n. 2: "יסד ist bereits im AT dann auch in Qumran terminus technicus für Gottes Schöpfungshandeln."

in concrete and recognizable behavior through a list of virtues and vices. In the table below, I have attempted to schematically describe the various components of this list:

Table 9: Schematic Overview of the List of Virtues and Vices in the Treatise IV, 2–14	
Now these are their paths in the world:	
to give light in the heart of man [cf. Gen 1:15,17 אוֹר] to straighten before his face the paths of righteousness of truth and to cause his heart to fear the ordinances of God	
	And to the spirit of falsehood there is:
<ul><li>a spirit of humility</li><li>patience</li><li>multitude of compassion</li><li>everlasting good</li><li>insight and understanding</li><li>mighty wisdom, trusting in all God's deeds, and depending upon the multitude of his mercy and the spirit of knowledge in all plans of deeds</li><li>zeal for the ordinances of righteousness and plans of holiness with firm inclination</li><li>abundance of loving-kindness upon all sons of truth</li><li>purity of glory, abhorring all idols of impurity</li><li>walking humbly in discernment of everything</li><li>to hide the truth, the mysteries of knowledge</li></ul>	<ul><li>a wideness of soul/breadth of self</li><li>a sloughiness of hands in the service of justice</li><li>wickedness and vanity</li><li>pride and arrogance</li><li>a lying heart and cruel deceit</li><li>much ungodliness</li><li>impatience and</li><li>a multitude of folly</li><li>a zeal for pride</li><li>deeds of abomination in a spirit of fornication/harlotry</li><li>paths of impurity in the service of uncleanliness/impurity</li><li>a slanderous tongue</li><li>blindness of eyes</li><li>heaviness of ear</li><li>hardness of neck</li><li>heaviness of heart</li><li>to walk in all the paths of darkness</li><li>craftiness of evil</li></ul>
These are the secret counsels/foundations of the spirit of the sons of truth (in) the world	
And the visitation of all walkers in it is:	The visitation of all walking in it is:

healing a multitude of peace in the length of days fruitful seed with all blessings of eternity everlasting joy in eternal life an ornament of glory with measure of honor in everlasting light	a multitude of plagues at the hand of all the angels of destruction eternal destruction with the anger of God's avenging wrath everlasting terror and reproach with the disgrace of complete destruction by fire of those who make dark And all their times of their generations are with agonizing sorrow/mourning and wickedness of bitterness in the threat/catastrophe of darkness until their complete destruction, for there is no remnant or escape for them

As table 9 makes clear, this section, containing the "list of vices and virtues" does not reflect a symmetrical structure. It is therefore unclear whether the first three infinitive constructs in IV, 2 (to shine, to straighten, to be fearful) are only connected to the spirit of light/truth or whether both spirits are envisioned. Wernberg-Møller argues that, since every human being is endowed with both spirits, no parallelism of introduction or content is needed.[103] The two lists then represent the behavior and conduct that are recognizably part of each realm. The text also describes the punishments and rewards that are attached to this variety of behaviors and thus inherently exhorts its audience to choose for or remain on the path of righteousness. As Licht has pointed out: "The two lists in themselves do not express any extreme dualistic theory: the juxtaposition of the righteous and the wicked, of deeds and rewards, could be used in any homily without predestinational tendencies."[104] Moreover, as we have already established that a mere contrasting of ethical terms is inherently part of religious theorizing, the list's oppositional language cannot be regarded as dualistic. Only if the ethical terminology would be connected to eschatological and/or cosmic dualistic layers does it become part of a larger dualistic realm. However, our preceding analysis of the Treatise seriously poses doubt on such a straightforward reading. Also, the notion that the spirits convey a variety of behaviors in which humans are inclined to "walk to and fro" prevents us from such an interpretation. Moreover, the strong emphasis on the eschatological punishments of the "spirit of false-

---

103. Wernberg-Møller, "Reconsideration of the Two Spirits," 429–31.
104. Licht, "Analysis of the Treatise," 94.

5. THE ZENITH OF QUMRAN THOUGHT

hood" possibly points to the author's preoccupation with the problem of sin and evil and reflects an exhortatory attempt to convince the righteous not to "walk in the spirit of iniquity."[105]

The next passage, 1QS IV, 15–26, returns to the author's main message:

> In these [אלה] are the natures [תולדות] of all the sons of man, and in their divisions [מפלגיהן] all their hosts will inherit for their generations. And in their paths they shall walk and every work of their deeds is in their divisions [מפלגיהן] according to the inheritance of man, great or small, for all eternal time. (IV, 15–16a)

The complexity of this passage has induced many scholars to evaluate lines IV, 15–26 as *the* example of Qumranite dualism. For instance, von der Osten-Sacken regards IV, 15–18a as the portrayal of "das Verhältnis zwischen Wahrheit und Frevel und die Stellung des Menschen zu ihnen in der Gegenwart."[106] Being the introduction to the last section of the Treatise, these first lines set the tone in which the remainder of the passage is interpreted. Even though this section is generally understood to (further) describe the sharp dualistic division between two classes of humans, Wernberg-Møller correctly noted that the actual word "two" only occurs once in the entire Treatise (III, 18) and thus is implied everywhere else.[107] Therefore, the plural forms in these lines do not necessarily need to be interpreted as dual and oppositional but might merely point to a plurality or variety, in accordance with the variety of behavioral manifestations as described in IV, 2–14.

The difficulty of translating and interpreting this passage lies in the various interconnected aspects of these sentences: (1) the reference of "these" (אלה) in IV, 15; (2) the translation of תולדות; (3) the use of the peculiar term מפלג; (4) the use of the third person feminine plural suffix in מפלגיהן in IV, 15. "These" in line IV, 15 corresponds either with "these" in line IV, 2 in which case they embrace the entirety of the virtues/vices catalog or, as many scholars have claimed, with the two spirits. Licht regards אלה as a reference to the "ways": "'in these' enumerated 'ways' are contained the *toladoth*—the pre-ordained nature and destiny—of all

---

105. Wernberg-Møller, "Reconsideration of the Two Spirits," 429–30.
106. Von der Osten-Sacken, *Gott und Belial*, 170.
107. Wernberg-Møller, "Reconsideration of the Two Spirits," 431; e.g., in *DSSSE* (1:79) the word "two" is added between brackets at IV 15, 79.

men."¹⁰⁸ Von der Osten-Sacken translates: "In diesen (sc. Geistern) ist der Usprung aller Menschen." He argues that IV, 15 functions to tie both earlier sections together, while at the same time ensuring that the succeeding passage clearly continues to emphasize the two spirits, "auch wenn ihr Gegensatz ab iv 17 ff. begrifflich durch die Abstrakta 'Wahrheit' und 'Frevel' ausgedrückt wird."¹⁰⁹ Wernberg-Møller more or less combines these views by arguing that in the virtues-and-vices catalog of 1QS IV, 2–14 רוח is used to describe "a great variety of moods and manifestations of the two 'spirits' mentioned in col. III."¹¹⁰ He argues that אלה in IV, 15 refers to that variety. In this elegant way, Wernberg-Møller can connect אלה with the succeeding terms ובדרכיהן, ומפלגיהן, and מפלגיהן, which he takes as parallel terms, syntactically connected by the preposition -ב. In such a way, the interpretation of אלה is connected to the interpretation of the third person plural feminine suffixes of these succeeding terms. Most scholars regard the gender of the suffixes as pointing exclusively to the "two spirits," thus forming the foundation for a further dualistic interpretation of the passage.¹¹¹ However, if Wernberg-Møller is correct, the feminine plural suffixes in this passage point both to the two spirits and to the variety of behavioral manifestations that color their ways. Moreover, if "these" (אלה) describe "the natures [תולדות] of all the sons of man" and hence can be taken as symbiotic terms, the feminine suffixes might just as well refer to the rich variety of human behavior covered by תולדות. Therefore, and in line with my argumentation regarding the meaning of תולדות above, the passage might simply recapture what is learned from the former two sections: the explanation of human nature as consisting of a variety of "inclinations."

In this light, the term מפלג (division) is more likely to refer to the variety of behavior within the two spiritual paths (truth/iniquity resp. light/darkness) than to a strictly dualistic division between two classes of

---

108. Licht, "Analysis of the Treatise," 94–95.
109. Von der Osten-Sacken, *Gott und Belial*, 170.
110. Wernberg-Møller, "Reconsideration of the Two Spirits," 431.
111. Only in 1QS IV, 17 do we find a masculine suffix attached to "divisions." However, the suffix is in superscript and hence might possibly be a later scribal correction, which might even be attributed to whoever incorporated the Treatise in 1QS and found a masculine suffix more appropriate for his purposes, thereby changing the original reference.

humans.[112] As such, "the word [מפלג], as applied to the spirits, is most naturally taken as referring to the various good and bad inclinations just enumerated [in IV, 2–14] in which all mankind, 'all the hosts of their generations', have their share."[113] The biblical language alluded to by the usage of terms, which in scripture are used to describe God's ordering of creation (מפלג) or his division of the land (נחל), might serve the author's purpose to demonstrate, once again, that "from the God of knowledge all exists and shall exist," a theme to which he will return shortly.[114]

Finally, it is important to notice that the humans are doing the walking, and, as such, we might deduce that they are held accountable as their every deed can be subscribed to the enumerated divisions in IV, 2–14. Thus, this part of the text leaves open the possibility to "walk on both paths" (cf. Sir 2:12). The next passage sets the spirits and their recognizable human behaviors over against one another:

> For God set them in equal portions, great to small, until the last time and he put eternal enmity between /their/ divisions.[115] An abomination of truth are the deeds of injustice and an abomination of injustice are all the paths of truth. And zealous dispute is upon their judgments/ordinances because they do not walk to and fro together. (IV, 16b–18a)

The declaration of "eternal enmity" is taken by most scholars as the ultimate evidence of the radical dualistic worldview of the Qumran sect.[116] However, this viewpoint can only be maintained if the divisions that oppose one another are interpreted as human divisions, which, as we established above, is precluded by the feminine suffixes.[117] Rather, the divisions refer to the two spirits, and, hence, this section of the Treatise still envisions the rather abstract concepts of "truth" and "iniquity" and their respective behavioral conducts as visible in human beings. A certain amount of tension between this section of the Treatise and the earlier classifica-

---

112. Von der Osten-Sacken, *Gott und Belial*, 171.
113. Wernberg-Møller, "Reconsideration of the Two Spirits," 432.
114. See von der Osten-Sacken, *Gott und Belial*, 171; he also points out that in 1 En. 72–82 and Jubilees, the term מפלג is used to describe the cosmological order of creation.
115. The verb שים again has a feminine suffix, but מפלג has a masculine suffix in superscript. Cf. n. 108.
116. E.g., Licht, "Analysis of the Treatise," 95; Frey, "Different Patterns," 293.
117. See also Wernberg-Møller, "Reconsideration of the Two Spirits," 431–32.

tion of humankind into two oppositional groups, the Sons of Righteousness/Light and the Sons of Iniquity/Darkness, cannot be denied. Whereas in the first part of the Treatise a fundamental distinction is being made between these two groups of humans, this part envisions both spirits to be active within every human being "in equal portions." This concept is repeated even more clearly in IV, 23b–25a:

> Until this point the spirits of truth and iniquity will strive in the heart of man. They will walk to and fro in wisdom and in folly. And corresponding to the inheritance of man in truth, he will be righteous and thus he shall hate injustice, and according to his possession in the lot of iniquity, he will act wickedly and thus he shall abhor truth. For God has set them in equal portions until the deciding time and the making of something new.

The idea of man being ruled by "portions" of both spirits has almost univocally been connected to 4Q186, a text that is also often referred to as an example of the Qumranites' dualistic ideology. Recently Popović has challenged this commonly held view, provocatively arguing that 4Q186's idea of "portions" of light and darkness reflects an astrological provenance, completely unrelated to the (ideology of) the Treatise.[118] Popović argues that the "spirit" (רוח) in 4Q186 does not refer to the human spirit, but rather reflects a zodiacal spirit. Moreover, he thinks that, unlike in the case of the Treatise, the terminology of "portions of light/darkness" is not meant metaphorically in 4Q186. Rather Popović holds the portions to function in a literal sense, namely, in an astrological framework, in which they are combined with the zodiacal term "house" (בית) to indicate the cosmological areas above and below the horizon. Therefore, he advocates that the terms light and darkness in 4Q186 should not be interpreted as dualistic, and the text's presumed ties to the Treatise need to be dissolved.[119]

If Popović is correct and we disconnect the Treatise's idea of portions within the human being from 4Q186, this passage might, again, touch upon the tension between the themes of free will and predestination. Indeed, Wernberg-Møller has argued that both 1QS IV, 16 and 1QS IV, 24

---

118. Popović, "Light and Darkness," 148–65.
119. Popović (ibid., 164) states that "4Q186 is not an example of a dualistic text from the Qumran community.... it most probably is not even a sectarian composition."

have the same person in view and speak about his position towards the various parts of his behavior. As such, he argues that "man was created with the two inclinations in perfect balance and equally strong."[120] There is no need to deny the existence of oppositional moral forces and/or behavior in every human being, leading to the (societal) evaluation of a "good" or "bad" person. Moreover, the theme of righteousness and wickedness's mutual hatred is not uncommon in scripture, especially in wisdom literature (e.g., Prov 29:27). Such a juxtaposition of ethical terms and behavior has elsewhere not been evaluated as dualistic, and there is no need to do so in this text.

A final statement against an evaluation of a thoroughly dualistic outlook is the Treatise's eschatological description of the end of iniquity in 1QS IV, 18–23a:

> And God, in the mysteries of his knowledge/understanding and in the wisdom of his glory has given a time to the being of injustice and on an appointed time of visitation he will destroy it forever. And then the truth of the world shall go out forever because she polluted herself on the paths of wickedness in the dominion of injustice, until the appointed time of the deciding judgment. And then God will purify, with his truth, all the deeds of man and he will refine for him the sons of man to end all spirit of injustice from the inner self of his flesh, cleansing him with the holy spirit from all deeds of wickedness. And he shall sprinkle upon him the spirit of truth like sprinkling waters, from all abominations of falsehood and its wallowing in the spirit of impurity, to instruct those who are upright in the knowledge of the most high and the wisdom of the sons of the heavens in order to instruct those of the perfect way. For God chose them for an eternal covenant and to them is all glory of Adam. And there is no injustice; all acts of deceit will be a shame.

Rather than the destruction of the perceived wicked people (for instance, the sons of iniquity), God will "purify all the deeds of man"; that is, he will end the existence of sin and injustice altogether. The text is almost impersonal in its purpose: wickedness rather than the wicked will be destroyed.[121] Since both spirits reside within every human being and the spirit of iniq-

---

120. Wernberg-Møller, "Reconsideration of the Two Spirits," 433.
121. The only personal element the text seems to envision is the special treatment of those who have been elected by God to be instructed in his special knowledge.

uity is destroyed by God in the end-time, no radical or moderate dualistic opposition that causes existence can be detected in this passage. Rather, the text is interested in the purification of humanity and creation in order to restore God's created world according to the "glory of Adam."

Dualism in the Treatise: Summary

When read on a superficial level, the Treatise of the Two Spirits demonstrates a rather stringent oppositional outlook, which at times tends justifiably to resemble Bianchi's definition of moderate dualism. Indeed, in its cosmological description of two oppositional angelic beings and their earthly counterparts, the Treatise might easily be evaluated as dualistic. From this first section, many scholars have interpreted the entirety of the Treatise in dualistic terms, even though syntactically and structurally many elements speak against such a straightforward evaluation of dualism.

Upon a closer investigation of the text's main purpose and primary focus, we detect that the author of the Treatise was predominantly occupied with the question of sin and transgression among "good" people. As in every tractate that concerns itself with the tension between free will and predestination, the omnipotence of God and the occurrence of sin and hardship, an explanation needs to be found for the presence of evil in the world. Moreover, the author finds such a solution in the oppositional, but variable, inclinations belonging to the "spirits of truth and iniquity," which are "put" within the very structure in which God has created man. This concept is not dualistic. Equally, the moral and ethical terms and behaviors that are attached to both oppositional forces can also not be evaluated as dualistic for the simple reason that (1) they are united within every human being and (2) they do not consist of irreducible causal principles which create existence. Also, to attach the oppositional terms "light" and "darkness" to the moral concepts of "truth" and "iniquity" can hardly be evaluated as dualistic as it is a commonly known phenomenon in scripture to use the concepts of light and darkness as metaphors (e.g., Isa 5:20; 9:2; 42:16; 45:7; Pss 18:28; 37:6; Qoh 2:13–14). To my knowledge, this metaphorical use of light/darkness in those instances has never led to an evaluation of dualism. Finally, those cosmological opposites that are often read dualistically are not perceived as impregnable: (1) the realm of the Prince of Darkness stretches out into the realm of the righteous (and perhaps vice versa); and (2) redemption is possible as God will purify all the works of man at the appointed time.

In this section, we have evaluated the common scholarly opinion that the Treatise is a dualistic text and have found that much of its oppositional language has an exhortatory function to persuade forcefully its audience to "walk the right path." Moreover, we have seen that the author of the Treatise is preoccupied with the question of why good people do bad things. Hence, our evaluation of the Treatise leads us to conclude that the text is better not regarded as having a dualistic outlook.

Nevertheless, because the text has long been understood as the pinnacle of Qumran dualism, the Treatise has been given a pivotal position in the perceived development of sectarian dualistic thought. As we already saw in chapter 4, scholars like Frey and Lange have placed the Treatise in a chronological framework that forms a "pattern of multidimensional sapiential dualism." This conceptualization of an ideological development from sapiential oppositionality to sectarian dualism has had an important influence on scholarly evaluations of oppositionality in certain texts. Also, it has introduced dualism as a cohesive force to link ideology to a sectarian social reality. For these reasons, we return to Frey's "pattern of dualism" to look at his argument in further detail.

5.5. The Treatise and Its Position in the Sapiential Pattern of Qumran Dualism

An important presupposition that underlies the evaluation of dualism as a key-concept of the Qumran sect is the notion of ideological development. As we have seen, Frey's evaluation of "the patterns of dualistic thinking" presents a model in which 1QS III, 13–IV, 26 and 1QM are the pre-*yahadic* linchpins that bound assumed precursory documents together through recognizable rudimentary elements of dualistic thinking. Moreover, they also are thought to have influenced the formation of a recognizable Qumran "sectarian form of dualism" that was primarily focused on sheer cosmic dualism and eternal election.[122] This pattern, reflecting a chronological development from late wisdom literature (e.g., Ben Sira) via multidimensional dualistic teaching (Treatise) into sheer cosmic dualism (various *yahadic* documents), is described as the "Qumran sect's ideo-

---

122. Frey follows to a large extent Lange's *Weisheit und Prädestination*, 127–29, 167–68.

logical radicalization process." Table 10 below schematically describes this pattern of development, from earliest work to latest.

Table 10: Overview of Frey's Pattern of Sapiential Dualism				
Proverbs	Ben Sira	4QInstruction 4QMysteries	Treatise	*Yahadic* reception in 1QS I, 16–26; II, 2–10 1QH^a VI, 11–12 4Q181 1, II, 1–5 CD II, 2–13 4Q280 2, 4–5 (4Q502 16)

5.5.1. The Precursors: Ben Sira, 4QInstruction, and 4QMysteries

Frey thinks that tradition-historically, the Treatise can be connected with early wisdom literature's "pronounced ethical dualism by the antithetical opposition of the scoffer and the wise or the wicked and the righteous with a mutual antipathy ... between the members of the respective groups (Prov 29:27)."[123] Frey also argues that, in the later wisdom text of Ben Sira, this notion of righteousness and wickedness is combined with the notion of a predestined order of creation and "the ethical dualities are interpreted in the context of the whole creation structured in pairs."[124] In this interpretation, Ben Sira is regarded as a possible precursor of the Treatise as it does "not teach any determinism of the destiny or even of the acts of human beings" but instead firmly advocates the freedom of the human will.[125] Hence, as we have seen, Ben Sira's predestined order of creation is thought to be the ideological background of the teaching in 1QS III, 13–IV, 26, which reflects this concept in a more developed form.[126]

As we already briefly discussed in chapter 4, two other sapiential texts from Qumran, 4QInstruction and 4QMysteries, are thought to be

---

123. Frey, "Different Patterns," 297; see also Gammie, "Spatial and Ethical Dualism," 372.

124. Frey, "Different Patterns," 297; Frey also thinks that Ben Sira connects his idea of a predestined order of creation with the created division between light and darkness (Gen 1:4).

125. Ibid., 297 n. 89.

126. Ibid., 298.

closely related to, but developmentally earlier than, the Treatise.[127] Frey has argued that the "mystery of existence" (רז נהיה) in these documents, to which the wise can gain special, revealed knowledge, is a further development of Ben Sira's predestined order of creation. He further thinks that because these texts do not reflect two spirits or an antagonism of cosmic powers they are to be considered earlier than the Treatise. In short, 4QInstruction and 4QMysteries are chronologically placed in between Ben Sira and the Treatise.

Hence, ideas and conceptualizations in Ben Sira, 4QInstruction, and 4QMysteries are thought to have influenced the development of early *yahadic* sapiential dualism in the Treatise. The next sections (§§5.1.1–3) will reevaluate Frey's conception of such a sapiential pattern of chronological development by studying those ideas in these texts that reflect the negotiation of oppositionality and/or dualism.

5.5.1.1. Ben Sira

The similarities in outlook between the Treatise and Ben Sira are indeed eye-catching as many scholars have pointed out. However, to place Ben Sira earlier in a direct developmental line to the Treatise brings up a series of difficulties. First, there is simply the matter of dating. Most scholars agree that Ben Sira was composed somewhere in the early part of the second century BCE and translated into Greek by his grandson towards the end of that same century. If Lange (see above) is right and the Treatise originates in the first quarter of the second century, both documents are of similar age, which makes it seemingly impossible to establish a chronological development between them in which the Treatise is perceived to be a modification of certain ideas in Ben Sira.[128]

In fact, Frey's argument that the Treatise is a later modification of ideas in Ben Sira, because the former conveys a deterministic outlook that the latter lacks, cannot be maintained in light of our analysis of the Trea-

---

127. Frey (ibid., 299) boldly states that these two documents "clearly represent the line of dualistic thought which can be found—somewhat more developed—in the Instruction on the Two Spirits."

128. A similar argument can be made with regard to 4QMysteries, which is commonly dated between 200–150 BCE. Moreover, scholars have implied that 4QInstruction might have a date in the early third century BCE, which makes the text unsuitable as a chronological buffer between Ben Sira and the Treatise.

tise above. Instead of reflecting a deterministic outlook, we find that the Treatise, in a way similar to Ben Sira, reflects an inherent tension between human free will and God's predestined order of creation, predominantly revolving around the question of the occurrence of sin in the world.[129]

Ben Sira seems to express a rather clear opinion as to where sin and evil belong. God gave man free will, and, hence, sinfulness belongs to the human realm: "When he made man in the beginning, he left him free to take his own decisions" and "He has commanded no man to be wicked, nor has he given license to commit sin" (Sir 15:11–20; cf. 37:18).[130] In Sir 17, the earlier declaration of free will and humans' capacity to discern between good and evil is, just like in the Treatise, firmly connected to Gen 1 (cf. Sir 17:1–8). However, the discernment between good and evil is not always easy to establish as a person can operate "with a double heart" and "full of deceit" (Sir 1:28, 30) and "sinners can walk on two paths at once" (Sir 2:12). Similarly to the Treatise, the possibility of being in two realms simultaneously (i.e., "to walk on two paths" or "to approach the Lord with a double heart" in Ben Sira), interferes with the neat division between sinners and godly and makes the oppositionality less symmetrical. Hence, sinners are not regarded as fully sinful as they can "walk on two paths" and thus are envisioned also to do good. As a solution to this problem, Ben Sira might understand double-heartedness as hypocrisy; it nevertheless leaves room for crossover. In a creation in which humans can choose to live "according to God's ways" or choose "the path of evil," they must be held fully accountable for their own conduct, behavior, and actions. However, the human accountability of which the text narrates seems to be in tension with Ben Sira's statement that "before the world was created, each man's deed was known to God" (Sira 23:20, cf. 1QS III, 15–16). In Sir 39, one can encounter tension or an intrinsic struggle between the conviction that God's creation is good, as Genesis tells us, and the more implicitly described experienced reality that the world is full of wickedness and evil. Ben Sira tries, on the one hand, to hold on to the old biblical notion of *Tun-Ergehen-Zusammenhang*, that is, the notion that good will lead to good and bad will lead to bad. On the other hand, he realizes that in the experienced social reality such causality is obviously not always the case. Possibly, Ben Sira attempts to explain the inexplicable by deferring

---

129. Contra Frey, who argues that Ben Sira univocally claims human free will.
130. Both passages, i.e., 15:16–17 and 37:18, might reflect Deut 30:15–20, which might also stand in the background of the Treatise.

the problem to some "appointed time," implicitly stating that man cannot comprehend God's plan. Hence, he expresses that all things will happen "in due time" (Sir 39:16) and "at the[ir] proper time" (Sir 39:17; 34). Such notions of primordial eschatology and the mystery of God's plan are very similarly negotiated in the Treatise.[131]

Just as in the Treatise, Ben Sira's account of what will happen to the wicked is inconsistent with his earlier statement that everything is good for the good and bad for the bad. The text seems most interested in the fate of the wicked over time in judgment and retribution, and again Ben Sira treats the "righteous" and "wicked" divisions asymmetrically. Moreover, the "spirits" or "winds" of retribution seem to be created exclusively for the wicked (e.g., Sir 39:16–34). Thus, just as in the Treatise, a complete antithesis is not achieved; the author simply does not seem to be interested in such a thoroughly oppositional scheme of creation. Moreover, the question behind Ben Sira's solution of judgment and retribution "over time" is, just like in the Treatise, how to evaluate the occurrence of sin and how to explain to the god-fearing that the wicked will not prosper, even though they probably do in the author's contemporary social reality.

The full scale of Ben Sira's problem regarding God's order of creation and his control over man in the face of man's sinful behavior leads him to insert a doctrinal passage regarding the "contradictory nature of God's world." In a manner similar to the Treatise, Ben Sira finds a solution for the existence of sin and evil as he conceives God having deliberately created the world in carefully balanced opposites:

> All man alike come from the ground.
> Adam was created out of earth.
> Yet in his great wisdom the Lord distinguished them,
> And made them go various ways.
> Some he blessed and lifted high,
> Some he hallowed and brought near to himself,
> Some he cursed and humbled,
> And removed from their place.
> As clay is in the potter's hands,

---

131. Sir 39:28 even has "spirits/winds of retribution." Unfortunately, we only have the Greek of this passage, as this passage is lacking in the Hebrew fragments. Moreover, the notion that God's plan is predestined and only he knows beginning and end is firmly established in both the Treatise and Ben Sira (e.g., 23:20, "Before the universe was created, it was known to him. And so it is since its completion").

> To be moulded just as he chooses,
> So are men in the hands of their maker,
> To be dealt with as he decides.
> Good is the opposite of evil, and life of death;
> Yes, and the sinner is the opposite of the godly.
> Look at all the works of the Most High;
> They go in pairs, one the opposite of the other. (Sir 33:10–15.)[132]

In Ben Sira's praise of creation (Sir 42), God's foreknowledge of his creation and the manner in which God has created the universe are intrinsically connected: "All things go in pairs, one the opposite of the other. He has made nothing incomplete. One thing supplements the virtues of the other" (Sir 42:24–25).

Moreover, the order of creation is now conceived as naturally oppositional in character, and hence oppositionality becomes a characteristic of completeness or perfection, which again forms a solution for the occurrence of sin and evil in the world. Indeed, one can now correlate the occurrence of sin and evil with the glory of God and the mystery of his creation. All ideas regarding God's plan of creation, human free will, the incomprehensibility of God's purpose, the exhortation for humans to be trusting, faithful, and law observant, and the idea of a final judgment of the wicked are now drawn together. In addition, God is recognized as the God of full knowledge, which remains a mystery to all of his creation (Sir 42:17–25).

Interestingly, and even though the similarities of themes and ideological outlooks between Ben Sira and the Treatise are most pronounced, I have not found any publication that characterizes Ben Sira's cosmology and anthropology as dualistic. Rather, Ben Sira's doctrine of opposites is often thought to explain the notion of the antinomies or polarities or opposites that are found in creation.[133] Recently, Gregory Schmidt Goering has argued that Ben Sira "bases his anthropology not on the notion of oppositions, but rather on the idea of Israel's election, a notion he derives from his observation of the cosmos."[134] He argues that, rather than evaluating Ben Sira's distinctions between anthropological and cosmological categories as oppositionality, they should be regarded from a viewpoint of

---

132. Translation from the Greek in Snaith, *Ecclecsiasticus*.

133. E.g., Patrick Skehan and Alexander Di Lella, *The Wisdom of Ben Sira*, AB 39 (New York: Doubleday, 1987).

134. Gregory Schmidt Goering, *Wisdom's Root Revealed: Ben Sira and the Election of Israel*, JSJ 139 (Leiden: Brill, 2009), 50.

set apartness. That is, he regards the contrasts in Ben Sira not as oppositional, but rather as expressions of election that are natural and visible in God's created world.[135] If Goering is correct, his observations demonstrate that the idea of binary oppositions in Ben Sira is not to be evaluated as strictly oppositional.

Even though my evaluations and Goering's stem from different perspectives, we both agree that the perceived oppositionality in Ben Sira cannot, for various reasons, function as a cradle for dualism. Moreover, the similarities in outlook and date of Ben Sira and the Treatise suggest that the ideas in both documents might possibly be more widespread in Second Temple society. Thus, similar ideas regarding God's plan for creation and the occurrence of sin can possibly be found in more or less modified forms in other contemporary documents. Such an observation might be preferred over the stringency of a chronological development scheme and the subsequent ideological straightjacket of dualism at Qumran.

5.5.1.2. 4QInstruction and 4QMysteries

Two other texts that are thought to be precursors to the Treatise are 4QInstruction and 4QMysteries. As we have already briefly discussed in chapter 4, Frey considers these two texts to fit ideologically in between Ben Sira and the Treatise, thus forming the chronological trajectory of the sapiential pattern of dualism that eventually made up part of Qumran dualistic thought. In his evaluation of these two "closely linked" documents, Frey follows Lange, who argues that the Treatise, 4QInstruction, and 4QMysteries demonstrate rather noticeable correspondences: (1) they share a significant amount of rather typical terminology; (2) the term מחשבה is used in both 4QInstruction and 1QS III, 13–IV, 26 for the preexistent order of the cosmos and history, that is, God's plan; (3) all three texts refer to "the God of Knowledge"; (4) the term תולדות is used in 4Q418 77, 2 and in 1QS III, 13 in its particular meaning of "human history"; (5) the dualism in the Treatise is comparable to the implicit oppositions in 4QInstruction; the Treatise and 4QMysteries share the "Theologenon von der eschatologischen Offenbarung der Weisheit."[136] On the basis of these similarities

---

135. Goering (ibid., 49–68) thinks that the distinction between righteous and wicked is similar to the distinction between "festival days" and "normal days," sun and moon, etc.

136. Lange, *Weisheit und Prädestination*, 127–29.

and correspondences, Lange concludes "daß die Zwei-Geister-Lehre aus den Kreisen stammt, die auch 4QSapA und Myst hervorgebracht haben. Jedoch stellt sie zumindestens gegenüber 4QSapA eine Weiterentwicklung dar, die die schon in diesem Text angelegten dualistischen Tendenzen stärker betont und das eschatologische Moment von Myst ausbaut."[137]

The editors of DJD XXXIV, who discuss 4QInstruction without specifically comparing 4QInstruction to the Treatise, tend to agree with this idea of ideological development, as they hold Instruction to have a theological framework that is "not developed to the level of sophistication found in the 'Instruction on the Two Spirits' (1QS III–IV); it could however, fit an early stage of development that led to such thinking."[138] However, the editors also extensively stress how 4QInstruction is different from the Treatise, while they are at the same time convinced of its "direct link" with 4QMysteries through the important term רז נהיה ("the mystery of existence"), a term that is not found in the Treatise.[139] For instance, the editors point out that 4QInstruction has "references to the 'evil inclination', without any talk of a corresponding 'good inclination' and without the psychological and metaphysical development of a dualism as found in the 'Instruction of the Two Spirits' in 1QS III–IV."[140] Furthermore, in 4QInstruction, "God is the creator and sustainer of all," and there are no "subordinate figures such as the Prince of Light or the Prince of Darkness (see 1QS III–IV) involved."[141] Even though the editors think these differences might possibly be signs of development, they demonstrate caution with regard to assumptions of dependency as they hasten to state that 4QInstruction's combination of "wisdom instructions with theological material is paralleled in many other Jewish and early Christian works."[142] Moreover, sociologically, 4QInstruction does not reflect a sectarian outlook, nor does it provide information regarding a specific community of addressees. Rather, the text seems concerned with the correct instruction

---

137. Ibid., 130.
138. John Strugnell, Daniel Harrington, and Torleif Elgvin, eds., *Sapiential Texts, Part 2: Cave 4.XXIV*, DJD XXXIV (Oxford: Clarendon, 1999), 33.
139. The term רז (mystery) occurs three times in the Treatise: רזי אל (the mysteries of God; 1QS III, 23), רזי דעת (the mysteries of knowledge; 1QS IV, 6), and ברזי שכלו (in the mysteries of his understanding; 1QS IV, 18).
140. DJD XXXIV, 33.
141. Ibid.
142. Ibid.

of a junior sage.¹⁴³ Finally, 4QInstruction is notoriously hard to position, both with regard to its date and its sociohistorical position, on both of which the text displays no concrete information.

Tigchelaar has argued that the correspondences between the Treatise and 4QInstruction are indeed conspicuous, but he thinks correspondences predominantly are found in those specific textual layers of the Treatise that he recognizes as later additions (i.e., 1QS III, 13–18; IV, 15–23a; and IV, 23b–26). Hence, according to Tigchelaar, 4QInstruction has few correspondences with 1QS III, 18–IV, 1, "which describes the basic spiritual protagonists in terms of light and darkness."¹⁴⁴ If Tigchelaar is correct, both documents may have a common background or 4QInstruction was influenced by the Treatise.

Hence, all these observations place serious doubt on Lange's straightforward identification of chronological development in which the Treatise is thought to represent a further ideological development of ideas, already present in crude form in 4QInstruction.

5.5.1.3. The Omission of 1 Enoch and Jubilees

Another feature of Frey's developmental analysis is his omission of two documents that ideologically and thematically demonstrate similarities with the Treatise: 1 Enoch, especially chapters 91–105, and Jubilees.

Even though the Treatise never explicitly mentions the myth of the Watchers as the origin of evil, the document has numerous points of reference with the Enochic writings. Within the Enochic writings themselves, tension can be observed between the Book of the Watchers, which explains the existence of evil on earth as a result of the fall of the Watchers, and the Epistle of Enoch, which takes a firm stand against an extraterrestrial origin of evil: "Sin was not sent upon the earth, but men created it by themselves" (1 En. 98:4).¹⁴⁵ In the eschatological framework of 1 Enoch, a strict division is made between the righteous and the wicked. In the Apocalypse of Weeks (1 En. 93:1–10; 91:11–17), we find the designation "sons of righteousness" (1 En. 93:1–3). Also, in 1 En. 94:1–5, which is often referred to

---

143. Ibid., 36.
144. Tigchelaar, *To Increase Learning*, 201.
145. For an integrated view on this ostensibly irresolvable contradiction within the Enochic tradition, see Loren T. Stuckenbruck, *1 Enoch 91–108: Translation and Commentary*, CEJL (Berlin: de Gruyter, 2007), 345–46.

as Enoch's Instruction on the Two Ways, we find the juxtaposition of walking in "paths of righteousness" or "paths of iniquity" as well as the respective fates of those who choose either path (1 En. 91:18-19, cf. 92:3-5, 99:10). Moreover, 1 Enoch envisions the possibility for someone to "draw near the truth with a double heart" instead of "walking in righteousness" (1 En. 91:4). Further, the Epistle of Enoch negotiates the ethical notions of righteousness and iniquity with the abstractions of light and darkness (e.g., 1 En. 92:5). Finally, the Epistle places the distinction between the righteous and the wicked in an eschatological frame that perceived the destruction of sin "forever" (e.g., 1 En. 91:8-10, 12-14, 18-19; 92:5).

Similarly, the book of Jubilees reflects certain ideas and concepts that resemble ideas within the Treatise. Von der Osten-Sacken has already pointed out the similar way in which Jub. 2:2 and the Treatise thematize a connection between God's creation act, especially the division of light and darkness (Gen 1:4), and the idea of a predestined order of creation in the division of the spirits:

> For on the first day he created the heavens, which are above, and the earth and the waters and all the spirits which minister before him:
> The angels of the presence,
> The angels of sanctification,
> The angels of the spirit of fire,
> The angels of the spirit of the winds,
> The angels of the spirit of the clouds and darkness and snow and hail and frost,
> The angels of resoundings and thunder and lightning,
> The angels of the spirits of cold and heat and winter and springtime and harvest and summer,
> And all the spirits of his creatures, which are in heaven and on earth.
> And he created the abysses and darkness—both evening and night—and light—both dawn and daylight—which he prepared in the knowledge of his heart. (Jub. 2:2)[146]

In addition, in the book of Jubilees we encounter the idea of spirits connected to righteousness and iniquity (e.g., Jub. 1:2). Moreover, Jub. 19:28 has the name "the spirit of Mastema" (cf. 1QS III, 23), while in other instances "Prince Mastema" seems to represent the ultimate evil leader

---

146. Translation from O.S. Wintermute, "Jubilees," in *The Old Testament Pseudepigrapha*, ed. James H. Charlesworth (New York: Doubleday, 1985), 2:35-142.

(e.g., Jub. 11:4–6; 17:15–16; and 48:1–3). Also, Jub. 7:26 envisions persons who might "walk in righteousness" but have chosen to "walk on the paths of corruption." Finally, in Jub. 10:6, the "sons of the righteous" are mentioned, who are to be kept safe from the ruling of evil spirits, who are said to be able to corrupt them (cf. Jub. 10:4–5).

The Treatise's closeness to these writings, which both negotiate similar ideas in their own particular way, cannot be ignored and therefore should be taken into account when considering the position of the Treatise within the larger body of Second Temple Jewish writings.

5.5.2. The *Yahadic* Reception: Radicalization and Rigidification

In the previous sections, we have dealt with texts that were thought to have influenced the sapiential dualistic pattern of the Treatise. According to this scheme, the ideological outlook of the Treatise has influenced later *yahadic* writings as they developed ideas further and demonstrate a clearly more radical dualistic thinking. It is therefore important that in this section we take a closer look at those texts that are commonly evaluated as *yahadic* developments beyond the Treatise.

With regard to the Treatise's presumed influence and "*yahadic* reception," Frey makes a sequence of observations, which he based on its incorporation into 1QS and the various citations of and allusions to the text in other sectarian documents.

(1) The position in which the Treatise is incorporated into 1QS, that is, after the liturgy of the renewal of the covenant, and its clear declaration of two opposing groups (1QS II, 2–10) following either God or Belial (1QS I, 16–26), reveals "a notion of sharpened cosmic dualism in the terminological framework of the community."[147]

(2) The *yahadic* reception of the Treatise is also established by it being cited or alluded to in other *yahadic* texts: 1QH^a VI, 11–12 and 4Q181 1, II, 5 are thought to reflect the idea in 1QS IV, 26 of "God's throwing of the lot"; CD II, 6–7 is perceived to cite the Treatise twice (cf. 1QS IV, 14–22); 4Q280 2, 4–5 apparently has a curse formula that cites 1QS IV, 14's phrase concerning the extinction of the wicked "without a remnant"; and finally, Frey mentions (with a question mark) a citation of the Treatise's virtues catalogue in 4Q502 16, a fragment which Tigchelaar has

---

147. Frey, "Different Patterns," 302.

recently identified as belonging to 4QS^c. Frey's analysis concludes that none of these texts contains the idea of two spirits or adopts the notion of their internal struggle within every human being. Moreover, they seem predominantly interested in the idea of eternal election, rather than in dualistic terminology regarding two spirits or angelic beings. Therefore, Frey concludes that the Treatise is only adopted in these *yahadic* texts in a "deeply modified and simplified form."[148]

(3) With regard to the Damascus Document, Frey observes that the spiritual teaching of CD II, 2–13 expresses the Treatise's ideas merely in ethical terms without any notion of angelic leaders. Rather than focusing on a fundamental opposition between the righteous and the wicked, the text divides people into those who have repented and joined the covenant (CD II, 2) and those who turned aside from the path and denounce the precepts (CD II, 6). Thus, an internal struggle within the human being has no place in this text that uses language reflecting a strong sense of sociological division between insiders and outsiders. Frey observes that CD integrates this sense of ethical division into a larger framework of "a dualistic conception of history." Further, he argues that the text interprets ethical oppositions in terms of cosmic dualism (e.g., Prince of Light vs. Belial; see CD IV, 13). As such, Frey regards CD as reflecting a developed ideology of the Treatise, since "any notion of internal ambivalence has been dropped" in favor of "a framework of reinforced cosmic dualism."[149]

(4) Frey thinks that 4Q181 1, II, 1–5 adopts the Treatise's "dualistic worldview of a predestined division of human and angelic beings into two strictly opposed classes."[150] Again, Frey concludes that in 4Q181 the ethical dualism is reduced in favor of a cosmic level of dualism and a reinforcement of rigid lines between "the elect righteous" and "the wicked."

Based on his observations with regard to these references and in view of the manner in which they represent the perceived dualisms in the Treatise, Frey concludes:[151]

> (1) The psychological dualism of "struggling spirits within the heart of every human being" is unique and not adopted in any other Qumran text.

---

148. Ibid., 303.
149. Ibid., 305.
150. Ibid., 306.
151. Ibid., 306–7.

(2) The ethical opposition of good/wicked and their corresponding virtues/vices become rigidified into sociological notions of insider/outsider groups. Hence, the ethical dimension that the Treatise's dualism inherited from the wisdom tradition becomes less important and "undergoes a transformation into a sheer cosmic dualism."[152]

(3) However, even this cosmic dualism is expressed in terms that are significantly different from the terminology in the Treatise. For instance, the notion of the "spirits" is dropped in favor of the name of Belial. Hence, also the Treatise's cosmic terminology undergoes a "thorough change in interpretation" in the sectarian writings.[153]

Frey's conclusions have serious implications for the overall evaluation of dualism at Qumran. Many of his conclusions can be seen as interpretations of the evidence that reflects a rather incongruent use of ideas and imagery with regard to the dualistic expressions in those *yahadic* texts that are perceived to be related to the Treatise. Since Frey holds the *yahadic* texts significantly change the dualism of the Treatise, we need to retrace his steps and evaluate how he finds and interprets his evidence and reaches his conclusions. This will be the topic of the next section.

5.5.2.1. An Evaluation of Frey's "Yahadic Reception" of Dualism

The basis on which Frey's analysis reaches its conclusion—that these documents can be chronologically structured within a later *yahadic* setting and thus form a pattern of development from the multidimensional sapiential dualism as witnessed in the Treatise into a more simplified and sharpened "cosmic" dualism—is questionable at best for the following reasons:

If we apply the definitions of dualism as we have determined in chapter 4, neither 1QS I, 16–26 nor II, 2–10 demonstrates signs of dualism. The proposed citation of the Treatise (1QS III, 22) in 1QS I, 23 leans on a similarity of only three words (חטאתם, ואשמתם, and ופשעי), while the context of these words is entirely different. Moreover, 1QS I, 16–26 envisions "all the children of Israel," including the new initiates into the community, as sinful (see 1QS I, 24), while in 1QS III, 22 the sins and transgressions

---

152. Ibid., 307.
153. Ibid.

point exclusively to the stumbling acts of the sons of righteousness. In 1QS I, 16–26, the term "the dominion of Belial" is used almost as a technical term in its own right, a term that could be commonly referred to as, for instance, our "Age of Aquarius." Hence, in this passage, Belial does not necessarily point to an anthropomorphic angelic being but might function on a higher level of abstraction. Finally, in contrast to the Treatise, both 1QS passages are concerned with the initiation rituals of a community and hence represent an entirely different genre, which makes comparison rather difficult. In fact, both passages seem most concerned with marking sociological boundaries between members and nonmembers, which inherently leads to (often oppositional) language that enhances the positive self-presentation of the "we" group over against the (exaggerated) otherness of the "they" group(s). Such insider/outsider language does not necessarily represent a social reality, nor does it guarantee an accurate reflection actual cosmology and anthropology of the in-group.

In the "citations" of the Treatise in the other texts identified by Frey, similar problems occur. Frey himself already notes that none of these texts (1QHᵃ VI, 11–12; 4Q181 1, II, 5; CD II, 6–7; and 4Q280 2, 4–5) contains the notion of either two spirits or a struggle between them within the heart of man.¹⁵⁴ Recently Davies has argued that "the presence of an explicit dualistic doctrine is confined to the S and M texts."¹⁵⁵ His arguments to exclude documents that are commonly thought to reflect dualistic thought, like 1QHᵃ, CD, and other parts of 1QS, generally revolve around the lack of a clear unsolvable division between two opposite but equally powerful forces. For instance, in 1QHᵃ, Davies finds terminology such as רוח and בליעל, but these terms are used in a totally different syntactical manner and have significantly different meanings. Also, Davies finds 1QHᵃ's light/darkness terminology not congruent with a dualistic framework: "The reference is to the periods of daylight and darkness, and though they can be metaphorically applied or can even inspire a dualistic opposition, this conception is not present."¹⁵⁶ Moreover, he asserts that, even though CD reflects Belial as an individual figure, he only occurs as a figure of temptation or destruction not as one of two equally powerful oppositional entities. Also, CD asserts a sense of predestination of the

---

154. In 1QHᵃ VI, 11–12 the word רוחות occurs close to the concepts of good and evil, but the text is highly reconstructed and partly illegible; see *DSSSE*, 1:153.

155. Davies, "Dualism in the Qumran War Texts," 8–19.

156. Ibid., 9.

elect and the idea of the dominance of evil in the present age; both concepts obviously flirt with dualism, but according to Davies, CD does not describe them in a dualistic manner.[157]

With Davies's evaluation in mind, we turn to the perceived citations of 1QS IV, 16–22 in CD II, 6–7 and the perceived progression of Qumran dualism in CD II, 2–13 (cf. 4Q266 2, II, 1–13a).[158] The inclusion of CD/DD in Frey's list of influenced *yahadic* documents is interesting. Frey seems unambiguously to define CD as a *yahadic* text, which he apparently places later than the Treatise and possibly even later than 1QS. Scholars have debated fiercely over the priority of these documents without having reached consensus. Hence, if we entertain the possibility that the sequence of these documents needs to be reversed, CD (and possibly also 1QM) might have influenced 1QS. In any case, Frey himself observes that CD speaks predominantly in ethical terms without any notion of two spirits or angelic beings and no mention of an internal struggle within the human heart. Moreover, the ethical criteria of good and evil are thought to be "firmly related to definite social groups."[159] According to Frey, the insider/outsider language therefore seeks to provide a reason for unambiguous belonging and thus can leave no room for psychological dualism that reflects an internal struggle within the human being. In order to evaluate Frey's reasoning, we need to revisit the passage in CD that he considers to be dualistic. If we assess CD II, 2–13, we suspect that Frey might possibly have interpreted the following as being dualistic:

Table 11: Possible Dualistic Elements in CD (following Frey)

3–7a	God loves knowledge; he has established wisdom and counsel before him; prudence and knowledge are at his service; patience is his and abundance of pardon to atone for those who repent from sin.	However, strength and power and a great anger with flames of fire by the hand of all the angels of destruction against those turning aside from the path and abominating the precept, without there being for them either a remnant or survivor.

---

157. Ibid., 9–10.
158. 4Q266 is very fragmentary and reconstructed with the aid of CD-A; see also Charlotte Hempel, *The Damascus Texts*, CQSS 1 (Sheffield: Sheffield Academic, 2000), 28.
159. Frey, "Different Patterns," 304.

11–13	He raised men up of renown for himself to leave a remnant for the land and in order to fill the face of the world with their offspring. He taught them by the hand of the anointed ones with his holy spirit and through seers of the truth, and their names were established with precision.	But those he hates, he causes to stray.

The entirety of this passage explains the origin of the community for which this text is written. It does not consciously reflect a dualistic worldview, but it merely explains God's order of creation and his system of election. Moreover, it contains the possibility of repentance and the chance to come back into God's mercy. As Davies has already argued, nowhere does this text reflect a dualistic worldview.

Another text that, according to Frey, holds a thoroughly dualistic framework, is 4Q181. The fragmentariness of this text makes interpretation rather difficult: the intended verse, 4Q181 1, II, 5, merely reflects one word (גרל) from which Frey wishes to establish an identification with the Treatise. Also, the extant text of 4Q181 clearly refers to the fallen angels of the Enochic Book of the Watchers. In the Treatise, the myth of the Watchers is not mentioned. Rather, the text seems to strongly support the view that iniquity and sin was created by God and was not the result of the rebellion of the angels.

Also, 4Q181 seems to preoccupy itself with the theme of divine election, rather than envision the irreducible opposition of two classes: from a world of evil and wickedness, God has "approached some among the sons of the world ... so that they can be considered with him in the com[munity of] the Gods" (4Q181 1, II, 3–4).[160] Hence, I fail to detect any dualistic worldview in 4Q181 and any unambiguous relationship to the Treatise.

Finally, in 4Q280 2, 4–5, the words "without a remnant" (לאין שרית) are thought to be a citation of 1QS IV, 14. However, this passage is followed by the words "you are damned, without a survivor" (cf. 4Q280 2, 5), which makes the entire passage much closer to 1QM I, 6 (cf. 4Q496 3,

---

160. The sister text of 4Q180 has a closer reference: "An Age to conclude ... and all that will be. Before creating them, he determined [their] operations." This text seems preoccupied with the predestined order of creation.

6).[161] Since Frey considers 1QM to belong to a different pattern of dualism, that is, the pattern of "sheer cosmic dualism," 4Q280 cannot be attributed to a developmental phase within the multidimensional sapiential pattern of the Treatise. Finally, the text uses rather eye-catchingly different terminology. Whereas the Treatise uses the "Angel of Darkness" and other texts frequently use a form of Belial, 4Q280 has "Melchiresha" as the evil source. Such a difference in terminology might well indicate a different social milieu. Finally, and most importantly, 4Q280 does not convey a dualistic worldview as it seems only interested in cursing its enemies—those who decline to enter the covenant. Most likely, the author sees his group as the righteous ones to the exclusion of all others. The exhortatory and accusatory tone of the text rather points to a literary strategy than that it is likely to contain any usable information about its author and its audience's worldviews.

In sum, when considering Frey's own evaluation of the *yahadic* texts that he ascribes to the sapiential multidimensional pattern of dualism, we find his conclusions to be rather at odds with the proposed existence of such a pattern. He himself already observes that:

(1) These texts do not have any notion of the two spirits, of oppositional angelic beings, or of an internal struggle within the heart of every human.
(2) Their dualisms are sometimes deeply modified and simplified.
(3) Some texts have heavily rigidified their dualistic outlook.
(4) The ambivalence of an internal struggle or emotional distress regarding good/bad conduct is simply dropped.
(5) Each one of Frey's three categories of dualism identified in the Treatise (i.e., cosmic, ethical, and psychological dualism) is either no longer existent or is severely modified in these *yahadic* texts.

These observations need subsequently to be evaluated in light of our earlier findings in both chapter 4 and this chapter, which can be recapitulated as follows: (1) Frey's three levels of dualism are inaccurate: two of them (psychological and ethical) can actually not be regarded as dualistic, while the third one (cosmic dualism) needs to be uncluttered of nondualistic elements (such as light/darkness) and brought in line with Bianchi's moderate

---

161. See also CD II, 3–7a.

dualism; (2) the Treatise turns out to be almost void of dualistic ideas and in fact seems to stay rather close to other late wisdom texts, such as Ben Sira and 4QInstruction, while it may reflect influences of apocalyptic texts such as the Book of Watchers (1 En. 9) and (to a lesser extent) Jubilees; (3) upon secondary evaluation, none of the "precursors" or "successors" of the Treatise convey a coherence of dualism that ties them to each other or to the Treatise. Hence, our conclusion simply must be that the establishment of dualism in the Treatise and in the other—supposedly related—Qumran documents, as well as the presumption of a chronological development reflected in a pattern of sapiential dualism, cannot be maintained without self-critical reflection. Rather, we might want to entertain the idea that the Treatise was part of a development and modification of ideas and traditions within the Judaism of the Second Temple. As such, the assessment of dualism with regard to this text might prevent us from openly evaluating the various negotiations regarding those ideas reflected in contemporary texts. The next section briefly deals with one of these ideas, the imagery of "Two Ways," in order to demonstrate how a text like the Treatise can be evaluated as part of a long tradition of shaping, negotiating, and modifying Jewish ideas, without necessarily holding on to its perceived dualistic outlook.

5.6. Two Ways: A Case Study

The imagery of two ways or two paths is considered to be one of the most distinctive features of the forms of dualism that scholars have identified in the Treatise of the Two Spirits. The idea of two strictly separated "walks of life" is thought to be extrapolated into the cosmic sphere as two angelic beings supposedly guide their respective two divisions of humans on their path of truth or iniquity. Moreover, the two paths are also thought to be internalized as the two spirits that represent the paths' struggle within the heart of every human being. In short, the imagery of the two ways is closely connected to scholarly evaluations of the Treatise as dualistic.

However, the imagery of the two ways is not uncommon within Jewish (and later Christian) writings, without necessarily being evaluated as reflecting a dualistic outlook. The idea of two ways or paths in which an individual can choose to walk is already encountered in Deut 30:15–20, which promises to those who "walk in the ways to the Lord" (i.e., those who keep his commandments) life and prosperity, while predicting a fate of death and destruction for those "who turn their hearts away." George

Nickelsburg has argued that Deut 30:15–20 connects the imagery of two ways with the observance and disobedience of the Mosaic torah. Also, he thinks that the terms "life" and "death" in this passage are constructed in order to connect the two ways to the already mentioned blessings and curses in Deut 28–29.[162]

These passages might have influenced Jer 21:8 in which the choice between life and death is taken quite literally, as the prophet proclaims that the Lord has set before the people two ways, the way of life and the way of death. The idea of two ways frequently occurs in the Psalms (e.g., Pss 1:1, 6; 119:29–30; 139:24). In Ps 119, the connection between a person's ways and his obedience to God's commandments is found again as it ties the moral categories of righteousness and deceit to their respective paths (e.g., Ps 119:1, 7, 9, 15, 21, 29–30, 32, 104).

Later, in the book of Tobit, such a moral categorization has taken the forefront, implicitly bringing the notion of observance and all its behavioral manifestations under the banners of righteousness: "I Tobit have walked all the days of my life in the ways of truth and righteousness" (Tob 1:3, cf. 4:5–6, 10, 19).

The imagery of the two ways is also prominent in Prov 1–9, where both ways are associated with wisdom and folly. For instance, Prov 2:12–22 envisions wisdom and understanding to be decisive factors in the ability of humans to choose the righteous path and stay out of the realm of the ways of wicked men and the paths of death. Hence, in Proverbs, the moral categories of righteousness and wickedness are expanded into the social categories of wise and foolish people.

Wisdom and knowledge also play a crucial part in the way the Epistle of Enoch negotiates the two paths, as it ties the ways of righteousness closely to the divine knowledge of the righteous chosen ones (1 En. 94:1–5). First Enoch's Two Ways Instruction exhorts its audience to "love righteousness and walk in it; for the paths of righteousness are worthy of acceptance, but the paths of iniquity will quickly be destroyed and vanish" (1 En. 94:1). Interestingly, the paths of righteousness are not the focal point, but rather "to certain people the paths of violence and death will be revealed," so they can avoid them (1 En. 94:2). Moreover, the instruction stresses the ability of the righteous (and perhaps all human beings?) to

---

162. George W. Nickelsburg, *1 Enoch 1: A Commentary on the Book of 1 Enoch, Chapters 1–36, 81–108*, Hermeneia (Minneapolis: Fortress, 2001), 455.

choose: "And now I say to you O righteous, walk not in the paths of evil, nor in the paths of death ... but seek and choose for yourselves righteousness and an elect life, and walk in the paths of peace so that you may live and flourish" (1 En. 94:3-4).

Other texts extend the imagery of the two ways to the realm of cosmological notions of light and darkness. For instance, Proverbs associates the two ways with light and darkness, attaching moral categories to these otherwise neutral cosmic phenomena: "The path of the righteous is like the first gleam of dawn, shining ever bright till the full light of day. But the way of the wicked is like deep darkness; they do not know what makes them stumble" (Prov 4:18-19; see also Prov 2:13). Also, Ps 112:4 has "unto the righteous the light arises in the darkness." In the Epistle of Enoch (1 En. 92:4), it is said of the righteous that "they shall walk in eternal light." Also, light and darkness terminology is frequently used in connection to walking in the book of Job. In Job 38:19-20, the paths are obscured and only known to God, who asks: "What is the way to the abode of light? And where does darkness reside?... Do you know the paths to their dwellings?" (cf. Isa 42:16).

Outside the scope of this section fall later occurrences of the two ways, reflected not only in rabbinic literature but also in early Christian literature, for instance in the Didache, Shepherd of Hermas, and the Epistle of Barnabas. Scholars have especially noticed the closeness of the Treatise to the Didache, and some have even suggested that the texts have a common source.[163]

In short, the imagery of two ways in which humans can walk is a rather widespread phenomenon in Judaism. Many of the texts that reflect the imagery of two ways negotiate oppositions without being evaluated as dualistic. Further, it is important to realize that an author's motive for contrasting the two ways often serves an exhortatory purpose, so as to advocate strategically ethically correct behavior. Therefore, instead of looking for dualistic constructions, it might be more fruitful to evaluate the Treatise against its Jewish background in which it represents one of the possibilities to negotiate the complexity and ambiguity of human life.

---

163. Huub van de Sandt and David Flusser, *The Didache: Its Jewish Sources and Its Place in Early Judaism and Christianity*, CRINT 3.5 (Assen: Van Gorcum, 2002), esp. 140-55.

5.7. The Cohesive Function of Dualism at Qumran

These scholarly enquiries into various aspects and examples of Qumran dualism leave us with rather devastating conclusions regarding theories of the (development of the) "Qumran Sect's characteristic dualistic thinking." In chapter 4, we have already seen that the definition of dualism was obscured by scholarly attempts to define perceived oppositions as various types of dualism. Moreover, these types of dualism have been perceived as developing within patterns of dualism. This chapter has evaluated one pattern of dualism and the perceived developments of its dualistic elements by analyzing not only the pattern but particularly its core text, the Treatise of the Two Spirits. In this regard, this chapter has brought the following critical points to light.

(1) The Treatise cannot successfully be used as a representative of Qumran dualism because of its problems regarding sources and redaction, which makes it more difficult to separate out what parts of the text do not originally belong.

(2) Moreover, the question of tradition also touches upon the problem of date. The traditional dating of the Treatise prevents this text from being the pivotal linchpin within a developmental chronology, especially if the text is considered to be reflecting a modification of certain ideas in contemporary wisdom texts like Ben Sira.

(3) The Treatise is often perceived as dualistic, because scholars start with the presupposition of a sectarian social reality and with dualism as their fitting radical ideology. However, the text itself conveys many ideas that speak against such a straightforward social setting. For instance, to allow every human being to be the battleground for good and evil can hardly be harmonized with the ideology of a sect.

(4) Furthermore, on evaluation, the Treatise reflects many ideas that are not dualistic and/or concur with similar ideas in contemporary Second Temple writings, such as Ben Sira, 1 Enoch (Book of the Watchers /Epistle of Enoch), and to some extent Jubilees.

(5) Scholarly research has revealed that the ethical component in the Treatise is probably the central focus of the text. Therefore, there is no reason to centralize the cosmic component in the text; rather, one must evaluate that the Treatise is concerned with why good people do bad things.

(6) Also, the section on the two ways has demonstrated that ideas such as this can have a long tradition in Judaism and that they might occur in texts that have never been regarded as dualistic. Surely, a concept like

the two ways could only be considered dualistic if the two ways had an existence in themselves, that is, if they were endemic to the fabric of the universe. The usage of the two ways imagery has, however, demonstrated enough ambiguity to discard such a construction of reality. Rather, the two ways imagery can be perceived as exhortational, a strategic device to induce ethical behavior.

In conclusion, the concept of dualism is better not used for the Treatise or as a means to tie a variety of texts together in a coherent ideological framework. Moreover, there is no denying that oppositionality can be observed in various texts, but the oppositions are often described and worked out in very different ways. Because of those differences and because the evaluation of dualistic thought in many of those text is incorrect, the concept of dualism is not suitable to tie all these texts together.

In his edited volume titled *Dualism in Qumran*, Géza Xeravits recognizes the inevitable fact that the notion of an eye-catchingly dualistic thinking of the Qumran sect can no longer be maintained but that reevaluation might cause problems for the larger theoretical framework of our understandings of Qumran. Therefore, he concludes that the perceived complexity of the material supports "the conviction that one cannot postulate compelling doctrines in the 'theology of Qumran'" and that "the group did not want to develop a sophisticated doctrinal system." Moreover, his subsequent conclusion that "they [the Qumran group] collected and mediated various aspects of the theology of their times without so much as being champions of several infallible dogmas"[164] seems to invest more in the preservation of the Qumran paradigm than it does justice to the richness of the Qumran manuscripts.

Xeravits's remarks are one step short of stating that a radical group like the *yahad* had no doctrine or ideology of its own but rather copied popular or appealing ideologies that floated around in Second Temple Judaism. Of course, such a theoretical framework might provide a solution for the perceived problems of variety and diversity within the framework of "dualism," but it hardly complies with the very nature of a religious sectarian group. Again, the Qumran paradigm of a community and a library is leading the theorizing and is preserved at all costs, even in the face of adversity.

---

164. Géza Xeravits, "Introduction," in Xeravits, *Dualism in Qumran*, 3.

6
THE QUMRAN PARADIGM:
TOWARD A REVISIONIST APPROACH

The current monograph has attempted to evaluate critically some of the foundational hypotheses of the Qumran paradigm. As we have seen, this paradigm connects the archaeological site of Khirbet Qumran to, on the one hand, the manuscripts from the eleven caves in its vicinity and, on the other hand, the descriptions of the Essenes by Philo, Josephus, and Pliny the Elder. Thus, the Qumran paradigm hypothesizes that the Qumran manuscripts reflect the sectarian library of a rather radical minority group (or sect), which was closely connected to the Essenes and resided at Khirbet Qumran. Part of this group's ideology is thought to be their self-identification as "the chosen righteous ones" awaiting the eschaton. Their exclusivist self-understanding is perceived to be demonstrated by modes of separatism and dualistic thinking as reflected in the manuscripts of their library.

Over the course of time, Qumran scholarship has undergone dramatic changes in the way the Scrolls and their social background are perceived. Early scholarship envisioned the Qumran sect to be a rather isolated or at least segregated social entity, while the steady publication of the Scrolls after the 1990s demonstrated that more recent enquiries into the social world of the Qumran texts and site allow for a more complex and multifaceted religious group. Whichever model of assembly one prefers, the central notion of the Qumran texts being the religious library of a sectarian Jewish group has remained steadfast. Within this Qumran paradigm, it has become commonly accepted to position certain key documents within an overarching interpretative framework, thus sustaining a theoretical ideology and a constructed social reality. Thus, there is a tendency to take as a point of departure a conceptual and constructed social reality and to impose this social reality on the (interpretation of) Qumran texts to the extent that their social world is not questioned but rather reified. Even though this book is set up as a critique of such reification, in many ways it wants to engage with the Qumran paradigm as a dialogue partner worthy of critique, while at the same time proposing a way forward that is more fundamentally revisionist with regard to its foundations.

In the preceding chapters, this book has laid bare some of the persistent building blocks that form the foundations of the Qumran paradigm: (1) the assumption of a coherent and meaningfully related library, (2) models of classification that imply (3) models of chronological development of the Qumran texts, and (4) the lack of clear definition of certain textual peculiarities, resulting in (5) presumed ideological coherence.

We have identified the problems attached to classifications and categorizations of texts and have recognized their inherent tendency to place texts in a framework of chronological development, thus positioning documents according to their presupposed place in the history of the Qumran sect in accordance with early theories regarding the Dead Sea Scrolls and site. Such fixed positions then become the driver from which further theorizing takes place and perceived ideological peculiarities are linked with the texts' presumed social reality. Another issue regarding the presupposition of a chronological development is that it encourages Qumran centrism; in other words, each text needs to be meaningfully related to the Qumran sect, even if the textual evidence does not fit. In practice, such Qumran centrism often pushes certain texts into a presectarian or formative realm. We have encountered a good example of this tendency in 4QMMT and its esteemed position as the foundational document of the Qumran sect. As we have seen, 4QMMT throws up so many difficulties and problems that we cannot comfortably use this text as the pinnacle of Qumran theology. Moreover, we have questioned the ideological notion of mild polemics as a contributing factor to its classification, since we have found no ground for any polemical reading of the text. In fact, there is nothing in this text that would prevent us from investigating other avenues of interpretation or from proposing an interpretation from a different vantage point or within a broader perspective.

The other building block in this book that questions an all-too-straightforward mirror reading of ideology and social reality is the presumption of the dualistic outlook of the Qumran sect. As we have seen, the broadening of the conceptual framework of dualism has permitted Qumran scholarship to recognize dualistic tendencies in documents that reflect paradoxes, oppositionality, contrasts, and authorial strategies of ethical or social stratification. Moreover, many of the documents that contain oppositionality reflect author strategies to define the Self over against the Other. Authorial strategies often negotiate the human experience of ambiguity and/or serve exhortatory purposes, rather than attempting to reflect an irresolvable oppositional worldview. Moreover, it must be questioned whether those concepts and occurrences in the Qumran texts to which the label dualism is applied can be divorced from their wider sociocultural concepts, such as apocalypticism and the wisdom tradition. Also, we have shown that many Second Temple texts demonstrate similar oppositional ideas without being evaluated as dualistic. For instance, our test case, the Treatise of the Two Spirits, has its closest analogies with Ben Sira, a text that has never been evaluated as dualistic. Thus, even though oppositionality can be observed within various texts in and outside of Qumran, dualism is not a suitable concept to tie these texts together as their oppositionality is often negotiated nondualistically in a very different way and with very different purposes. And moreover, the Treatise cannot be used as a representative of all those texts that contain oppositionality. Finally, it must be concluded that ideology, in this case dualism, cannot be used as a sociological boundary marker. Therefore, we have to dissolve the cohesive forces of the Qumran paradigm that try to tie sometimes very different texts together within a notion of ideological sameness.

Having evaluated classification and ideology as building blocks of the Qumran paradigm, a broader perspective of theorizing needs to be addressed. These two investigated building blocks often ultimately and implicitly reconstruct social reality as well as working from presupposed assumptions of social reality.[1] As a result, these theories become self-fulfilling prophecies as they are built out of a fair amount of circular reasoning and retrospective theorizing, which can only lead to the reinforcement of the Qumran paradigm and its adjustments; the foundations of the theorized sectarian group and library remain untouched.

6.1. THE PYRAMID STRUCTURE OF THE QUMRAN PARADIGM

There is no reason why scientific research should invent the wheel over and over again. Building upon the results of former research often brings

---

1. See Peter Berger and Thomas Luckmann, *The Social Construction of Reality: A Treatise in the Sociology of Knowledge* (London: Penguin, 1966).

further insight to the materials at hand. However, the foundations of research need not become unmovable objects or impregnable dogmas. In many ways, the foundations of the Qumran paradigm have become the unspoken rules from which scholars begin. Such an inherent set of rules resemble what Michel Foucault has called the "archaeology of knowledge": those systems of regularities within the scientific discourse that function outside the customary boundaries but which are so profoundly dominating that they have become the informal structures that partly determine the scholarly discourse.[2] In other words, the informal structure of Qumran scholarship dictates that research begins from within the prevalent Qumran paradigm and hence reinforces the finding of results that sustain this paradigm.

Figure 7. The Pyramid Structure.

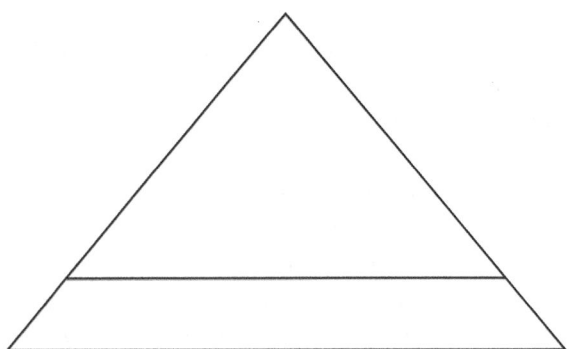

To use an image, Qumran scholarship has erected a pyramid structure, which has a foundation upon which all further research is constructed. This foundation has proven to be so broad that it has become very difficult to back away from it, even in the face of evidence that does not fit. Hence, what happens is that one can play with and form theories at the top of the pyramid, but the base will remain untouched, simply because it is the structure that provided the foundation for the paradigm. It has not been my aim categorically to dispense with all aspects of the Qumran paradigm,

---

2. See Michel Foucault, *The Order of Things: An Archaeology of the Human Sciences*, 13th ed. (London: Routledge, 2010).

6. TOWARD A REVISIONIST APPROACH

but rather to question whether the descriptions of its social world that stem from its foundation—its parameters of sect and sectarian library—do justice to the complexity of Qumran. This study has demonstrated that we cannot comfortably proceed on the basis of the Qumran paradigm to evaluate the evidence, simply because currently there are just too many unanswered difficulties that prevent us from maintaining an inflexible interpretative framework.

6.2. The Proposed Alternatives: Protest Reinforces the Paradigm

Over the years, there have been scholars who have attempted to discard the Qumran paradigm and its adjusted theories altogether. The most famous one of these attempts is the theory of Golb. Golb, whose ideas have been received with great criticism and ardent opposition, denied the relationship between the Qumran site and the Scrolls in its entirety and argued that all Qumran manuscripts came from different Jerusalemite libraries, and, hence, they were representative of Judaism as a whole.[3] Even though his theories have received the most attention in the field, Golb was not the first one to propose that the Scrolls originally came from Jerusalem. In 1960, Karl Heinrich Rengstorf published a theory in which he argued that the Qumran manuscripts had no connection to the Essenes (or any other sect) but were part of the library of the Jerusalem Temple, which were brought to Qumran as a precaution before the Jewish revolt.[4]

Golb and Rengstorf's theories were not the only ones to deny the validity of the Qumran paradigm. From the side of archaeology, we have already discussed scholarly theories that disconnect the site from the caves and/or pose alternative destinations for the Qumran site, such as a "villa rustica," a fortress, or a commercial center.[5] During the last decades even more variant theories have surfaced. For instance, the elaborate water installations were thought to have a very different purpose than ritual bathing; supposedly, they supported agriculture, pottery manufacturing, balm produce, or

---

3. Norman Golb, *Who Wrote the Dead Sea Scrolls*.
4. Karl H. Rengstorf, *Hirbet Qumran und die Bibliothek vom Toten Mer*, Studia Delitzschiana 5 (Stuttgart: Kohlhammer, 1960).
5. These proposals were respectively made by Donceel-Voûte, Golb, and Hirschfeld; Magen; and Peleg; see ch. 1.

similar industry. Lately, David Stacey has even suggested the installations might have been used seasonally for glue manufacturing, preparation, and dyeing of wool.[6] Also, the seclusion and uniqueness of the Qumran site has been called into question. Recently, Rachel Bar-Nathan has argued that the ceramics found at Qumran do not point to a sectarian occupancy as similar pottery has been found on other sites in the Jericho region.[7]

The most ardent critic of the Qumran paradigm from an archaeological point of view might be Jürgen Zangenberg, who objects to the parameters of the Qumran paradigm on methodological grounds. He argues that the collection of Qumran manuscripts we have now cannot and should not be regarded as representative of the original collection, but rather as an incidental remainder of an original collection. According to him, "der ursprüngliche Charakter des ehemaligen Corpus [ist] unerreichbar vergangen," and, therefore, he regards it as methodologically unwise to make the library (or collection) "zum Kennmerkmal der Schriften insgesamt." He consequently warns against comfortably inferring conclusions about the common social world of these texts.[8] Moreover, Zangenberg doubts whether Qumran can be connected to the Essenes, even if some of the manuscripts might have an Essene origin. He argues that even though there is a certainty that Jews inhabited the Qumran site, doubt should be cast as to whether they were Essene sectarians.[9]

The methodological questions that are inherently raised within the theories of critics like Golb and Zangenberg are invaluable to the progress of Qumran scholarship, but their alternative theories tend to emphasize that they were born out of protest and resistance. To put it in an image, they attempt to overturn the pyramid structure altogether and alternatively create an antipyramid structure.

---

6. See Magen and Peleg, *The Qumran Excavations*; Yizhar Hirschfeld, *Qumran in Context*; David Stacey and Gregory Doudna, *Qumran Revisited: A Reassessment of the Site and Its Texts*, BARIS 2520 (Oxford: Archaeopress, 2013).

7. Bar-Nathan, "Qumran and the Hasmonean and Herodian Winter Palaces," 263-77.

8. Jürgen Zangenberg, "Zwischen Zufall und Eigenartigkeit: Bemerkungen zur jüngsten Diskussion über die Funktion von Khirbet Qumran und die Rolle einiger ausgewählter archäologischer Befunde, in *Qumran und die Archäologie: Texte und Kontexte*, ed. Jörg Frey, Carsten Claussen, and Nadine Kessler, WUNT 278 (Tübingen: Mohr Siebeck, 2011), 129.

9. Ibid., 145-46.

6. TOWARD A REVISIONIST APPROACH

Figure 8. The Antipyramid Structure.

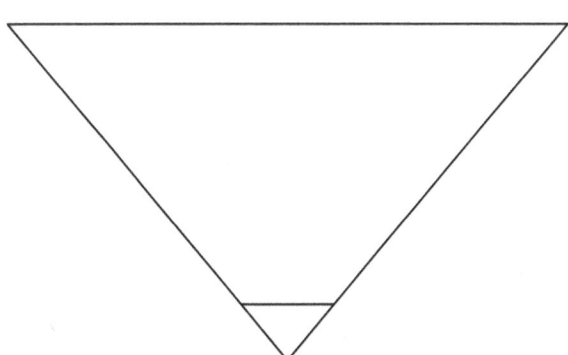

Not only does an antipyramid structure have a very skimpy base to hold and ground its alternative explanations; such a structure often also provokes an unwanted side effect: the reinforcement of the established pyramid structure. In the case of Golb, we have seen that not so much his critical questions but rather the radicality of his resistance has provoked negative reactions. The radical discarding of the prevalent paradigm in its entirety and the protest-induced alternative proposals have often contributed to the theoretical strengthening of the Qumran paradigm as they deny the probability that aspects of the paradigm might provide scholarship with valuable information about (some of) these texts.

The strength of the critical questions that both Golb (from a literary point of view) and Zangenberg (from an archaeological point of view) have posed lies in their hesitation to combine and categorize texts and material evidence in order to establish a clear-cut history of origins. Indeed, they inherently question whether a precise and more accurate analysis of sources might speak against too swiftly conflating various social groups and sociohistorical circumstances. Thus, perceived similarities between texts with regard to social backgrounds or ideological outlooks might often be explained by similar and contemporary sociocultural circumstances, but they cannot be comfortably used to draw conclusions about possible dependencies and affiliations of social groups.

With such caution in mind, this book has attempted not only to point to certain weaknesses in the prevalent paradigm but also to unhook certain documents from an all-too-stringent interpretative framework and to advocate the development of a methodology in which the individual texts themselves are a point of departure when researching their possible social environment(s).

6.3. What Can We Learn from 4QMMT and the Treatise?

The two case studies of chapters 3 and 5, 4QMMT and the Treatise, have demonstrated how certain documents have become domesticated by the prevalent paradigm and hence interpreted accordingly. The analysis of these texts has demonstrated that, even though scholarship has linked 4QMMT and the Treatise to similar phases of development in relation to a *yahad*, there is nothing in those documents themselves that suggests such provenance without the presupposition of the Qumran paradigm. Neither of these texts refers to a *yahad* and neither of them contains terminology that is commonly associated with a *yahad*. Rather, through classification systems and perceived inceptions of ideological boundary-markers, scholars have domesticated these texts within a sectarian paradigm. Even more so, there is nothing in either 4QMMT or the Treatise that suggests that these two documents should be linked to each other, even though scholars proceeding on the assumption of a Qumran paradigm want to assign them to an analogous period of chronological development in the making of a Qumran community. However, these very different documents have nevertheless become linked through the back door, because scholars have treated them from the same interpretative framework. Through this framework, both documents are not only linked within a certain time frame and provenance; they are similarly made to fit the paradigm's presumed social world.

On the content level of these documents, a certain deregulation of ideological definitions has taken place. In the case of 4QMMT, scholars speak of "mild polemics," while in the Treatise a "multidimensional dualistic outlook" is perceived. In this book, we have seen that both concepts need to be questioned with regard to (1) the way they are perceived and defined within the context of these texts and (2) the sociohistorical reality that they are perceived to reflect. The ideas of mild polemics and dualism serve the paradigmatic notion of sectarianism well, because they support the idea of tension and radicality. Within current scholarship, the perceived sectarian tensions within these texts are thought to reflect a sociohistorical reality. However, within the world of the text, perceived oppositionality need not necessarily reflect a conflictual social reality. Texts create symbolic worlds that have their own coherence, rather than reflecting an external order of reality. Literary strategies might convey authorial attempts to make sense of a messy world by describing reality in terms of a reversal of power or a hyperbolic dividing of things that in real life are not so easily separated. Moreover, ambiguities, paradoxes, and contradictions are part of everyday life. This book has shown that these texts, in very different ways, try to negotiate, change, and complement these experiences.

Another problem this study has detected is the widening of definitions. If we depart from our definitions and broaden concepts like polemics and dualism to such an extent that they can be applied to almost every occurrence of discussion or contrast, these concepts lose their explanatory power. Moreover, the broadened definition of polemics and dualism might stand in the way of investigating particular or unique information within these texts about the way the ancient authors negotiate the human experience of ambiguity and their conceptualization of and interaction with the larger sociohistorical reality. Indeed, the broadening of definitions and the conflating of concepts serve the purpose of reiterating the notion of sectarianism and high social boundaries in these texts in order to make them fit a certain theoretical framework of reality. In this constructed reality of segregation and sectarianism, texts are not perceived as contributing to developments in larger society. Letting go of such a construct of social reality might open up some of these texts—4QMMT and the Treatise among them—to the possibility that they contributed to the negotiations and transformations of the larger contemporary Jewish society as their symbolic worlds negotiated various forms of ambiguity in real life. In the case of 4QMMT, a more formal legal approach might be detected that tries to inform, influence, and participate in the larger society. In the case of the Treatise, the focus might be more on answering eternal questions of theodicy and ethical behavior, maybe even in a hortatory or persuasive fashion.

6.4. Proposals for Future Research

How, then, are we to approach the nine hundred manuscripts from the Qumran caves without making use of the theorization of the Qumran paradigm? Surely, the criticism to my *modus operandi* would be: but these texts have been found at Qumran, and even if it is an interesting heuristic exercise to see how we would evaluate them if they were not, how can we read them so innocently (i.e., outside of their "hermeneutical circle")? Such a critique is fair enough, but I am convinced that such an exercise of methodological innocence (or methodological doubt) can provide scholarship with new insights as to the complexity of the contemporary

Jewish world. Surely, we may attempt to read these texts more innocently than we are doing now. We could, for instance postpone the question of why these texts have been found at Qumran and first and foremostly begin with a larger hermeneutical circle, namely, the certainty that these texts were produced in the Palestinian Judaism of the Second Temple. As such, we might indeed take them as known and formerly unknown representatives of this turbulent time and age. I think that Qumran scholarship has raised enough questions and is convinced of enough doubt with regard to the early theories to no longer insist on the sustainment of the Qumran paradigm.

It is my contention that the problems start with an all-too-quick assignment of these texts to a sectarian milieu. If we presuppose the Qumran scrolls are the library of a sectarian social entity, it begs the questions: What sect? Whose library? However, if we would, in the first instance, evaluate the Qumran scrolls as an opportunity to learn more about the shaping of Jewish ideas and traditions in this historical period, instead of immediately conflating these texts by ascribing them to one sectarian social entity, nothing really stands in the way of our taking the primary evidence, namely, the individual texts themselves, as our point of departure. There might be reasons why Qumran scholarship has, as of yet, not undertaken such a hermeneutical exercise. In her philosophical inquiry into Qumran scholarship, Edna Ullmann-Margalit has noted that the socioreligious and political reasons that (both Christian and Jewish) scholars were invested in the concept of sect, might have played an important part in the adoption of the early theories of Qumran sectarianism, thereby inducing a self-fulfilling prophecy which maintained both the idea of an orthodoxy over against existing heterodoxy (Jewish scholars) and the originality of Jesus (Christian scholars).[10]

Naturally, not only socioreligious and political reasons lie behind the initial reluctance of scholars to contemplate that these texts—even though they are found at Qumran—might represent and reflect a wider section of contemporary Jewish society and that studying them individually would be a good way forward into gaining insight into its complexity. There are indeed also genuine analytical difficulties with regard to the text-types and underlying literary sources. As many scholars have pointed out, a large portion of the Qumran texts take authoritative scripture as their point of

---

10. Ullmann-Margalit, *Out of the Cave*, 136–51.

departure and rework, interpret, or use texts we have come to know as scripture in new literary forms. Due to their variant use of scripture, complex webs of allusions and citations are woven, from which the dependency and direction of interpretation is hard to establish. In a 1994 article, Brooke addresses this problem with regard to the difficulties of establishing a historical reconstruction from the pesharim:

> If we have such difficulty knowing how to relate the historical significance of two texts [1QpHab and 4QpPs^a] of the same genre, in the same language, with the same formulae and the same vocabulary, probably from the same community, in the same place, at roughly the same time, how much more problematic is discerning the relationship between the varying motifs and supposed history lying behind texts in different languages, of different genres, almost certainly from different communities and different times and places. It is only with much care in asserting how texts relate to one another that we can avoid naïve historicism, namely that wherever there are two phenomena with even the vaguest correspondences they must be related in some way in terms of cause and effect.[11]

Brooke's warning against too easily conflating perceived textual similarities, which in his article predominantly relates to the pesharim, can be just as valid with regard to the entirety of the Qumran corpus, even though we have seen that scholars have comfortably conflated various texts with very different outlooks on the basis of similarly perceived terminology, ideology, and lexical locutions. Similarly, the evaluation of quite different usage and names of sobriquets and epithets in certain texts as basically speaking about the same (historical) figures is a case in point. Would it not be helpful to investigate the different forms and uses of (nick)names individually and contemplate how they might be developed as important analytical tools to open up these different texts so that they might provide a fruitful beginning to shed light on their social worlds, rather than assuming that the different usages have no meaning (or point to the same figures)?

---

11. George Brooke, "The Pesharim and the Origins of the Dead Sea Scrolls," in *Methods of Investigation of the Dead Sea Scrolls and the Khirbet Qumran Site: Present Realities and Future Prospects*, ed. Michael O. Wise et al., ANYAS 722 (New York: The New York Academy of Sciences, 1994), 339–52.

In taking the individual texts as the point of departure (instead of the notion of a Qumran sect and library), scholars can focus on the literary traditions and textual peculiarities that may provide information about these texts' social worlds without immediately reading them in light of one another. In order to prevent the circular reasoning and retrospective theorizing which we have identified in the preceding chapters and in light of the many questions and difficulties we have detected throughout, this book advocates rather to push these Qumran texts apart and evaluate them with an open perspective that appreciates their differences and often unique outlooks. In short, in order to investigate the social world behind these unique texts, we need to return to their individuality, studying their literary traditions, form, genre, and content and juxtapose those markers with linguistic peculiarities and dominant themes.

In taking the text's individuality as a point of departure, the answers to literary questions might possibly demonstrate the diversity among the Scrolls: What sort of author writes this text? What kind of text is it? Is it a discourse, and if so, what are the dominant themes? How do the (biblical) references interplay or weave their semantic webs? Who or what does the text see as authority? What is the purpose of the writing? How does the author construct his literary world and the main players in it? Of course, I am not the first one to advocate such a back-to-the-basics approach. In his aforementioned article on the Dead Sea Scrolls pesharim, Brooke equally promotes the study of literary traditions while avoiding historical reconstructions. Moreover, he is convinced that by studying these often juxtaposed literary traditions within the world of the text, a social location will surface, which will eventually help to identify a "suitable historical backdrop."[12] I agree that such a "history of literary traditions" approach is an important and vital step toward understanding the Qumran texts. However, my contention would be not to

---

12. Ibid., 349–50. Notably, Brooke leaves open the possibility that such a "history of literary traditions" approach might lead to the conclusion that "not all the so-called 'sectarian' scrolls necessarily reflect a homogeneous group." Hence, even though Brooke does not contemplate first analyzing the Qumran manuscripts individually and outside of their proposed hermeneutical circle, he allows for the possibility of a larger diversity as he concludes. "As our appreciation of the literature of the late Second Temple period increases, we can begin to see that the commentator in these texts [i.e., the pesharim] refers to and uses his selected scriptural traditions often through the filter of their use in other texts which reflected his own ethos."

take as a point of departure the Qumran paradigm, because in doing so, one might run the risk of assessing the materials at hand accordingly and thus interpret the rich allusions in the various texts in light of this overarching theory and in light of seemingly similar themes and allusions in other Qumran texts. Rather I would advocate analyzing the Qumran texts individually.

Moreover, I am not convinced that analyzing the literary traditions with the help of historical critical methods alone will provide us with much usable information about the social reality behind the text. Apart from the fact that many of the Qumran texts give us little concrete information about their social worlds, I agree with Davies that "sects, no less than [religious] establishments, need to rewrite history in support of their view of the world," and, as such, they "cannot be relied upon to give an authentic account of their own history,"[13] however skillfully it is negotiated in webs of allusions to authoritative traditions.

Therefore, in order to theorize anew about the possible rich social worlds behind the various Qumran texts, we need to—apart from textual analysis through the usual textual methodology—address the politics and inherent functioning of religious groups and thus turn to knowledge that can be obtained from other fields, such as semantics, cultural studies, sociology, and anthropology. Since our interpretations are very much focused on the explanation of sociological phenomena, I believe that a social-scientific approach is invaluable to the better understanding of the habitus of religious groups. Two things might be gained from such an approach. First, by studying the sociology of religious groups and sects, we might gain invaluable insights in how religious groups function, why they come into being, and how they generally behave. In understanding the sociology (and anthropology) of religious groups, we might be better equipped to recognize certain behavioral traits, characteristics, practices, and social constructions and thus make more grounded evaluations about the nature of the social groups behind the scrolls. Second, studying groups and group behavior in antiquity inherently limits our certainty of getting it right simply by the lack of living communities that can be interviewed or observed with regard to their worldviews and social reality (and the relationship between them). However, social-scientific and linguistic methods may help to shed light on the fact that

---

13. Davies, "Sects from Texts," 75, 81.

social reality in Qumran times might not have been so bounded and well-defined as the Qumran paradigm wishes to describe it. Also, it can profoundly aid in the realization that life is often complex, contradictory, and paradoxical and that—even though we do not have actual living communities—human strategies to survive, cope with, and give meaning to life and its experiences might not change so much over time. Thus, by studying the politics of social groups, their group dynamics, and the strategies they (and their authors) develop to negotiate their social reality, we might step away from an all too serious or literal interpretation of what is being described in the text. Texts, then, can be seen as devices to comfort, persuade, exhort, and such, without necessarily having to reflect a social reality.

In order to maintain and strengthen their identity and in order to comply with authoritative boundary markers, religious groups (and societies as a whole) develop tools to aid them in this quest. As such, religious texts can be seen as expressions, not only of beliefs, ideas, and ideologies but also of strategies to achieve the purpose of the group's self-definition. Thus, in a sense, texts are symbols, as they create imagery that provokes group cohesion as it creates a world of meaning. The creation of symbolic worlds is a highly complex process in which literary strategies and group dynamics play an important role. Notably, even though textual symbolic worlds undoubtedly have some sort of connection to the sociohistorical times in which they are written, they are not the direct result (or even causal effect) of real social worlds and hence cannot be read as such. Thus, the language within a text "creates a symbolic universe which transforms and re-presents social *realia* in terms of its own order."[14] As such, and in agreement with Brooke earlier in this chapter, the world of the text can best be understood by analyzing the themes connected to the literary traditions within the text, rather than taking the symbolic world as a literary mirror to the real world. The text's connection to this social reality can only be understood once the themes in the world of the text are explored and understood from the emic perspective of the author and his audience.[15]

---

14. Leonard Thompson, "A Sociological Analysis of Tribulation in the Apocalypse of John," *Semeia* 36 (1986): 147.

15. This even goes for rule texts, which can be seen as ideal-typical codes of conduct. Without a living community, it becomes hard to establish social reality. A good example that teaches us to approach such historical rule books with caution is the

Leonard Thompson has observed that scholars "make a sharp distinction between social, institutional entities on the one hand, and symbolic literary entities on the other."[16] Further, he argues that the literary sources to describe sociohistorical circumstances (as in our case the classical authors)[17] are often taken as politically and historically correct, rather than reflecting "certain tendencies and motivations stemming from the … writers themselves and their social, historical situation."[18] Another important presupposition in the perceived mirror between text and social reality is the fact that scholars tend to perceive the sociohistorical situation as given, which "'causes' or 'occasions' religious and literary expressions. Causality is seen as flowing uni-directionally."[19] Two consequences of such an approach come to mind: First, in such a unilateral view, the symbolic world of the text can only be a reflection of a "more real" social reality; as such, intrinsic socioreligious or culturally complex worldviews of the authors and audiences are not fully considered as possibly to a large extent determining the text's outlook. Second, a unidirectional notion of certain sociohistorical circumstances causing socioreligious literary expressions does not allow for the possibility that text and social reality interact and might both be transformed as they mutually influence one another (consciously or incidentally). Hence, with Thompson, I would propose to study the themes, symbols, and social constructions of the individual Qumran texts, while putting the sources of our current knowledge of the contemporary social reality of the texts under extreme scrutiny with regard to their underlying motivations and tendencies. As a result, we can start to envision two perceptions or models of the contemporary world, two very particular interpretations of order. Then, we

---

Book of the Rule of the Lord, written by James Strang, who founded the Strangite schismic church of Mormons after the death of Joseph Smith. Upon arrival at Strang's self-proclaimed kingdom at Beaver Island, anthropologists observed that his ideal-typical rulebook did not at all reflect the group's social reality; see Doyle C. Fitzpatrick, *The King Strang Story: A Vindication of James J. Strang, The Beaver Island Mormon King* (Lansing, MI: National Heritage, 1970).

16. Thompson, "Sociological Analysis of Tribulation," 163.
17. And, of course, to a certain extent 1 Maccabees.
18. Thompson, "Sociological Analysis of Tribulation," 155.
19. Ibid., 163; rather, Thompson advocates that the text and the social world mutually transform one another and that they both participate in a "myriad of qualities, behavioural traits, religious commitments, psychosocial understandings, and social and political interactions."

can start asking: What do these worlds communicate about social reality, social history, and religious traditions?

Now, it becomes evident that, especially with regard to the multiple voices within the Qumran manuscripts and their rather insecure socio-historical background, Thompson's notion of the scholarly unidirectional model from reality to text is an even more pregnant warning sign as, in Qumran studies, we currently have only considered these texts within our paradigmatic theories of social reality. Taking the symbolic world of the individual texts as our point of departure, we can no longer proceed to model the world of the text on the constructed model of Qumran reality and thus come up with the self-fulfilling prophecy of a fitting social world. Moreover, it would be equally unwise to combine peculiarities in various, often very different, texts in order to make them fit the Qumran paradigm without questioning how, to what extent, and for what purpose their individual symbolic worlds were constructed. Additionally, one needs to question how these symbolic expressions relate to the individual social worlds of these texts.

In both exercises—learning about the nature of social groups and learning about their strategies to negotiate life (and thus read the text behind the text)—social-scientific approaches can help interpret the information from the literary analysis and enhance and enrich this interpretation by their insights into human behavior. Therefore, social-scientific theories of group formation and linguistic strategies are two additional and vital methodological steps, which, on top of enquiries into the textual and traditional history of the Qumran texts, can aid positioning them within the multifaceted world of the Second Temple period. However, most importantly, we need to start analyzing individual Qumran texts using the methodologies at hand, without presuming the chronology or social history of a Qumran sect. If on such a basis some texts should be linked, that is valuable, but we need to let go of theories that link up texts that are not obviously linked, be it through categorizations or ideology.

6.5. Conclusion

The Qumran paradigm has demonstrated its tendency to create large theoretical umbrellas to shelter very different documents and link them together in an inceptive or formative period. Moreover, it has created a sect-based framework in which all Qumran texts need to be meaningfully linked to the social history of this sect, thus creating a framework of chronological development and coherent ideology.

Realizing that the question of relationship between ideology (or symbolic, textual reality) and social reality needs to leave room for flexibility and complexity, the test cases of 4QMMT and the Treatise make clear that we need to rethink the whole question of library, the question of sectarianism, the question of chronological development, and the question of ideology. In short, we need to rethink what sort of paradigm we are working with, what to maintain, and what to leave behind.

This study demonstrates that—for a certain number of texts—scholarship needs to take a step back from the Qumran paradigm and make space for the possibility that these texts functioned in a larger social environment than previously thought, possibly even with various notions of audience and readership. As such, I am calling for a kind of reasoning that is prepared to start closer to the foundations of Qumran theories. This fundamentally revisionist approach should be an attempt not only to question the parameters of the Qumran paradigm more thoroughly; it should also be an attempt to dereify some of the points of departure that have been taken for granted in most of the theories of Qumran. For such a fundamentally revisionist evaluation, we need to take the individual texts, their peculiarities, and their symbolic expressions as our point of departure and hence investigate how they might fit within the larger picture of what we know about the Second Temple period. As such, this fundamentally revisionist approach leaves behind the constructed social reality of a sectarian paradigm and attempts to recover the complexity of Judaism in this period by advocating a reevaluation of the Qumran texts as a rich assemblage of varied witnesses to such a complexity.

Bibliography

Alexander, Philip. "The Redaction-History of the Serekh ha-Yahad: A Proposal." *RevQ* 17 (1996): 437–53.
Alexander, Philip, and Géza Vermes, eds. *Qumran Cave 4.XIX: Serekh ha-Yahad and Two Related Texts.* DJD XXVI. Oxford: Clarendon, 1998.
Atkinson, Kenneth, and Jodi Magness. "Josephus's Essenes and the Qumran Community." *JBL* 129 (2010): 317–42.
Baillet, Maurice, József T. Milik, and Roland de Vaux. *Les "Petites Grottes" de Qumrân: Explorations de la falaise, les grottes 2Q, 3Q, 5Q, 6Q, 7Q à 10Q, le rouleau de cuivre.* DJD III. Oxford: Clarendon, 1962.
Bar-Nathan, Rachel. "Qumran and the Hasmonean and Herodian Winter Palaces of Jericho: The Implication of the Pottery Finds on the Interpretation of the Settlement at Qumran." Pages 263–77 in *Qumran, The Site of the Dead Sea Scrolls: Archaeological Interpretations and Debates; Proceedings of a Conference Held at Brown University, November 17–19, 2002.* Edited by Katherina Galor, Jean-Baptiste Humbert, and Jürgen Zangenberg. STDJ 57. Leiden: Brill, 2006.
Barth, Fredrik. *Ethnic Groups and Boundaries: The Social Organization of Culture Difference.* Prospect Heights, IL: Waveland, 1998.
Barton, Stephen. "Early Christianity and the Sociology of the Sect." Pages 140–62 in *The Open Text: New Directions for Biblical Studies?* Edited by Francis Watson. London: SCM, 1993.
Baumgarten, Albert I. *The Flourishing of Jewish Sects in the Maccabean Era: An Interpretation.* JSJSup 55. Leiden: Brill, 1997.
———. "Reflections on the Groningen Hypothesis." Pages 256–62 in *Enoch and Qumran Origins: New Light on a Forgotten Connection.* Edited by Gabriele Boccaccini. Grand Rapids: Eerdmans, 2005.
———. "Who Cares and What Does It Matter? Qumran and the Essenes, Once Again!" *DSD* 11 (2004): 174–90.
Baumgarten, Joseph M. "The Laws of the Damascus Document—Between Bible and Mishnah." Pages 17–26 in *The Damascus Document: A Cen-

tennial of Discovery; Proceedings of the Third International Symposium of the Orion Center for the Study of the Dead Sea Scrolls and Associated Literature, 4–8 February 1998. Edited by Joseph M. Baumgarten, Esther G. Chazon, and Avital Pinnick. STDJ 34. Leiden: Brill, 2000.

Beall, Todd. *Josephus' Description of the Essenes Illustrated by the Dead Sea Scrolls.* Cambridge: Cambridge University Press, 1988.

Beentjes, Pancratius C. *The Book of Ben Sira: A Text Edition of All Extant Hebrew Manuscripts and a Synopsis of All Parallel Hebrew Ben Sira Texts.* VTSup 68. Leiden: Brill, 1997.

Ben-Dov, Jonathan, and Stéphane Saulnier. "Qumran Calendars: A Survey of Scholarship 1980–2007." *CurBR* 7 (2008): 131–79.

Bernstein, Moshe J. "The Employment and Interpretation of Scripture in 4QMMT: Preliminary Observations." Pages 29–51 in *Reading 4QMMT: New Perspectives on Qumran Law and History.* Edited by John Kampen and Moshe J. Bernstein. SymS 2. Atlanta: Scholars Press, 1996.

Bernstein, Moshe J., Florentino García Martínez, and John Kampen, eds. *Legal Texts and Legal Issues: Proceedings of the Second Meeting of the International Organization for Qumran Studies, Cambridge 1995; Published in Honour of Joseph M. Baumgarten.* STDJ 23. Leiden: Brill, 1997.

Berger, Peter L., and Thomas Luckmann. *The Social Construction of Reality: A Treatise in the Sociology of Knowledge.* London: Penguin, 1966.

Bianchi, Udo. "Dualism." Pages 4506–12 in vol. 4 of *The Encyclopedia of Religion.* Edited by Mircea Eliade. New York: MacMillan, 1987.

———. *Selected Essays on Gnosticism, Dualism and Mysteriosophy.* SHR 38. Leiden: Brill, 1978.

Bianchi, Udo, and Yuri Stoyanov. "Dualism." Pages 2504–17 in vol. 4 of *The Encyclopedia of Religion.* Edited by Mircea Eliade. New York: MacMillan, 2005.

Blenkinsopp, Joseph. "The Qumran Sect in the Context of Second Temple Sectarianism." Pages 10–25 in *New Directions in Qumran Studies: Proceedings of the Bristol Colloquium on the Dead Sea Scrolls, 8–10 September 2003.* Edited by Jonathan Campbell, William John Lyons, and Lloyd Pietersen. LSTS 52. London: T&T Clark, 2005.

Boccaccini, Gabriele. *Beyond the Essene Hypothesis: The Parting of the Ways between Qumran and Enochic Judaism.* Grand Rapids: Eerdmans, 1998.

———, ed. *Enoch and Qumran Origins: New Light on a Forgotten Connection.* Grand Rapids: Eerdmans, 2005.

Brooke, George. "The Pesharim and the Origins of the Dead Sea Scrolls." Pages 339–52 in *Methods of Investigation of the Dead Sea Scrolls and the Khirbet Qumran Site: Present Realities and Future Prospects*. Edited by Michael O. Wise et al. ANYAS 722. New York: The New York Academy of Sciences, 1994.

Brownlee, William H. "The Historical Allusions of the Dead Sea Habakkuk Midrash." *BASOR* 126 (1952): 10–20.

———. "The Wicked Priest, the Man of Lies, and the Righteous Teacher: The Problem of Identity." *JQR* 73 (1982): 1–37.

Burrows, Millar. *The Dead Sea Scrolls*. London: Secker & Warburg, 1956.

Callaway, Phillip. *The History of the Qumran Community: An Investigation*. JSPSup 3. Sheffield: JSOT Press, 1988.

Charlesworth, James H. "A Critical Comparison of the Dualism in 1QS 3:13–4:26 and the 'Dualism' contained in the Gospel of John." Pages 76–106 in *John and Qumran*. Edited by James H. Charlesworth. London: Chapman, 1972.

Collins, John J. *The Apocalyptic Imagination: An Introduction to Jewish Apocalyptic Literature*. 2nd ed. Grand Rapids: Eerdmans, 1998.

———. *Apocalypticism in the Dead Sea Scrolls*. London: Routledge, 1998.

———. *Beyond the Qumran Community: The Sectarian Movement of the Dead Sea Scrolls*. Grand Rapids: Eerdmans, 2010.

———. "Forms of Community in the Dead Sea Scrolls." Pages 97–112 in *Emanuel: Studies in Hebrew Bible, Septuagint and Dead Sea Scrolls in Honor of Emanuel Tov*. Edited by Shalom M. Paul, Robert A. Kraft, Lawrence H. Schiffman, and Weston W. Fields. VTSup 94. Leiden: Brill, 2003.

———. "Introduction: Towards the Morphology of a Genre." *Semeia* 14 (1979): 1–20.

———. "The Yaḥad and the 'Qumran Community.'" Pages 81–96 in *Biblical Traditions in Transmission: Essays in Honour of Michael A. Knibb*. Edited by Charlotte Hempel and Judith Lieu. JSJSup 111. Leiden: Brill, 2006.

Craffert, Pieter. "An Exercise in the Critical Use of Models: The 'Goodness of Fit' of Wilson's Sect Model." Pages 21–46 in *Social Scientific Models for Interpreting the Bible: Essays by the Context Group in Honor of Bruce J. Malina*. Edited by John J. Pilch. BibInt 53. Leiden: Brill, 2001.

Cross, Frank Moore. *The Ancient Library of Qumran and Modern Biblical Studies*. 3rd ed. BibSem 30. Sheffield: Sheffield Academic, 1995.

Davies, Philip. "Dualism in the Qumran War Texts." Pages 8–19 in *Dualism in Qumran*. Edited by Géza G. Xeravits. LSTS 76. London: T&T Clark, 2010.

———. "Eschatology at Qumran." *JBL* 104 (1985): 39–55.

———. "Sect Formation in Early Judaism." Pages 133–55 in *Sectarianism in Early Judaism: Sociological Advances*. Edited by David Chalcraft. London: Equinox, 2007.

———. *Sects and Scrolls: Essays on Qumran and Related Topics*. Atlanta: Scholars Press, 1996.

———. "Sects from Texts: On the Problems of Doing Sociology of the Qumran Literature." Pages 69–82 in *New Directions in Qumran Studies: Proceedings of the Bristol Colloquium on the Dead Sea Scrolls, 8–10 September 2003*. Edited by Jonathan Campbell, William John Lyons, and Lloyd Pietersen. LSTS 52. London: T&T Clark, 2005.

Dimant, Devorah. "Between Qumran Sectarian and Non-sectarian Texts: The Case of Belial and Mastema." Pages 235–56 in *The Dead Sea Scrolls and Contemporary Culture: Proceedings of the International Conference Held at the Israel Museum, Jerusalem (July 6–8, 2008)*. Edited by Adolfo D. Roitman, Lawrence H. Schiffman, and Shani Tzoref. STDJ 93. Leiden: Brill, 2011.

———. "Between Sectarian and Non-sectarian: The Case of the *Apocryphon of Joshua*." Pages 105–134 in *Reworking the Bible: Apocryphal Texts at Qumran; Proceedings of a Joint Symposium by the Orion Center for the Study of the Dead Sea Scrolls and Associated Literature and the Hebrew University Institute for Advanced Studies Research Group on Qumran, 15–17 January, 2002*. Edited by Esther G. Chazon, Devorah Dimant, and Ruth A. Clements. STDJ 58. Leiden: Brill, 2005.

———. "The Composite Character of the Qumran Sectarian Literature as an Indication of Its Date and Provenance." *RevQ* 22 (2006): 615–30.

———. "Israeli Scholarship on the Qumran Community." Pages 237–80 in *The Dead Sea Scrolls in Scholarly Perspective: A History of Research*. Edited by Devorah Dimant. STDJ 99. Leiden: Brill, 2012.

———. "New Light on Jewish Pseudepigrapha—4Q390." Pages 405–48 in *The Madrid Qumran Congress: Proceedings of the International Congress on the Dead Sea Scrolls, Madrid, 18–21 March, 1991*. Edited by Julio Trebolle Barrera and Luis Vegas Montaner. STDJ 11. Leiden: Brill, 1992.

———. "The Qumran Aramaic Texts and the Qumran Community." Pages 197–205 in *Flores Florentino: Dead Sea Scrolls and Other Early Jewish*

Studies in Honour of Florentino García Martínez. Edited by Anton Hilhorst, Émile Puech, and Eibert J. C. Tigchelaar. Leiden: Brill, 2007.

———. "The Qumran Manuscripts: Contents and Significance." Pages 23–58 in *Time to Prepare the Way in the Wilderness: Papers on the Qumran Scrolls by Fellows of the Institute for Advanced Studies of the Hebrew University, Jerusalem, 1989–1990*. Edited by Devorah Dimant and Lawrence H. Schiffman. STDJ 16. Leiden: Brill, 1995.

———. "Qumran Sectarian Literature." Pages 483–550 in *Jewish Writings of the Second Temple Period: Apocrypha, Pseudepigrapha, Qumran Sectarian Writings, Philo, Josephus*, Edited by Michael E. Stone. CRINT 2. Assen: Van Gorcum, 1984.

———. "Sectarian and Non-sectarian Texts from Qumran: The Pertinence and Usage of a Taxonomy." *RevQ* 24 (2009): 7–18.

Doering, Lutz. *Ancient Jewish Letters and the Beginnings of Christian Epistolography*. WUNT 298. Tübingen: Mohr Siebeck, 2012.

Donceel-Voûte, Pauline. "'Coenaculum': La sale a l'étage du locus 30 a Khirbet Qumrân sur la mer morte." Pages 61–84 in *Banquets d'orient*. Edited by Rika Gyselen. ResOr 4. Leuven: Peeters, 1992.

Duhaime, Jean. "Dualistic Reworking in the Scrolls from Qumran." *CBQ* 49 (1987): 32–56.

Dupont-Sommer, André. *The Dead Sea Scrolls: A Preliminary Survey*. Translated by M. Rowley. Oxford: Blackwell, 1952.

———. *The Essene Writings from Qumran*. Gloucester: Smith, 1973.

Elgvin, Torleif. "The Yaḥad Is More Than Qumran." Pages 273–79 in *Enoch and Qumran Origins, New Light on a Forgotten Connection*. Edited by Gabriele Boccaccini. Grand Rapids: Eerdmans, 2005.

Elman, Yaakov. "4QMMT and the Rabbinic Tradition, or, When Is a Parallel Not a Parallel?" Pages 99–128 in *Reading 4QMMT: New Perspectives on Qumran Law and History*. Edited by John Kampen and Moshe J. Bernstein. SymS 2. Atlanta: Scholars Press, 1996.

Eshel, Hanan. *The Dead Sea Scrolls and the Hasmonean State*. Grand Rapids: Eerdmans, 2008.

———. "The Historical Background of the Pesher Interpreting Joshua's Curse on the Rebuilder of Jericho." *RevQ* 15 (1992): 409–20.

Fernández, Miguel Pérez. "4QMMT: Redactional Study." *RevQ* 18 (1997): 191–205.

Fitzpatrick, Doyle C. *The King Strang Story: A Vindication of James J. Strang, The Beaver Island Mormon King*. Lansing, MI: National Heritage: 1970.

Fontaine, Petrus. "What Is Dualism, and What Is It Not?" Pages 266–76 in *Light against Darkness: Dualism in Ancient Mediterranean Religion and the Contemporary World.* Edited by Armin Lange, Eric M. Meyers, Bennie Reynolds, and Randall Styers. JSJSup 2. Göttingen: Vandenhoeck & Ruprecht, 2011.

Foucault, Michel. *The Order of Things: An Archaeology of the Human Sciences.* 13th ed. London: Routledge, 2010.

Fraade, Steven. *Legal Fictions: Studies of Law and Narrative in the Discursive Worlds of Ancient Jewish Sectarians and Sages.* JSJSup 147. Leiden: Brill, 2011.

Frey, Jörg. "Different Patterns of Dualistic Thought in the Qumran Library: Reflections on Their Background and History." Pages 275–335 in *Legal Texts and Legal Issues: Proceedings of the Second Meeting of the International Organization for Qumran Studies, Cambridge, 1995; Published in Honour of Joseph M. Baumgarten.* Edited by Moshe J. Bernstein, Florentino García Martínez, and John Kampen. STDJ 23. Leiden: Brill, 1997.

———. "Flesh and Spirit in the Palestinian Jewish Sapiential Tradition and in the Qumran Texts: An Inquiry into the Background of Pauline Usage." Pages 367–404 in *The Wisdom Texts from Qumran and the Development of Sapiential Thought: Studies in Wisdom at Qumran and Its Relationship to Sapiential Thought in the Ancient Near East, the Hebrew Bible, Ancient Judaism, and the New Testament.* Edited by Charlotte Hempel, Armin Lange, and Hermann Lichtenberger. Leuven: Peeters, 2002.

Galor, Katharina, Jean-Baptiste Humbert, and Jürgen Zangenberg, eds. *Qumran, the Site of the Dead Sea Scrolls: Archaeological Interpretations and Debates; Proceedings of a Conference Held at Brown University, November 17–19, 2002.* STDJ 57. Leiden: Brill, 2006.

Gammie, John G. "Spatial and Ethical Dualism in Jewish Wisdom and Apocalyptic Literature." *JBL* 93 (1974): 356–85.

García Martínez, Florentino. "4QMMT in a Qumran Context." Pages 15–27 in *Reading 4QMMT: New Perspectives on Qumran Law and History.* Edited by John Kampen and Moshe J. Bernstein. SymS 2. Atlanta: Scholars Press, 1996.

———. "Beyond the Sectarian Divide: The 'Voice of the Teacher' as an Authority-Conferring Strategy in Some Qumran Texts." Pages 227–44 in *The Dead Sea Scrolls: Texts and Context.* Edited by Charlotte Hempel. STDJ 90. Leiden: Brill, 2010.

———. "Dos Notas Sobre 4QMMT." *RevQ* 16 (1993): 293–97.
———. "The Groningen Hypothesis Revisited." Pages 17–29 in *The Dead Sea Scrolls and Contemporary Culture: Proceedings of the International Conference Held at the Israel Museum, Jerusalem (July 6–8, 2008)*. Edited by Adolfo D. Roitman, Lawrence H. Schiffman, and Shani Tzoref. STDJ 93. Leiden: Brill, 2011.
———. *Qumranica Minora I: Qumran Origins and Apocalypticism*. Edited by Eibert J. C. Tigchelaar. STDJ 63. Leiden: Brill, 2007.
———. "Qumran Origins and Early History: A Groningen Hypothesis." *FO* 25 (1988): 113–36.
———. "Sectario, No-Sectario, O Qué? Problemas de una taxonomía correcta de los textos qumránicos." *RevQ* 23 (2008): 383–94.
———. *Textos de Qumrán*. Madrid: Editorial Trotta, 1992.
García Martínez, Florentino, and Adam van der Woude, "A 'Groningen' Hypothesis of Qumran Origins and Early History." *RevQ* 14 (1990): 521–42.
Ginzberg, Louis. *An Unknown Jewish Sect*. New York: Jewish Theological Seminary of America, 1970.
Goering, Gregory Schmidt. *Wisdom's Root Revealed: Ben Sira and the Election of Israel*. JSJSup 139. Leiden: Brill, 2009.
Goff, Matthew J. "Looking for Sapiential Dualism at Qumran." Pages 20–38 in *Dualism in Qumran*. Edited by Géza G. Xeravits. LSTS 76. London: T&T Clark, 2010.
Golb, Norman. *Who Wrote the Dead Sea Scrolls? The Search for the Secret of Qumran*. London: O'Mara, 1995.
Goodman, Martin. "Josephus and Variety in First-Century Judaism." Pages 33–46 in *Judaism in the Roman World: Collected Essays*. AGJU 66. Leiden: Brill, 2007.
———. "A Note on the Qumran Sectarians, the Essenes and Josephus." Pages 137–44 in *Judaism in the Roman World: Collected Essays*. AGJU 66. Leiden: Brill, 2007.
Grabbe, Lester. *Judaic Religion in the Second Temple Period: Belief and Practice from the Exile to Yavneh*. London: Routledge, 2000.
———. *Yehud: A History of the Persian Province of Judah*. Vol. 1 of *A History of the Jews and Judaism in the Second Temple Period*. LSTS 47. London: T&T Clark, 2005.
Grossman, Maxine. "Cultivating Identity: Textual Virtuosity and 'Insider' Status." Pages 1–12 in *Defining Identities: We, You and the Other in the Dead Sea Scrolls: Proceedings of the Fifth Meeting of the IOQS in Gron-*

ingen. Edited by Florentino García Martínez and Mladen Popović. STDJ 70. Leiden: Brill, 2008.

———. "Reading *4QMMT*, Genre and History." *RevQ* 20 (2001): 3–22.

Heger, Paul. "Another Look at Dualism in Qumran Writings." Pages 39–101 in *Dualism in Qumran*. Edited by Géza G. Xeravits. LSTS 76. London: T&T Clark, 2010.

Hempel, Charlotte. "1QS 6:2c–4a: Satellites or Precursors of the Yahad?" Pages 31–40 in *The Dead Sea Scrolls and Contemporary Culture: Proceedings of the International Conference Held at the Israel Museum, Jerusalem (July 6–8, 2008)*. Edited by Adolfo D. Roitman, Lawrence H. Schiffman, and Shani Tzoref. STDJ 93. Leiden: Brill, 2011.

———. "The Community and Its Rivals according to the Community Rule from Caves 1 and 4." *RevQ* 21 (2003): 47–81.

———. "The Context of 4QMMT and Comfortable Theories." Pages 275–92 in *The Dead Sea Scrolls: Texts and Contexts*. Edited by Charlotte Hempel. STDJ 90. Leiden: Brill, 2010.

———. *The Damascus Texts*. CQS1. Sheffield: Sheffield Academic, 2000.

———. "Emerging Communal Life in the S Tradition." Pages 43–61 in *Defining Identities: We, You and the Other in the Dead Sea Scrolls; Proceedings of the Fifth Meeting of the IOQS in Groningen*. Edited by Florentino García Martínez and Mladen Popović. STDJ 70. Leiden: Brill, 2008.

———. "The Groningen Hypothesis: Strengths and Weaknesses." Pages 249–55 in *Enoch and Qumran Origins: New Light on a Forgotten Connection*. Edited by Gabriele Boccaccini. Grand Rapids: Eerdmans, 2005.

———. "Kriterien zur Bestimmung 'essenischer Verfasserschaft' von Qumrantexten." Pages 71–85 in *Qumran Kontrovers: Beiträge zu den Textfunden vom Toten Meer*. Edited by Jörg Frey and Hartmut Stegemann. Einblicke 6. Paderborn: Bonifatius, 2003.

———. "The Laws of the Damascus Document and 4QMMT." Pages 69–84 in *The Damascus Document: A Centennial of Discovery; Proceedings of the Third International Symposium of the Orion Center for the Study of the Dead Sea Scrolls and Associated Literature, 4–8 February 1998*. Edited by Joseph M. Baumgarten, Esther G. Chazon, and Avital Pinnick. STDJ 34. Leiden: Brill, 2009.

———. "The Qumran Sapiential Texts and the Rule Books." Pages 277–95 in *The Wisdom Texts from Qumran and the Development of Sapiential Thought*. Edited by Charlotte Hempel, Armin Lange, and Hermann Lichtenberger. BETL 159. Leuven: Peeters, 2002.

———. "The *Treatise on the Two Spirits* and the Literary History of the *Rule of the Community*." Pages 102–20 in *Dualism in Qumran*. Edited by Géza G. Xeravits. LSTS 76. London: T&T Clark, 2010.
Hirschfeld, Yizhar. *Qumran in Context: Reassessing the Archaeological Evidence*. Peabody, MA: Hendrickson, 2004.
Horsley, Richard. *Scribes, Visionaries and the Politics of Second Temple Judea*. Louisville: Westminster John Knox, 2007.
Humbert, Jean-Baptiste. "Interpreting the Qumran Site." *NEA* 63 (2000): 140–43.
———. "Some Remarks on the Archaeology of Qumran." Pages 19–39 in *Qumran, The Site of the Dead Sea Scrolls: Archaeological Interpretations and Debates; Proceedings of a Conference Held at Brown University, November 17–19, 2002*. Edited by Katharina Galor, Jean-Baptiste Humbert, and Jürgen Zangenberg. STDJ 57. Leiden: Brill, 2006.
Jokiranta, Jutta. "Identity on a Continuum: Constructing and Expressing Sectarian Social Identity in Qumran *Serakhim* and *Pesharim*." PhD diss., University of Helsinki, 2005.
———. "'Sectarianism' of the Qumran 'Sect': Sociological Notes." *RevQ* 20 (2001): 223–39.
———. *Social Identity and Sectarianism in the Qumran Movement*. STDJ 105. Leiden: Brill, 2013.
Kampen, John. "4QMMT and New Testament Studies." Pages 129–44 in *Reading 4QMMT: New Perspectives on Qumran Law and History*. Edited by John Kampen and Moshe J. Bernstein. SymS 2. Atlanta: Scholars Press, 1996.
Kampen, John, and Moshe J. Bernstein, eds. *Reading 4QMMT: New Perspectives on Qumran Law and History*. SymS 2. Atlanta: Scholars Press, 1996.
Kister, Menahem. "Studies in 4QMiqsat Maʿase Ha-Torah and Related Texts: Law, Theology, Language and Calendar." *Tarbiz* 68 (1999): 317–71.
Klinghardt, Matthias. "The Manual of Discipline in the Light of Statutes of Hellenistic Associations." Pages 251–70 in *Methods of Investigation of the Dead Sea Scrolls and the Khirbet Qumran Site: Present Realities and Future Prospects*. Edited by Michael O. Wise, Norman Golb, John J. Collins, and Dennis G. Pardee. ANYAS 722. New York: The New York Academy of Sciences, 1994.
Lange, Armin. "From Paratext to Commentary." Pages 195–216 in *The Dead Sea Scrolls and Contemporary Culture: Proceedings of the Inter-*

national Conference Held at the Israel Museum, Jerusalem (July 6–8, 2008). Edited by Adolfo D. Roitman, Lawrence H. Schiffman, and Shani Tzoref. STDJ 93. Leiden: Brill, 2011.

———. "Kriterien essenischer Texte." Pages 59–69 in *Qumran Kontrovers: Beiträge zu den Textfunden vom Toten Meer*. Edited by Jörg Frey and Hartmut Stegemann. Einblicke 6. Paderborn: Bonifatius, 2003.

———. *Weisheit und Prädestination: Weisheitliche Urordnung und Prädestination in den Textfunden von Qumran*. STDJ 18. Leiden: Brill, 1995.

Lenski, Gerhard E. *Power and Privilege: A Theory of Social Stratification*. McGraw-Hill Series in Sociology. New York: McGraw-Hill, 1966.

Leonhardt-Balzer, Jutta. "Dualism." Pages 553–56 in *The Eerdmans Dictionary of Early Judaism*. Edited by John J. Collins and Daniel C. Harlow. Grand Rapids: Eerdmans, 2010.

Licht, Jacob. "An Analysis of the Treatise on the Two Spirits in DSD." Pages 88–100 in *Aspects of the Dead Sea Scrolls*. Edited by Chaim Rabin and Yigael Yadin. ScrHier 4. Jerusalem: Magnes, 1958.

Lichtenberger, Hermann. *Studien zum Menschenbild in Texten der Qumrangemeinde*. SUNT 15. Göttingen: Vandenhoeck & Ruprecht, 1980.

Lim, Timothy, and John J. Collins, eds. *The Oxford Handbook of the Dead Sea Scrolls*. Oxford: Oxford University Press, 2010.

Magen, Yizhak, and Yuval Peleg. *The Qumran Excavations 1993–2004: Preliminary Report*. Jerusalem: Israel Antiquities Authority, 2007.

Magness, Jodi. *The Archaeology of Qumran and the Dead Sea Scrolls*. Grand Rapids: Eerdmans, 2002.

Mason, Steve. "What Josephus Says about the Essenes in His *Judean War*." http://orion.mscc.huji.ac.il/symposiums/programs/Mason00-1.shtml; http://orion.mscc.huji.ac.il/symposiums/programs/Mason00-2.shtml.

Metso, Sarianna. *The Textual Development of the Community Rule*. STDJ 21. Leiden: Brill, 1997.

———. "Whom Does the Term Yahad Identify?" Pages 213–35 in *Biblical Traditions in Transmission: Essays in the Honour of Michael A. Knibb*. Edited by Charlotte Hempel and Judith Lieu. JSJSup 110. Leiden: Brill, 2003.

Metzger, Bruce M. "The Fourth Book of Ezra: A New Translation and Introduction." Pages 517–59 in vol. 1 of *The Old Testament Pseudepigrapha*. Edited by James H. Charlesworth. New York: Doubleday, 1985.

Meyers, Eric M. "From Myth to Apocalyptic: Dualism in the Hebrew Bible." Pages 92–106 in *Light against Darkness: Dualism in Ancient Mediter-*

ranean Religion and the Contemporary World. Edited by Armin Lange, Eric M. Meyers, Bennie Reynolds III, and Randall Styers. JAJSup 2. Göttingen: Vandenhoeck & Ruprecht, 2011.

Milik, Józef T. *Ten Years of Discovery in the Wilderness of Judaea*. SBT 26. London: SCM, 1959.

Murphy-O'Connor, Jerome. "The Essenes and Their History." *RB* 81 (1974): 215–44.

Needham, Rodney. *Symbolic Classification*. Goodyear Perspectives in Anthropology. Santa Monica, CA: Goodyear, 1979.

Neusner, Jacob. *Judaism and Its Social Metaphors, Israel in the History of Jewish Thought*. Cambridge: Cambridge University Press, 1989.

Newsom, Carol. "'Sectually Explicit' Literature from Qumran." Pages 167–87 in *The Hebrew Bible and Its Interpreters*. Edited by William H. C. Propp, Baruch Halpern, and David N. Freedman. BJSUCSD 1. Winona Lake, IN: Eisenbrauns, 1990.

———. *The Self as Symbolic Space: Constructing Identity and Community at Qumran*. STDJ 52. Leiden: Brill, 2004.

Nickelsburg, George W. E. *1 Enoch 1: A Commentary on the Book of 1 Enoch, Chapters 1–36, 81–108*. Hermeneia. Minneapolis: Fortress, 2001.

Osten-Sacken, Peter von der. *Gott und Belial: Traditionsgeschichtliche Untersuchungen zum Dualismus in den Texten aus Qumran*. SUNT 6. Göttingen: Vanderhoeck & Ruprecht, 1969.

Parry, Donald W., and Emanuel Tov, eds. *The Dead Sea Scrolls Reader*. 6 vols. Leiden: Brill, 2004.

Popović, Mladen. "Light and Darkness in the Treatise on the Two Spirits (1QS III 13–IV 26) and in 4Q186." Pages 148–65 in *Dualism in Qumran*. Edited by Géza G. Xeravits. LSTS 76. London: T&T Clark, 2010.

Puech, Émile. "L'Épilogue de *4QMMT* Revisité." Pages 309–39 in *A Teacher for All Generations: Essays in Honor of James C. VanderKam*. Edited by Eric F. Mason. 2 vols. JSJSup 153. Leiden: Brill, 2012.

———. "The Essenes and Qumran, the Teacher and the Wicked Priest, the Origins." Pages 298–302 in *Enoch and Qumran Origins: New Light on a Forgotten Connection*. Edited by Gabriele Boccaccini. Grand Rapids: Eerdmans, 2005.

Qimron, Elisha. "The Nature of the Reconstructed Composite Text of 4QMMT." Pages 9–13 in *Reading 4QMMT: New Perspectives on*

Qumran Law and History. Edited by John Kampen and Moshe J. Bernstein. SymS 2. Atlanta: Scholars Press, 1996.

Qimron, Elisha, and John Strugnell. *Qumran Cave 4.V: Miqsat Ma'ase Ha-Torah*. DJD X. Oxford: Clarendon, 1994.

Regev, Eyal. *Sectarianism in Qumran: A Cross-Cultural Perspective*. RelSoc 45. Berlin: de Gruyter, 2007.

———. "The Yahad and the Damascus Covenant: Structure, Organization, and Relationship." *RevQ* 21 (2003): 233–62.

Rengstorf, Karl Heinrich. *Hirbet Qumran und die Bibliothek vom Toten Mer*. Studia Delitzschiana 5. Stuttgart: Kohlhammer, 1960.

Sandt, Huub van de, and David Flusser. *The Didache: Its Jewish Sources and Its Place in Early Judaism and Christianity*. CRINT 3.5. Assen: Van Gorcum, 2002.

Schechter, Solomon. *Fragments of a Zadokite Work*. Documents of Jewish Sectaries 1. Cambridge: Cambridge University Press, 1910.

Schiffman, Lawrence H. *The Halakhah at Qumran*. SJLA 16. Leiden: Brill, 1975.

———. "Prohibited Marriages in the Dead Sea Scrolls and Rabbinic Literature." Pages 113–25 in *Rabbinic Perspectives: Rabbinic Literature and the Dead Sea Scrolls, Proceedings of the Eight Symposium of the Orion Center for the Study of the Dead Sea Scrolls and Associated Literature (7–9 January 2003)*. Edited by Steven Fraade, Aharon Shemesh, and Ruth Clements. STDJ 62. Leiden: Brill, 2006.

———. *Qumran and Jerusalem: Studies in the Dead Sea Scrolls and the History of Judaism*. Grand Rapids: Eerdmans, 2010.

———. *Reclaiming the Dead Sea Scrolls: Their True Meaning for Judaism and Christianity*. Philadelphia: Jewish Publication Society, 1994. Repr., New York: Doubleday, 1995.

Schofield, Alison. *From Qumran to the Yaḥad: A New Paradigm of Textual Development for the Community Rule*. STDJ 77. Leiden: Brill, 2008.

Schofield, Alison, and James VanderKam. "Were the Hasmoneans Zadokites?" *JBL* 124 (2005): 73–87.

Schürer, Emil. *History of the Jewish People in the Age of Jesus Christ (175 B.C.–A.D. 135)*. Edited by Géza Vermes, Fergus Millar, and Martin Goodman. Rev. and enl. ed. Edinburgh: T&T Clark, 2004.

Scott, James C. *Domination and the Arts of Resistance: Hidden Transcripts*. New Haven: Yale University Press, 1990.

Sharp, Carolyn. "Phinean Zeal and Rhetorical Strategy in 4QMMT." *RevQ* 18 (1997): 207–22.

Shemesh, Aharon. *Halakhah in the Making: The Development of Jewish Law from Qumran to the Rabbis*. Taubman Lectures in Jewish Studies. Berkeley: University of California Press, 2009.
Shemesh, Aharon, and Cana Werman. "Halakhah at Qumran: Genre and Authority." *DSD* 10 (2003): 104–29.
Siegal, Elitzur Bar-Asher. "Who Separated from Whom and Why? A Philological Study of 4QMMT." *RevQ* 25 (2011): 229–56.
Skehan, Patrick, and Alexander Di Lella. *The Wisdom of Ben Sira*. AB 39. New York: Doubleday, 1987.
Snaith, John G. *Ecclesiasticus, or The Wisdom of Jesus Son of Sirach*. CBC. Cambridge: Cambridge University Press, 1974.
Stacey, David, and Gregory Doudna. *Qumran Revisited: A Reassessment of the Site and Its Texts*. BARIS 2520. Oxford: Archaeopress, 2013.
Stark, Rodney, and William Sims Bainbridge. *A Theory of Religion*. Toronto Studies in Religion 2. New York: Peter Lang, 1987.
Stegemann, Hartmut. "Die Bedeutung der Qumranfunde für die Erforschung der Apokalyptik." Pages 495–530 in *Apocalypticism in the Mediterranean World and the Near East: Proceedings of the International Colloquium on Apocalypticism, Uppsala, August 12–17, 1979*. Edited by D. Hellholm. Tübingen: Mohr Siebeck, 1983.
Stern, Sacha. "Qumran Calendars and Sectarianism." Pages 232–53 in *The Oxford Handbook of the Dead Sea Scrolls*. Edited by Timothy H. Lim and John J. Collins. Oxford: Oxford University Press, 2010.
Strugnell, John. "MMT: Second Thoughts on a Forthcoming Edition." Pages 57–73 in *The Community of the Renewed Covenant: The Notre Dame Symposium on the Dead Sea Scrolls*. Edited by Eugene Ulrich and James VanderKam. CJA 10. Notre Dame: University of Notre Dame Press, 1994.
Strugnell, John, Daniel J. Harrington, and Torleif Elgvin, eds. *Sapiential Texts, Part 2: Cave 4.XXIV*. DJD XXXIV. Oxford: Clarendon, 1999.
Stuckenbruck, Loren T. *1 Enoch 91–108: Translation and Commentary*. CEJL. Berlin: de Gruyter, 2007.
———. "The Interiorization of Dualism within the Human Being in Second Temple Judaism: The Treatise of the Two Spirits (1QS iii 13–iv 26) in Its Tradition-Historical Context." Pages 145–68 in *Light against Darkness: Dualism in Ancient Mediterranean Religion and the Contemporary World*. Edited by Armin Lange, Eric M. Meyers, Bennie Reynolds III, and Randall Styers. JAJSup 2. Göttingen: Vandenhoeck & Ruprecht, 2011.

Sukenik, Eleazer L. *Megillot Genuzot.* Jerusalem: Bialak Institute, 1948.
Sussman, Jacob. "The History of *Halakhah* and the Dead Sea Scrolls—Preliminary Observation on *Miqsat Ma'ase Ha-Torah* (4QMMT)." *Tarbiz* 59 (1990): 11–76.
Talmon, Shemaryahu, Jonathan Ben-Dov, and Uwe Glessmer. *Qumran Cave 4.XVI: Calendrical Texts.* DJD XXI. Oxford: Clarendon, 2001.
Thompson, Leonard. "A Sociological Analysis of Tribulation in the Apocalypse of John." *Semeia* 36 (1986): 147–74.
Tigchelaar, Eibert J. C. "Classifications of the Collection of the Dead Sea Scrolls and the Case of *Apocryphon of Jeremiah C.*" *JSJ* 43 (2012): 519–50.
———. "The Dead Sea Scrolls." Pages 163–80 in *Eerdmans Dictionary of Early Judaism.* Edited by John J. Collins and Daniel C. Harlow. Grand Rapids: Eerdmans, 2010.
———. "'These Are the Names of the Spirits of…': A Preliminary Edition of *4QCatalogue of Spirits* (4Q230) and New Manuscript Evidence for the *Two Spirits Treatise* (4Q257 and 1Q29a)." *RevQ* 21 (2004): 529–47.
———. *To Increase Learning for the Understanding Ones: Reading and Reconstructing the Fragmentary Early Jewish Sapiential Text 4QInstruction.* STDJ 44. Leiden: Brill, 2001.
Tov, Emanuel. "Hebrew Biblical Manuscripts from the Judaean Desert: Their Contribution to Textual Criticism." *JJS* 39 (1988): 5–37.
———. *Scribal Practices and Approaches Reflected in the Texts Found in the Judean Desert.* STDJ 54. Leiden: Brill, 2004.
Troeltsch, Ernst. *The Social Teaching of the Christian Churches.* Translated by Olive Wyon. New York: Macmillan, 1931.
Ullmann-Margalit, Edna. *Out of the Cave: An Inquiry into the Dead Sea Scrolls Research.* Cambridge: Harvard University Press, 2006.
VanderKam, James C. *Calendars in the Dead Sea Scrolls: Measuring Time.* New York: Routledge, 1998.
———. *The Dead Sea Scrolls Today.* Grand Rapids: Eerdmans, 1994.
Vaux, Roland de. *Archaeology and the Dead Sea Scrolls.* London: Oxford University Press, 1973.
Vermes, Géza. *The Dead Sea Scrolls: Qumran in Perspective.* Cleveland: Collins World, 1977.
———. "Preliminary Remarks on Unpublished Fragments of the Community Rule from Cave 4." *JSS* 42 (1991): 250–55.
Weber, Max. *Wirtschaft und Gesellschaft.* Tübingen: Mohr Siebeck, 1925.

Weissenberg, Hanne von. *4QMMT: Reevaluating the Text, the Function and the Meaning of the Epilogue*. STDJ 82. Leiden: Brill, 2009.
Wernberg-Møller, P. "A Reconsideration of the Two Spirits in the Rule of the Community (1QSerek III, 13–IV, 26)." *RevQ* 3 (1961): 413–41.
Werrett, Ian. *Ritual Purity and the Dead Sea Scrolls*. STDJ 72. Leiden: Brill, 2007.
Wills, Lawrence M. *Not God's People: Insiders and Outsiders in the Biblical World*. Lanham, MD: Rowman & Littlefield, 2008.
Wilson, Bryan. *Religious Sects: A Sociological Study*. World University Library. London: Weidenfeld and Nicholson, 1970.
Wilson, Edmund. "The Scrolls from the Dead Sea." *The New Yorker* (May 14, 1955): 45–121.
Wintermute, O. S. "Jubilees." Pages 35–142 in vol. 2 of *The Old Testament Pseudepigrapha*. Edited by James H. Charlesworth. New York: Doubleday, 1985.
Woude, Adam van der. "Wicked Priest or Wicked Priests? Reflections on the Identification of the Wicked Priest in the Habakkuk Commentary." *JSS* 33 (1982): 349–59.
Xeravits, Géza G., ed. *Dualism in Qumran*. LSTS 76. London: T&T Clark, 2010.
Zanella, Francesco. "Sectarian and non-sectarian Texts: A Possible Semantic Approach." *RevQ* 24 (2009): 19–34.
Zangenberg, Jürgen. "Zwischen Zufall und Einzigartigkeit: Bemerkungen zur jüngsten Diskussion über die Funktion von Khirbet Qumran und die Rolle einiger ausgewählter archäologischer Befunde." Pages 121–46 in *Qumran und die Archäologie: Texte und Kontexte*. Edited by Jörg Frey, Carsten Claussen, and Nadine Kessler. WUNT 278. Tübingen: Mohr Siebeck, 2011.

Index of Primary Texts

Hebrew Bible

Genesis 234
  1   155–56, 206–7, 213, 234, 219
  1:4   232, 240
  1:15   223
  1:17   223
  1:26–28   213
  2:4   216–17
  2:4–9   216
  2:8–9   216
  5:1   216

Leviticus   99, 104, 113
  22:16   117

Numbers   104, 113

Deuteronomy   97, 99, 104, 106–7, 113, 119, 134
  1–3   105
  7   134
  12:5   104
  26:15   220
  28–29   249
  30–31   106
  30:15–20   234, 248–49

Ezra-Nehemiah   25

Ezra   134
  9–10   134

Nehemiah
  9–10   105

Job   250
  38:19–20   250

Psalms   249
  1:1   249
  1:6   249
  8:7   213
  18:28   230
  36:9   218
  37   127
  37:6   230
  37:32–33   109, 129
  44   155
  44:24–25   159
  68:26   218
  112:4   250
  119   249
  119:1   249
  119:7   249
  119:9   249
  119:15   249
  119:21   249
  119:29–30   249
  119:32   249
  119:104   249
  139:24   249

Proverbs   162, 166–67, 232, 249–50
  1–9   159, 249
  2:12–22   249
  2:13   250
  4:18–19   250
  10:11   218
  13:14   218
  14:27   218

Proverbs (cont.)

16:22	218
18:4	218
25:26	218
29:27	162, 183, 222, 229, 232

Qoheleth

2:13–14	230
3:1–8	155, 159

Isaiah

5:20	230
9:2	230
12:3	220
24–27	155, 159
25–26	159
40–55	156
40:3	67
42:16	230, 250
45:7	219, 230
55–66	156, 159
59:20	41

Jeremiah

2:13	218
9:10	220
10:22	220
17:13	218
21:8	249
25:30	220
49:33	220
51:37	220

Ezekiel

	155
40–48	159

Daniel 141, 151, 155, 160, 164, 184

Hosea

13:15	218

Haggai 159

Zechariah 155, 159

DEUTEROCANONICAL WORKS AND PSEUDEPIGRAPHA

1 Enoch	43, 75, 136–37, 155, 176, 239
1–36	147, 152–54, 184, 239, 246, 248, 251
9	248
72–82	136, 227
83–90	70
85–90	68
91–105	239
91–108	222, 239–40, 249, 250–51
91:1–10, 18–19	222
91:3–4	222
91:4	240
91:8–10	240
91:11–17	239
91:12–14	240
91:18–19	222, 240
92:3–5	240
92:4	250
92:5	240
93:1–3	239
93:1–10	222, 239
94:1	249
94:1–5	222, 239, 249
94:2	249
94:3–4	250
98:4	239

1 Maccabees	43, 54–55, 110, 267
10:18–20	110
13:33–42	28
14:27	28
14:41	28

4 Ezra	176
7:50	176

Apocryphal Psalms 43

Ben Sira	43, 81, 149, 162, 164–66, 179, 206, 231–37, 248, 251, 255
1:28	165, 234
1:30	234

2:12	165, 227, 234	Judith	43, 54
11:16	159		
15:11	159	Letter of Jeremiah	43
15:11–20	214, 222, 234		
15:14	159, 165	Psalms of Solomon	55
15:16–17	234		
16:16	159	Testament of Levi	43
17	234		
17:1–8	234	Testament of Naphtali	43
21:6	165		
21:10–11	214	Tobit	43, 81, 249
23:2–3	165	1:3	249
23:20	235	4:5–6	249
33:9	149	4:10	249
33:10–15	165, 214, 235–36	4:19	249
33:11–15	159		
33:14–15	149, 162, 183, 222	Wisdom of Solomon	43, 54–55
37:18	234		
39	234	DEAD SEA SCROLLS	
39:16	162, 183, 206, 235		
39:16–34	235	1Q26 (*see also* 4Q415–418)	167, 197, 204
39:17	235		
39:24–34	162, 183, 206		
39:28	235	1Q27 (1QMysteries) (*see also* 4Q299–300)	149, 162, 167, 183, 186, 204
39:34	235	I, 2–II, 10	148
42	236		
42:17–25	236		
42:22–25	162, 183, 206	1Q29a	201
42:24	149, 183		
42:24–25	159, 236	1QH^a (Hodayot)	46, 72, 141, 143, 162–63, 196, 204, 244
		VI	148
Book of Giants	43	VI, 11–12	150, 183, 232, 241, 244
		VI, 17	218
Jubilees	19, 43, 47, 67–68, 70, 73, 75, 83, 136, 152–53, 164, 184, 227, 239–40, 248, 251	VI, 22–23	205
		VII	148
		X, 31	218
1:2	240	XI, 20–37	148
2:2	240	XII, 6–13	148
7:26	241	XVI, 15	218
10:4–5	241		
10:6	241		
11:4–6	241	1QM (War Scroll) (*see also* 4QM)	46, 72, 126, 141–43, 146–48, 150–54, 173, 176, 184–85, 187, 196, 231, 245, 247
17:15–16	241		
19:28	240		
48:1–3	241	I	142, 148, 150

1QM (cont.)	201	III, 13–14	212
I, 2	150	III, 13–15	195–96, 216
I, 5	173	III, 13–15a	211
I, 6	246	III, 13–18	197, 213, 239
VIII, 1b–7	173	III, 13–18a	196
XIII	148	III, 13–IV, 14	142, 147, 196
XIII, 10b–12b	173	III, 13–IV, 25	195
XV–IXX	148	III, 13–IV, 26 (Treatise of the Two Spirits) 34–35, 60, 140–43, 147–54, 162–67, 177, 179, 183, 185–188, 189–253, 255, 260–61, 269	
1QpHab xiii, 2, 65, 77, 81, 111, 163, 263			
IV, 17b–V, 12a	148		
V, 9–12	66	III, 14	217
VII, 14	163	III, 15	173, 196
VIII, 8b–11a	111	III, 15–16	234
XI, 2–8	65, 83	III, 15–17	212
		III, 15–18	195
1QS (1Q28) (*see also* S and 4QS)		III, 17–19	199
xiii, 2, 8–9, 11, 27, 31, 46, 67, 71–72, 74, 96, 109, 126, 142–43, 148–49, 151, 190–204, 208–9, 218, 224, 226, 241, 244–45		III, 17c–18	213, 215
		III, 18	216, 222, 225
		III, 18–19	215
		III, 18–IV, 1	195, 197, 205, 239
I–IV	191, 200, 202–3, 241	III, 18–IV, 14	197
I, 1–5	203	III, 18b–23a	196, 219
I, 1–II, 18	148, 222	III, 19	59, 199, 215–20
I, 1–III, 12	209	III, 20–21	219, 221
I, 1–III, 13	191, 193	III, 21–22	205
I, 2–3	203	III, 21c–25a	221
I, 10	203	III, 22	243
I, 15–19	203	III, 23	238, 240
I, 16–26	232, 241, 243–44	III, 23–25	221
I, 21–23	203	III, 23b–25a	196, 219, 228
I, 23	243	III, 24	193, 208, 210
I, 24	243	III, 25	222
II, 2–10	232, 241, 243	III, 25–IV, 1	222
II, 4–5	203	III, 25b–26a	196
II, 4–11	203	IV, 1–14	196
II, 4–25	153, 184	IV, 2	224–25
II, 6–11	203	IV, 2–11	201
II, 26	203	IV, 2–14	196–97, 200, 205, 222–27
III	204, 226	IV, 4–10	191, 203
III–IV	207, 238	IV, 6	238
III, 1–10	203	IV, 6–8	205
III, 4–5	203	IV, 12–15	191
III, 7–12	203	IV, 13–15	203
III, 13	197, 212, 215–17, 237	IV, 14	241, 246

IV, 14–22	241	4Q175	47
IV, 15	215–17, 225–26	23	148
IV, 15–16a	225		
IV, 15–18	196, 205	4Q177	148, 153, 184
IV, 15–18a	222		
IV, 15–23a	142, 196–97, 239	4Q180	148, 246
IV, 15–26	196–97, 225		
IV, 16	228	4Q181	148, 162, 205, 242, 246
IV, 16–22	245	1, II, 1–5	232, 242
IV, 16b–18a	227	1, II, 3–4	246
IV, 17	226	1, II, 5	150, 183, 232, 241, 244, 246
IV, 17ff.	226		
IV, 18	238	4Q184	148, 167, 173
IV, 18–23a	196, 229		
IV, 22	193	4Q185	167
IV, 23	215		
IV, 23–24	59, 167	4Q186	141, 148, 228
IV, 23–25	191, 203		
IV, 23b–26	142, 196–97, 239	4Q251	126
IV, 24	228		
IV, 25	196	4Q265	126
IV, 26	241		
V–XI	191, 195, 198, 219	4Q280	148, 162, 205, 247
VI, 1–8	11–12	2, 2	153, 184
VI, 2	11	2, 5	246
VI, 3	11	2, 4–5	150, 183, 232, 241, 244, 246
VI, 18	128		
VIII, 12b–16a	67	4Q286	148
IX, 16–17	109	7, II, 1–13	153, 184
X, 12	218		
XI, 2b–22	148	4Q287	148
XI, 3–6	218		
XI, 11	173	4Q299–4Q301 (4QMysteries)	148, 167, 179, 201, 204–5, 232–33, 237–38
1Q28a (1QSa)	11, 46, 126	4Q299	148
		4Q300	148
1Q28b (1QSb)	11, 46, 126		
		4Q319	96, 136
4Q171 (4QpPs^a)	109, 111, 127, 129, 263		
II, 1–IV, 18	148	4Q327	94
IV, 3, II, 8–9	109		
IV, 8c–9a	128–29	4Q378–4Q379 (Apocryphon of Joshua) 47, 73	
4Q174	148, 153, 184		
1–2, I, 7	128		

4Q386		4Q522	47
1, II, 3	148	4Q525	167
4Q400–4Q407	59–60	4Q561	148
4Q413	148		

4QM (War Scroll, 4Q491–497) (see also
   1QM)   147, 150
   4Q496 3, 6   246–47

4Q414   126

4Q415–4Q418 (4QInstruction)   59,
  166–67, 179, 186, 197, 201, 204–5,
  232–33, 237–39, 248

4QMMT (4Q394–4Q399) 14–15, 33–35,
  60, 66, 68–70, 75, 77, 80–81, 83, 87,
  89–102–39, 189–90, 254, 260–61, 269

4Q417	149		
4Q417 2, I, 15–18	162, 183	4QMMT A	93–98, 100, 118, 135
4Q418	41, 148	1–18 (see 4Q394 1–2)	94, 95, 97
4Q418 81/8a, 1	218	19–21 (see 4Q394 3–4)	94, 96–97
4Q418 77, 2	237		

4QMMT B   15, 93, 95, 97–102, 104–8,
  116–21, 124, 127, 131–32, 135, 137

4Q252	60	1	102, 128
V, 5	60	2	127–28
4Q253		12–13	104, 117
3, 2	148	26–27	104, 117, 135
4Q254	60	35	99, 105
4, 4	60	68	105–6, 117
		68–70	99
4Q320–4Q330	84	70	105–6
		75–82	135
4Q423 (see also 4Q415–418)	167, 197	80	117
		80–82	99
4Q448	55		

4QMMT C   93, 95, 97–100, 102, 104–7,
  111, 116–20, 122, 124

4Q487		1–8	132, 134
37	191, 203	7	98, 109, 133
4Q502	183	7–8 (see 4Q397 14–21)	105, 111,
16	191, 203, 232, 241	118–20, 130–35	
		7b 8a	69
4Q504	67	8	105–6, 131
		9–16 (see 4Q398 14–17)	103
4Q510–511	148	10–12a	103
4Q510 1, 4–6	153, 184	14–15	132
4Q511	205	18–24 (see 4Q398 11–13)	103
		23	106, 119, 127–28

INDEX OF PRIMARY TEXTS

25–32 (see 4Q398 14–17)	103	4Q258 (4QS^d)	11, 191, 202–3
26–30	102	4Q259 (4QS^e)	84, 96, 136, 191, 202–3
27	127–28, 135	4Q260 (4QS^f)	203
28	106, 111, 119	4Q261 (4QS^g)	203
30	104	4Q262 (4QS^h)	191, 198, 203–4
31–32	104, 106, 119, 135	4Q263 (4QS^i)	203
32	111	4Q264 (4QS^j)	203

4QMMT^a (4Q394) 8–10, 15, 84, 93–98, 102, 135–37
  1–2 (see 4QMMT A 1–18) 93–97, 135
  3–4 (see 4QMMT A 19–21) 93–97
  3–7, I, 4 102

4QMMT^b (4Q395) 93–94, 97

4QMMT^c (4Q396) 93–94, 97, 105

4QMMT^d (4Q397) 93–94, 97–98, 102–3, 105, 117, 132
  14–21 105
  14–21, 7b–8c 111, 130
  14–21, 10–12a 103

4QMMT^e (4Q398) 97–98, 102–3
  1–3 93
  1–3, 5, 7 94
  1–9 98
  11–13 (see 4QMMT C 18–24) 92, 103
  11–17 93–94, 98
  14–17 (see 4QMMT C 9–16, 25–32) 103
  14–17, I, 2–4 103
  14–17, II, 3 102
  14–17, II, 5 148
  14–17, II, 6 102

4QMMT^f (4Q399) 93, 102–3

4QS (4Q255–264) (see also S and 1QS) 126, 191, 194, 197–200, 203–4
  4Q255 (4QpapS^a) 190–92, 198, 201–3
  4Q256 (4QS^b) 11, 191, 202–3
  4Q257 (4QS^c) 191, 201–3, 242

4QTestament of Levi 148, 152, 184

4QTestament of Qahat 148, 152, 184

4QVisions of Amram 148, 152–53, 184
  4Q544 152

5Q9 47

5Q11 (see also S and 1QS) 191

11Q5
  XVIII 167
  XXI 167

11Q11 147–48, 152–54, 184
  V, 3–14 152

11Q13 148, 153, 184

11Q17 59

11QT^a (Temple Scroll) 8, 10, 14–15, 19, 47, 68–70, 73, 75, 77, 81, 90, 93, 95, 97, 113–14, 124–26
  LV, 3 148

Aramaic Levi Document 20, 73

Copper Scroll 24

CD (Cairo Genizah Damascus Document) xiii, 2, 4, 8–9, 11, 22, 31, 46, 53, 60, 66–68, 70–72, 74–75, 102, 111, 113, 126, 133, 142, 148, 162–63, 204, 242, 244–45
  I, 5b–12 68

CD (cont.)		5.408–412	110
II, 2	242		
II, 2–13	148, 163, 232, 242, 245	Josephus, *Vita*	
II, 3f.	163	10–12	2
II, 3–7	163		
II, 3–7a	245, 247	Philo, *Pro judaeis defensio*	2
II, 6	242		
II, 6–7	150, 183, 205, 241, 244–45	Philo, *Quod omnis probus liber sit*	
II, 7–8	205	72–91	2
II, 11–13	246		
IV, 12–VI, 11	148	EARLY CHRISTIAN LITERATURE	
IV, 13	242		
XVI, 3–4	184	Didache	250

D (Damascus Document tradition) 10–14

Shepherd of Hermas — 250

Epistle of Barnabas — 250

DD (Qumran Damascus Document)
xiii, 8–9, 11, 53, 102, 111, 113, 133, 245

Eusebius, *Praep. ev.* 8.11.1–8 — 2

4Q266 2, II, 1–13a — 245

GRECO-ROMAN AUTHORS

S (Rule of the Community/Serekh tradition) (*see also* 1QS and 4QS)
5, 10–14, 126, 190–92, 194, 197–200, 202, 204, 206

Pliny the Elder, *Naturalis historia*
5.17.4 — 3

Plutarch, *On Isis and Osiris* — 160

Sapiential Work A and B (*see* 4Q418)

ZOROASTRIAN LITERATURE

ANCIENT JEWISH WRITERS

Avesta	155, 160
Vohuman Yast	160
Stutkar Nask	160

Josephus, *Antiquitates judaicae*
12.10	110
18.18–22	2
Bahman Yast	160

Josephus, *Bellum judaicum*
1.78–80	2
2.111–113	2
2.119	3
2.119–161	2
2.122	3
2.124	3
2.137	3
2.141–142	3
2.160	9

Bundahisn	160
Gathas	160
Oracle of Hystaspes	160
Zand-I Vohuman	160

Index of Modern Authors

Alexander, Philip	195, 200	Doering, Lutz	108
Atkinson, Kenneth	52	Donceel-Voûte, Pauline	13, 257
Baillet, Maurice	39	Doudna, Gregory	258
Bainbridge, William Sims	139	Duhaime, Jean	142, 146, 161, 196–97, 219
Bar-Nathan, Rachel	13, 258		
Barth, Fredrik	23	Dupont-Sommer, André	2, 5–6, 17
Barton, Stephen	23, 24	Elgvin, Torleif	18–19, 76, 238
Baumgarten, Albert	6, 21, 26–28, 71, 76	Elman, Yaakov	126–27
Baumgarten, Joseph M.	107	Eshel, Hanan	47, 130
Beall, Todd	9	Fernández, Miguel Pérez	131
Beentjes, Pancratius C.	164	Fitzpatrick, Doyle C.	267
Ben-Dov, Jonathan	84, 94	Flint, Peter	24
Berger, Peter L.	255	Flusser, David	250
Bernstein, Moshe J.	92, 93, 97, 101, 107–8, 111, 114, 122, 127–28, 141, 190	Fontaine, Petrus	172
		Foucault, Michel	256
Bianchi, Udo	144, 168–71, 173–78, 180–82, 187, 211, 215, 230, 247	Fraade, Steven	101, 106, 108, 110, 112, 119, 131
Blenkinsopp, Joseph	21, 25	Frey, Jörg	17–18, 141, 144–55, 161–62, 164, 168–69, 174–85, 187–91, 193, 195, 204–6, 209–11, 213, 219, 227, 231–34, 237, 239, 241–47, 258
Boccaccini, Gabriele	7, 10, 19, 76, 77		
Brooke, George	111, 263–64, 266		
Brownlee, William H.	65		
Burrows, Millar	2		
Callaway, Phillip	3, 6, 9	Galor, Katharina	13–14
Charlesworth, James H.	143, 145, 168, 176–78, 240	Gammie, John G.	143–45, 168, 232
		García Martínez, Florentino	4, 7–10, 12, 15–16, 18–20, 23, 37–38, 49, 59, 62–77, 79, 81–82, 84–87, 90–92, 95–96, 100, 103, 112, 128–30, 140–41, 158, 185, 190, 192, 222
Collins, John J.	6, 7, 9, 11–12, 67–68, 157–58, 160–61, 163		
Craffert, Pieter	23, 24		
Cross, Frank Moore	2, 16		
Davies, Philip	7, 14, 21, 24–25, 27–28, 67–68, 150, 244–46, 265	Ginzberg, Louis	4–5, 22, 53
		Glessmer, Uwe	94
Di Lella, Alexander	236	Goering, Gregory Schmidt	236–37
Dimant, Devorah	4, 16–17, 19–20, 37–62, 77–78, 80, 85–87, 90–91, 131, 133, 140, 153, 190–91, 195	Goff, Matthew J.	166–67, 178
		Golb, Norman	48–49, 257–59
		Goodman, Martin	118, 137

Grabbe, Lester 24, 26
Grossman, Maxine 23, 108, 112
Harlow, Daniel C. 19, 168
Harrington, Daniel J. 238
Heger, Paul 215
Hempel, Charlotte 7, 10, 12–13, 18, 41, 44–45, 72, 101, 105, 107–8, 117, 119, 131, 133–35, 137, 147, 179, 191, 194, 197–98, 200, 203, 219–20, 245
Hirschfeld, Yizhar 13, 247, 258
Horsley, Richard 25, 28, 29
Humbert, Jean-Baptiste 13–14
Jokiranta, Jutta 4, 22, 24, 139
Kampen, John 92, 93, 97, 107–8, 111, 127–28, 141, 190
Kister, Menahem 96
Klinghardt, Matthias 27
Lange, Armin 17–18, 41, 149, 154, 162–64, 172, 179, 186, 191, 193–96, 201, 203–4, 209, 231, 233, 237–39
Lenski, Gerhard E. 25, 28–29
Leonhardt-Balzer, Jutta 168
Licht, Jacob 155, 194, 199, 215–16, 222, 224–27
Lichtenberger, Hermann 41, 142–43, 179, 213, 217
Lim, Timothy 137
Luckmann, Thomas 255
Magen, Yizhak 13, 257–58
Magness, Jodi 52, 65, 83
Mason, Steve 6, 104
Metso, Sarianna 11–12, 191–92, 197–203
Metzger, Bruce M. 176
Meyers, Eric M. 154–56
Milik, Józef T. 2, 16, 39, 48–49, 202
Murphy-O'Connor, Jerome 192
Needham, Rodney 171, 172, 206
Newsom, Carol 6, 206–9, 213
Nickelsburg, George W. E. 249
Osten-Sacken, Peter von der 141–42, 146, 161, 189, 196, 198–99, 216–20, 222, 225–27, 240
Parry, Donald W. 194
Peleg, Yuval 13, 257–58

Popović, Mladen 12, 23, 141, 194, 228
Puech, Émile 16, 77, 103
Qimron, Elisha 91–93, 96–99, 102–3, 105, 107–10, 114, 117–18, 122–23, 125, 127–28, 131–33
Regev, Eyal 10–12, 129
Rengstorf, Karl Heinrich 257
Sandt, Huub van de 250
Saulnier, Stéphane 84
Schechter, Solomon 22, 53
Schiffman, Lawrence H. 4–5, 7, 12, 14–16, 18, 21, 68, 71, 90, 99–100, 112, 119, 125–26, 129, 131
Schofield, Alison 2, 4, 10, 12, 21, 199, 202
Schürer, Emil 26–27
Scott, James C. 207
Sharp, Carolyn 131
Shemesh, Aharon 15, 100–101, 126, 131
Siegal, Elitzur Bar-Asher 133–35
Skehan, Patrick 236
Snaith, John G. 165, 236
Stacey, David 258
Stark, Rodney 139
Stegemann, Hartmut 17, 18, 92, 192
Stern, Sacha 137
Stoyanov, Yuri 168–70, 174, 178
Strugnell, John 91–95, 97–99, 102–3, 105–10, 117–18, 125, 129–30, 238
Stuckenbruck, Loren T. 164–66, 177, 192–93, 200, 208–9, 239
Sukenik, Eleazer L. 1, 5
Sussman, Jacob 15, 100
Talmon, Shemaryahu 94
Thompson, Leonard 266–68
Tigchelaar, Eibert J. C. 9, 16, 19, 37, 63, 114, 191, 194, 197, 199, 201, 212, 216, 219, 222, 239, 241
Tov, Emanuel 7, 18, 49, 194
Trebolle Barrera, Julio 153
Troeltsch, Ernst 22
Ullmann-Margalit, Edna 32, 262
VanderKam, James C. 15, 24, 91, 104, 136
Vaux, Roland de 1–3, 5, 31, 39, 65

Vermes, Géza   17, 26, 195, 200
Weber, Max   22
Weissenberg, Hanne von   92–99, 101–6,
    108–9, 114–15, 118–19, 129, 132–34,
    137–38
Werman, Cana   15, 101
Wernberg-Møller, P.   212, 214, 216, 220,
    222, 224–29
Werrett, Ian   97, 125
Wills, Lawrence M.   206
Wilson, Bryan   21
Wilson, Edmund   2
Wintermute, O. S.   240
Wise, Michael O.   263
Woude, Adam van der   62, 65, 76
Xeravits, Géza G.   142, 145, 150, 166,
    191, 215, 252
Zanella, Francesco   49
Zangenberg, Jürgen   3, 13–14, 258–59

www.ingramcontent.com/pod-product-compliance
Lightning Source LLC
Chambersburg PA
CBHW021820300426
44114CB00009BA/245